# The 70-294 Cram Sheet

This cram sheet provides the distilled, key facts about Exam 70-294, "Windows Server 2003 Active Directory Infrastructure." Review these important points as the last thing you do before entering the test center. Pay close attention to those you feel you need to review. A good exam strategy is to transfer all the facts you can recall from this tool onto a piece of paper once you sit down for the exam.

## PLANNING AND IMPLEMENTING FORESTS AND DOMAINS

1. The SYSVOL folder must reside on an NTFS partition.

2. Use `convert.exe c: /fs:ntfs` to convert a FAT or FAT32 partition to NTFS.

3. Use `dcpromo.exe` to promote and demote servers to and from a domain controller.

4. Running dcpromo will do the following:
   - Create a domain controller for a new domain
   - Create a new domain tree or join an existing domain as a child domain
   - Create a new forest of domain trees or join an existing forest

5. Domains in Windows 2003 support four functional levels and Forests support three functional levels. The Windows Server 2003 Functional Levels are as follows:
   - *Windows 2000 Mixed Functional Level*
   - *Windows 2000 Native Functional Level*
   - *Windows 2003 Interm Functional Level*
   - *Windows 2003 Functional Level*

6. To create an alternate UPN suffix, open the Active Directory Domains and Trusts administrative console.

7. An *application data partition* is a partitioned section of Active Directory that is replicated only to specified domain controllers. It can only be hosted on Windows Server 2003 domain controllers in a Windows 2003 Forest.

8. The four ways to create, delete, and manage Application Data Partitions include application-specific tools supplied by software vendors, NTDSUtil command-line utility, LDP Graphical tool included on the installation CD, and Active Directory Service Interfaces (ADSI).

9. The types of trusts in Windows 2003 are Transitive, Forest, External, Realm, and Shortcut.

10. Domains map the *logical structure* of your organization, whereas sites relate to the *physical layout* of the network. The domain namespace is likewise unrelated to the physical sites.

## IMPLEMENTING AND MANAGING ACTIVE DIRECTORY SITES

1. Because of the separation of physical and logical structures, a site can support multiple domains.

2. The primary function of a site is to consolidate directory service requests within a high-speed connection area and to control replication with external domain controllers.

3. Sites are created via the Active Directory Sites and Services snap-in. Windows Server 2003 creates the first site automatically when AD is installed. This site is named Default-First-Site-Name and includes all the domain controllers.

4. The sites themselves are connected via site links, which are typically lower-bandwidth than the LAN speeds within the Site or unreliable/occasional connections between sites.

5. The server that is responsible for evaluating and creating the topology for the intersite replication is known as the *Intersite Topology Generator*.

6. The replication topology among sites is generated automatically by Windows Server 2003 through a service known as the *Knowledge Consistency Checker (KCC)*.

7. A *site link bridge* is a collection of site links. You create site links and add them to the site link bridge.

8. You should be familiar with two site parameters:
   - *The schedule* • *The replication interval*

9. Two different protocols can be used:
   - *Remote Procedure Call (RPC)*
   - *Simple Mail Transfer Protocol (SMTP)*

## OPERATIONS MASTERS AND GLOBAL CATALOG SERVERS

1. Operation masters have specific roles in AD:

| Operations Master | Scope |
|---|---|
| Schema Master | Forestwide |
| Domain Naming Master | Forestwide |
| Primary Domain Controller (PDC) Emulator | Specific to adomain |
| Relative Identifier (RID) Master | Specific to a domain |
| Infrastructure Master | Specific to a domain |

9. Windows Server 2003 uses "Version 2" templates, whereas Windows 2000 uses "Version 1" templates. These two are not completely interchangeable—Windows 2000 Active Directory cannot use Version 2 certificates because of some schema components that are missing.

## TROUBLESHOOTING GROUP POLICY

1. GPUpdate is a command-line tool that ships with Windows Server 2003. Its purpose is to allow you to manually trigger the refresh of Group Policies from a client machine (be it a server or workstation).

2. Loopback processing is designed to reverse the usual processing rules.

3. There are two settings for loopback: Loopback with Replace and Loopback with Merge. Replace gives settings applied to the computer precedence over the user-configuration settings targeting the logged-on user. Merge applies those settings aimed at the computer and then combines them with those targeting the user.

4. RSoP snap-in works with Windows Management Instrumentation (WMI) to allow you to work out which policies are currently being applied to a given environment.

5. GPResult is a precursor to RSoP. It is command-line driven. It allows for two modes of operation: Planning and Logging. Planning simulates the effect of Group Policies while Logging Mode reports on existing policies.

6. The GPMC tool offers a plethora of features, such as the ability to administer policies across domains and forests, the ability to perform backups and restores of policy data, and the ability to import or copy policy data.

7. GPmonitor comes in two parts. The first is a service that runs on the client computers. This service collects policy data from the client and forwards it to a central repository. The second is a viewer tool.

8. GPOTool allows you to check consistency, within a domain or across domains, of the Group Policy Container (GPC) and Group Policy Template (GPT) data. This can be used to determine whether you have replication issues.

## ACTIVE DIRECTORY MAINTENANCE

1. Active Directory uses the Extensible Storage Engine (ESE). It uses the concept of transactions to ensure that the database does not become corrupted by partial updates and to recover in the case of a power failure. Each transaction is a call to modify the database.

2. Five files make up the AD database system: ntds.dit, edb*.log, ebd.chk, res1.log, and res2.log.

3. Data is never immediately deleted from AD. Instead, the object's attributes are deleted and the object is moved to a container called Deleted Objects. The object is then assigned a tombstone. By default, this tombstone is 60 days, although this can be changed. The tombstone indicates that the physical deletion of the object will occur by the configured interval.

This gives AD time to replicate this change to all DCs. It also means that the deletion can take place at around the same time, no matter how distant the DCs may be.

4. The nonauthoritative restore is the simplest form of restore when you are using backup media. A nonauthoritative restore is simply a restore of data from backup. Because the data will probably be out of date (presumably, some changes were made to the data in AD after the last backup), normal AD replication processes make sure that the missing data elements are updated.

5. An authoritative restore allows an administrator to restore deleted OU objects from backup.

6. You can move the database with the Ntdsutil command-line utility. For this to work, you must have booted your server in Directory Services Restore Mode.

7. AD defragmentation can occur in two modes:
   - *Online mode*
   - *Offline mode*

8. The three main tools you can use to troubleshoot replication problems with AD are Event Viewer, the command-line utility Repadmin, and the Graphical User Interface tool Replmon.

9. Event Viewer contains log files generated by the operating system.

10. Replication Administrator is a tool that ships with the resource kit. It has many of the same functions as Replmon, with the added benefit of being command-line based. Repadmin can provide a lot of information and functions, including the following:
    - Give the status of the Knowledge Consistency Checker (KCC)
    - Provide the last replication event received from a DC's partner or partners
    - Can be used to delete objects restored accidentally with an authoritative restore (such as when the tombstone value has been exceeded)
    - Disable compression of AD replication data intersite

11. Replication Monitor is basically the same tool as Repadmin, with the addition of a Graphical User Interface. This makes it easier to use while you are at a server console. Replmon is provided with System Tools in a Windows Server 2003 installation.

## PLANNING AND IMPLEMENTING AN OU STRUCTURE

1. There are essentially two main uses for OUs:
   - To allow subadministrators control over a selection of users, computers, or other objects
   - To control desktop systems through Group Policy Objects (GPOs) associated with an OU
2. Windows Server 2003 allows you to delegate various levels of control on parts of a domain.
3. Group Policies are used to define default settings for computers and users. In general, Group Policies are not applied at the domain or site level, but applied at the OU level in order to generate a specific combination of user and computer environmental factors for specific organization roles, locations, and groups.

## PLANNING A GROUP POLICY IMPLEMENTATION

1. The benefits of Intellimirror technologies are as follows:
   - Enables administrators to define environment settings for users, groups, and computers.
   - Allows Windows 2003 Server and Professional to be installed remotely onto compatible computers.
   - Enables users' local folders to be redirected to a shared server location, and they enable files to be synchronized automatically between the server and local hard drive for working offline.
   - Enables users' desktop settings and applications to roam with them.
   - Enables administrators to centrally manage the process of installing, updating, and removing applications. Self-healing applications replace missing or corrupted files automatically.
   - Makes the computer a commodity. A system can be replaced with a new one with less administration.
2. Group Policy supports Windows 2000 clients and up, so Windows 9x and NT 4.0 and earlier systems cannot realize the benefits of a Group Policy implementation.
3. Group Policy is processed by Windows Server 2003 in the following order: Site, Domain, OU.
4. Group Policy Objects require two steps to take effect: They must be created and they must be linked. When creating Group Policies through AD Users and Computers, both steps are completed for you, but you can still link the policy to other OU's without having to re-create it. Creation can be done via a custom MMC with the Group Policy snap-in or by editing an existing policy. Linking is done at the site, domain, or OU level.
5. Note that GPOs cannot be linked to the generic Active Directory containers: Builtin, Computers, and Users.

6. The Delegation of Control Wizard is used to delegate control to users or groups that will manage GPO links.
7. Windows Server 2003 has two methods to change the default behavior of setting inheritance:
   - *Block Policy Inheritance*    • *No Override*
8. Two permissions are required for an object to be able to receive policy settings from a GPO, and by default all authenticated users have Read and Apply Group Policy permissions.
9. Windows Server 2003 Group Policy gives you the option of disabling either the Computer Configuration container or the User Configuration container within a GPO if you are not using it. Doing so will speed up Group Policy processing.
10. Microsoft has introduced a new MMC snap-in called RSoP. It can query about an object (such as a computer or user) and determine what policies have been applied to it. It does this by utilizing Windows Management Instrumentation.

## UNDERSTANDING SECURITY SETTINGS WITH GROUP POLICY

1. Administrative templates provide the primary means of administering the user environment and defining the end-user computing experience.
2. There are two different administrative template sections within a Group Policy Object: Computer Configuration container and User Configuration container.
3. Group Policy can also be used to manage security settings on a Windows Server 2003 network.
4. Security templates in Windows Server 2003 are a set of profiles that can be imported into a GPO.
5. The types of security templates available are as follows:
   - *Compatible*    • *Secure*    • *High Secure*
6. With Windows Server 2003, scripts can be run at any or all of the following times:
   - *Startup*    • *Logon*    • *Logoff*
   - *Shutdown*
7. Folder Redirection allows user folders to be stored on a network share. The folders that can be redirected are: Application Data, Desktop, My Documents, Start Menu.
8. There are two options for Folder Redirection:
   - *Basic—Redirect Everyone's Folder to the Same Location*—This policy will redirect all folders to the same network share.
   - *Advanced—Specify Locations for Various*
   - *Groups*—The Advanced policy allows you to redirect folders based on security group memberships.

2. The Schema Master is responsible for maintaining the only writable copy of the schema in AD.

3. The Domain Naming Master manages the addition and deletion of domains from the forest.

4. The Primary Domain Controller (PDC) Emulator processes requests for password changes, replication, and user authentication to clients that do not run Active Directory client software.

5. The Relative Identifier (RID) Master is assigned from a pool of RIDs stored at each DC. The DCs aquire their RIDS from the RID Master.

6. Infrastructure Master—If a change is made to a referenced object in a Domain, this change needs to be consistent throughout all Domains. It is the job of the Infrastructure Master to receive these reference changes within its Domain and to update them throughout all Domains.

7. You can use the AD Users and Computers tool to find out which server or servers are holding the roles of RID Master, Infrastructure Master, and PDC Emulator.

8. For the Domain Naming Master, you use the AD Domains and Trusts administrative tool to view which Server is holding the role.

9. For the Schema Master, you must create a custom MMC Console after registering `schmmgmt.dll`. Run the command `regsvr32.exe schmmgmt.dll`.

10. You can transfer a role through the appropriate tool (AD Users and Computers for the RID Master, PDC Emulator, and Infrastructure Master). To seize a role, you use `ntdsutil.exe` for the Schema Master, Domain Naming Master, or RID Master role.

11. Global Catalog servers are used as part of the process of login such as determining group membership in environments running at the Mixed Functional level. They should be placed close to larger groups of users to speed up login. If the domain is operating at the Windows 2003 functional level, you can enable the caching of Universal group membership so users can log in even if no GC server is available.

## USER AND GROUP ADMINISTRATION

1. *Groups* are collections of user accounts (although they can also include computers) that are used to ease administration.

2. A Windows Server 2003 network has three different types of user accounts:

   • *Domain user account* • *Local user account*

   • *Built-in user accounts*

3. Two options exist for login:

   • *User Principal Name*—The *user principal name* has two parts, and is the new-style logon name on Windows Server 2003 networks. One uniquely identifies the user object in AD; the second part identifies the domain where the user object was created such as:

   WWillis@Inside-Corner.com

   • *User Login Name*—The *user logon name* is used to describe backward-compatible usernames. It is used by clients logging on to a Windows Server 2003 network from an older operating system, such as Windows 9*x* or Microsoft Windows NT 4.

4. Renaming a user account is convenient when a user's function is being taken over by someone else.

5. Disabling an account temporarily prevents a user from logging in to the network.

6. The required elements that must be in place in order for users to log on using smartcards are as follows:

   • Install and configure at least one Enterprise Certificate Authority (CA) on your Windows Server 2003 network.

   • Configure the permissions in each domain that will contain smartcard users with the enroll permission for the smartcard user, smartcard logon, and Enrollment Agent certificate templates.

   • Configure the CA to issue smartcard certificates and Enrollment Agent certificates.

   • Install smartcard readers at each workstation and server that will be used with smartcard logons.

   • Prepare a smartcard enrollment station, including getting an Enrollment Agent certificate.

   • Set up each required smartcard to be used for user logon and distribute the smartcards and train users on how to log on with them.

7. Security groups differ from distribution groups. They can be used to assign security rights— You cannot use distribution groups for this purpose.

8. A feature of Windows Server 2003 is the ability to *nest* groups. When a group is nested within another group, it inherits all the security permissions from its parent. This requires that the Functional Level (FL) of the Domain supports nesting (Windows 2000 FL Native, Windows 2003 FL).

9. With a single domain, you can achieve all the simplification you need using only Domain Local and Global groups. Use Microsoft's acronym AGDLP to understand group nesting. This acronym stands for the following:

   • **A**—Accounts (user)
   • **G**—Global group
   • **DL**—Domain Local group
   • **P**—Permissions

9. The practical limit on the number of users a group can contain is 5,000 members.

10. Both the Universal group name and the membership list are replicated to every Global Catalog server. If you add a single user to a universal group, the *entire* membership list must be replicated. That is why you should always add a Global group to the Universal group.

# Windows®
# Server™ 2003
# Active Directory®
# Infrastructure

David Watts

Will Willis

CERTIFICATION

# Windows® Server™ 2003 Active Directory® Infrastructure Exam Cram 2 (Exam 70-294)

Copyright © 2004 by Que Publishing

International Standard Book Number: 0-7897-2950-4

Library of Congress Catalog Card Number: 2003103166

Printed in the United States of America

First Printing: November 2003

06   05   04   03          4   3   2   1

## Trademarks

All terms mentioned in this book that are known to be trademarks or service marks have been appropriately capitalized. Que Publishing cannot attest to the accuracy of this information. Use of a term in this book should not be regarded as affecting the validity of any trademark or service mark.

## Warning and Disclaimer

Every effort has been made to make this book as complete and as accurate as possible, but no warranty or fitness is implied. The information provided is on an "as is" basis. The author(s) and the publisher shall have neither liability nor responsibility to any person or entity with respect to any loss or damages arising from the information contained in this book or from the use of the CD or programs accompanying it.

## Bulk Sales

Que Publishing offers excellent discounts on this book when ordered in quantity for bulk purchases or special sales. For more information, please contact

**U.S. Corporate and Government Sales**

**1-800-382-3419**

**corpsales@pearsontechgroup.com**

For sales outside of the U.S., please contact

**International Sales**

**1-317-428-3341**

**international@pearsontechgroup.com**

**Publisher**
Paul Boger

**Executive Editor**
Jeff Riley

**Acquisitions Editor**
Jeff Riley

**Development Editor**
Steve Rowe

**Managing Editor**
Charlotte Clapp

**Project Editor**
Tricia Liebig

**Copy Editor**
Bart Reed

**Indexer**
Erika Millen

**Proofreader**
Juli Cook

**Technical Editors**
Marc Savage
Bill Ferguson

**Team Coordinator**
Pamalee Nelson

**Multimedia Developer**
Dan Scherf

**Interior Designer**
Gary Adair

**Cover Designer**
Anne Jones

**Page Layout**
Bronkella Publishing

**CERTIFICATION**

Que Certification • 800 East 96th Street • Indianapolis, Indiana 46240

## *A Note from Series Editor Ed Tittel*

You know better than to trust your certification preparation to just anybody. That's why you, and more than two million others, have purchased an Exam Cram book. As Series Editor for the new and improved Exam Cram 2 series, I have worked with the staff at Que Certification to ensure you won't be disappointed. That's why we've taken the world's best-selling certification product—a finalist for "Best Study Guide" in a CertCities reader poll in 2002—and made it even better.

Best Study Guides

As a "Favorite Study Guide Author" finalist in a 2002 poll of CertCities readers, I know the value of good books. You'll be impressed with Que Certification's stringent review process, which ensures the books are high-quality, relevant, and technically accurate. Rest assured that at least a dozen industry experts—including the panel of certification experts at CramSession—have reviewed this material, helping us deliver an excellent solution to your exam preparation needs.

We've also added a preview edition of PrepLogic's powerful, full-featured test engine, which is trusted by certification students throughout the world.

As a 20-year-plus veteran of the computing industry and the original creator and editor of the Exam Cram series, I've brought my IT experience to bear on these books. During my tenure at Novell from 1989 to 1994, I worked with and around its excellent education and certification department. This experience helped push my writing and teaching activities heavily in the certification direction. Since then, I've worked on more than 70 certification-related books, and I write about certification topics for numerous Web sites and for *Certification* magazine.

In 1996, while studying for various MCP exams, I became frustrated with the huge, unwieldy study guides that were the only preparation tools available. As an experienced IT professional and former instructor, I wanted "nothing but the facts" necessary to prepare for the exams. From this impetus, Exam Cram emerged in 1997. It quickly became the best-selling computer book series since "...*For Dummies*," and the best-selling certification book series ever. By maintaining an intense focus on subject matter, tracking errata and updates quickly, and following the certification market closely, Exam Cram was able to establish the dominant position in cert prep books.

You will not be disappointed in your decision to purchase this book. If you are, please contact me at etittel@jump.net. All suggestions, ideas, input, or constructive criticism are welcome!

*Ed Tittel*

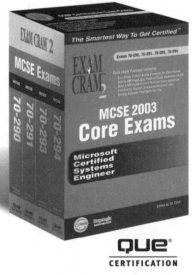

# About the Authors

## Lead Authors

**Will Willis (MCSE, A+ Certified Technician, Network+, B.A.)** is a Senior Network Administrator for an international software-development company in the Dallas, Texas area. He is responsible for the network and server infrastructure, for documentation, maintaining disaster recovery preparedness, antivirus strategies, firewalls/network security, infrastructure (servers, routers, switches, hubs) maintenance and upgrades, and ensuring the reliability and availability of network resources.

Will started out as a help desk tech, providing technical support over the phone for PC hardware and software and later moved up to a desktop/LAN support specialist position working on a team of eight to support a 3,000+ user multiple-site network. From that position, Will moved into a job as a network manager, where he also administered multiple Active Directory domains and servers running BackOffice applications Exchange Server, IIS, Site Server, SQL Server, and SMS. He enjoys spending time with his family and writing and recording original music when not busy being a techie; he can be reached at WWillis@Inside-Corner.com. Will has co-authored eight books and scores of technical articles to date. He has also written practice exams and tech edited many titles. His first album of guitar-based instrumental music, *Darkness into Light*, was released in late 2002. Will is also a seminary student, pursuing a Master of Arts in Theology. More information on Will can be found at www.willwillis.us.

**David V. Watts (MCSE, MCSD, CNE, and Network+)** currently directs customer and professional services for the European, Middle Eastern, and African (EMEA) headquarters of Altiris, Inc., a software company dedicated to developing and implementing systems-management software for both small businesses and global enterprises.

Born in Basildon, Essex, United Kingdom, David relocated to the United States in 1988, where he worked for 14 years in information technology as both a project lead for and consultant to enterprise-level deployments of

Microsoft technologies. In 2002, he relocated once again—to Landau, Germany, a small city located amid the vineyards of the Rhineland—to fill the Director of Customer Services position Altiris had just created in conjunction with its expanding presence throughout the European market. In this role, David travels widely and frequently.

David has played with, exploited, and (sometimes) cursed Windows 2003 since its beta version. Along the way, he accumulated expertise with Altiris Notification Server 6.0 and Altiris Deployment Server. Along with these, he has worked extensively with Microsoft BackOffice products, including Microsoft Systems Management Server, Microsoft SQL Server, and Microsoft Exchange.

When not accumulating frequent-flyer miles, David monopolizes his home theatre system with marathon screening sessions for the worst (and thus the best) horror films produced within the last 70 years. His long-suffering wife and three mutts have noted an especially rabid passion for Italian giallos and gorefests and prefer his other obsessions: music (especially modern and experimental jazz) and photography. David can be reached at `dwatts@altiris.com`.

# Contributing Author

**Brian McCann** is a trainer and consultant specializing in Active Directory and network security. He is the owner of Diesel Technologies, a training and consulting company dedicated to helping small-to-medium-size businesses with their IT needs.

He has worked in the IT field for 10 years and started his career in the U.S. Army. His teaching credits have come from local training centers, community colleges, and also just under 3 years of experience teaching live synchronous training over the Web. Brian has spent the last 5 years teaching students from all over the world on technologies such as Active Directory, PKI, DNS, IIS, and many more.

Brian has been recognized by Microsoft as one of its "Go to Trainers" and holds an MCSE and MCT certification.

# Technical Editors

**Marc Savage** is the Senior National Technical Advisor and Technical Trainer for Polar Bear Corporate Education Solutions. Combined with more than seven years experience in microcomputer training and systems development in the private, public, and non-profit organization sector his professional expertise is focused particularly on providing companies with a clear vision and direction in regards to Microsoft products. Marc currently holds the following certifications: MCT, MCSE NT4, MCSE W2K, MCSA, CNE 4.11, A+, NETWORK+. Marc lives in Ottawa, Canada with his lovely wife Lynne and two daughters Isabelle and Carolyne.

**Bill Ferguson**, MCT, MCSE, MCSA, MCP+I, CCSI, CCNA, A+, Network+, Server+, Security+, has been in the computer industry for more than 15 years. Originally in technical sales and sales management with Sprint, Bill made his transition to Certified Technical Trainer in 1997 with ExecuTrain. Bill now runs his own company as an independent contractor from Birmingham, Alabama, teaching classes for most of the national training companies and some regional training companies. In addition, Bill writes and produces technical training videos for Virtual Training Company, Inc. and Specialized Solutions, Inc. He currently has titles including A+, Network+, Windows 2000 Management, Windows XP Management, Windows 2000 Security, Server+, and Interconnecting Cisco Network Devices. Bill keeps his skills sharp by being a technical reviewer for books and sample tests for Que Certification and McGraw-Hill Technical. He is currently co-authoring the 70-297 Exam Cram 2 title for Que Publishing and producing a training video for the 70-292 MCSA Skills Upgrade test for QuickCert. Bill says, "My job is to understand the material so well that I can make it easier for my students to learn than it was for me to learn."

# Acknowledgments

. . . . . . . . . . . . . . . . . . . . . . . . . . . . . . . . . . . . . . . . . . . . . . . . . . . . . . . . . . . . . . . . . . . .

**David Watts**

Writing a book, like most things of value in life, takes time, dedication, and commitment. When we fall short in any of these areas, it then becomes a matter of faith that things will reach an adequate conclusion. When writing this particular title, I had to lean on the publishers, and particularly on Jeff Riley, much more than I had planned. Jeff has been patient and even aggrieved at times, and yet he has always held the course on the title. Kudos then to the commitment of Jeff, and the staff around him who no doubt felt pain as we worked on this title.

As always, there are lots of people who have worked around this book who never get credit. My wife, Siobhan, whose ideas are always welcome, my parents Len and Kit, suffering through the hottest summer in the UK, my brother who sometimes finds time to get back to the UK from Thailand. My wife's mother, Moira, and her brother, Peter, both in the U.S., deserve mention too!

I also have had the honor of working on a team that excels in everything it does. Special thanks to Volker Wiora, Ron Porter, Poul Neilsen, Dwain Kinghorn, and Greg Butterfield—all leaders for team Altiris. Within EMEA, it is my pleasure to work with Christof Mayer and Colin Martin (we know how to steer this boat!), Bertram Rawe, who champions excellence, and Lorena Lardon, who organizes us and keeps everything in balance.

And what of the ground troops: Scott Keatinge, Eric Girard, Younes Dallol, and Dennis Leibich? You guys are a team, and as a team have achieved much—it is very much appreciated by the entire organization. And to Paul Butler and Justin Rodino, who have brought experience, dedication, and commitment to their tasks: As long as we do what we know is right, we shall reap the benefits.

Along with these people are those who daily support our message and help our customers realize concrete, meaningful benefits from engaging with Altiris. Nick Shaw—tireless, relentless. Maarten Van Hintum—independent, driven. Frederic Pierresteguy—hard-working, focused. Stephan Kurz—

big-thinking, determined. And Lars Norballe, for putting a stake in the ground and carving out his niche. Along with these people we also have staff supporting them too numerous to mention each by name. You know who you are. As long as we remember that we are all working toward the same ultimate goal, then alliances can be formed. We all form part of this team; we all contribute. Without the key ingredient of wanting and having to succeed, we'd make no progress at all. And as our organization matures over time, and our roles change, we must stay focused on what really counts. Kudos then to Mark Boggia and Arie Joosse who work each day to ensure success.

A company like Altiris cannot be successful without everyone pulling together, and often it is the unsung heroes who contribute the most. Christine Roggenbuck has worked tirelessly and deserves credit. Esther Helwig helped me tremendously, and still does to this day. Esther experienced a life-defining moment this year, and although these moments can create great challenges, she is working through them and remaining remarkably not "balla-balla." We thought we'd lost her for a while, and the gravity of that loss was so great, I think it made us all realize how important she is to us. When it comes to unsung heroes, it is high time we took a moment out of our day to thank them.

Finally, I want to thank the Altiris Partners and customers out there. As part of our Customer Services team, I want you to know that my defined goal is for this team to be there when you need them, to offer all the aid and assistance you might require to achieve your own goals. By engaging at a grassroots level for the coming year, we will share in the benefits of moving from good to great, from great to greater.

# Contents at a Glance

# Table of Contents

. . . . . . . . . . . . . . . . . . . . . . . . . . . . . . . . . . . . . . . . . . .

# We Want to Hear from You!

As the reader of this book, *you* are our most important critic and commentator. We value your opinion and want to know what we're doing right, what we could do better, what areas you'd like to see us publish in, and any other words of wisdom you're willing to pass our way.

As an executive editor for Que Publishing, I welcome your comments. You can email or write me directly to let me know what you did or didn't like about this book—as well as what we can do to make our books better.

*Please note that I cannot help you with technical problems related to the topic of this book. We do have a User Services group, however, where I will forward specific technical questions related to the book.*

When you write, please be sure to include this book's title and author as well as your name, email address, and phone number. I will carefully review your comments and share them with the author and editors who worked on the book.

Email:  feedback@quepublishing.com

Mail:  Jeff Riley
Executive Editor
Que Publishing
800 East 96th Street
Indianapolis, IN 46240 USA

For information about the Exam Cram 2 series, visit www.examcram2.com. Type the ISBN (excluding hyphens) or the title of a book in the Search field to find the page you're looking for.

# Introduction

· · · · · · · · · · · · · · · · · · · · · · · · · · · · · · · · · · · · · · · · · · · ·

Welcome to *The 70-294 Exam Cram 2*! This book aims to help you get ready to take—and pass—exam 70-294, "Planning, Implementing, and Maintaining a Microsoft Windows Server 2003 Active Directory Infrastructure." This Introduction explains Microsoft's certification programs in general and talks about how the *Exam Cram 2* series can help you prepare for Microsoft's Windows 2003 certification exams.

*Exam Cram 2* books help you understand and appreciate the subjects and materials you need to pass Microsoft certification exams. *Exam Cram 2* books are aimed strictly at test preparation and review. They do not teach you everything you need to know about a topic. Instead, we (the authors) present and dissect the questions and problems we've found that you're likely to encounter on a test. We've worked to bring together as much information as possible about Microsoft certification exams.

Nevertheless, to completely prepare yourself for any Microsoft test, we recommend that you begin by taking the Self-Assessment included in this book immediately following this Introduction. This tool will help you evaluate your knowledge base against the requirements for an MCSE under both ideal and real circumstances.

Based on what you learn from that exercise, you might decide to begin your studies with some classroom training or some background reading. On the other hand, you might decide to pick up and read one of the many study guides available from Microsoft or third-party vendors on certain topics, including Que's *Training Guide* series. We also recommend that you supplement your study program with visits to www.examcram2.com to receive additional practice questions, get advice, and track the Windows 2003 MCSE program.

We also strongly recommend that you install, configure, and fool around with the software you'll be tested on, because nothing beats hands-on experience and familiarity when it comes to understanding the questions you're likely to encounter on a certification test. Book learning is essential, but hands-on experience is the best teacher of all!

# The Microsoft Certified Professional (MCP) Program

The MCP Program currently includes the following separate tracks, each of which boasts its own special acronym (as a certification candidate, you need to have a high tolerance for alphabet soup of all kinds):

➤ *MCSE (Microsoft Certified Systems Engineer)*—Anyone who has a current MCSE is warranted to possess a high level of networking expertise with Microsoft operating systems and products. This credential is designed to prepare individuals to plan, implement, maintain, and support information systems, networks, and internetworks built around Microsoft Windows 2000 or Windows Server 2003 and its BackOffice Server family of products.

To obtain an MCSE 2003, an individual must pass six core exams and one elective exam. The six core exams are broken up into three sections; there are four networking system exams, one operating system exam, and one design exam. These six exams are the core exams to the Windows Server 2003 MCSE. Besides the core exams there is a requirement for one elective exam that must be passed to fulfill the requirements to obtain an MCSE 2003.

The four networking system core exams on the Windows Server 2003 track are "70-290: Managing and Maintaining a Microsoft Windows Server 2003 Environment," "70-291: Implementing, Managing, and Maintaining a Microsoft Windows Server 2003 Network Infrastructure," "70-293: Planning and Maintaining a Microsoft Windows Server 2003 Network Infrastructure," and "70-294: Planning, Implementing, and Maintaining a Microsoft Windows Server 2003 Active Directory Infrastructure."

The one client operating system core exam can be either one of the following exams: "Exam 70–270: Installing, Configuring, and Administering Microsoft Windows XP Professional" or "Exam 70-210: Installing, Configuring, and Administering Microsoft Windows 2000 Professional."

The one design core exam can be either one of the following exams: "Exam 70-297: Designing a Microsoft Windows Server 2003 Active Directory and Network Infrastructure" or "Exam 70-298: Designing Security for a Microsoft Windows Server 2003 Network."

To fulfill your MCSE 2003 you have a lot of choices to choose from for your elective exam. This is where you can really start to specialize in certain areas, such as SQL, security, Exchange, or even design engineering. If you are on your way to becoming an MCSE and have already taken some exams, visit www.microsoft.com/traincert/mcp/mcse/windows2003 for information about how to complete your MCSE certification.

➤ *MCSA (Microsoft Certified Systems Administrator)*—This certification program is designed for individuals who are systems administrators but have no need for network design skills in their current career path. An MCSA on Windows Server 2003 candidate must pass three core exams—70-270, 70-290, and 70-291—and must also pass an elective exam, for a total of four exams.

➤ *MCP (Microsoft Certified Professional)*—This is the least prestigious of all the certification tracks from Microsoft. Passing one of the major Microsoft exams qualifies an individual for the MCP credential. Individuals can demonstrate proficiency with additional Microsoft products by passing additional certification exams.

➤ *MCSD (Microsoft Certified Solution Developer)*—The MCSD credential reflects the skills required to create multitier, distributed, and COM-based solutions, in addition to desktop and Internet applications, using new technologies. To obtain an MCSD, an individual must demonstrate the ability to analyze and interpret user requirements; select and integrate products, platforms, tools, and technologies; design and implement code as well as customize applications; and perform necessary software tests and quality-assurance operations.

To become an MCSD, you must pass a total of four exams: three core exams and one elective exam. Each candidate must choose one of three desktop application exams—"70-016: Designing and Implementing Desktop Applications with Microsoft Visual C++ 6.0," "70-156: Designing and Implementing Desktop Applications with Microsoft Visual FoxPro 6.0," or "70-176: Designing and Implementing Desktop Applications with Microsoft Visual Basic 6.0"—*plus* one of these three distributed application exams: "70-015: Designing and Implementing Distributed Applications with Microsoft Visual C++ 6.0," "70-155: Designing and Implementing Distributed Applications with Microsoft Visual FoxPro 6.0," or "70-175: Designing and Implementing Distributed Applications with Microsoft Visual Basic 6.0." The third core exam is "70-100: Analyzing Requirements and Defining Solution Architectures." Elective exams cover specific Microsoft applications and languages, including Visual Basic, C++, the Microsoft Foundation Classes, Access, SQL Server, Excel, and more.

➤ *MCDBA (Microsoft Certified Database Administrator)*—The MCDBA credential reflects the skills required to implement and administer Microsoft SQL Server databases. To obtain an MCDBA, an individual must demonstrate the ability to derive physical database designs, develop logical data models, create physical databases, create data services by using Transact-SQL, manage and maintain databases, configure and manage security, monitor and optimize databases, and install and configure Microsoft SQL Server.

To become an MCDBA, you must pass a total of three core exams and one elective exam. The required core exams are broken into three sections; there is one exam needed under SQL Server Administration, one exam needed for SQL Server Design, and another exam for Networking Systems.

The SQL Server Administration section has two exams to choose from: "Exam 70–228: Installing, Configuring, and Administering Microsoft SQL Server 2000 Enterprise Edition" and "Exam 70–028: Administering Microsoft SQL Server 7.0."

The SQL Server Design section has two exams to choose from: "Exam 70–229: Designing and Implementing Databases with Microsoft SQL Server 2000 Enterprise Edition" and "Exam 70–029: Designing and Implementing Databases with Microsoft SQL Server 7.0."

The Networking Systems section has three exams to choose from: "70-290: Managing and Maintaining a Microsoft Windows Server 2003 Environment," "70-291: Implementing, Managing, and Maintaining a Microsoft Windows Server 2003 Network Infrastructure," and "Exam 70–215: Installing, Configuring, and Administering Microsoft Windows 2000 Server."

The elective exams you can choose from cover specific uses of SQL Server, and all of them can be found at www.microsoft.com/traincert/mcp/mcdba/requirements.asp#D.

➤ *MCT (Microsoft Certified Trainer)*—Microsoft Certified Trainers are deemed able to deliver elements of the official Microsoft curriculum, based on technical knowledge and instructional ability. Therefore, it is necessary for an individual seeking MCT credentials (which are granted on a course-by-course basis) to pass the related certification exam for a course and complete the official Microsoft training in the subject area, as well as to demonstrate an ability to teach.

This teaching skill criterion may be satisfied by proving that one has already attained training certification from Novell, Banyan, Lotus, the

Santa Cruz Operation, or Cisco, or by taking a Microsoft-sanctioned workshop on instruction. Microsoft makes it clear that MCTs are important cogs in the Microsoft training channels. Instructors must be MCTs before Microsoft will allow them to teach in any of its official training channels, including Microsoft's affiliated Certified Technical Education Centers (CTECs) and its online training partner network. As of January 1, 2001, MCT candidates must also possess a current MCSE or MCSD.

Once a Microsoft product becomes obsolete, MCPs typically have to recertify on current versions. (If individuals do not recertify, their certifications become invalid.) Because technology keeps changing and new products continually supplant old ones, this should come as no surprise.

The best place to keep tabs on the MCP Program and its related certifications is on the Web. The URL for the MCP Program is www.microsoft.com/traincert. But Microsoft's Web site changes often, so if this URL doesn't work, try using the Search tool on Microsoft's site with either "MCP" or the quoted phrase "Microsoft Certified Professional" as a search string. This will help you find the latest and most accurate information about Microsoft's certification programs.

# Taking a Certification Exam

Once you've prepared for your exam, you need to register with a testing center. Each computer-based MCP exam costs $125, and if you don't pass, you may retest for an additional $125 for each additional try. In the United States and Canada, tests are administered by Prometric and by Virtual University Enterprises (VUE). Here's how you can contact them:

➤ *Prometric*—You can sign up for a test through the company's Web site at www.2test.com, or you can register by phone at 800-755-3926 (within the United States and Canada) or at 410-843-8000 (outside the United States and Canada).

➤ *Virtual University Enterprises*—You can sign up for a test or get the phone numbers for local testing centers through the Web page at www.vue. com/ms/.

To sign up for a test, you must possess a valid credit card, or you can contact either company for mailing instructions to send in a check (in the U.S.). Only when payment is verified, or your check has cleared, can you actually register for a test.

To schedule an exam, call the number or visit either of the Web pages at least one day in advance. To cancel or reschedule an exam, you must call before 7 p.m. pacific standard time the day before the scheduled test time (or you may be charged, even if you don't appear to take the test). When you want to schedule a test, have the following information ready:

➤ Your name, organization, and mailing address.

➤ Your Microsoft Test ID. (Inside the United States, this means your Social Security number; citizens of other nations should call ahead to find out what type of identification number is required to register for a test.)

➤ The name and number of the exam you wish to take.

➤ A method of payment. (As we've already mentioned, a credit card is the most convenient method, but alternate means can be arranged in advance, if necessary.)

Once you sign up for a test, you'll be informed as to when and where the test is scheduled. Try to arrive at least 15 minutes early. You must supply two forms of identification—one of which must be a photo ID—to be admitted into the testing room.

All exams are completely closed-book. In fact, you will not be permitted to take anything with you into the testing area, but you will be furnished with a blank sheet of paper and a pen or, in some cases, an erasable plastic sheet and an erasable pen. We suggest that you immediately write down on that sheet of paper all the information you've memorized for the test. In *Exam Cram 2* books, this information appears on a tear-out sheet inside the front cover of each book. You will have some time to compose yourself, record this information, and take a sample orientation exam before you begin the real thing. We suggest you take the orientation test before taking your first exam, but because they're all more or less identical in layout, behavior, and controls, you probably won't need to do this more than once.

When you complete a Microsoft certification exam, the software will tell you whether you've passed or failed. If you need to retake an exam, you'll have to schedule a new test with Prometric or VUE and pay another $100.

The first time you fail a test, you can retake it the next day. However, if you fail a second time, you must wait 14 days before retaking that test. The 14-day waiting period remains in effect for all retakes after the second failure.

# Tracking MCP Status

As soon as you pass any Microsoft exam (except Networking Essentials), you'll attain Microsoft Certified Professional (MCP) status. Microsoft also generates transcripts that indicate which exams you have passed. You can view a copy of your transcript at any time by going to the MCP secured site and selecting Transcript Tool. This tool will allow you to print a copy of your current transcript and confirm your certification status.

Once you pass the necessary set of exams, you'll be certified. Official certification normally takes anywhere from six to eight weeks, so don't expect to get your credentials overnight. When the package for a qualified certification arrives, it includes a Welcome Kit that contains a number of elements (see Microsoft's Web site for other benefits of specific certifications):

➤ A certificate suitable for framing, along with a wallet card and lapel pin.

➤ A license to use the MCP logo, thereby allowing you to use the logo in advertisements, promotions, and documents, and on letterhead, business cards, and so on. Along with the license comes an MCP logo sheet, which includes camera-ready artwork. (Note: Before using any of the artwork, individuals must sign and return a licensing agreement that indicates they'll abide by its terms and conditions.)

➤ A subscription to *Microsoft Certified Professional Magazine*, which provides ongoing data about testing and certification activities, requirements, and changes to the program.

Many people believe that the benefits of MCP certification go well beyond the perks that Microsoft provides to newly anointed members of this elite group. We're starting to see more job listings that request or require applicants to have an MCP, MCSE, and so on, and many individuals who complete the program can qualify for increases in pay and/or responsibility. As an official recognition of hard work and broad knowledge, one of the MCP credentials is a badge of honor in many IT organizations.

# How to Prepare for an Exam

Preparing for any Windows Server 2003–related test requires that you obtain and study materials designed to provide comprehensive information about the product and its capabilities that will appear on the specific exam for which you are preparing. The following list of materials will help you study and prepare:

➤ The Windows Server 2003 product CD-ROM includes comprehensive online documentation and related materials; it should be a primary resource when you are preparing for the test.

➤ The exam-preparation materials, practice tests, and self-assessment exams on the Microsoft Training & Services page at `www.microsoft.com/ trainingandservices/default.asp?PageID=mcp`. The Testing Innovations link offers examples of the new question types found on the Windows 2003 MCSE exams. Find the materials, download them, and use them!

➤ The exam-preparation advice, practice tests, questions of the day, and discussion groups on the ExamCram2.com e-learning and certification destination Web site (`www.examcram2.com`).

In addition, you'll probably find any or all of the following materials useful in your quest for Active Directory Infrastructure expertise:

➤ *Microsoft training kits*—Microsoft Press offers a training kit that specifically targets Exam 70-294. For more information, visit `www.microsoft.com/ mspress/`. This training kit contains information that you will find useful in preparing for the test.

➤ *Microsoft TechNet CD*—This monthly CD-based publication delivers numerous electronic titles that include coverage of Active Directory Infrastructure and related topics on the Technical Information (TechNet) CD. Its offerings include product facts, technical notes, tools and utilities, and information on how to access the Seminars Online training materials for Active Directory Infrastructure. A subscription to TechNet costs anywhere from $349 to $999 per year, but it is well worth the price. Visit `www.microsoft.com/technet/` and check out the information under the "TechNet Subscription" menu entry for more details.

➤ *Study guides*—Several publishers—including Que—offer Windows Server 2003 titles. Que Certification includes the following:

    ➤ *The Exam Cram 2 series*—These books give you information about the material you need to know to pass the tests.

    ➤ *The Training Guide series*—These books provide a greater level of detail than the *Exam Cram 2* books and are designed to teach you everything you need to know from an exam perspective. Each book comes with a CD-ROM that contains interactive practice exams in a variety of testing formats.

Together, the two series make a perfect pair.

➤ *Multimedia*—The PrepLogic Practice Tests CD-ROM that comes with each *Exam Cram 2* and *Training Guide* title features a powerful, state-of-the-art test engine that prepares you for the actual exam. PrepLogic Practice Tests are developed by certified IT professionals and are trusted by certification students around the world. For more information, visit www.preplogic.com.

➤ *Classroom training*—CTECs, online partners, and third-party training companies (such as Wave Technologies, Learning Tree, Data-Tech, and others) all offer classroom training on Windows Server 2003. These companies aim to help you prepare to pass Exam 70-294. Although such training runs upwards of $350 per day in class, most of the individuals lucky enough to partake find it to be quite worthwhile.

➤ *Other publications*—There's no shortage of materials available about Active Directory Infrastructure. The resource sections at the end of each chapter should give you an idea of where we think you should look for further discussion.

By far, this set of required and recommended materials represents a nonpareil collection of sources and resources for Active Directory Infrastructure and related topics. We anticipate you'll find that this book belongs in this company.

# About This Book

Each topical *Exam Cram 2* chapter follows a regular structure, along with graphical cues about important or useful information. Here's the structure of a typical chapter:

➤ *Opening hotlists*—Each chapter begins with a list of the terms, tools, and techniques you must learn and understand before you can be fully conversant with that chapter's subject matter. We follow the hotlists with one or two introductory paragraphs to set the stage for the rest of the chapter.

➤ *Topical coverage*—After the opening hotlists, each chapter covers a series of topics related to the chapter's subject title. Throughout this section, we highlight topics or concepts likely to appear on a test using a special Exam Alert layout, like this:

This is what an Exam Alert looks like. Normally, an Exam Alert stresses concepts, terms, software, or activities that are likely to relate to one or more certification test questions. For that reason, we think any information found offset in Exam Alert format is worthy of unusual attentiveness on your part. Indeed, most of the information that appears on The Cram Sheet appears as Exam Alerts within the text.

Pay close attention to material flagged as an Exam Alert; although all the information in this book pertains to what you need to know to pass the exam, we flag certain items that are really important. You'll find what appears in the meat of each chapter to be worth knowing, too, when preparing for the test. Because this book's material is very condensed, we recommend that you use this book along with other resources to achieve the maximum benefit.

In addition to the Exam Alerts, we have provided tips that will help you build a better foundation for Active Directory Infrastructure knowledge. Although the information may not be on the exam, it is certainly related and will help you become a better test-taker.

This is how tips are formatted. Keep your eyes open for these, and you'll become a Active Directory Infrastructure guru in no time!

➤ *Practice questions*—Although we talk about test questions and topics throughout the book, a section at the end of each chapter presents a series of mock test questions and explanations of both correct and incorrect answers.

➤ *Details and resources*—Every chapter ends with a section titled "Need to Know More?" This section provides direct pointers to Microsoft and third-party resources offering more details on the chapter's subject. In addition, this section tries to rank or at least rate the quality and thoroughness of the topic's coverage by each resource. If you find a resource you like in this collection, use it, but don't feel compelled to use all the resources. On the other hand, we recommend only resources we use on a regular basis, so none of our recommendations will be a waste of your time or money (but purchasing them all at once probably represents an expense that many network administrators and would-be MCPs and MCSEs might find hard to justify).

The bulk of the book follows this chapter structure slavishly, but there are a few other elements we'd like to point out. Chapters 11 and 13 include sample tests that provide a good review of the material presented throughout the book to ensure you're ready for the exam. Chapters 12 and 14 are the answer keys to these questions.

Finally, the tear-out Cram Sheet attached next to the inside front cover of this *Exam Cram 2* book represents a condensed and compiled collection of facts and tips we think you should memorize before taking the test. Because you can dump this information out of your head onto a piece of paper before taking the exam, you can master this information by brute force—you need to remember it only long enough to write it down when you walk into the test room. You might even want to look at it in the car or in the lobby of the testing center just before you walk in to take the test.

# How to Use This Book

We've structured the topics in this book to build on one another. Therefore, some topics in later chapters make more sense after you've read earlier chapters. That's why we suggest you read this book from front to back for your initial test preparation. If you need to brush up on a topic or you have to bone up for a second try, use the index or table of contents to go straight to the topics and questions you need to study. Beyond helping you prepare for the test, we think you'll find this book useful as a tightly focused reference to some of the most important aspects of Active Directory Infrastructure.

Given all the book's elements and its specialized focus, we've tried to create a tool that will help you prepare for—and pass—Microsoft Exam 70-294. Please share your feedback on the book with us, especially if you have ideas about how we can improve it for future test-takers.

Thanks, and enjoy the book!

# Self-Assessment

The reason we included a Self-Assessment in this *Exam Cram 2* book is to help you evaluate your readiness to tackle MCSE certification. It should also help you understand what you need to know to master the topic of this book—namely, Exam 70-294, "Planning, Implementing, and Maintaining a Microsoft Windows Server 2003 Active Directory Infrastructure." But before you tackle this Self-Assessment, let's talk about concerns you may face when pursuing an MCSE for Windows Server 2003 and what an ideal MCSE candidate might look like.

## MCSEs in the Real World

In the next section, we describe an ideal MCSE candidate, knowing full well that only a few real candidates will meet this ideal. In fact, our description of that ideal candidate might seem downright scary, especially with the changes that have been made to the program over the years. But take heart: Although the requirements to obtain an MCSE may seem formidable, they are by no means impossible to meet. However, be keenly aware that it does take time, involves some expense, and requires real effort to get through the process.

Increasing numbers of people are attaining Microsoft certifications, so the goal is within reach. You can get all the real-world motivation you need from knowing that many others have gone before, so you will be able to follow in their footsteps. If you're willing to tackle the process seriously and do what it takes to obtain the necessary experience and knowledge, you can take—and pass—all the certification tests involved in obtaining an MCSE. In fact, we've designed *Training Guides*, the companion to the *Exam Cram 2* series, to make it as easy on you as possible to prepare for these exams. We've also greatly expanded our Web site, www.examcram2.com, to provide a host of resources to help you prepare for the complexities of Windows Server 2003.

Besides MCSE, other Microsoft certifications include the following:

➤ MCSD, which is aimed at software developers and requires one specific exam, two more exams on client and distributed topics, plus a fourth elective exam drawn from a different, but limited, pool of options.

➤ Other Microsoft certifications, whose requirements range from one test (MCP) to several tests (MCP+SB, MCDBA).

# The Ideal Windows Server 2003 MCSE Candidate

Just to give you some idea of what an ideal MCSE candidate is like, here are some relevant statistics about the background and experience such an individual might have. Don't worry if you don't meet these qualifications or don't even come that close—this is a far-from-ideal world, and where you fall short is simply where you'll have more work to do:

➤ Academic or professional training in network theory, concepts, and operations. This includes everything from networking media and transmission techniques through network operating systems, services, and applications.

➤ Three-plus years of professional networking experience, including experience with Ethernet, token ring, modems, and other networking media. This must include installation, configuration, upgrade, and troubleshooting experience.

 The Windows Server 2003 MCSE program is rigorous; therefore, you'll really need some hands-on experience. Some of the exams require you to solve real-world case studies and network design issues, so the more hands-on experience you have, the better.

➤ Two-plus years in a networked environment that includes hands-on experience with Windows Server 2003, Windows XP Professional, Windows 2000 Server, Windows 2000 Professional, Windows NT Server, Windows NT Workstation, and Windows 95 or Windows 98. A solid understanding of each system's architecture, installation, configuration, maintenance, and troubleshooting is also essential.

➤ Knowledge of the various methods for installing Windows Server 2003, including manual and unattended installations.

➤ A thorough understanding of key networking protocols, addressing, and name resolution, including TCP/IP, IPX/SPX, and NetBEUI.

➤ A thorough understanding of NetBIOS naming, browsing, and file and print services.

➤ Familiarity with key Windows Server 2003–based, TCP/IP-based services, including HTTP (Web servers), DHCP, WINS, and DNS, plus familiarity with one or more of the following: Internet Information Services (IIS), Index Server, and Internet Security and Acceleration Server.

➤ An understanding of how to implement security for key network data in a Windows Server 2003 environment.

➤ Working knowledge of NetWare 3.x and 4.x, including IPX/SPX frame formats, NetWare file, print, and directory services, and both Novell and Microsoft client software. Working knowledge of Microsoft's Client Service for NetWare (CSNW), Gateway Service for NetWare (GSNW), the NetWare Migration Tool (NWCONV), and the NetWare Client for Windows (NT, 95, and 98) is essential.

➤ A good working understanding of Active Directory. The more you work with Windows Server 2003, the more you'll realize that this operating system is quite different from Windows NT. Newer technologies such as Active Directory have really changed the way that Windows is configured and used. We recommend that you find out as much as you can about Active Directory and acquire as much experience using this technology as possible. The time you take learning about Active Directory will be time very well spent!

Fundamentally, this boils down to a bachelor's degree in computer science, plus three years' experience working in a position involving network design, installation, configuration, and maintenance. We believe that well under half of all certification candidates meet these requirements, and that, in fact, most meet less than half of these requirements—at least when they begin the certification process. But because all the people who already have been certified have survived this ordeal, you can survive it, too, especially if you heed what our Self-Assessment can tell you about what you already know and what you need to learn.

# Put Yourself to the Test

The following series of questions and observations is designed to help you figure out how much work you must do to pursue Microsoft certification and what kinds of resources you may consult on your quest. Be absolutely honest in your answers; otherwise, you'll end up wasting money on exams you're not yet ready to take. There are no right or wrong answers, only steps along the path to certification. Only you can decide where you really belong in the broad spectrum of aspiring candidates.

Two things should be clear from the outset, however:

➤ Even a modest background in computer science will be helpful.

➤ Hands-on experience with Microsoft products and technologies is an essential ingredient to certification success.

# Educational Background

1. Have you ever taken any computer-related classes? [Yes or No]

   If Yes, proceed to question 2; if No, proceed to question 4.

2. Have you taken any classes on computer operating systems? [Yes or No]

   If Yes, you will probably be able to handle Microsoft's architecture and system component discussions. If you're rusty, brush up on basic operating system concepts, especially virtual memory, multitasking regimes, user mode versus kernel mode operation, and general computer security topics.

   If No, consider some basic reading in this area. We strongly recommend a good general operating systems book, such as *Operating System Concepts, 6th Edition*, by Abraham Silberschatz and Peter Baer Galvin (John Wiley & Sons, 2001, ISBN 0-471-41743-2). If this title doesn't appeal to you, check out reviews for other, similar titles at your favorite online bookstore.

3. Have you taken any networking concepts or technologies classes? [Yes or No]

   If Yes, you will probably be able to handle Microsoft's networking terminology, concepts, and technologies (brace yourself for frequent departures from normal usage). If you're rusty, brush up on basic networking concepts and terminology, especially networking media, transmission types, the OSI Reference Model, and networking technologies such as Ethernet, token ring, FDDI, and WAN links.

   If No, you might want to read one or two books in this topic area. The two best books that we know of are *Computer Networks, 4th Edition*, by Andrew S. Tanenbaum (Prentice-Hall, 2002, ISBN 0-13-066102-3) and

*Computer Networks and Internets, with Internet Applications, 3rd Edition*, by Douglas E. Comer (Prentice-Hall, 2001, ISBN 0-13-091449-5).

Skip to the next section, "Hands-on Experience."

4. Have you done any reading on operating systems or networks? [Yes or No]

If Yes, review the requirements stated in the first paragraphs after questions 2 and 3. If you meet those requirements, move on to the next section. If No, consult the recommended reading for both topics. A strong background will help you prepare for the Microsoft exams better than just about anything else.

# Hands-on Experience

The most important key to success on all the Microsoft tests is hands-on experience, especially with Windows Server 2003 and Windows XP Professional, plus the many add-on services and BackOffice components around which so many of the Microsoft certification exams revolve. If we leave you with only one realization after taking this Self-Assessment, it should be that there's no substitute for time spent installing, configuring, and using the various Microsoft products upon which you'll be tested repeatedly and in depth.

5. Have you installed, configured, and worked with:

➤ Windows 2000 Server or Windows Server 2003? [Yes or No]

If Yes, make sure you understand basic concepts as covered in Exam 70-215 and/or 70-290. You should also study the TCP/IP interfaces, utilities, and services for Exam 70-216 or 70-291 and 70-293, plus implementing security features for Exam 70-220.

You can download objectives, practice exams, and other data about Microsoft exams from the Training and Certification page at www.microsoft.com/traincert. Use the "Exams" link to obtain specific exam information.

If you haven't worked with Windows Server 2003, you must obtain one or two machines and a copy of the operating system. Then, learn the operating system and any other software components on which you'll also be tested.

In fact, we recommend that you obtain two computers, each with a network interface, and set up a two-node network on which to practice. With decent Windows Server 2003–capable computers selling for about $500 to $600 apiece these days, this shouldn't be too much of a financial hardship. You may have to scrounge to come up with the necessary software, but if you scour the Microsoft Web site you can usually find low-cost options to obtain evaluation copies of most of the software you'll need.

➤ Windows XP Professional? [Yes or No]

If Yes, make sure you understand the concepts covered in Exam 70-270.

If No, you will want to obtain a copy of Windows XP Professional and learn how to install, configure, and maintain it. You can use *MCSE Windows XP Professional Exam Cram 2* (ISBN 0789728745) to guide your activities and studies, or you can work straight from Microsoft's test objectives if you prefer.

For any and all of these Microsoft exams, the Resource Kits for the topics involved are a good study resource. You can purchase soft cover Resource Kits from Microsoft Press (search for them at www.microsoft.com/mspress), but they also appear on the TechNet CDs (www.microsoft.com/technet). Along with the *Exam Cram 2* and *Training Guide* series, we believe that Resource Kits are among the best tools you can use to prepare for Microsoft exams.

**6.** For any specific Microsoft product that is not itself an operating system (for example, SQL Server), have you installed, configured, used, and upgraded this software? [Yes or No]

If the answer is Yes, skip to the next section. If it's No, you must get some experience. Read on for suggestions on how to do this.

Experience is a must with any Microsoft product exam, be it something as simple as FrontPage or as challenging as SQL Server. For trial copies of other software, search Microsoft's Web site using the name of the product as your search term. Also, search for bundles such as "BackOffice" or "Small Business Server."

If you have the funds, or your employer will pay your way, consider taking a class at a Certified Training and Education Center (CTEC) or at an Authorized Academic Training Partner (AATP). In addition to classroom exposure to the topic of your choice, you get a copy of the software that is the focus of your course, along with a trial version of whatever operating system it needs, with the training materials for that class.

Before you even think about taking any Microsoft exam, make sure you've spent enough time with the related software to understand how it may be installed and configured, how to maintain such an installation, and how to troubleshoot that software when things go wrong. This will help you in the exam, and in real life!

# Testing Your Exam-Readiness

Whether you attend a formal class on a specific topic to get ready for an exam or use written materials to study on your own, some preparation for the Microsoft certification exams is essential. At $125 a try, pass or fail, you want to do everything you can to pass on your first try. That's where studying comes in.

We have included a practice exam in this book, so if you don't score that well on the test, you can study more and then tackle the test again. We also have exams that you can take online through the ExamCram2.com Web site at www.examcram2.com. If you still don't hit a score of at least 70% after these tests, you'll want to investigate the other practice test resources we mention in this section.

For any given subject, consider taking a class if you've tackled self-study materials, taken the test, and failed anyway. The opportunity to interact with an instructor and fellow students can make all the difference in the world, if you can afford that privilege. For information about Microsoft classes, visit the Training and Certification page at www.microsoft.com/traincert/training/find/find.asp for Microsoft Certified Education Centers or www.microsoft.com/education/msitacademy for the Microsoft IT Academy Program.

If you can't afford to take a class, visit the Training and Certification page anyway, because it also includes pointers to free practice exams and to Microsoft Certified Professional Approved Study Guides and other self-study tools. And even if you can't afford to spend much at all, you should still invest in some low-cost practice exams from commercial vendors.

7. Have you taken a practice exam on your chosen test subject? [Yes or No]

If Yes, and you scored 70% or better, you're probably ready to tackle the real thing. If your score isn't above that threshold, keep at it until you break that barrier.

If No, obtain all the free and low-budget practice tests you can find and get to work. Keep at it until you can break the passing threshold comfortably.

When it comes to assessing your test readiness, there is no better way than to take a good-quality practice exam and pass with a score of 70% or better. When we're preparing ourselves, we shoot for 80% or better, just to leave room for the "weirdness factor" that sometimes shows up on Microsoft exams.

# Assessing Readiness for Exam 70-294

In addition to the general exam-readiness information in the previous section, you can do several things to prepare for the Planning, Implementing, and Maintaining a Microsoft Windows Server 2003 Active Directory Infrastructure exam. As you're getting ready for Exam 70-294, visit www.examcram2.com for the latest information on this exam, and be sure to sign up for the Question of the Day. You'll also find www.cramsession.com to be an excellent resource for your exam preparation. We also suggest that you join an active MCSE mailing list. One of the better ones is managed by Sunbelt Software. Sign up at www.sunbelt-software.com (look for the "Subscribe to..." button).

Microsoft exam mavens also recommend checking the Microsoft Knowledge Base (available on its own CD as part of the TechNet collection, or on the Microsoft Web site at http://support.microsoft.com/support/) for "meaningful technical support issues" that relate to your exam's topics. Although we're not sure exactly what the quoted phrase means, we have also noticed some overlap between technical support questions on particular products and troubleshooting questions on the exams for those products.

# Onward, Through the Fog!

Once you've assessed your readiness, undertaken the right background studies, obtained the hands-on experience that will help you understand the products and technologies at work, and reviewed the many sources of information to help you prepare for a test, you'll be ready to take a round of practice tests. When your scores come back positive enough to get you through the exam, you're ready to go after the real thing. If you follow our assessment regime, you'll not only know what you need to study, but when you're ready to make a test date at Prometric or VUE. Good luck!

# Planning and Implementing Forests and Domains

## Terms you'll need to understand:

✓ Forest
✓ Domain
✓ Workgroup
✓ Member server
✓ Forest root
✓ Domain controller
✓ Trust relationship

✓ Schema
✓ UPN suffix
✓ dcpromo
✓ SYSVOL
✓ Application data partitions
✓ Forest and domain functional levels

## Techniques/concepts you'll need to master:

✓ Implementing an Active Directory forest and domain structure
✓ Creating the forest root domain
✓ Creating a child domain
✓ Creating and configuring application data partitions
✓ Installing and configuring an Active Directory domain controller

✓ Setting forest and domain functional levels
✓ Establishing trust relationships, including external trusts, shortcut trusts, and cross-forest trusts
✓ Managing trust relationships
✓ Managing schema modifications
✓ Adding and removing a UPN suffix

After the installation of Windows Server 2003, the system will exist in one of two settings. The server will be a member server (or standalone server) of a workgroup, or it will be a member server of an existing domain. In either state, the server will have the capability of holding several roles. For example, a standalone server would be able to handle the sharing of folders and files, Web services through IIS, media services, database services, print services—the list of functional uses is long. However, directory services are not part of a member server's functionality. For that reason, you may need to consider implementing a "domain" environment.

What are some of the immediate advantages of a domain environment? Perhaps your company requires a single point of logon, centralized management of resources, scalability, or your network and directory infrastructure to be able to grow with your company over time. Making that first move toward a domain begins with establishing your first domain controller (DC). To accomplish this with Windows Server 2003, you need to install the Windows Server 2003 Active Directory (AD) service and configure it properly to suit your company's needs. This endeavor requires some forethought and planning to allow for a smooth domain deployment.

# The Windows Server 2003 Domain

The term *domain* is not new to the networking vernacular. The way Windows Server 2003 utilizes the concept, however, is quite advanced. The Windows Server 2003 domain is defined as being a boundary for security that provides an organized means of structuring users, resources, and directory information. It also provides a method for replicating that information, and it provides the core administrative services in a Windows Server 2003 network. In Windows Server 2003, only one directory database, called the *Active Directory (AD)*, stores all the user accounts and other resources for the domain. This centralized structure means that users need only have one account that will provide access to all resources for which they are given permission.

In the actual creation of a domain, you identify a Domain Name System (DNS) name for the domain. This requires some planning to choose a name that is appropriate from both a corporate and legal standpoint. Windows Server 2003 domains utilize the DNS naming convention to maintain an organized structure. Because the first domain created will be the top-level domain in your directories' infrastructure, this domain is the most crucial, especially if you will be implementing additional domains in the network. Another term for the first domain is the *root domain*, so named because it is the root of the  first domain tree in the forest and, by extension, the entire forest.

Even though it is small, a single domain without child domains is still considered its own domain tree. In addition, this single domain is called the *forest root* because it becomes the first tree of a possible new forest. The forest root can be likened to the foundation of a building, which holds up the rest of the structure. The foundation of a domain must be solid, and it begins by the promotion of a member server to be a domain controller. You accomplish this promotion by installing AD. Before installation can proceed, however, you must ensure that certain requirements have been met on the server that will be your DC.

# Requirements for AD

Whenever you implement a new feature within a Windows product, minimum hardware and software requirements must be met so that the feature will work adequately. The first requirement is fairly obvious: You must have a computer running Windows Server 2003. Meeting this AD requirement ensures that your system meets the minimum hardware for your operating system.

 There are actually four versions of Windows Server 2003—Standard Edition, Enterprise Edition, Datacenter Edition, and Web Edition, as well as 64-bit versions of the Enterprise and Datacenter editions for Intel Itanium processors. Some of the key differences in versions relate to the number of processors supported, the amount of RAM supported, and clustering/load balancing support. For this book and exam, the Standard Edition and Enterprise Edition of Windows Server 2003 are interchangeable.

The following list identifies the requirements for the installation of Windows Server 2003:

➤ *CPU*—Pentium 133MHz or higher (733MHz or higher recommended)

➤ *Memory*—128MB minimum (256MB recommended)

➤ *Hard disk space*—1.5GB of free space

➤ *Display*—VGA resolution or higher

➤ *CD-ROM or network installation*—Supported

The primary difference between versions of Windows Server 2003 is the number of processors supported. The Web Edition supports up to two processors, Standard supports up to four processors, Enterprise up to eight, and Datacenter up to 64 (eight minimum).

Once the operating system is installed, the following requirements are necessary to install AD:

➤ Depending on the partition of the hard disk where you plan to install your AD database and transaction log files, you will need 200MB for the database and 50MB for the transaction logs. The files can reside on a partition that is formatted with the FAT (file allocation table), FAT32, or NTFS (NT File System) file system. These files will grow over time as more objects are added, so you need to ensure the space is sufficient. Additional space is required if your DC is also configured to be a Global Catalog server.

➤ Along with the database and transaction logs, a special folder structure is created during the installation, and the root folder is called SYSVOL. This folder must reside on an NTFS partition. If your system doesn't have an NTFS partition, the AD installation will fail.

 If you would like to install your SYSVOL folder on a partition that you already have allocated as FAT and you cannot reformat the partition without losing critical data (as in the case of your boot and system partitions), you need to use the **convert** command. Go to a command prompt and type **convert.exe c: /fs:ntfs**, where **c:** should be replaced with the drive letter you require.

➤ Another requirement is that your system is functioning under TCP/IP and utilizing a Domain Name System (DNS) server. If you've forgotten to establish a DNS server, this will be provided as an option during AD installation.

Once you've established that your server meets the requirements to install AD and you have invested the necessary time in planning your first DC, it's time to kick off the installation.

# The AD Installation Wizard

The actual creation of the first domain of your network is not a difficult task. You are simply promoting a Windows Server 2003 server to be a domain controller by using the AD Installation Wizard. You are creating your forest root as the first DC of your new domain.

The AD Installation Wizard, unlike some wizards, does not have an icon or shortcut to execute. It requires that you select Start, Run. In the Run box, type dcpromo.exe (or just dcpromo for short) and hit Enter.

This wizard offers the following directory service installation options:

➤ Create a domain controller for a new domain.

➤ Create a new domain tree or join an existing domain as a child domain.

➤ Create a new forest of domain trees or join an existing forest.

The next three sections discuss the different functions of this wizard.

# Installing Your First Domain

To install the first DC by promoting a member server, follow these steps:

> If you install Windows Server 2003 on a server that is a primary or backup domain controller for an NT 4 domain, upgrading the server will automatically make it as a Windows Server 2003 DC that includes the user and group accounts and configurations, unless you specify that the install is not an upgrade of the NT 4 domain controller. It is important to note, though, that the first Windows NT 4 domain controller to be upgraded must be the PDC.

1. Begin the promotion by selecting Start, Run and typing dcpromo.exe. Press Enter.

2. Once your AD Installation Wizard has initialized, you will see a screen that welcomes you to the wizard. Select Next.

3. The first screen you are presented with, shown in Figure 1.1, is a warning telling you that Windows 95 and Windows NT 4.0 SP3 and earlier computers are unable to log on to Windows Server 2003 domain controllers. If this is a consideration on your network, you will have to address this prior to implementing a Windows Server 2003 domain controller.

![Active Directory Installation Wizard - Operating System Compatibility screen showing warning about improved security settings in Windows Server 2003 affecting older versions of Windows. Lists Windows 95 and Windows NT 4.0 SP3 or earlier as versions that cannot meet the new requirements.]

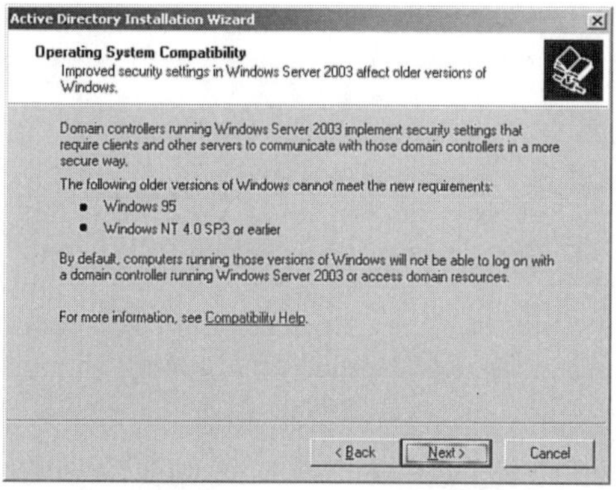

**Figure 1.1**   Security compatibility warning about Windows 95 and NT 4.0 SP3 and earlier clients.

**4.** As shown in Figure 1.2, you are presented with two options: creating a DC of a new domain (either a child domain, new domain tree, or new forest) and creating an additional DC for an existing domain (which will take on the account information of the domain joined). Because this is the first domain of a new forest, select the first radio button and click the Next button.

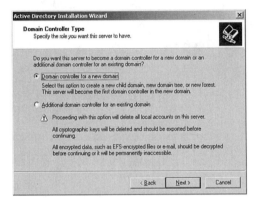

**Figure 1.2** Domain Controller Type screen.

**5.** You are now asked whether you want to create a new domain tree in a new forest, a new child domain in an existing domain tree, or a new domain tree in an existing forest. This is shown in Figure 1.3. In the case of creating a new domain in a new forest, you select the first radio button and click the Next button.

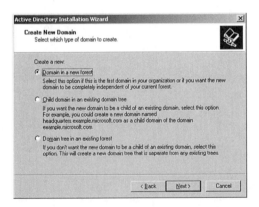

**Figure 1.3** Create new domain trees in a new or existing forest, or create a child domain.

**6.** The next screen is short, as shown in Figure 1.4. You are asked to supply the full DNS name of your domain. If you've planned your naming strategy and registered a name for your company's domain, use that name. If you are implementing your directory structure in a test environment without a registered domain name, use a fictitious DNS name. Click the Next button.

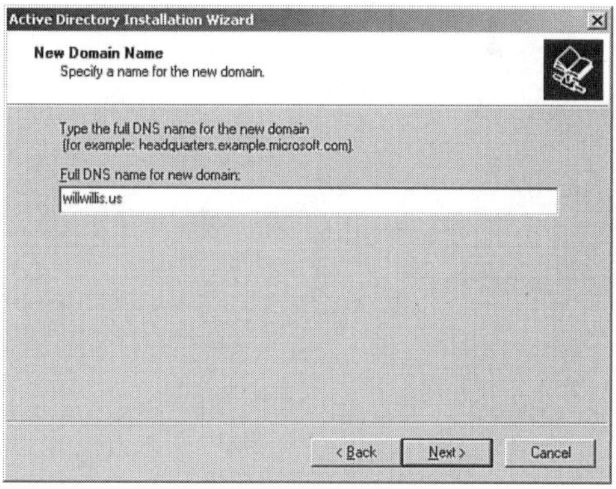

**Figure 1.4**    Your forest root domain name.

7. The next screen, shown in Figure 1.5, requests your NetBIOS name. This name is used for clients running earlier versions of Windows or Windows NT that utilize NetBIOS for the location of their DCs. It is usually the same as the first part of your domain name. Enter the name and click the Next button.

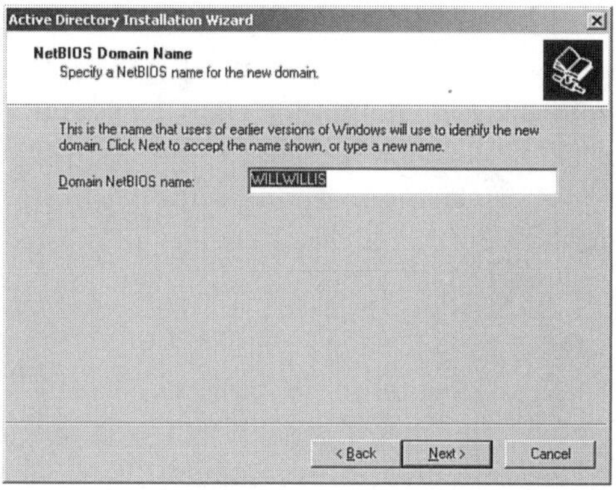

**Figure 1.5**    The NetBIOS name provides for backward compatibility with legacy clients.

8. The next screen, shown in Figure 1.6, specifies the location of the AD database and log files. These files can exist on any of the supported file systems for Windows Server 2003. Remember, the minimum requirement for AD is 200MB for the database and 50MB for the log files.

Also, remember that minimum requirements should usually be exceeded to allow for flexibility and growth. Choose your location and then click the Next button.

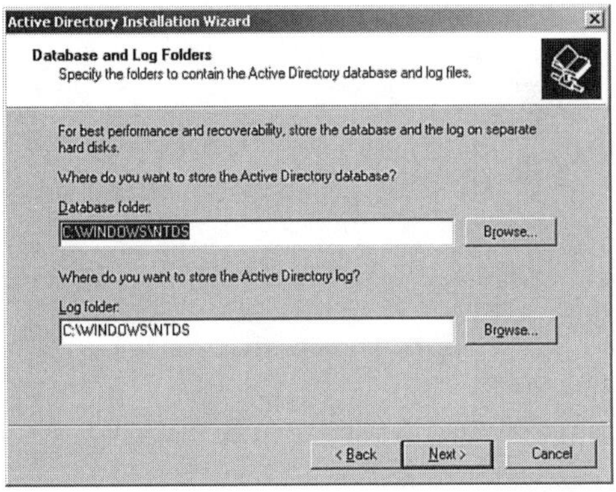

**Figure 1.6** Database and log files.

Placing your database files and your log files on separate hard drives is recommended. Your database holds your directory, whereas your log file holds your temporary database changes before they are written to the actual database. This creates a conflict of interest for your hard drive as information is written back and forth. Placing the files on different drives (not partitions) will ensure equal time to both files.

9. The next screen, shown in Figure 1.7, is quite important and necessary to your AD installation. Here you specify the location for the SYSVOL folder. This folder, which will be shared, allows the DCs to receive replicas of the information within. Therefore, it must be on an NTFS partition. Indicate the location of this folder and then click the Next button.

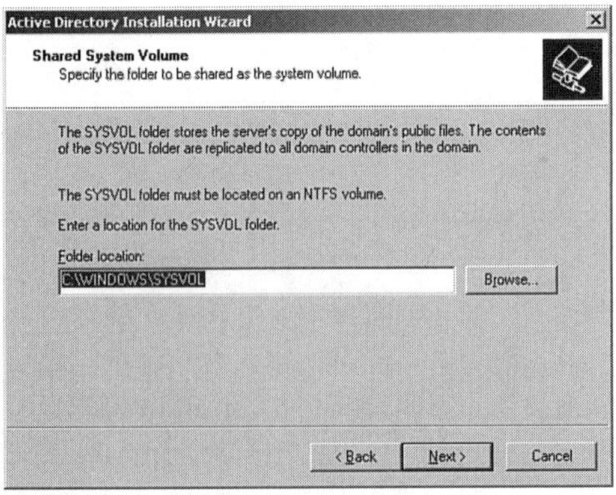

**Figure 1.7** The placement of the SYSVOL folder.

10. The next step in the installation process is the DNS Registration Diagnostics screen, shown in Figure 1.8. The purpose of this is to determine whether an existing DNS server has already been configured or if the Active Directory Installation Wizard needs to install and configure the DNS service as part of the installation. Figure 1.8 shows a DNS server that has already been set up for use by AD. If no DNS server is located, the AD Installation Wizard will install it behind the scenes as part of the actual installation.

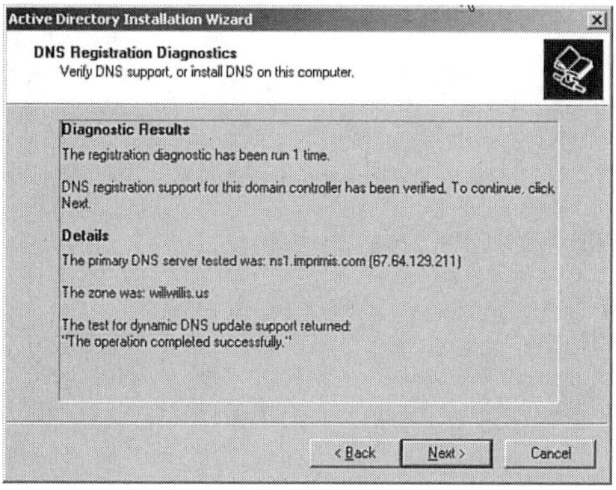

**Figure 1.8**   The AD Installation Wizard needs to determine the status of DNS prior to installation.

11. The next screen, shown in Figure 1.9, asks whether you want to allow permissions to be compatible with pre–Windows 2000 servers or if you want to allow Windows 2000– and Windows Server 2003–compatible permissions only. The first selection comes with a warning. If you enable this option, anonymous users will be able to read information on the domain. This can be beneficial in some cases—for example, if you are migrating toward Windows Server 2003 from a Windows NT 4 platform and will have a mixed environment of remote access servers. With this type of situation, your users dialing in from home will have difficulty logging in to the domain if they contact a Windows Server 2003 DC, unless the permissions are oriented toward a pre–Windows 2000 or 2003 system. Select your choice and then click the Next button.

12. The next screen, shown in Figure 1.10, is where you specify the password for the administrative account that is used during Directory Services Restore Mode. Because the AD service is not started when entering this mode, it will be necessary for you to be authenticated by the server through another means. A non-AD database containing the administrator's name and password allows authentication under these circumstances. Specify your administrative password and then click the Next button.

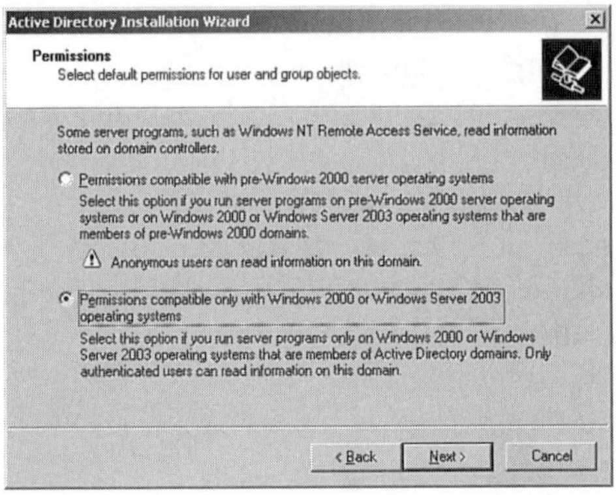

**Figure 1.9**    The permissions screen allows you to set the default permissions for user and group objects.

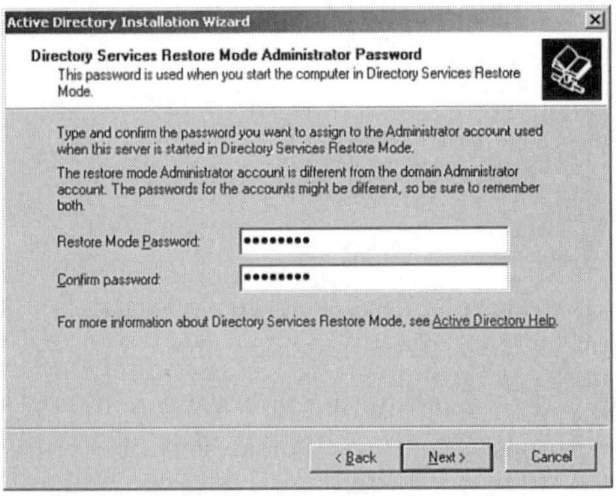

**Figure 1.10**    Configuring the password for the administrative account used in Directory Services Restore Mode.

**13.** When all your information is complete, you get the final screen, shown in Figure 1.11, which is customized to your choices. Look them over before clicking the Next button. After you do, the installation will follow through until you see a final screen of completion, where you should click Finish.

Your installation will now proceed by establishing your system as the first DC for your new domain tree under a new forest root.

**Figure 1.11**   The final promotion screen.

# Deciding Which Type of DNS to Use

As already mentioned, having a DNS server for your AD installation is a pre-requisite. However, you can determine which type of DNS server you will use. Although your choices are limited, they do exist. Let's assume that you haven't made your decision by the time you install AD. Not a problem—Windows Server 2003 will make the decision for you.

After you've indicated the location of the SYSVOL folder, the wizard will begin a search for the DNS in the IP stack to see whether it exists and whether it supports dynamic updates. In our scenario, a DNS server already existed, so it was unnecessary for the AD Installation Wizard to install and configure DNS. However, if DNS is not located, you will receive an inform-ative prompt that it will be created for you. Click OK at this point.

Once the DNS service is configured and supports dynamic updates (which would be automatically done during the installation), the rest of your instal-lation can proceed.

Active Directory installation does not automatically set the DNS to allow automatic updates unless you tell the wizard to do so. Microsoft recommends that you set this or allow the AD Installation Wizard to set it for you if the wizard is also installing DNS as part of AD installation. However, AD will work without enabling dynamic updates. If you do not allow dynamic updates, you have to manually synchronize the SRV resource records when you add or remove additional domain controllers.

# The Lesser-Known Roles of the Wizard

On the surface, the AD Installation Wizard appears merely to handle the various screens that require user input. However, this understates its full role. Prior to an installation, the wizard performs the following checks:

1. Before the wizard even opens, it makes sure the user is a member of the local Administrators group and is on a Windows Server 2003 server. It also checks that the server is ready to move forward without needing to reboot or complete some previously begun procedure. If the User Interface portion clears, the wizard moves on.

2. The wizard verifies that the NetBIOS and server names are unique in the forest.

3. The wizard checks the TCP/IP configuration to ensure that the system is fully functional and capable of reaching the DNS server. That DNS server must be able to provide dynamic updates or have manually provided an SRV resource record within your DNS; otherwise, the AD Installation Wizard will prompt you later to create a DNS server.

4. The wizard checks to ensure that the DNS and NetBIOS domain names are unique.

5. The final stages of verification involve checking the user's credentials to ensure he or she has the correct security permissions and, finally, that the files can be located where the user has specified.

In configuring the directory service, the AD Installation Wizard handles the following tasks:

➤ Making Registry changes for the AD

➤ Setting up Kerberos

➤ Setting the Local Security Authority (LSA) policy

➤ Placing the new tools into Administrative Tools (accessed through Start, Programs, Administrative Tools)

➤ Establishing performance counters for AD

➤ Setting up X.509 certificate acceptance

In addition, depending on the installation, the wizard might create the schema directory partition, the configuration directory partition, and the domain directory partition. These are all portions of the directory that are held in a hierarchical fashion and replicated out to other DCs. If the installation is the first in the forest, the wizard will create the forest root domain, and as part of the process it will create the DNS root zone and the forward lookup zone for the domain.

# Fault-Tolerant Replicas

The concept of *fault-tolerant replicas* is simple: It refers to creating additional DCs within a single domain. Additional DCs in a domain help share the load and improve performance. They also provide fault tolerance, because if one DC goes down, the other DCs can authenticate the users and provide normal operations while the damaged DC is repaired.

When adding more DCs to a domain, keep the following factors in mind:

➤ The more DCs you have in a domain, the greater the logon authenticity, because when users log on to the domain, they can gain authentication from any one of the DCs. Client computers will attempt to log on first to a DC in their own site and then look to DCs in other sites if they cannot locate a DC in their own site.

➤ Each of the DCs will replicate or share its copy of the AD database with other DCs in the domain that it is configured to replicate with by the Knowledge Consistency Checker (KCC), or configured manually by the administrator. Adding more DCs to a domain also increases the following, thereby degrading network performance:

➤ The amount of replication that takes place within the domain

➤ The amount of bandwidth that is used on the network

When deciding how many DCs are going to be on the domain, you must consider both of these factors. You need to balance increased speed of logon authentication against bandwidth usage due to directory replication.

Adding DCs to a domain is not a difficult task. Starting with a Windows Server 2003 server, you promote it using the `dcpromo.exe` command, which executes the AD Installation Wizard. Instead of selecting the option Domain Controller for a New Domain, you select Additional Domain Controller for an Existing Domain (refer back to Figure 1.2).

Additionally, you could create a child domain under an existing domain by following much the same process as outlined earlier in the chapter. The main difference in the process is selecting the option to create a child domain at the first part of the AD Installation Wizard. An example of child domains would be to take the willwillis.us domain we created previously during the installation and to create marketing.willwillis.us, support.willwillis.us, and sales.willwillis.us child domains underneath it. Child domains are useful for delegating administrative roles to a particular division, without giving permissions over the entire domain tree, as well as for controlling replication.

Once you have created the first domain, how do you know that your installation was a successful one? This topic is discussed in the next section.

# Troubleshooting Your AD Installation

Any number of things can cause your AD installation to fail. Here are a few scenarios:

➤ *You get an Access Denied error message when creating or adding DCs*—These types of error messages usually indicate an incorrect user account. Perhaps you have logged on with an account that doesn't have permissions in the Local Administrators group of the server on which you are trying to create a new domain. Or, as in the case of adding a DC to a preexisting domain, it's possible that you are not a member of the Domain Administrators group.

Be conscious of situations where you are not a member of the Domain Administrators group, especially if you are asked about the accounts needed to install AD on a system.

➤ *Your DNS and NetBIOS names are not unique*—Not much of a choice here; you must have unique names, so you need to change them to names that are unique. The only exception to this rule would be in a testing/training situation, where you are testing the various options for the domain structure in a lab environment (not a production environment, we hope), and you've added systems to the domain and then failed to remove them correctly, perhaps by merely formatting the drive. Now your AD domain tree might still see these nonexistent names as being present. To resolve this problem, you need to edit AD with some additional tools that Microsoft provides, such as ADSI Edit, a snap-in for the Microsoft Management Console (MMC) that acts as a low-level AD editor. A potential gotcha is that NetBIOS names are limited to 15 characters (plus two hidden hex characters assigned by the operating system), whereas DNS domain names don't have that limitation. For example, if you have a domain called WINDOWS2003NETWORK1.COM and try to create WINDOWS2003NETWORK2.COM, the creation of the NetBIOS name for the second domain will fail if you leave it at the default. This is because only the first 15 characters of the DNS name would be used for the NetBIOS name.

➤ *The DC cannot be contacted, and you are sure a DC is up and running*—This situation might indicate that DNS is not set up correctly. Several areas of concern with DNS have already been discussed, but you should ensure that SRV resource records are present for the domain being contacted. Check your DNS server first to make certain these records exist. If they do exist, use the NSLOOKUP tool to determine whether you can resolve DNS names on the computer where you are installing AD. These records are created when the first domain controller is successfully installed with Active Directory.

➤ *You have an insufficient amount of disk space or you don't have an NTFS partition*—You must have a minimum of 250MB of disk space for the database and transaction logs. You must also have an NTFS partition for the SYSVOL folder. If you can't free enough space, consider using another volume or partition to store these files. If you do not have an NTFS partition and cannot create one, you need to convert your existing partition. If you are running Windows Server 2003 Server in a dual-boot situation with Windows 98 on a FAT32 partition, you will not be able to make the move toward a DC and retain your Windows 98 operating system under FAT32; you must convert your partition or remain a member server with FAT32. Naturally, you wouldn't run a dual-boot with Windows 98 and Windows Server 2003 outside of a lab environment, but it's something to consider if you are practicing for the exam using your home computer or another computer with an existing Windows 98 installation.

Microsoft does not recommend having a Windows Server 2003 server in a dual-boot configuration.

# Verifying Your AD Installation

Once your installation is complete and the system has rebooted, you may want to verify your installation. Verification can be accomplished in a number of ways, the easiest being a check of your newly acquired Administrative Tools. However, you have a few other options to ensure a valid installation.

## File Verification

One way to verify that your installation is complete is to ensure that the AD files are located where you've specified. The following is a list of files that are necessary for AD:

➤ NTDS.DIT—The directory database file.

➤ EDB.LOG *and* EDB.CHK—The EDB files are the transaction logs and the checkpoint files. Transaction logs temporarily hold transactions before they are written to the directory. The checkpoint files are pointer files that track transaction logs once they have been committed to the database. These files work in harmony to ensure an accurate database with multiple points of strength.

➤ RES1.LOG *and* RES2.LOG—RES files are reserved files that are used for low-disk-space situations. These two files are 10MB in size, as are all transaction logs. Because these files are permanent, there is always a way to write to a file, even when disk space is low.

## SYSVOL

Another way to make sure you've had a successful install is to ensure the SYSVOL folder structure is on an NTFS partition and contains a server copy of all shared files, including Group Policy and scripts. The SYSVOL folder should include several subfolders, including these:

➤ Domain

➤ Staging

➤ Staging Areas

➤ Sysvol

The SYSVOL folder within should be shared out as, you guessed it, SYSVOL. Another necessary folder that should be shared is the Scripts folder under the Domain folder, which is under the SYSVOL folder. The Scripts folder is shared out as NETLOGON and is used for backward compatibility with Windows NT systems that search for scripts during logon in the NETLOGON share.

## Final Checkpoints

You can investigate many avenues to ensure your AD install was successful, but the most direct method is to check within the event logs. Event logs retain several different types of logs that help you quickly pinpoint a failure, whether it's on the system itself or with one of the services, such as DNS. A Directory Services log is even created when you install Active Directory.

If DNS doesn't seem to be functioning properly, you'll have to troubleshoot your DNS installation (such as verifying records with the NSLOOKUP tool and monitoring your DNS forward and recursive queries within the DNS properties on the Monitoring tab). That's beyond the scope of this exam, though, and is covered on the 70-291 Network Infrastructure Exam.

# AD Removal

At times, you might want to remove your AD, especially if you've done some restructuring of your accounts and find that some domains require unnecessary administrative overhead, or if certain DCs are simply not required and are creating a strain on the network because of an overabundance of replication. You remove AD with the same tool you used to install it—the AD Installation Wizard. Logically, not just any user can remove AD from the DC. If you are removing the last DC in a domain (meaning you are removing the domain), you must be logged on as a member of the Enterprise Admins group. If the DC you are removing is not the last DC in a domain, you must be a member of either the Domain Admins group or the Enterprise Admins group.

## What Removing AD Entails

When you remove AD, the following actions occur (which are reversals of what took place when you installed AD):

➤ Group Policy security settings are removed, and Local Security is reenabled for local security settings.

➤ Any Flexible Single Master Operations (FSMO) roles are transferred over to other DCs, if any exist.

> ➤ The SYSVOL folder hierarchy is removed, along with any related items within, including the NetLogon share.

> ➤ The DNS is updated to remove DC Locator service records.

> ➤ The local Security Accounts Manager (SAM) is now used for user authentication.

> ➤ Services related to AD are stopped and configured not to start automatically.

> ➤ If there is another DC, final changes are replicated to that controller before AD is shut down. The system that is removing AD will notify the remaining DCs to remove it from the DC's OU.

# Troubleshooting AD Removal

Follow these hints if you run into problems during AD removal:

> ➤ If your DC cannot verify that no child domains exist and you believe there aren't any, you probably had these child domains at one time and failed to remove them the correct way from the domain. Your AD database still holds records for these domains, although they have been physically taken offline. Now your DC won't allow you to uninstall AD without cleaning these out with some effort and searching.

> ➤ If you cannot connect to a DC in the parent domain to replicate changes, the removal may not proceed smoothly or any final changes may not replicate. In either case, your parent DC would not be notified properly of the removal, and a dilemma similar to the preceding one would exist.

Sometimes removing AD is a problem, for whatever reason the removal doesn't work. In most cases there are reasons, such as data not having finished replicating to other domain controllers. However, in a production environment you can't always wait and you might need to do a removal immediately, or in a lab environment you might not need to wait at all. In such cases you can force the removal of Active Directory. You must be running Windows 2000 SP4 or later (or at minimum you must have SP3 and the Q332199 hotfix installed) or Windows Server 2003 to forcibly remove AD. Simply run dcpromo /forceremoval to get the process to go through.

Now that we've covered the usual procedures for the installation and removal of AD, let's go back and explore some other types of installation, such as an unattended installation of AD.

# Unattended Installation of AD

An unattended installation is not a new idea, although the AD portion of it is completely new. The concept is simple. Instead of manually answering the questions posed by the installation wizard, an unattended installation of Windows Server 2003 provides all the answers to the installation questions automatically. These questions are answered through the use of an answer file and usually a uniqueness database file (UDF file) so that both the standard questions and the unique ones are given responses without human intervention.

Because the installation of Windows Server 2003 only completes to the point where the server is assigned as either a member server of a workgroup or a member server of a domain, the final portion of the installation, the promotion, is still manually handled. Microsoft, however, has established a method of directory services installation that can be either completely automated from start to finish or at least automated for the promotion to AD.

The installation of Windows Server 2003 is not our primary concern at this point, although you should have a thorough understanding of the two executable programs that begin the installation (namely, `winnt.exe` and `winnt32.exe`) and the various switches that allow for the selection of an answer file and a UDF file for an unattended installation. You should also know that the Setup Manager program (which can be found in the Windows Server 2003 Resource Kit, officially titled `setupmgr.exe`) is used to create these important files. Finally, you should be aware that you can automate the installation of AD in one of these two ways:

➤ You can provide additional information within the answer file that is used to automate the installation of Windows Server 2003.

➤ You can create a separate answer file to be run in conjunction with the `dcpromo.exe` program.

Regardless of the option you choose, the command executed is the same:

```
dcpromo/answer:<answer file>"
```

# The GuiRunOnce Section

To automate a complete installation of both the operating system and AD, you will need to make some configuration changes to the answer file under a section titled [GuiRunOnce]. This section contains a list of commands to be executed the first time a user logs on to the computer after GUI (Graphical

User Interface) mode setup has completed. Each line specifies a command to be executed by the GuiRunOnce entry. One of those entries could include the command to begin the AD Installation Wizard with dcpromo.exe. In addition, the command could include the request to reach out for another answer file (named by the administrator who created it) so that the installation creates a complete DC under Windows Server 2003. It is worth noting that performing an unattended installation, though, won't get you around the prerequisite of needing to have the required level of permissions to install AD. Therefore, the user account you use to run DCPROMO must still be a member of the Enterprise Admins group.

A side point to keep in mind when running commands using the GuiRunOnce key is that they will run in the context of the user who is currently logged in. Therefore, the user must have the permissions to run such a command. However, this is usually not an issue in establishing a complete unattended installation of Windows Server 2003 with AD.

Here is an example of an unattended installation file that uses the GuiRunOnce key to search for the AD answer file:

```
[Unattended]
  OemSkipEula = Yes

[GuiUnattended]
  AutoLogon = Yes
  AdminPassword = *
  OEMSkipRegional = 1
  OemSkipWelcome = 1
  TimeZone = 33

[UserData]
  FullName = "Polo DC Servers"
  OrgName = "Polo Fuzzball Suppliers, Inc."
  ComputerName = DC-Polo1

[LicenseFilePrintData]
  AutoMode = PerSeat

[GuiRunOnce]
  Command0 = "dcpromo /answer:dcanswer.txt"

[Identification]
  DomainAdmin = "CORPDOM\InstallAcct"
  DomainAdminPassword = 12345678A
  JoinDomain = "POLODOM"
```

Logically, if the unattended file can contain a line that utilizes dcpromo with an answer file for AD, two things must be true. First, you must create that AD answer file; otherwise, the command won't work. Second, you can utilize that answer file at any time by typing in the command and path from the Run option in the Start menu.

# The **DCInstall** Section

This section of the answer file is necessary for the AD Installation Wizard to have its questions answered automatically. Below this section are many keys that hold values that allow for the questions to be answered without human intervention. If a key doesn't have a value specified, a default value will be used. Here are descriptions of a few of the keys; their values and defaults are listed in Table 1.1.

> The keys are listed alphabetically, not according to the order in which they are used in the answer file. Also, this is an abbreviated list of important keys. To learn a great deal more about unattended installation files and the keys involved, refer to the \Support\Tools folder on the Windows Server 2003 installation CD-ROM. When executed, the **deploy.cab** file allows you to view a document called **unattend.doc**. This document contains about 150 pages of information on unattended installs.

➤ `AutoConfigDNS`—Answers the question as to whether or not DNS should be configured automatically, if dynamic DNS updates aren't available.

➤ `ChildName`—Indicates the name of the child domain. This name would be added to the portion of the domain name that is the parent domain. For example, if the domain you are joining is que.com and the name specified here is sales, the total domain would be sales.que.com.

➤ `CreateOrJoin`—Indicates whether the new domain that is created is part of an existing forest or would become a separate forest of domains.

➤ `DatabasePath`—Specifies the location of the database files. Logically, enough disk space should be available on the disk that you specify. As mentioned in the "Deciding Which Type of DNS to Use" section earlier in this chapter, for performance purposes, placing the database files on a separate disk from the log files is best.

➤ `DomainNetBiosName`—Indicates the NetBIOS name within the domain. This must be a unique name.

➤ `LogPath`—Specifies the location of the log files. Logically, enough disk space should be available on the disk you specify. As mentioned in the "Deciding Which Type of DNS to Use" section earlier in this chapter, for performance purposes, placing the database files on a separate disk from the database files is best.

➤ `NewDomainDNSName`—Specifies the full name of a new tree within a preexisting domain. This could also specify the full name when a new forest is being created.

➤ ReplicaDomainDNSName—Indicates the DNS name of the domain that will be replicated from. This name must be accurate because the installation will search for the DC that is considered its replication point of contact. That DC must be up and running to handle the request for the replication.

➤ ReplicaOrNewDomain—Indicates whether a new DC will be the first DC of a new domain or will be a replica of a preexisting domain.

➤ SysVolPath—Provides the path for the Sysvol folder structure. By extension, the path must lead toward an NTFS Version 5 partition for the install to be functional.

➤ TreeOrChild—Indicates whether the new domain will be a root domain of a new tree or will become a child domain beneath a preexisting parent domain.

| Table 1.1 Values and Defaults of Keys | | |
|---|---|---|
| Key | Value | Default |
| AutoConfigDNS | Yes I No | Yes |
| ChildName | Value: <child domain name> | — |
| CreateOrJoin | Create I Join | Join |
| DatabasePath | <path to database files> | "%systemroot%\NTDS" |
| DomainNetBiosName | <domain NetBIOS name> | — |
| LogPath | <path to log files> | "%systemroot%\NTDS" |
| NewDomainDNSName | <DNS name of domain> | — |
| ReplicaDomainDNSName | <DNS name of domain> | — |
| ReplicaOrNewDomain | Replica I Domain | Replica |
| SysVolPath | <path to database file> | "%systemroot%\sysvol" |
| TreeOrChild | Tree I Child | Child |

You may be wondering whether remembering all these options is absolutely necessary. That is not the reason they are listed. These only comprise a portion of the entire list of options you can research when and if you plan on creating your unattended installation file for AD. They are provided to help you realize the amount of work that can go into setting up the file correctly so that it deploys smoothly.

# Post-AD Installation Options

Once AD is installed and running correctly, you might want to investigate several different options.

# Integrated Zones

Now that AD is installed, perhaps you would like to implement AD integrated zones within your DNS structure. Integrated zones allow the DNS zone files to be replicated by the AD replication engine, as opposed to being replicated through DNS zone transfers, because the zone database files will be included within AD rather than stored in their usual systemroot/System32/DNS folder.

Once your server is supporting AD integrated zones, you will be able to configure your zones for secure dynamic updates with the DNS Secure Update Protocol. This will allow a greater level of security on your DNS updates.

# Domain Mode Options

Windows Server 2003 supports four different types of domain modes: Windows 2000 mixed mode, Windows 2000 native mode, Windows Server 2003 interim, and Windows Server 2003 mode. Upon first installing or upgrading your domain to Windows Server 2003, you will be running in Windows 2000 mixed mode, which supports having Windows NT 4, Windows 2000, and Windows Server 2003 domain controllers in your domain. This mode does not allow for all the functionality of Active Directory though, so you may decide to change over to Windows 2003 mode to take advantage of added functionality that becomes available. The differences between the three modes are described in the following sections.

## Windows 2000 Mixed Mode

Mixed mode is used for supporting DCs that are Windows NT 4 controllers. While moving your current structure toward Windows Server 2003, there may be a period of time during which you will continue to use Windows NT 4 backup domain controllers (BDCs), and by running in mixed mode, the Windows Server 2003 DCs will be able to synchronize information. Although there is no timetable for how long you must run in mixed mode, Microsoft recommends that you switch to native mode when you no longer have Windows NT 4 DCs in your domain so that you can take advantage of native mode's additional functionality. Windows 2000 mixed mode also supports having Windows 2000 domain controllers.

 You can continue to run in mixed mode even if there are no Windows NT 4 DCs in the domain. Also, you can make the move toward native mode even if you still have remaining Windows NT 4 member servers present in your domain because they do not require the synchronization between the servers.

## Windows 2000 Native Mode

If you are installing Windows Server 2003 in an environment with no preexisting Windows NT 4 DCs, but one that had Windows 2000 domain controllers, you should consider native mode. Native mode provides several enhancements, including the following:

➤ *Group nesting*—Allows you more flexibility to place groups within other groups to allow permissions to flow through, such as placing global groups into other global groups, or local groups into other local groups, or nesting universal groups. Prior to this, the only nesting supported was placing global groups into local groups.

➤ *Universal groups*—Enables another level of group possibilities, allowing for forestwide group implementations. Universal groups are covered in detail in Chapter 4, "User and Group Administration."

➤ *Security ID (SID) history*—Used during migrations to retain the original SID of the objects that are moved.

## Windows Server 2003 Interim Mode

A special functional level exists specifically for the purpose of upgrading the first Windows NT 4 domain to become the forest root domain in a Windows Server 2003 forest: the Windows Server 2003 interim functional level. When you upgrade a Windows NT 4 PDC to Windows Server 2003, you are given the option of setting the functional level to Windows Server 2003 during setup, provided you choose to create a new forest.

This functional level only supports domain controllers running Windows Server 2003 and Windows NT 4; Windows 2000 domain controllers are not supported. The Windows Server 2003 interim mode affords the same level of forest-level functionality as the Windows 2000 forest functional level (forest functional levels are discussed next), but with the added benefit of improved replication scalability and efficiency.

## Windows Server 2003 Mode

If you have only Windows Server 2003 domain controllers in your domain, and after you've upgraded any preexisting Windows NT 4 and Windows 2000 domain controllers, you can convert your domain to a Windows Server 2003 functional level. The term *functional level* is used in Windows Server 2003 rather than *mode*. As with changing from Windows 2000 mixed mode to Windows 2000 native mode, raising the functional level to Windows Server 2003 is irreversible.

Windows Server 2003 though goes further than Windows 2000 in that there are *domain functional levels* and *forest functional levels*. As you would expect, the differences between the two relate to functionality at the domain and forest levels, respectively.

You cannot raise the functional level of the forest until all domains in the forest are operating at the Windows Server 2003 functional level.

When you raise the domain functional level of a domain, you get the benefits of going from Windows 2000 mixed mode to Windows 2000 native mode, plus the following:

➤ *Domain Rename*—The ability to rename domain controllers without having to remove and reinstall AD.

➤ *Update Logon Timestamp*—Allows you to track a user account's logon history.

➤ *User password on InetOrgPerson*—The InetOrgPerson object class is used in some LDAP and X.500 directory services to represent people within an organization. This feature allows you to set the password just like you would any other user account, and it makes migrating from other directory services to AD more efficient.

If all your domains are raised to the Windows Server 2003 functional level, you can then raise your forest functional level from the default Windows 2000 to Windows Server 2003. As with raising the domain functional level, once you raise the forest functional level you cannot revert back to the Windows 2000 level without rebuilding your forest from scratch (not a pleasant thought in a production environment). The Windows Server 2003 functional level gains you the following forest-level functionality:

➤ Improved Global Catalog (GC) replication, such as the preservation of the synchronization status of the GC, which reduces the amount of data to be replicated

➤ The ability to deactivate schema classes and attributes, and to reactivate them later if desired

➤ Forest-level trust relationships

➤ The ability to rename domains without removing them and reinstalling

➤ Linked value replication to improve AD replication efficiency

➤ Support for linking dynamic auxiliary classes directly to individual objects and not just classes of objects

It is important to remember that although you can raise functional levels, you cannot lower them. So, if you are going to make the move, ensure your readiness. You can change functional levels in one of two ways:

➤ Through Active Directory Users and Computers

➤ Through Active Directory Domains and Trusts

In either tool the options will be the same. Open either AD Users and Computers or AD Domains and Trusts. To raise the domain functional level, right-click the domain and then select Raise Domain Functional Level. The dialog box shows you the current domain functional level, with a drop-down list to choose any higher levels to which you can raise the domain. In our scenario, shown in Figure 1.12, we're in Windows 2000 mixed mode still and have the choices of Windows 2000 native mode and Windows Server 2003 on the drop-down list. Once you select a higher level and click the Raise button, you cannot go back to the previous level without removing the domain and reinstalling it.

Raising the forest functional level is very similar. The only difference is that instead of right-clicking the domain to select the option, you right-click the root container of the Active Directory Domains and Trusts console and select Raise Forest Functional Level.

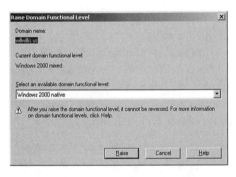

**Figure 1.12**   Raising the domain functional level is easy, but there is no going back.

You are still in the early stages of the installation at this point. Now you can move on to thinking about the next stage: Organizational Units.

# UPN Suffixes

One of the tasks you will need to know for the exam is how to add and remove a user principle name (UPN) suffix. The UPN is in most cases the full DNS domain name of the object. Windows Server 2003 is fully backward compatible so you can still use the traditional Windows *domain\user* format for logon authentication, or you can use the UPN. The UPN suffix is the domain portion of the UPN, such as @willwillis.us in user1@willwillis.us. Windows Server 2003 allows you to configure alternate UPN suffixes for logon, which can be used to provide additional security (having the user log in with the alternate rather than the primary suffix), or to simplify the naming in multiple-level child domains. For example, if you had the child domain Lewisville.texas.studio.willwillis.us, the default UPN suffix would be that same lengthy name with an "at" (@) symbol in front of it. A user named Meli logging in to that domain would have a UPN of Meli@lewisville.texas. studio.willwillis.us. As an administrator you might create an alternate UPN suffix for logon purposes called *Lewisville*, whereby the user's UPN would instead just be Meli@Lewisville. This is much easier to work with, and more secure if someone is trying to authenticate using the default UPN.

To create an alternate UPN suffix, open the Active Directory Domains and Trusts administrative console, right-click the root container, and select Properties. This will bring you to the UPN Suffixes dialog box, shown in Figure 1.13. Simply type in the name of the UPN suffix you wish to add and then click Add. Note that it is not necessary to type in the @ symbol here. It will be added for you automatically. Including it here will actually cause problems because you'll end up with a UPN suffix such as @@willwillis.us.

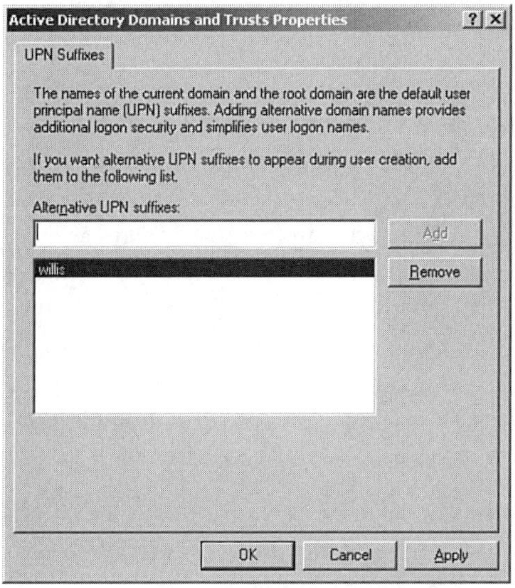

**Figure 1.13**   You can easily add and remove alternate UPN suffixes for your domain.

Something important to consider is that if you remove a suffix that is in use, user accounts that reference that suffix will not be able to authenticate.

To test the results of your new suffix, open up the Active Directory Users and Computers administrative console and either go through the process of creating a new user or go into the properties of an existing user account and access the Account tab. In either case you should have your new alternate UPN available as an option on the drop-down list next to the logon name.

# Application Data Partitions

Another new feature in Windows Server 2003's version of Active Directory that wasn't available in Windows 2000 is the concept of *application data partitions*. An application data partition is a partitioned section of Active Directory that is replicated only to specified domain controllers. The advantages of such a configuration is that replication traffic is reduced and therefore more efficient. Application data partitions can only be hosted on Windows Server 2003 domain controllers. In addition to replication efficiency, application data partitions provide fault tolerance by storing replicas on specified domain controllers in the forest. In this sense they differ from the domain directory partitions AD uses, because AD directory partitions are replicated to all domain controllers in a domain.

Application data partitions are typically created by applications that can use them, because they store application-specific data. As an administrator you may never have to manually create or configure an application data partition, but Microsoft gives you the ability to do so anyway through the NTDSUTIL command-line utility (there are a couple of other ways as well, which we'll discuss a bit later). Because you'll likely be tested on configuring application data partitions, we'll walk through the process of it at the end of this section. Furthermore, replication of application data partitions is managed automatically through Active Directory's Knowledge Consistency Checker (KCC), which is a built-in AD process that runs on all domain controllers and manages the replication topology for the forest.

As far as naming goes, an application data partition is part of the overall DNS namespace in your forest. Similar to creating a domain, there are three possible ways you can place your application data partition:

➤ As a child of a domain directory partition

➤ As a child of another application data partition

➤ As a new tree in a forest

Naming an application data partition requires following the same rules and conventions as naming DNS domains. One thing to note is that you cannot create a domain directory partition as a child of an application data partition. For example, if you have an application data partition named app1.quepublishing.com, you cannot create a domain that has a DNS name of domain1.app1.quepublishing.com.

Previously we mentioned that although applications typically handle the management of their own application data partitions, and replication is handled by the KCC, Windows Server 2003 provides administrators with the ability to manually create and manage application data partitions. You have a total of four ways to create, delete, and manage your application data partitions:

➤ By using application-specific tools supplied by software vendors

➤ By using the `ntdsutil.exe` command-line utility

➤ By using `LDP.exe`

➤ By using Active Directory Service Interfaces (ADSI)

Using ADSI typically involves some level of programming, and for the exam you will only need to concern yourself with the NTDSUTIL utility, which we will discuss next.

# Creating an Application Data Partition

You can use the NTDSUTIL command-line utility to manually create application data partitions. Simply open a command prompt and type `ntdsutil` and press Enter. When you do so, you will be presented with a cryptic prompt that just reads `ntdsutil:` and a flashing cursor. If you press the ? key and hit Enter, you will see a menu like the one shown in Figure 1.14.

In order to perform the following steps, the user account you use must be a member of the Domain Admins or Enterprise Admins groups.

1. To begin the process of creating an application data partition, type `domain management` and press Enter. You will see the prompt change from `ntdsutil:` to `domain management:`.

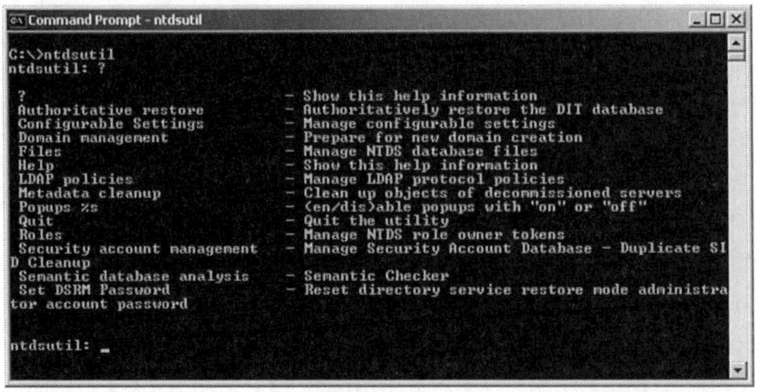

**Figure 1.14** NTDSUTIL provides a number of options for managing your server.

**2.** Next, type the following:

```
create nc ApplicationDataPartition DomainController
```

Here, you would substitute *ApplicationDataPartition* with the distinguished name of the partition you want to create, and you would substitute *DomainController* with the fully qualified domain name (FQDN) of the domain controller you want to create the application data partition on. Putting it all together, if we wanted to create an application data partition named adptest1.willwillis.us on a domain controller named studio1.willwillis.us, we would type the following line at the prompt:

```
create nc dc=adptest1,dc=willwillis,dc=us studio1.willwillis.us
```

**3.** At this point, assuming you substituted names that are valid on your network, you would see a message that the object is being added to Active Directory. When the process has completed you will be returned to the `domain management:` prompt.

Deleting an application data partition follows the same procedure; you simply substitute `create` with `delete` in the preceding syntax. Once you remove the last replica of an application data partition, any data it contained will be lost.

# Trust Relationships

On a small network, you might only have a single Active Directory forest and domain. However, larger companies often divide their networks into multiple forests and domains. This can be for delegation of administration, for political boundaries, or for any number of other reasons. As a network grows more complex, so does the administration of the network. In order to facilitate network usability and management, Windows Server 2003 uses the concept of *trust relationships* between domains and forests.

A trust relationship at its basic level is simply a configured link that allows a domain to access another domain, or a forest to access another forest. A typical use is to allow users in one domain or forest to access resources in another domain or forest without having to have a separate user account in the other domain or forest. When a trust relationship is established between domains, users in one domain can be granted permissions to shared resources (such as folders or printers) in the other domain. This simplifies both the management of the network, in that administrators don't have to duplicate accounts, and network usability from an end-user standpoint, because they don't have to keep track of multiple accounts and passwords to access the resources they need.

Depending on your needs, Windows Server 2003 offers the following types of trusts:

➤ Transitive trusts

➤ Forest trusts

➤ External trusts

➤ Realm trusts

➤ Shortcut trusts

# Transitive Trusts

Transitive trusts were first introduced in Windows 2000, and they were a great improvement over the older Windows NT–style trusts that required explicitly defining each and every trust relationship (something that could be unwieldy in a large enterprise environment). For example, prior to Windows 2000, if Domain1 trusted Domain2, and Domain2 trusted Domain3, there was no implicit relationship between Domain1 and Domain3. That is, a trust would also need to be manually configured between Domain1 and Domain3 if needed.

With Windows 2000 and Windows Server 2003, transitive trusts simplify administration. In the preceding example, if Domain1 trusts Domain2, and Domain2 trusts Domain3, then Domain1 would automatically trust Domain3. Two-way transitive trusts are automatically configured by Windows Server 2003 whenever a new domain is added to an existing domain tree. For instance, if you add a child domain called texas.studio.will-willis.us, a two-way transitive trust would automatically be created between the new child and the parent domain (studio.willwillis.us) and its parent (willwillis.us). Likewise, when a new domain tree is added to an existing forest, two-way transitive trusts are created automatically between the new domain tree and each tree in the forest.

Transitive trusts are created automatically by Windows Server 2003 and do not require administrative management. The other four types of trust, which we'll discuss next, require the administrator to configure them manually. A command-line tool called netdom is provided by Windows Server 2003, and a graphical application called the New Trust Wizard is available as well. For the exam you won't need to know the specifics of netdom, so in this chapter we will focus on using the New Trust Wizard. After discussing each type of trust we'll look at the process of actually creating a trust relationship.

## Forest Trusts

As the name suggests, forest trusts are used to share resources between forests. The trust relationship can either be one-way or two-way, and it's transitive in nature. It is important to note that forest trusts must be created between the forest root domains in each Windows Server 2003 forest, and trusts created between non-forest root domains in different forests are not forest trusts but rather *external trusts*, which are discussed in the next section.

A one-way forest trust allows users in one forest to access resources in another forest (assuming permission is given to the desired resources), but not the other way around. A two-way forest trust allows users in domains in both forests to access resources in the trusting forest. Because forest trusts are transitive, child domains in a forest receive the benefit of the trust relationship between forest root domains. That is, if a trust relationship is established between willwillis.us and virtual-realm.com, users in the child domain studio.willwillis.us would automatically be a part of the trust through the transitive nature of forest trusts.

It is important to note that to create a forest trust, both forests must be operating at the Windows Server 2003 forest functional level.

## External Trusts

External trusts are similar to forest trusts in that they must be explicitly configured by an administrator, but that's where the similarity ends. External trusts are *nontransitive*, meaning you use them to explicitly define a one-to-one relationship between domains. They are commonly used when you still have Windows NT 4 domains on your network, because Windows NT 4 did not support transitive trust relationships and used a flat domain structure rather than the hierarchical tree structure of Active Directory. You would therefore use an external trust to set up a trust relationship between a Windows Server 2003 domain and a Windows NT 4 domain.

External trusts have another use as well. We noted earlier that forest trusts need to be configured between forest root domains and are transitive. If you happen to not want that but still want to create a trust relationship between domains in different forests, you would use an external trust. For example, if you only want the Windows Server 2003 domains studio.willwillis.us and design.virtual-realm.com to have a trust relationship, without involving the parent domains, you would configure external trusts between the two.

External trusts, naturally, can be configured as one-way or two-way. The New Trust Wizard, which we will discuss later, allows you to specify at the time of creating the trust whether it is two-way, one-way outgoing, or one-way incoming.

# Realm Trusts

One of the more exciting new features of Windows Server 2003 is the ability to create *realm trusts*, which allow for interoperability between a Windows Server 2003 Active Directory forest and any non-Windows realm that supports Kerberos 5 (such as Unix). In the past, Microsoft has taken the approach of closing off domains to only being able to enter into trust relationships with other Windows domains. Now, if you have a heterogeneous environment that can utilize Kerberos 5, you have the opportunity to exploit the benefits of trust relationships.

Realm trusts have extra flexibility in that you can define them as either transitive or nontransitive, depending on your needs. When you use the New Trust Wizard you are given the choice of transitivity as well as whether to make the trust one-way or two-way.

# Shortcut Trusts

Shortcut trusts are useful administrative trusts that help speed up the time it takes for user authentication. For example, consider a situation where a forest contains the domain trees willwillis.us and virtual-realm.com. Users in the child domain texas.studio.willwillis.us regularly access a shared folder in texas.design.virtual-realm.com to collaborate on projects. When a user attempts to access the resource, the authentication request has to travel the path of the trust relationship. That means the authentication token passes through texas.design.virtual-realm.com, design.virtual-realm.com, virtual-realm.com, willwillis.us, studio.willwillis.us, and finally texas.studio.will-willis.us. Because this can become cumbersome, especially in an even more complex forest, shortcut trusts were created.

In the preceding scenario, a shortcut trust could be configured between texas.studio.willwillis.us and texas.design.virtual-realm.com to speed up the authentication processing. They shorten the path necessary for authentication to travel, thus speeding up performance. Shortcut trusts are transitive in nature and like other manually configured trusts can be configured either as one-way or two-way.

It is important to note the difference between external trusts and shortcut trusts. Shortcut trusts are used to connect domains in domain trees within the same forest. External trusts are used to connect domains in different forests.

# New Trust Wizard

Now that we've discussed the various kinds of trust relationships that can be configured in Windows Server 2003, let's use the New Trust Wizard to configure a trust relationship. In our example, we will configure a forest trust between two distinct Windows Server 2003 Active Directory forests: willwillis.us and virtual-realm.com. To complete the task on your end, you need a lab environment with two domains configured in their own forests. If you have that, just substitute the names of your domains for what we have here.

Before we begin, you should note that in order to configure a trust, you need to have administrative privileges in both domains or forests, depending on at what level you are configuring the trust.

Now here are the steps to follow:

1. Open the Active Directory Domains and Trusts administrative console on a domain controller in one of the domains that will be participating in the trust. In this scenario, where we're are creating a forest trust between the forest root domains willwillis.us and virtual-realm.com, we will open the console on the domain controller wmdr.virtual-realm.com.

2. Right-click the forest root domain (in this case, virtual-realm.com) and click Properties. When the Domain Properties window opens, click the Trusts tab. You will see a dialog box similar to the one shown in Figure 1.15.

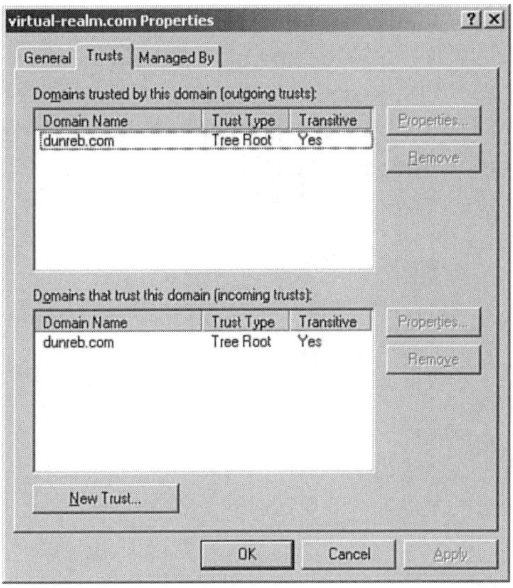

**Figure 1.15**    The Trusts tab of the domain properties is where you manually configure trust relationships.

**3.** Click the New Trust button to launch the New Trust Wizard. When the welcome screen appears, click next.

**4.** The first screen, shown in Figure 1.16, is where you specify the DNS name of the domain or forest for the trust. You can use a NetBIOS name if the destination is a domain, but if it is a forest you must use the DNS name. Type in the name and click next.

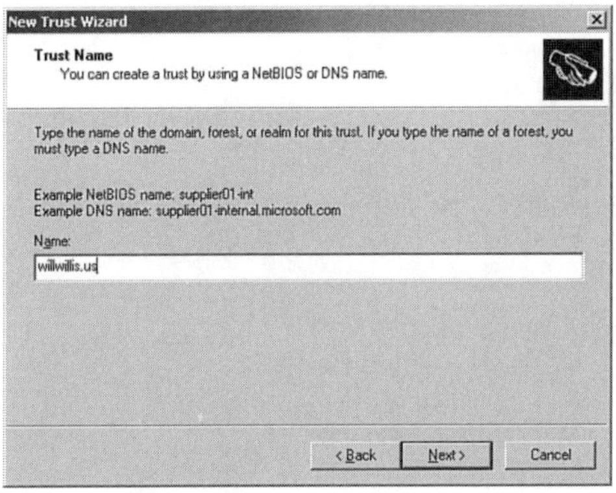

**Figure 1.16**    The first step in creating a trust is to specify the domain or forest on the other end of the domain you are configuring.

**5.** The next screen, shown in Figure 1.17, is where you choose whether to create an external trust or a forest trust. If the domain you specified in step 4 is not a forest root domain, you would not have the option of creating a forest trust. Likewise, if it is a Windows NT domain or a Unix realm, the options here would be to create a realm trust or external trust. Essentially the wizard tailors itself to your choices. Because we are creating a forest trust, select that and click Next.

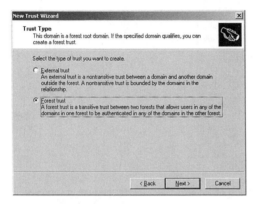

**Figure 1.17**   Once the wizard identifies the destination domain, you are given relevant choices as to the type of trust to create.

6. After choosing the trust type, you are presented with the screen shown in Figure 1.18. Here you choose whether to create a two-way trust or a one-way trust (incoming or outgoing). Select a two-way trust and click Next.

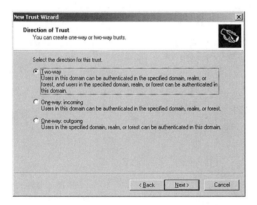

**Figure 1.18**   Trusts can be two-way, one-way incoming, or one-way outgoing.

7. On the next screen you can choose whether to create both sides of the trust simultaneously (if you have the appropriate permissions) or just this side of the trust. In our example, we know the administrator account in the destination domain, so we will choose to create both

sides now. If you were working in conjunction with another administrator in the other domain/forest, you would create just this side of the trust and have the other administrator repeat the process in the other domain. Figure 1.19 shows this step.

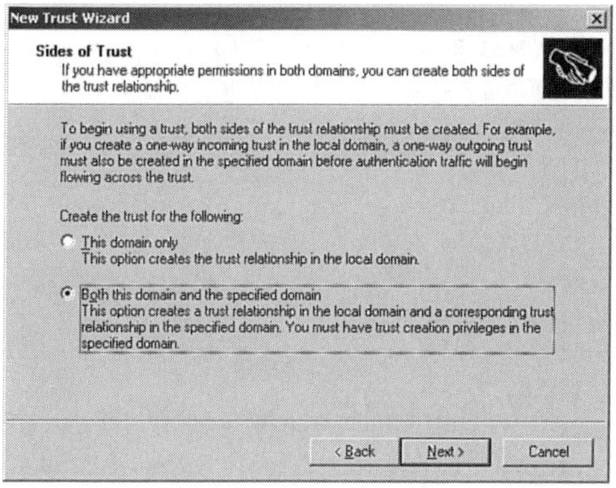

**Figure 1.19**    You can create both sides of a trust if you have the administrator permissions in both domains, or you can create just one side of the trust.

8. Because we chose to create both sides of the forest trust, we are prompted for a valid administrative username and password for the destination forest root domain (willwillis.us). This is shown in Figure 1.20. Supply the account information and click Next.

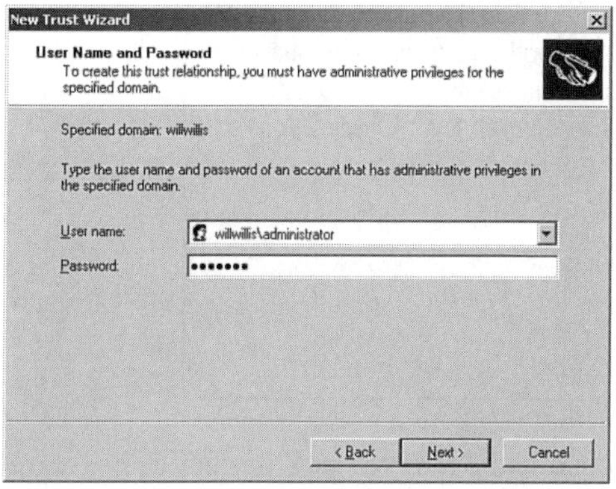

**Figure 1.20**    To create the trust in the destination forest root domain, you must supply a valid administrative username and password for that forest.

At this point the New Trust Wizard will proceed with configuring the forest trust relationship, and when it is finished you will be able to view the trust status on the Trust tab of each domain's property sheet (similar to what's shown in Figure 1.15, earlier in this section).

# Exam Prep Questions

## Question 1

You install Active Directory on a server and you want it to be a separate domain that is part of an existing tree structure with a forest root containing a contiguous namespace. What is this type of domain called?

- O A. A replica
- O B. A parent domain
- O C. A child domain
- O D. A forest root

Answer C is correct. A child domain is one that exists below a parent domain and continues to use a contiguous namespace. Answer A is incorrect because a secondary domain controller, as a replica, would not be a "separate domain." Answer B is incorrect because there is already an existing domain in the domain tree. As a result, it cannot have another parent created above it. Answer D is incorrect because the forest root would have been established first in order to add a child domain.

## Question 2

In order to troubleshoot an installation problem with a particular application, the vendor asks you to manually create an application data partition on your domain controller. What utilities could you use to accomplish this? [Check all correct answers.]

- ❑ A. ADSI
- ❑ B. Active Directory Users and Computers
- ❑ C. NTDSUTIL
- ❑ D. DNS administrative console

Answers A and C are correct. You can use ADSI to programmatically create application data partitions, or you can use the ntdsutil.exe command-line utility. Answer B is incorrect because Active Directory Users and Computers does not give you the ability to manage application data partitions, and answer D is incorrect because although application data partitions are required to be in DNS name formats and resemble DNS domain names, you cannot create them with the DNS console.

# Question 3

You are giving a presentation to executive management on upgrading your
Active Directory domains from Windows 2000 to Windows Server 2003. You
are asked how this upgrade will improve connectivity with the Unix users. Which
of the following features would you describe for the executive committee?

○ A.  Realm trusts

○ B.  Forest trusts

○ C.  Shortcut trusts

○ D.  External trusts

Answer A is correct. Realm trusts in Windows Server 2003 provide you with
the ability to create trust relationships between Windows Server 2003 and
any outside realm that supports the Kerberos 5 protocol. As a result, you
could establish trust relationships between your Unix environment and the
Windows Server 2003 domains, improving administrative efficiency and
end-user usability. Answer B is incorrect because forest trusts can only be
established between Windows Server 2003 forests, which doesn't meet the
needs of the question. Answer C is likewise incorrect because shortcut trusts
are for connecting domains in different trees within the same Windows
Server 2003 forest. Answer D is incorrect because external trusts are used for
connecting Windows Server 2003 domains to Windows NT 4 domains and
for connecting Windows Server 2003 domains from separate forests that are
not connected by a forest trust.

# Question 4

Your installation of Active Directory halts because the SYSVOL folder cannot
seem to be placed where you've specified. What is the most likely cause of the
problem?

○ A.  You've requested that it go on a partition that doesn't have enough
         space.

○ B.  You've formatted the partition with NTFS.

○ C.  The drive letter you've specified doesn't exist.

○ D.  The partition you are specifying is FAT or FAT32.

Answer D is correct. The SYSVOL folder structure must be on an NTFS partition. Answers A and C are incorrect because, although they are possible causes, the question asks for the "most likely" cause. Answer B is incorrect because
putting the SYSVOL folder on an NTFS partition would have actually been
the correct thing to do.

# Question 5

> In selecting the locations of your database and log files, which two of the following options would enhance the performance of these files?
>
> ❑ A. Placing them on the same NTFS partition
>
> ❑ B. Ensuring plenty of hard disk space for these files to expand
>
> ❑ C. Placing them on separate physical disks
>
> ❑ D. Restricting them to small-sized partitions for additional control over their size

Answers B and C are correct. Plenty of room and separate physical disks will make for a healthy database and log file configuration. Answer A is incorrect because, although placing the files on an NTFS partition isn't a bad idea, it doesn't enhance performance. Answer D is incorrect because you don't want to prevent your database and log files from growing. This is a normal part of the directory service.

# Question 6

> Which of the following is not a valid domain functional level for a Windows Server 2003 domain?
>
> ○ A. Windows 2000 mixed mode
>
> ○ B. Windows 2000 native mode
>
> ○ C. Windows Server 2003 functional level
>
> ○ D. Windows Server 2003 native mode

Answer D is correct. When domain functional levels are discussed, the term *native mode* refers to Windows 2000 native mode. In Windows 2000, this is the highest mode the domain can run at. In Windows Server 2003, the "native mode" is simply called the Windows Server 2003 *functional level*. Answers A, B, and C are all valid functional levels in Windows Server 2003.

# Question 7

You are the senior network administrator for an enterprise that has four Windows Server 2003 forests consisting of 15 domains. A junior administrator is struggling with some concepts and asks if you can explain why you have trust relationships configured between some domains when they are in the same forest. Which of the following would be the best answer?

○ A.  Shortcut trusts improve the efficiency of user authentication.

○ B.  Shortcut trusts are required in order to connect child domains in different domain trees, even in the same forest.

○ C.  External trusts are required in order to connect child domains in different domain trees, even in the same forest.

○ D.  Transitive trusts allow for automatic trusting within a domain tree, but not across trees in the same forest.

Answer A is correct. By establishing shortcut trusts between domains that are already connected with transitive trusts, you can improve authentication times. This is especially true in complex forest/domain environments. Answer B is incorrect because shortcut trusts are not required in the strictest sense; authentication would still take place over the transitive trust paths (albeit slower). Answer C is incorrect because within a forest you would not use external trusts, and answer D is incorrect because transitive trusts apply to all domains within the same tree, not just within an individual domain tree.

# Question 8

What utilities would you use to raise the domain functional level from Windows 2000 mixed mode to Windows Server 2003? [Check all correct answers.]

❑ A.  Group Policy Editor

❑ B.  Active Directory Users and Computers

❑ C.  Delegation of Control Wizard

❑ D.  Active Directory Domains and Trusts

Answers B and D are correct. AD Users and Computers and AD Domains and Trusts both allow for raising the domain functional level. Answer A is incorrect because Group Policy Editor allows you to specify the settings for a user or computer that relate to desktop views or software and security policy. Answer C is incorrect because the Delegation of Control Wizard provides a graphical way to assign Active Directory access permissions to individuals with trusted administrative control.

# Question 9

---

You are the administrator for a Windows Server 2003 domain tree that goes five levels deep in child domains. Users at the deeper levels have complained about how much typing they have to do to enter their login info. Management has also inquired as to whether there's anything that can be done to strengthen authentication security without incurring any additional cost. What can you use to simplify logons as well as make logon authentication more secure in one fell swoop without incurring an added expense?

- O A. Change the DNS domain name to something more manageable.
- O B. Implement a smart card solution for authentication.
- O C. Implement an alternate UPN suffix.
- O D. Consolidate the child domains into the parent domain.

Answer C is correct. Alternate UPN suffixes simplify logon names because you can take a complex child domain such as @lewisville.texas.studio.inside-corner.com and create the UPN suffix @Lewisville for users to use. In addition to being easier for users, it improves the logon security because users aren't using the default logon domains for their authentication. Answer A is incorrect because renaming a child domain four levels deep would still result in a lengthy name. Removing the domain and reinstalling it as a child higher up the tree or as a new domain tree would have other repercussions that might not be desirable (and wouldn't improve security). Answer B is incorrect because it doesn't meet the requirement of not incurring any extra expense. Answer D is incorrect because it doesn't improve security, and it could have other consequences in the management of the network (the child domains probably existed as child domains for a reason).

# Question 10

---

Under which part of the answer file for an unattended installation of both Windows Server 2003 and Active Directory would you specify the command to install Active Directory?

- O A. **GuiRunPromo**
- O B. **GuiRunOnce**
- O C. **DCInstall**
- O D. **ADInstall**

Answer B is correct. The GuiRunOnce section within the answer file would specify the command dcpromo and then specify an additional answer file that is specific to the Active Directory install. Answer C is incorrect because, although DCInstall is a section of the Active Directory answer file, it is not the section that installs the operating system. Answers A and D are simply invalid answers.

# Need to Know More?

 Honeycutt, Jerry. *Introducing Microsoft Windows Server 2003.* Microsoft Press. Redmond, WA, 2003. ISBN 0-7356-1570-5.

 Microsoft Corporation. *Microsoft Windows Server 2003 Resource Kit.* Microsoft Press. Redmond, WA, 2003. ISBN 0-7356-1471-7.

 Mulcare, Mike and Stan Reimer. *Active Directory for Microsoft Windows Server 2003 Technical Reference.* Microsoft Press. Redmond, WA, 2003. ISBN 0-7356-1577-2.

# Implementing and Managing Active Directory Sites

## Terms you'll need to understand:

✓ Sites
✓ Site link bridge
✓ Bridgehead server
✓ Knowledge Consistency Checker (KCC)
✓ Intersite Topology Generator (ISTG)
✓ Well-connected
✓ Connection object
✓ Site link costs
✓ Domain controller (DC)

## Techniques/concepts you'll need to master:

✓ Implementing an Active Directory site topology
✓ Configuring site links
✓ Configuring preferred bridgehead servers
✓ Managing an Active Directory site
✓ Configuring replication schedules
✓ Configuring site link costs
✓ Configuring site boundaries

The core concept of the physical structure of Windows Server 2003 Active Directory is the *site*, which is a collection of computers connected via a high-speed network. Typically, the computers within a site are connected via LAN-style technology and are considered to be "well-connected." Well-connected generally means constant, high-speed connectivity within an IP subnet, though a site can include multiple subnets. By "high-speed," we mean a minimum of a 10MBps connection between computers.

It is important to understand that sites and domains do not have a direct relationship. Domains map the *logical structure* of your organization, whereas sites relate to the *physical layout* of the network. Domain namespace is likewise unrelated to the physical sites, though many times administrators will choose to align the namespace and the physical sites during the planning phase of a Windows Server 2003 rollout or migration.

A site can contain multiple domains, and likewise a domain can cross several sites. In most cases, sites will mirror the actual physical layout of the network, with a site at each of the major business locations of a company. If a company is using a single-domain structure, that domain will cross the sites as shown in Figure 2.1.

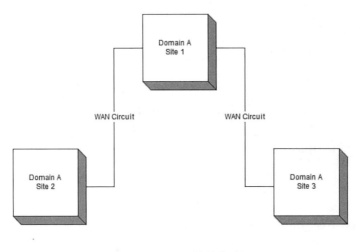

Single Domain over Multiple Sites

**Figure 2.1**   A single domain across multiple sites.

Because of the separation of the physical and logical structure, a site can also support multiple domains. In Figure 2.2, Site 1 has computers in both Domain A and Domain B.

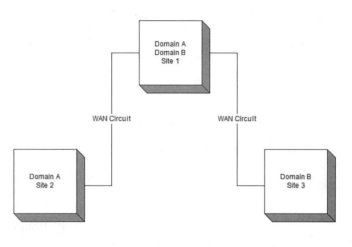

Multiple Domains over Multiple Sites

**Figure 2.2**    Multiple domains across multiple sites.

# Why Use Sites?

If you are a network administrator who has supported WAN-connected Windows NT domains, you may be wondering about the purpose of defined sites within Windows Server 2003. After all, the use of remote networks, backup domain controllers, and WAN circuits certainly is nothing new, nor is the concept of multiple domains at a particular location. The problem with the older Windows NT network lay in the replication of security information between the domain controllers. Whenever there were changes to the security policy within a domain, such as new user accounts, new groups, or even group membership changes, the entire SAM database had to be replicated across the WAN link. In large or active network environments, this replication could consume a majority of the bandwidth between locations.

Windows Server 2003, like Windows 2000, corrects this issue by replicating data between domain controllers differently depending on the relationship between the domain controllers. Within a site, the primary goal of replication is to keep the domain controllers updated with as little latency as possible. Between sites, the replicated data is compressed (if it is greater than 50MB in size) and sent periodically. The compression helps save bandwidth, but it does require more processing overhead on the part of the domain controllers.

The primary function of a site is to consolidate directory service requests within a high-speed connection area and to control replication with external domain controllers. Sites provide the following features:

➤ Directory services are provided by the closest DC, if one is located within the site.

➤ Latency is minimized for replication within a site.

➤ Bandwidth utilization for replication is minimized between sites.

➤ Replication can be scheduled between sites to better suit the network utilization.

Sites are used for many different tasks in Active Directory. Aside from their use in Active Directory replication, they are also used to optimize logon traffic and to select shared folders that use the Distributed File System (Dfs). They are also used for Remote Installation Services (RIS). In all cases, they are used to calculate the local server that can most efficiently provide the service. If a client contacts a server on the same subnet as itself, it is safe to assume processing time will be reduced.

# Sites and Domain Controllers

A domain controller is automatically placed within a site during the server-promotion process. Dcpromo checks for the defined sites during the promotion process, and if the server's IP address falls within the range of a defined subset, the server is automatically placed within the site associated with that subnet.

If no subnets are associated with site objects, the server is placed in the default site, which is named Default-First-Site-Name. If the IP address of the server does not fall within a range that is defined, the server is placed in the Default-First-Site-Name. Sites are automatically assigned only during the initial promotion; if a domain controller configuration or physical location changes significantly, the domain controller must also be moved to another site via the Active Directory Sites and Services snap-in.

Multihomed servers can only belong to a single site. When a multihomed server is promoted, dcpromo selects the site at random from the ones the server matches. If you do not agree with the selection, the domain controller can be moved to another site via the Active Directory Sites and Services snap-in. We'll walk through the process of moving a domain controller from one site to another later in this chapter.

When client computers log on to an Active Directory domain controller, they query DNS for domain controllers that are on the same subnet as the client. Once a domain controller is located, the client computer establishes communication with a DC using the Lightweight Directory Access Protocol (LDAP). As part of the process, the domain controller identifies which Active Directory site the client computer belongs to. If the domain controller in question isn't in the closest site to the client computer, it indicates this to the client computer and the client begins the DNS lookup process again. This step is especially useful for client computers that travel between sites regularly (mobile users) to keep their contact with domain controllers at an optimum performance level.

# Creating a Site

Sites are created via the Active Directory Sites and Services snap-in. Windows Server 2003 creates the first site automatically when AD is installed. This site is named Default-First-Site-Name and includes all the domain controllers. It is possible to rename the default site, but it should never be deleted. Additional sites must be created manually. To create a site, open the snap-in, shown in Figure 2.3, and right-click to open the context menu of the Sites folder. Select the New Site option to create a new site.

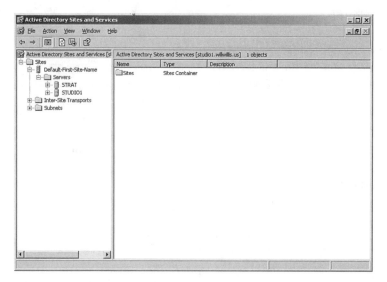

**Figure 2.3**   The AD Sites and Services snap-in.

The New Object-Site dialog box allows you to enter the name of the remote site and to select the site link for the site. Windows Server 2003 creates a default site link called DEFAULTIPSITELINK that can be used to establish the replication process of the Active Directory service, which is shown in Figure 2.4. This default site link uses RPC over TCP/IP, and it will use any available route to the remote site for replication. If explicit site links have been previously defined, those site links will show up in the lower portion of the New Object-Site dialog box.

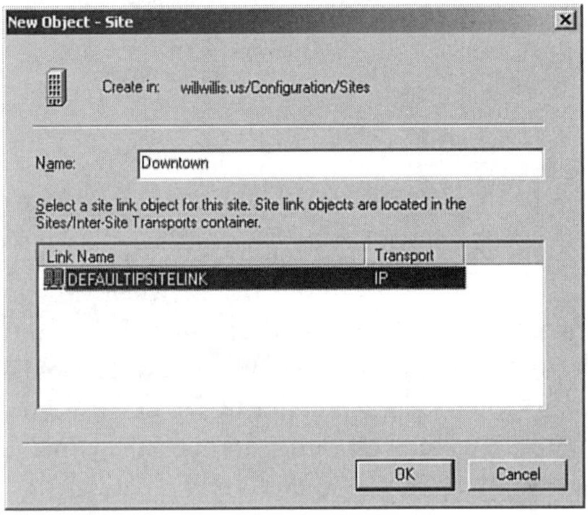

**Figure 2.4**   Creating a new site.

Once the site is defined, several other steps must be undertaken before the site can be activated within the Active Directory structure. These steps are nicely delineated in the dialog box that follows the creation of a new site, as shown in Figure 2.5. To finish configuring a site, you must do the following:

➤ Add appropriate IP subnets to the site.

➤ Install or move a domain controller or controllers into the site. Although a domain controller is not required for a site, it is strongly recommended.

➤ Connect the site to other sites with the appropriate site link.

➤ Select a server to control and monitor licensing within the site.

Once these steps are completed, the site is then added to the Active Directory structure and the replication is automatically configured by Windows Server 2003.

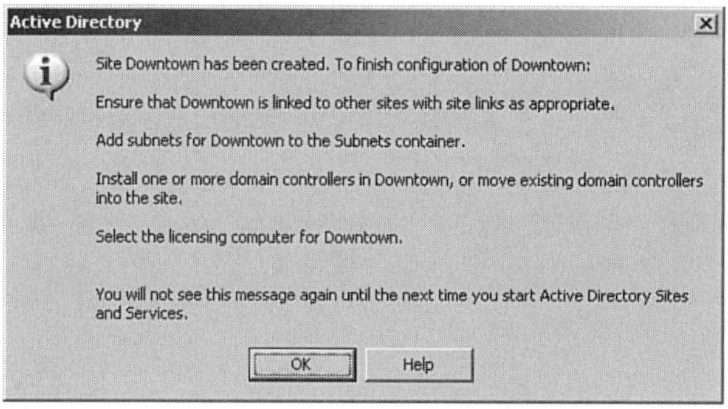

**Figure 2.5**    Required configuration steps for a new site.

# Moving Domain Controllers Between Sites

We discussed earlier how subnets could be associated with particular sites. After a site has been associated with a subnet, any new domain controller with an IP address within that subnet will automatically be assigned to the site. For example, if site Downtown has the 192.168.0.0/24 subnet associated with it, a new domain controller with the IP address 192.168.0.5 will automatically become part of the Downtown site. If a domain controller is assigned an IP address that is not associated with a particular site, the new domain controller will be assigned to the default site.

There will be situations where the automated assignment does not fit the needs of the network environment, or situations where preexisting domain controllers need to be moved to the correct sites. Fortunately, this is a very easy process.

To move a domain controller between two sites, first open the AD Sites and Services snap-in. Navigate to the server you wish to relocate (the server "STRAT" in our example) and then open the context menu for that server, as shown in Figure 2.6.

Select Move from the context menu and then select the destination site, as shown in Figure 2.7.

Clicking the OK button will move the server to the destination site. Obviously, this does not change the actual network settings on the domain controller itself. If IP address changes or other network-configuration changes are necessary, those changes will need to be made on the domain controller before it will be able to communicate with the rest of the network environment.

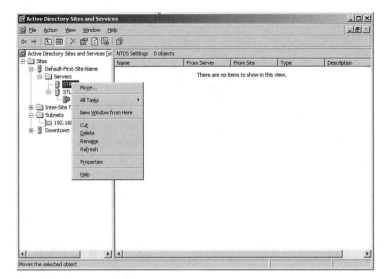

**Figure 2.6**   Moving a domain controller between sites.

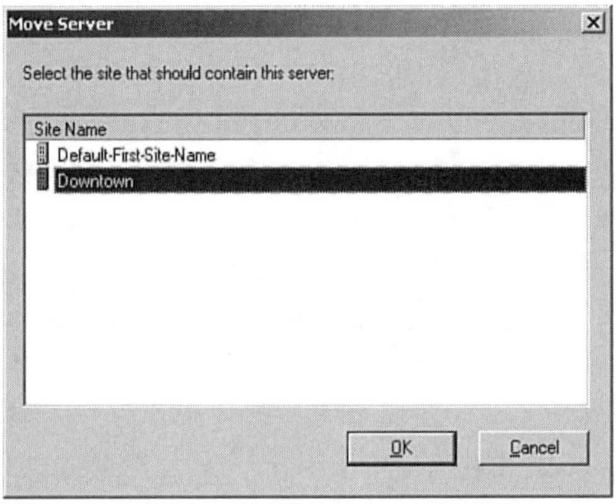

**Figure 2.7**   Select the destination site for the domain controller.

The new configuration of the sites will automatically be displayed within the AD Sites and Services snap-in, as shown in Figure 2.8. Note the new location of the moved domain controller: STRAT is now in the Downtown site rather than in the default site.

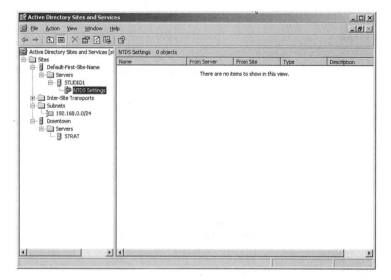

**Figure 2.8**   New site location for the domain controller.

# Site Connections

A site is a physical subnet or selection of physical subnets that are connected via a high-speed connection. Sites themselves are connected via *site links*, which are low-bandwidth or unreliable/occasional connections between sites. In general, any connection between locations slower than LAN speeds is considered a site link. WAN links such as Frame Relay connections are examples of site links, as are high-speed links that are saturated and have a low effective bandwidth.

Site links are not automatically generated by Windows Server 2003. Instead, the administrator creates the site links through the Active Directory Sites and Services snap-in. The site links are the core of the Active Directory replication. The links can be adjusted for replication availability, bandwidth costs, and replication frequency. Windows Server 2003 uses this information to generate the replication topology for the sites, including the schedule for replication.

Windows Server 2003 domain controllers represent the inbound replication through a special object known as a *connection object*. Active Directory uses site links as indicators for where it should create connection objects, and connection objects use the physical network connections to replicate directory information. Each domain controller creates its own connection objects for replication within a site (intrasite replication), through the Knowledge

Consistency Checker (KCC). For replication between sites (intersite replication), one domain controller within each site is responsible for evaluating the replication topology. The domain controller creates the connection objects appropriate to that topology. The server that is responsible for evaluating and creating the topology for the intersite replication is known as the *Intersite Topology Generator (ISTG)*.

Site links, like trusts, are transitive, which means domain controllers in one site can replicate with domain controllers in any other site within the enterprise through these transitive links. In addition, explicit links can be created to enable specific replication paths between sites.

# Creating and Configuring a Site Link

Windows Server 2003 creates a default site link named, naturally enough, DefaultIPSiteLink. This site link can be used to connect sites in simple network environments, but in more complicated enterprise environments, explicit site links should be established by the administrator.

To create a site link, perform the following tasks:

➤ Open the Active Directory Sites and Services snap-in.

➤ Open the Inter-Site Transports folder and then right-click the appropriate transport protocol, as indicated in Figure 2.9.

➤ Select New Site Link from the context menu to form a new link.

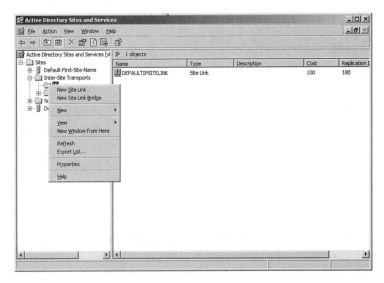

**Figure 2.9** Creating a new site link.

In our example, the name of the new site link is Uptown Frame Link. Although the name of the link is arbitrary, good administrative practice dictates the name should be something that identifies the link, the connected sites, and the type of link. Of course, the link could be named "bob," but that would tend to confuse successors and coworkers.

The next step is to select the linked sites from the left column and click the Add button to associate them with the link, as shown in Figure 2.10. A link must contain at least two sites; in general a link will connect only two sites. However, if there are multiple sites at one physical location or connected via a particular network path, those sites could all share a single site link.

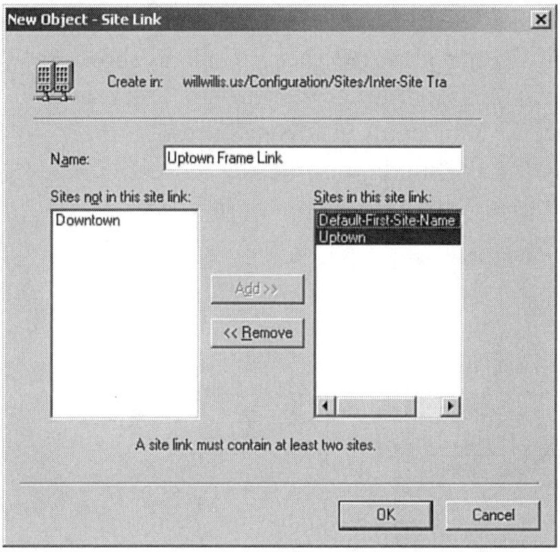

**Figure 2.10**  Naming the site link and associating the sites.

Each site link has four important properties as well as an optional descriptor. To get into the properties of a site link, right-click the site link in the Inter-Sites Transport folder in Active Directory Sites and Services and then select Properties. The properties are described in the following list:

➤ *Name*—A name that uniquely identifies the site link. As discussed earlier, this name should clearly indicate the sites being linked and the speed/type of circuit.

➤ *Cost*—The cost is the relative speed of the link in relation to the other links within the topology. This cost has nothing to do with the actual monetary costs of the bandwidth. When you configure site link costs, you should assign a lower cost to a fast link and a higher cost to a slow link. The cost defaults to 100 on a new circuit.

➤ *Transport*—This property indicates the type of transport used to replicate the directory information between the domain controllers. There two options: synchronous Remote Procedure Call (RPC) over a routed TCP/IP connection and an asynchronous Simple Mail Transport Protocol (SMTP) connection over the underlying mail transport network. This property is not set within the link properties but is instead determined when the site link is first created. (See page 65 for more information.)

➤ *Schedule*—This option allows you to configure the replication schedule your sites will follow. The schedule determines when the directory information is replicated between sites. This is determined by two elements: the replication frequency and the available times. The replication frequency is adjusted within the properties of the site link, as shown in Figure 2.11. The schedule is a listing of times that the site link is available to pass replication data. This schedule is adjusted through the Change Schedule option within the site link properties.

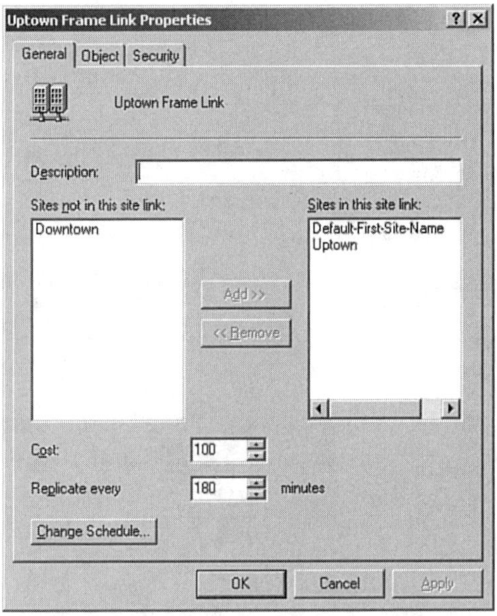

**Uptown Frame Link Properties**                                          ? X

General | Object | Security |

    Uptown Frame Link

Description: [                                                          ]

Sites not in this site link:              Sites in this site link:
Downtown                                  Default-First-Site-Name
                                          Uptown

              Add >>
              << Remove


Cost:            [100]
Replicate every  [180]   minutes

Change Schedule...

              OK        Cancel      Apply

**Figure 2.11**  Site link properties.

# Bridgehead Servers

The replication topology between and among sites is generated automatically by Windows Server 2003. This is generated via a service known as the *Knowledge Consistency Checker (KCC)*. The KCC service tries to establish at least two inbound replication connections to every domain controller so that if a server becomes unavailable or uncommunicative, replication can still occur.

Within a site, all domain controllers are treated equally, but replication between sites is another matter. Windows Server 2003 prefers to funnel intersite replication to only a single domain controller. These preferred servers are known as *bridgehead servers*. The replicated data is first sent to the bridgehead server of a site and then is replicated from that bridgehead server to the other domain controllers within the site. Bridgehead servers are chosen automatically by Windows Server 2003 through a process called the *Intersite Topology Generator (ISTG)*.

## Configuring Preferred Bridgehead Servers

You can also select a bridgehead server or even a group of preferred servers. You simply select the servers you want to use as preferred within the site.

 If the preferred bridgehead server is unavailable, Active Directory will use an alternate replication path if the KCC is automatically configuring bridgehead servers. If you are manually assigning bridgehead servers and the preferred bridgehead server fails, replication will fail along with it.

# Site Link Bridge

The site link bridge is an extension of the *sites* concept we covered earlier in this chapter. You use site link bridges when your physical network topology requires them. For instance, your corporate network is likely divided by a firewall. In that case, the network is not fully routed—that is, every subnet cannot communicate directly with every other subnet. For AD replication to work, AD must model the normal routing behavior of your network.

A *site link bridge* is a collection of site links. Before you create a site link bridge, you must first create the site links. You then create the site link bridge and add those site links to the bridge. For instance, let's assume you have a site link that contains both Downtown and Midtown. The cost of this link is 2. You have a second site link that contains Uptown and Midtown. The cost of this link is 6. You could create a site link bridge and add both of these site links to it. This would enable Downtown to communicate with Uptown with a cost of 8.

A site link bridge does not dictate the physical path the network packets take. This aspect of the communication cannot be controlled from within AD.

Notice that the two site links we added to the site link bridge have a site in common—Midtown. Having a common site link among all the site links in your site link bridge is a requirement of creating a site link bridge. If this were not the case, the site link bridge would have no way of working out the total cost of moving a message from Downtown to Uptown.

Because site links are by default transitive, in most cases you will not have to create site link bridges. However, by creating site link bridges and manually designating DCs that will communicate, you can alleviate some of the problems you may encounter from working on a nonrouted network.

To use site link bridges, you must turn off the Bridge All Site Links feature. Because this is an all-or-nothing affair (sites are either transitive or not), doing so increases the amount of administration you are expected to do yourself. The transitive link feature can be turned off within each transport by unselecting the Bridge All Site Links option within the property sheet of each transport, as shown in Figure 2.12. Once the option is unselected, a site link bridge allows transitive replication routing within the bridged links, but not outside the bridge.

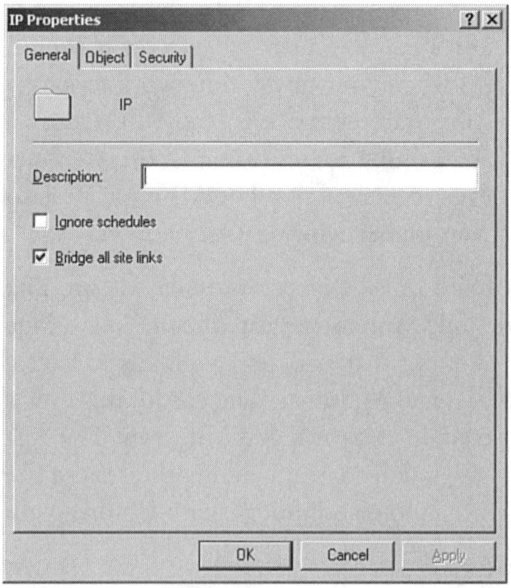

**Figure 2.12** In order to use site link bridges, you first must disable the Bridge All Site Links option.

# Creating Site Link Bridges

To create a new site link bridge, first the site links themselves must be defined, as discussed earlier. Once the site links have been defined, open the Inter-Site Transports folder and select the desired transport. This transport can be either IP or SMTP (the differences between the two are discussed later in the chapter). From the context menu of the selected transport, choose New Site Link Bridge, as shown in Figure 2.13.

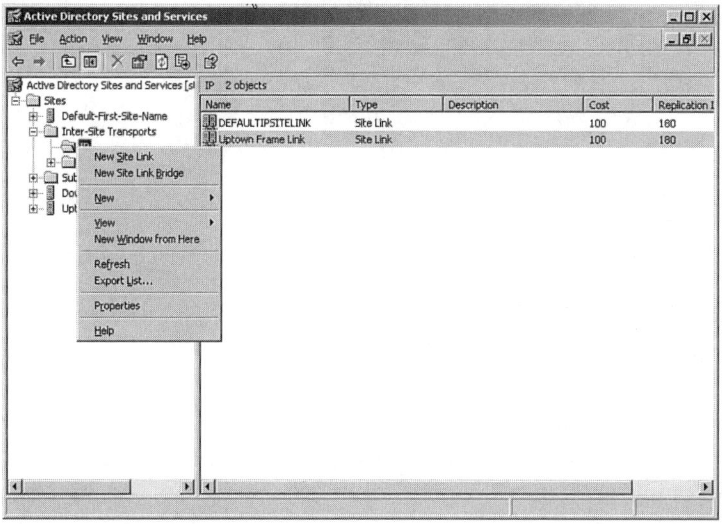

**Figure 2.13**   Creating a new site link bridge.

The new site link bridge requires at least two site links. When these site links are bridged, a transitive replication link is generated across both the links. In the case of the example shown in Figure 2.14, the Downtown link connects the corporate center with the downtown center, and the Uptown link connects the corporate center with the uptown center. Through the site link bridge, the uptown site can now replicate directly with the downtown site, even though there is no direct physical link between the sites.

Two Active Directory server components are responsible for the topology of sites. The first one we've touched on already: the Knowledge Consistency Checker (KCC). The server that is responsible for evaluating and creating the topology for the intersite replication is known as the *Intersite Topology Generator (ISTG)*. Note that depending on the size and complexity of your network, the KCC and ISTG may become overwhelmed and be unable to build a full replication topology on a regular schedule. This happens when there are many paths on your network, and the KCC must sort through each of them to find the optimal route. In these rare cases, you could disable the Bridge All Site Links option and build site link bridges.

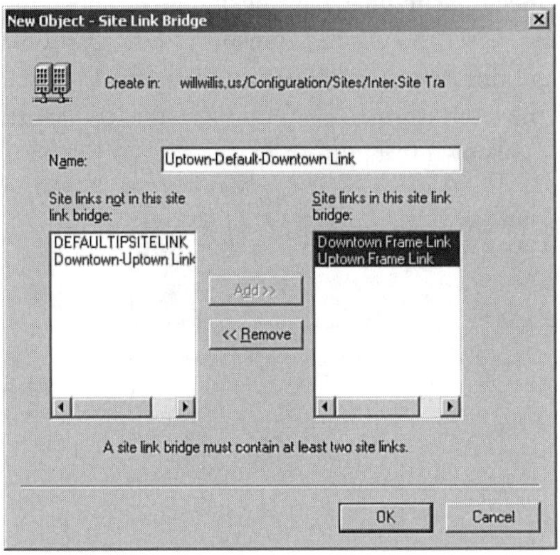

**Figure 2.14** Adding site links to a site link bridge.

You can also prevent the KCC from building a site-to-site topology. However, this increases the overhead of managing your network. One of the best features of the KCC is that it runs on a regular schedule. This means it can recover from sudden changes on your network, such as a site disappearing because a router is down. If the KCC has had its feature set trimmed, you need to take care of these situations yourself. Keep in mind, however, that such situations can be difficult to detect and will take a lot of time to configure. In almost all cases, you are better off using the KCC than performing the task yourself.

# Connection Objects

Windows Server 2003 domain controllers represent the inbound replication through a special object known as a *connection object*. Active Directory uses site links as indicators for where it should create connection objects, and connection objects use the physical network connections to replicate directory information. Each domain controller creates its own connection objects for replication within a site (intrasite replication). For replication between sites (intersite replication), one domain controller within each site is responsible for evaluating the replication topology. The domain controller creates the connection objects appropriate to that topology. As mentioned earlier, the server that is responsible for evaluating and creating the topology for the intersite replication is the Intersite Topology Generator (ISTG).

In general, the connection objects will be automatically generated both within sites and between sites. However, if the Knowledge Consistency Checker (KCC) is not used to generate replication topology, the connection objects will have to be generated manually. To generate these objects, first open the AD Sites and Services snap-in, as shown in Figure 2.15, and then navigate to the domain controller on which you wish to form a connection object.

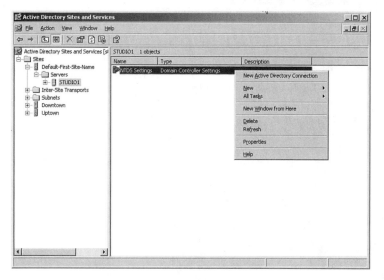

**Figure 2.15**  Creating a new connection object.

Select the NTDS settings and then choose New Active Directory Connection from the context menu. The resulting dialog box shows a list of the domain controllers that can be used for inbound replication (see Figure 2.16).

Choose the desired domain controller and then click OK. The selected domain controller will be shown in the resulting dialog box (see Figure 2.17). If this is the correct DC for inbound replication, click OK to finish creating the site connector.

Once the connection object is created, it can be viewed through the NTDS settings for each domain controller, as shown in Figure 2.18. Remember that connection objects are usually created automatically, and they can be dynamically modified to change replication if new domain controllers and sites are created. Connection objects should only be manually created if the administrator is absolutely confident that the connection object is needed and will be needed on a permanent basis.

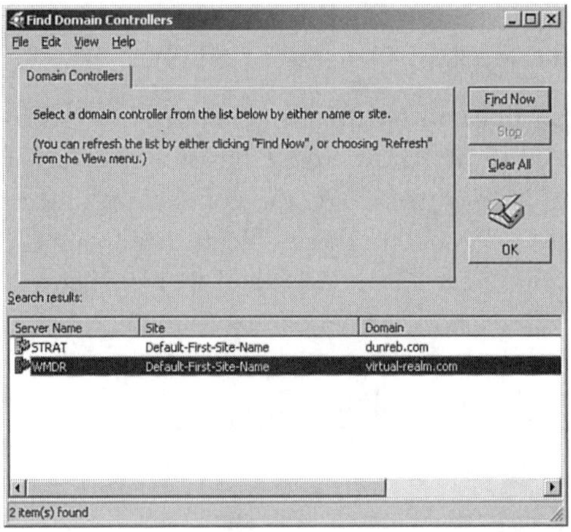

**Figure 2.16** Available domain controllers for replication.

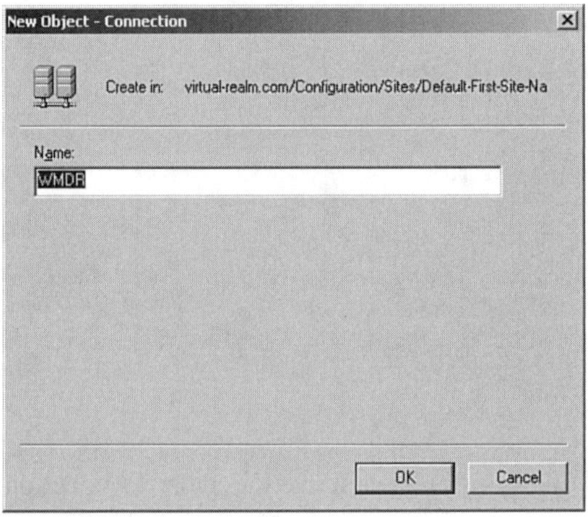

**Figure 2.17** Finish creating the connection object.

Manually created connection objects will remain until they are manually deleted.

Both manually and automatically created connection objects can be viewed through the NTDS settings for each of the domain controllers. In this example, you will notice that the manually created object and the automatic object are identical, due to the fact we only had two DCs to work with. In a larger real-world environment, your manually configured connection objects would be better suited toward connecting domain controllers not already automatically connected by the KCC.

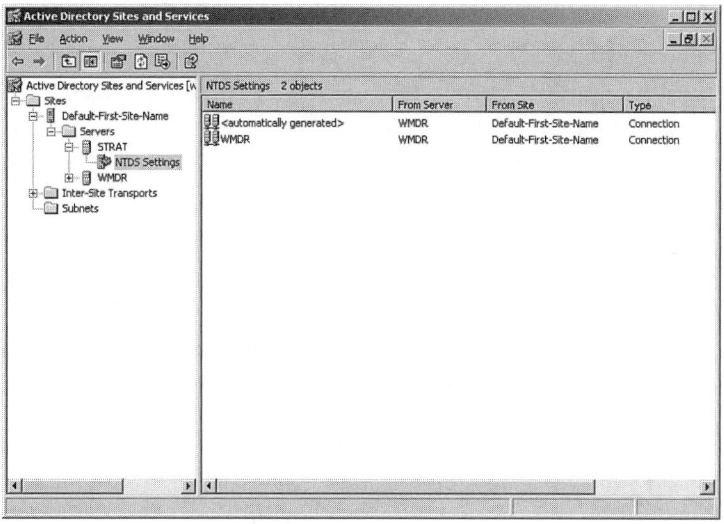

**Figure 2.18**   Viewing connection objects.

# Optimizing Active Directory Replication with Sites

Before the KCC can do its work, it requires some basic information about your network, including data on the physical aspects of the infrastructure. You supply this data by creating sites. Once your sites have been created, you must create connection objects between them. The KCC then uses this information to build the necessary replication infrastructure. By creating sites, you are effectively controlling replication on your network—albeit via an automatic process.

By adding subnets to a site, you are implying that these subnets have fast and reliable connectivity among them. You add server objects to site objects. Once a server is part of a site, the KCC can calculate a path through the network in question, with the assumption that the servers can talk to each other quickly.

## Replication Within a Site and Between Sites

Although replication occurs both within a site and between sites, subtle differences exist between the two situations. Replication within a site assumes a highly available network with a lot of bandwidth. Therefore, the replicated data is sent uncompressed. Because the DC does not have to take time to compress data, there is less of a load on each DC. However, your network bandwidth suffers because a lot more data goes across the wire. The replication process is triggered by the notification process mentioned earlier in this chapter.

In contrast, replication between sites occurs on a schedule. In addition, the data greater than 50MB is compressed before being sent. This means that the load on servers is greater, but the bandwidth requirement is reduced. Additionally, you can configure a threshold that must be reached before replication takes place. This helps optimize replication based on your needs.

You need to be concerned about two parameters:

➤ *The schedule*—Defines how often replication takes place. This option allows you to configure replication to take place during off-hours or times when the most bandwidth is available.

➤ *The replication interval*—Defines how often DCs check for changes during periods when replication is allowed to occur.

Keep in mind that an incorrectly configured schedule and interval can prevent replication from ever occurring. For instance, if the schedule allows replication to occur only between 6:00 a.m. and 7:00 a.m., replication will only ever occur during a single hour of the day. If the interval is set for every two hours, starting at 7:00 a.m., the interval gets checked only on odd hours (7:00 a.m., 9:00 a.m., 11:00 a.m., 1:00 p.m., 3:00 p.m., and so on). Notice that there is no overlap between the schedule and the interval. In this case, the interval is not starting during the scheduled window; therefore, replication would not take place.

 You must have an overlapping schedule for replication to work. In the case of multiple sites, the replication schedule may not be overlapping, but it could cause replication to be slow. For instance, suppose you have three sites—A, B, and C. If the replication schedule between A and B is 7:00 a.m. to 8:00 a.m., and the replication schedule between B and C is 2:00 p.m. to 4:00 p.m., then the updated data from A won't arrive in C until 2:00 p.m. at the earliest. This will cause it to appear that you have a replication problem.

# Protocols That Support Replication

It might seem obvious to state that DCs that want to communicate must use the same protocol. However, you should note that in terms of replication, we are referring to the protocol used specifically by Active Directory to achieve our goal.

Two different protocols can be used:

➤ *Remote Procedure Call (RPC)*—This primary protocol is used exclusively for replication within a site.

➤ *Simple Mail Transfer Protocol (SMTP)*—This protocol has a limited implementation and is used when connections between DCs are unreliable. To use SMTP, the DCs must be in different domains and in different sites.

When replicating between sites, you can use RPC or SMTP. The preferred protocol is RPC over IP (which means the RPC calls are wrapped in IP packets for transport across the wire).

In addition to the aforementioned limitations of using SMTP, also note that SMTP cannot be used to replicate all partitions of Active Directory. Because the domain partition has dependencies that fall outside of simply replicating Active Directory data, such as file transfer using the File Replication Service (FRS), SMTP cannot be used for the domain partition. However, SMTP is useful when a direct connection cannot be made between DCs, because SMTP data can be stored and forwarded by mail servers. This capability can sometimes compensate for poor connections.

# Exam Prep Questions

## Question 1

You have three distinct subnets on your network. Two of these subnets are in the United States, and they have a 10Mbps connection between them. The third subnet is in England over a 128Kbps link. You want to make sure that replication works efficiently on your network. How many sites would you create on your network?

○ A. You would create three sites: two for the United States and one for England. AD will work out an efficient replication topology.

○ B. You would create a single site and add all DCs to it. AD will then configure replication.

○ C. You would create two sites. One site would include a single subnet from the United States. The second site would include both England and one of the subnets from the United States. This allows the subnet in England to replicate with the site in the United States.

○ D. You would create two sites: one in the United States that includes the two subnets there, and one for the subnet in England. AD will work out the replication topology based on this data.

Answer D is correct. Sites can be defined as a group of subnets that have fast connectivity. Because the subnet in England is on the other side of a 128Kbps link, this is a slow connection and should therefore be its own site. Answers A, B, and C are all incorrect.

## Question 2

The replication topology can be created automatically on a Windows 2000 network. An automatic process takes place that generates the topology. This process will even regenerate the topology should it become necessary. What is the name of the process that automatically creates the replication topology?

○ A. The Replication Topology Generator

○ B. The Knowledge Consistency Checker

○ C. The Knowledge Constant Changer

○ D. The Knowledge Replication Strategy

Answer B is correct. The automatic process is known as the *Knowledge Consistency Checker*. Although this process can be overridden, doing so is not a good idea. Most of the time, you should let the KCC make decisions about replication partners, because it requires very little configuration and can work in near real time. Answers A, C, and D are all invalid answers.

# Question 3

You have two sites that need to be on different subnets. The network connection between these two sites is 128Kbps. Because the connection is slow and these sites contain DCs in different subnets, they will be connected to ensure replication. What is the name of the process that automatically decides which DCs in each of these sites will be replication partners with each other?

○ A. The Knowledge Consistency Checker

○ B. The Replication Topology Generator

○ C. The Internet Site Topology Generator

○ D. The Intersite Topology Generator

Answer D is correct. It is the job of the Intersite Topology Generator to decide which specific DCs within a site will replicate with each other. Once these two servers have replicated data, normal replication practices take place to ensure that all other DCs within a site receive the updates. Answer A is incorrect because the Knowledge Consistency Checker is the process that automatically generates the topology. Answers B and C are simply invalid answers.

# Question 4

Which of the following statements are true concerning replication within an Active Directory site? [Check all correct answers.]

❑ A. Bridgehead servers are used to replicate data.

❑ B. All domain controllers are treated as equal in the replication process.

❑ C. Replication occurs on a schedule.

❑ D. Replication occurs whenever needed.

Answers B and D are correct. It is important to understand how replication differs when it is working within a site versus between sites. Within a site, replication takes place whenever it is needed because the topology assumes well-connected domain controllers. Also, as a result of expecting all domain controllers to have plenty of available bandwidth within a site, each DC is treated as equal. Answers A and C are incorrect because they describe between-site replication, not within-site replication.

# Question 5

You have decided to use site link bridges to manually configure some specific replication paths. However, during testing you find that they are not functioning like you anticipated. What are you likely doing wrong?

- ○ A. You must define the site link costs so traffic will flow in the desired manner.
- ○ B. You need to disable the automatic bridging of site links.
- ○ C. Site link bridges are configured automatically and therefore you cannot configure them manually.
- ○ D. You need to enable the automatic bridging of site links.

Answer B is correct. By default, Windows Server 2003 bridges all site links (making Answer D incorrect), so unless you disable this feature, your site link bridges will not have the intended effect. Answer A is incorrect because although costs are used in determining the path traffic will take, there are default costs associated with every site link, and the automatic bridging is taking precedence over the manually configured bridges. Answer C is incorrect because although bridging occurs automatically, you can disable automatic bridging and configure it manually.

# Question 6

You have a multihomed Windows Server 2003 server in Domain1, servicing subnets 192.168.1.0/24, 192.168.2.0/24, and 192.168.3.0/24. After running dcpromo and promoting the server to a domain controller, you notice in Active Directory Sites and Services that the server is in the wrong site, even though you have subnets defined. Why might that be?

- ○ A. Multihomed servers confuse Windows Server 2003 and have to be manually placed in sites.
- ○ B. Multihomed servers can belong to multiple sites. Just add the servers to the other sites they should belong to.
- ○ C. Your subnet mask in Active Directory Sites and Services is defined as 255.255.0.0, which causes all three subnets to be treated as the same.
- ○ D. Windows Server 2003 will make a best guess as to what site to place a server in.

Answer D is correct. The KCC will examine the topology and determine what site to place a server in. If you want the server to be in a different site than what was chosen, simply move it with the AD Sites and Services utility. Answer A is incorrect because the KCC will examine all subnets of a multihomed server and choose the one it thinks best fits. Answer B is incorrect because a server can only belong to a single site, even if it is multihomed. Answer C is incorrect because intended to mislead you into looking at the wrong place for the problem—a subnet can only be associated with a single site.

# Question 7

Users at remote offices are reporting difficulties in locating Active Directory resources that you have notified are supposed to be available to them. After doing a little troubleshooting you find out that replication is configured and working within the corporate site, but it's not taking place between sites. You have 128Kbps circuits between corporate and each location and have not had any recent outages. What might be the problem? [Check all correct answers.]

❑ A. The replication schedule is too short.

❑ B. The replication interval and schedule overlap.

❑ C. You should reconfigure between-site replication to use the SMTP transport rather than IP.

❑ D. The replication interval and schedule do not overlap.

Answers A and D are correct. If the replication schedule is too short, there might not be sufficient time for replication to take place, especially over a slower 128K link. Also, if the replication interval and schedule do not overlap, replication will never occur. Answer B is incorrect because the interval and schedule must overlap, and Answer C is incorrect because the SMTP transport is used primarily when there is irregular/inconsistent network connectivity. The situation states a reliable link exists between sites, so the IP transport is appropriate.

# Question 8

Which of the following is *not* a benefit of using sites?

○ A. Directory services are provided by the closest domain controller.

○ B. Bandwidth utilization by replication is limited.

○ C. Delegation of administrative authority to remote sites is possible without giving permissions on the main site.

○ D. Replication can be scheduled.

Answer C is correct. It's the only choice that isn't a benefit of using sites. Delegation of authority is related to domains, which can either span sites or be contained entirely within a site. Answers A, B, and D are all benefits you get from using sites.

# Question 9

Your network consists of four sites: Dallas, Houston, Omaha, and Boston. You have configured site links to reflect the geography, so replication traffic will take the shortest possible path. To that end you've set the site link cost between shorter paths to 100 and the cost between longer paths to 10. A few days later you notice that replication is inconsistent and seems to take longer than it should. What would you look at first in troubleshooting?

- ○ A. You need to configure site link bridges to bridge the links on the longer paths.
- ○ B. You need to reverse the site link costs.
- ○ C. You need to use the SMTP transport rather than the IP transport.
- ○ D. You should change bridgehead servers at each site to the most powerful servers you have, to accommodate the increased traffic burden.

Answer B is correct. With site link costs, the lower the number, the faster/more preferred the link is. In this scenario, you've given preference to a slower path, which could have negative performance consequences. Answer A is incorrect because, by default, site links are bridged and managed by the KCC. Answer C is incorrect because the SMTP transport is used when there is unreliable communication across links. Answer D is incorrect because although a bridgehead server could become burdened, the ISTG and KCC work to choose the most appropriate domain controller.

# Question 10

If you need to manually configure the inbound replication in your network topology, what would you configure?

- ○ A. Site link
- ○ B. Connection object
- ○ C. Site link bridge
- ○ D. Bridgehead server

Answer B is correct. Connection objects represent inbound replication partners and normally are generated by the KCC. They can also be configured manually. Answers A and C are incorrect because site links are used by Active Directory as indicators of where connection objects should be placed, and site link bridges are collections of site links. Answer D is incorrect because a bridgehead server is the domain controller that intersite replication is funneled through at each site, but connection objects on these servers are more specifically involved with inbound replication.

# Need to Know More?

 Honeycutt, Jerry. *Introducing Microsoft Windows Server 2003*. Microsoft Press. Redmond, WA, 2003. ISBN 0-7356-1570-5.

 Mulcare, Mike and Stan Reimer. *Active Directory for Microsoft Windows Server 2003 Technical Reference*. Microsoft Press. Redmond, WA, 2003. ISBN 0-7356-1577-2.

Microsoft Corporation. *Microsoft Windows Server 2003 Resource Kit*. Microsoft Press. Redmond, WA, 2003. ISBN 0-7356-1471-7.

# Operations Masters and Global Catalog Servers

## Terms you'll need to understand:

✓ Single-master replication
✓ Operations master
✓ PDC Emulator
✓ RID Master
✓ Infrastructure Master
✓ Schema Master
✓ Domain Naming Master
✓ Transferring a role
✓ Seizing a role
✓ Ntdsutil
✓ Global Catalog (GC)
✓ Universal group

## Techniques/concepts you'll need to master:

✓ Identifying operations master role dependencies
✓ Planning for business continuity of operations master roles
✓ Planning a strategy for placing Global Catalog servers
✓ Evaluating network traffic considerations when placing Global Catalog servers
✓ Evaluating the need to enable Universal Group Membership Caching

Although it's true to say that all domain controllers (DCs) act as peers on a Windows Server 2003 network when Active Directory (AD) replication is used, at times the peer model does not achieve the desired result. Some functions on a network are best suited to being controlled by a single DC. These functions include implementing security measures, ensuring compatibility with down-level (Windows 2000 and Windows NT 4) servers, and ensuring that the security identifiers (SIDs) of the clients created in a domain are unique.

To this end, Microsoft has implemented *operations masters*. Operations masters have a unique role to play on your network. Management of operations masters is essential to ensuring that you have a healthy and efficient Windows Server 2003 network. In this chapter, we define the operations masters and what they do. We also discuss what actions you should take if an operations master fails or becomes unavailable. In addition, we talk about how the role of an operations master can be moved from one DC to another and what you should do if the original operations master comes back online.

# Introducing Operations Masters

When replicating AD data, Windows Server 2003 uses a *multimaster* concept. This means that any DC can accept a change to AD data, and this change will then be replicated to all partner DCs, who replicate with their partners in the domain and/or forest, and so on, until all domain controllers have received the change. Replication conflicts can, and do, occur. Additionally, some operations that occur on a Windows Server 2003 network could be harmful if conflicts were to occur. In the case of these operations, Windows Server 2003 reverts to using single-master replication. This means that a single DC on the network takes responsibility for performing a specific task. Microsoft uses the term *role* to describe the task that this DC performs. There are five distinct roles, collectively known as *Flexible Single Master Operations (FSMO) roles*, or simply *operations master roles*. When a DC has been assigned a role, it becomes the *operations master* for that role.

Data regarding which DCs are functioning as operations masters is stored in AD. When a client needs to get in touch with an operations master, the client simply queries AD. There are no specific requirements a DC must meet to function as an operations master. This gives you flexibility in deciding which DC takes on the task. It also means that roles can be moved from one DC to another. This becomes more important when a DC acting as an operations master fails.

Although there are no requirements for which DC can act as a specific operations master, pay particular attention to the section "Recommendations for Operations Masters" later in this chapter. For efficiency reasons, it makes sense to assign specific roles to particular DCs.

# Identifying Operations Master Role Dependencies

Each of the five operations master roles that exist on your network has a scope—that is, some of the roles are specific to a domain, whereas others play a role in the entire forest. The five operations masters and their corresponding scopes are set out in Table 3.1. Your Windows Server 2003 network may have five servers that are acting as operations masters (this would be the case in a single-domain environment), or it could have more.

Knowing this fact becomes important when you are deciding which DC should play a specific role on your network. Once you understand each of the roles, you can decide where best to have a role placed for maximum efficiency.

| Table 3.1 Operations Masters and Their Scopes | |
|---|---|
| **Operations Master** | **Scope** |
| Schema Master | Forestwide |
| Domain Naming Master | Forestwide |
| Primary Domain Controller (PDC) Emulator | Specific to a domain |
| Relative Identifier (RID) Master | Specific to a domain |
| Infrastructure Master | Specific to a domain |

Because three of the five types of operations masters are domainwide, you will have several servers in your environment playing that role. Working out the correct placement of the domainwide roles is easier than doing the same thing for the forestwide roles. This is because the forestwide roles must be placed in a location that offers administrators easy and fast access, which can be difficult on wide area networks (WANs).

All Windows Server 2003 installations start with a single server (if this is a migration, it is the first server upgraded). The first server installed takes on all roles. This is unlikely to be optimal for your network, and you should move the roles to other servers as they come online. (We talk about moving roles to other servers in the "Determining Operations Master Roles" section later in this chapter.) Because the first server also operates as a Global Catalog server and DC, the first server installed will be a little overloaded.

When you install a second domain into your Windows Server 2003 network, the first DC that joins the forest for this new domain assumes the three roles that are domain based. Once again, this may not be feasible from a performance standpoint. These default behaviors should be considered carefully when you are designing your network.

Now let's define what each role achieves. Once you fully understand why these roles exist, you can better plan their placement on your network.

## Schema Master

AD is a database built up of instances of objects and objects' attributes. The class of objects and the attributes these objects can have are defined in the schema for the directory. There must be no conflicts when changes are being made to the schema. For instance, with multimaster replication, any DC can make an update to AD data. If any DC were able to make additions or deletions from the schema, you would end up with replication problems. For example, let's say you created a new object type called Database Servers. Replication should take care of letting all other DCs know about this change. But what happens if replication is not yet able to replicate out this schema change to all DCs? You could end up with a situation where one DC is attempting to replicate AD data, but its replication partner doesn't even know the object type is possible!

To go one step further, the schema is obviously a very important piece of AD. Because it defines what can exist within the directory, managing the process of updating it with new objects and attributes should be a closely monitored process. To ensure that this process is limited, there is a single read/write copy of the schema on your Windows Server 2003 network, stored on the Schema Master. In addition, only members of the Schema Admins group can make changes to the schema. Once a change has been made to the schema, the Schema Master then takes on the task of replicating this change to all DCs in the forest.

There is a single Schema Master per forest.

## Domain Naming Master

All objects within AD must be unique. That is, you cannot create two objects in a container with the same name. To make sure this is the case, Windows Server 2003 must ensure that new domains added to your Windows Server 2003 network have unique names. This is the job of the Domain Naming Master.

The Domain Naming Master manages the addition and deletion of domains from the forest. This means that whenever you want to add a domain to your

Windows Server 2003 network, a call must be made to the Domain Naming Master. You will not be able to add or remove a domain if this connection cannot be made. Domains are added to Windows Server 2003 by running dcpromo.exe. This wizard contacts the Domain Naming Master on your network automatically.

In Windows 2000, the Domain Naming Master was also required to be a Global Catalog (GC) server. As a result, if you are running your forest at the Windows 2000 mixed mode or Windows 2000 native mode functional level, you are required to have the Domain Naming Master on a GC server. Once you are running at the Windows Server 2003 functional level, the GC server requirement for the Domain Naming Master is lifted. Global Catalog servers are discussed later in this chapter.

There is a single Domain Naming Master per forest.

## Primary Domain Controller (PDC) Emulator

The PDC Emulator plays several important roles on your Windows Server 2003 network. To understand these roles, remember that a Windows Server 2003 network can operate at one of three functional levels: Windows 2000 mixed mode, Windows 2000 native mode, and Windows Server 2003. Windows 2000 mixed mode means that you have Windows NT 4 servers acting as backup domain controllers (BDCs) alongside Windows 2000 and/or Windows Server 2003 DCs. You cannot change to Windows 2000 native mode until these Windows NT 4 domain controllers have been eliminated from your network. You can have Windows NT 4 member servers in a Windows 2000 native mode domain, just not domain controllers.

The PDC Emulator acts as a conduit between the newer Windows Server 2003 DCs and the older-style Windows NT 4 BDCs. The PDC Emulator is, in effect, the PDC for older Windows NT computers. It takes care of replicating AD data to Windows NT BDCs.

The role of synchronizing older-style DCs with the newer DCs is a two-way street. For instance, if a user object is created within AD, the PDC Emulator makes sure this object is also replicated to older-style DCs. Also, if an older client—a Windows 95 client, for instance—makes a password change, the PDC Emulator accepts the change in the context of being the PDC and replicates that data to AD.

Another area of importance for the PDC Emulator has to do with *replication latency*, which is the amount of time it takes for a change made in AD to be copied to all replicas. Despite your best efforts, there is no way for this to be done in real time; it takes time for data to be processed and for packets to travel across the cable. Generally, this is not a problem, but in the case of users' passwords, it can be debilitating. For instance, say a user changes her password. This change is made at a DC in Houston. Before this DC has had a chance to replicate this password change to all other DCs, the user logs off and tries to log on again. This time, the user connects to a different DC. Because this DC does not have a copy of the new password, the logon attempt is declined.

To prevent this from happening, all password changes on a Windows Server 2003 network are preferentially replicated to the PDC Emulator. Before a DC rejects a logon attempt, it contacts the PDC Emulator to see if any recent changes to the password have taken place. If they have, the PDC Emulator can replicate this data immediately.

The PDC Emulator in a domain also operates as the time-synchronization master. All DCs in a Windows Server 2003 domain synchronize their time with the PDC Emulator. The PDC Emulator in a domain synchronizes its time with the PDC Emulator in the root domain (the first domain installed on your network). The PDC Emulator for the root domain should be synchronized with an external source.

One final area of concern is Group Policy Objects (GPOs). These objects are automatically edited on the PDC Emulator. Although this is not essential for your network, editing these objects on a single server helps eliminate any possible conflicts. This is the default action.

There is a single PDC Emulator per domain.

## RID Master

AD is made up of objects known as *security principals*. A security principal is essentially something that can be assigned permissions within a Windows Server 2003 network. This includes users, groups, and computers. Each security principal is assigned a *security identifier* (SID) so it can be identified. This descriptor is unique to the object and must always remain unique.

A SID is made up of two components. The first component, the *domain SID*, is common to all security principals in a domain. Because it is common to all objects within a domain, the domain SID alone does not allow objects to have a unique SID. The uniqueness comes from the addition of a second number, the *relative identifier* (RID). The RID is assigned from a pool of RIDs stored at each DC. The RIDs in this pool are assigned to each DC by the RID Master.

RIDs are assigned to each DC in blocks. Once the block of RIDs is exhausted, the DC requests another block from the RID Master. The RID Master keeps track of which RID blocks have been assigned. This ensures uniqueness.

If the RID pool on a DC is exhausted and the RID Master is not available, you will not be able to create security principals on that server, which could lead to seemingly strange errors when trying to add objects from a client workstation. You can view the pools by using the Dcdiag utility.

The RID Master also has a role to play when objects are being moved from one domain to another. In this case, the RID Master ensures that an object is not moved to multiple domains. Further, it deletes the object from the previous domain.

There is a single RID Master per domain.

## Infrastructure Master

The domain partition of AD contains data about objects that exist within the domain only. It might also contain references to objects from other domains. This occurs, for instance, when you grant permissions for users that exist in other domains to resources in your domain. Universal groups can be used for this purpose (groups are discussed in detail in Chapter 4, "User and Group Administration").

If a change is made to a referenced object, these changes need to be replicated to all domains. It is the job of the Infrastructure Master to receive these changes and to replicate them to all DCs in its domain.

Let's use an example to clarify this process. A user object named Lisa Arase exists in the Asia domain, and it is referenced in the Europe domain. The Lisa Arase object is then moved from the Asia domain to the Americas domain. This means the SID for the user changes. (Don't forget, the SID is made up of two components: the domain SID, which in this case will change, and the RID.) This change must be made in both the Asia domain and the Americas domain, and the reference in Europe must also be updated. The Infrastructure Master will make this change in Europe.

The Infrastructure Master records references to objects that it does not contain in its directory partition. In our example, this means that although it contains a reference to the user object Lisa Arase, it does not contain any other object data. It is this distinction that allows the Infrastructure Master to work. If the Infrastructure Master is also a Global Catalog server (which contains a reference to all objects created in a forest), the Infrastructure Master will know about all objects in the forest, and the comparison will not work. This breaks the Infrastructure Master's operation. Therefore, the Infrastructure Master cannot also be a Global Catalog server.

Because there will be no references to external objects in a single domain, there is no need to worry about the Infrastructure Master in a single-domain environment.

There is a single Infrastructure Master per domain.

# Planning for Business Continuity of Operations Master Roles

Because the first DC installed in a domain (or the forest) assumes all the FSMO roles by default, it is highly likely that you will want to transfer at least some of the roles to other domain controllers later.

Before you can do this, however, you must determine which servers in your environment are currently performing each role. You can then gracefully move a role from one DC to another (known as *transferring* the role), or you can *seize* a role. Seizing a role is the act of taking control away from one DC and assigning it to another without the current operations master relinquishing its role first. You would do this if the DC acting as an operations master had failed and was no longer online. Because the server is not operational, it cannot gracefully give up its role; instead, the role must be seized.

## Determining Operations Master Roles

The tools you use to determine which server is performing a specific role depend on the scope of the role. Remember that two of the five roles are forestwide. The remaining three are domain specific. You can use a single tool to determine the domain-level roles, but you must use different tools to figure out the forestwide roles.

### Domain-Level Operations Master Roles

As mentioned, the three domain-level operations master roles are PDC Emulator, RID Master, and Infrastructure Master. You can use the Active Directory Users and Computers tool to find out which server or servers are playing this role. To do this, right-click Active Directory Users and Computers, navigate to All Tasks, and select Operations Masters, as shown in Figure 3.1.

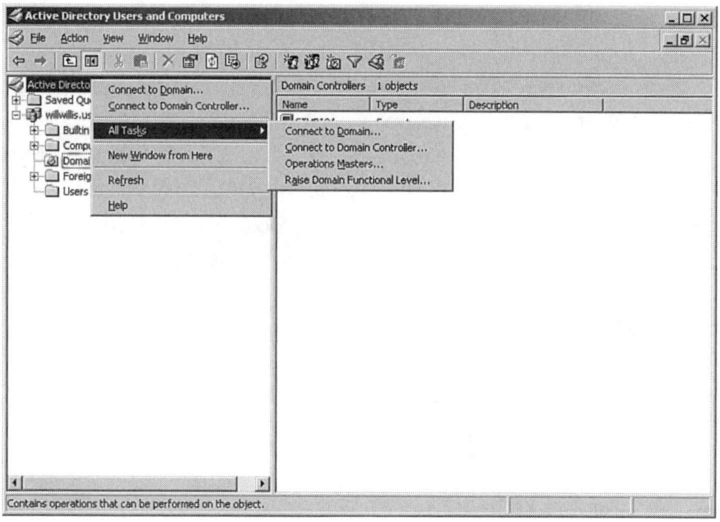

**Figure 3.1**   Using AD Users and Computers to determine a role owner.

When you make this selection, you are presented with the Operations Masters dialog box, shown in Figure 3.2. There are three domain-level operations master roles, and each is displayed on its own tab. Along with the name of the system playing the role is a Change button, which you use to change the server playing the role, that is transfer the role.

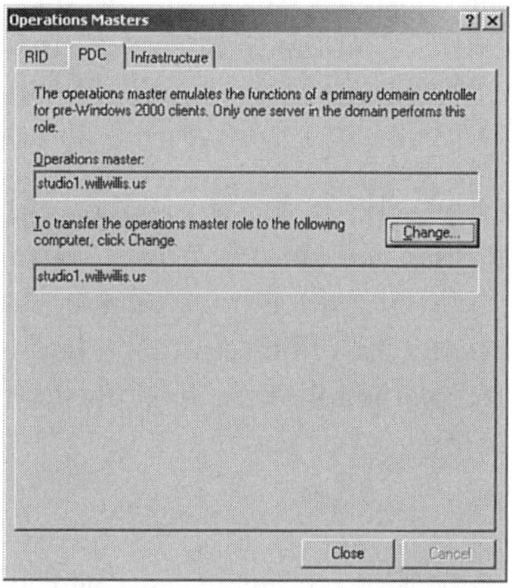

**Figure 3.2**   The Operations Masters dialog box.

# Forest-Level Operations Master Roles

As mentioned previously, two roles are forestwide: the Domain Naming Master and the Schema Master. You use two different tools to determine which DC is playing these roles. For the Domain Naming Master, you use Active Directory Domains and Trusts, which is found in the Administrative Tools menu. You navigate to the Change Operations Master dialog box, shown in Figure 3.3, in much the same way you reached the Operations Masters dialog box in the last section. In this case, right-click Active Directory Domains and Trusts and then select Operations Master. This brings up the Change Operations Master dialog box. You can change the name of the server that plays the role by clicking the Change button.

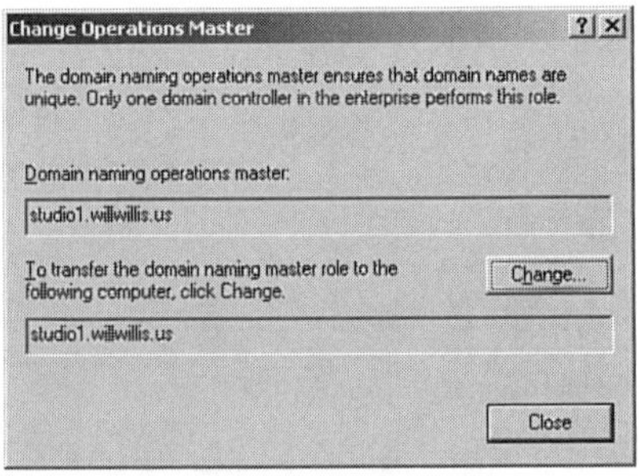

**Figure 3.3**  The Change Operations Master dialog box.

The Schema Master role is a little different. Editing the AD schema should be a very controlled process for several reasons. First, when a change is made to the schema, the change must be replicated to all DCs in the forest. This generates a lot of activity on those servers and consumes bandwidth. Second, you can never delete anything from the schema. You can only "deactivate" parts of the schema. That means an object can be deactivated but will still take up space within the schema definition.

To find out which server is playing the role of Schema Master, and also to change the name of the DC playing the role, you must use the Active Directory Schema MMC snap-in. By default, this snap-in is not available. To use it, you must first register the schema dynamic link library (DLL). To do this, open a Command Prompt window and type the following (you must be a Domain Admin or Enterprise Admin to complete this task):

```
regsvr32.exe schmmgmt.dll
```

This registers the DLL for use on your system. This command must be run on a Windows Server 2003 server. If the system root is not in your path, make sure you give the full path to the schmmgmt.dll file. The path should be <systemroot>\system32.

Once you have registered the DLL, you must create a custom MMC console. Follow these steps to create a custom console:

1. Select Start, Run and type **MMC**.

2. This brings up an empty console. Click the Console menu and select Add/Remove Snap-In.

3. This brings up the Add/Remove Snap-In dialog box. Click the Add button.

4. This displays the Add Standalone Snap-In dialog box. Select Active Directory Schema and click Add. Click Close and then OK.

To display the name of the DC playing the Schema Master role, right-click Active Directory Schema in the right-side panel and select Operations Master. This displays the Change Schema Master dialog box, shown in Figure 3.4. You can change the server name by clicking the Change button.

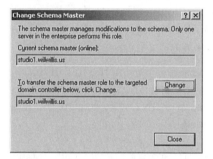

**Figure 3.4**    The Change Schema Master dialog box.

Each of the methods given in this "Determining Operations Masters" section includes an option to connect to an alternative DC on the context-sensitive menu from which you chose the Operations Master option. Use this option to connect to other domains and to view or change the operations master in those domains.

# Permissions for Changing an Operations Master Server

Before you can transfer a role from one server to another, you must make sure you have sufficient permissions. Table 3.2 details what these permissions should be. Pay particular attention to the Schema Master, because this is a special group within the domain.

| Table 3.2 Required Permissions for Changing an Operations Master Role | |
|---|---|
| **Role** | **Group with Permission** |
| PDC Emulator | Domain Admins group |
| RID Master | Domain Admins group |
| Infrastructure Master | Domain Admins group |
| Schema Master | Schema Admins group |
| Domain Naming Master | Enterprise Admins group |

# Seizing a Role

Transferring an operations master role from one server to another using the methods outlined in the previous sections is a graceful exchange—that is, an assumption is made that both servers are functioning. With both online, normal AD replication can take care of transferring necessary data from one server to another so it can perform its new role.

This is not always the case, however. If the server playing the role of operations master fails or becomes unavailable, it may be necessary to seize control of it. Seizing the role forces the transfer from one system to another. This is a last resort and is not recommended.

 Seizing a role is a serious matter and should be done in emergencies only. The server currently playing the role must not come back online. If it does, you will have a serious conflict on your network. If you want to reuse a server that previously played a role that has been seized, reformat the partition that contains Windows Server 2003 and reinstall the operating system.

The method used to seize a role depends on the operations master you are working with. If you need to seize the role for the PDC Emulator or the Infrastructure Master, you can go ahead and use the Active Directory Users and Computers console. Use the method outlined previously when viewing and changing the current DC playing the role.

Things get more complicated if you are changing the Schema Master, Domain Naming Master, or RID Master role. For these, you must use the Ntdsutil command-line utility. This utility is a powerful tool that has many uses. The help screen displaying the various options is shown in Figure 3.5 (along with the steps to seize a role, which are described in the following section).

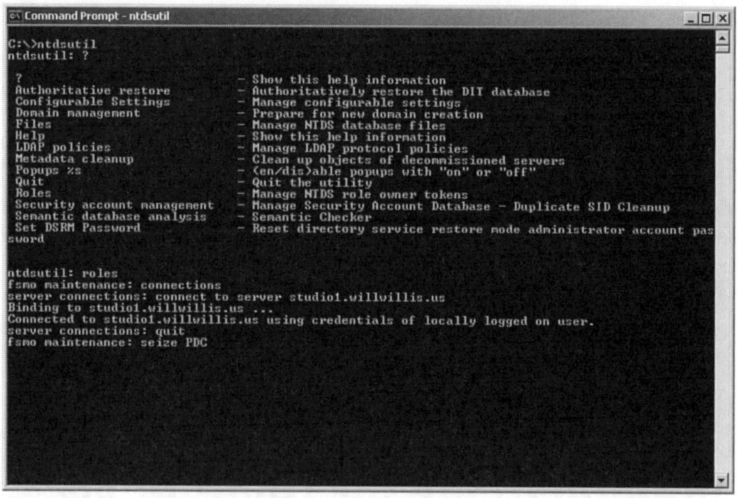

**Figure 3.5**   Using the Ntdsutil utility to seize a role.

As you can see, the ntdsutil command has a host of options. The following steps walk you through seizing a role as well as how to get help with this utility at any time by using the help command:

1. Select Start, Run and then type **ntdsutil**. Click OK.

2. At the ntdsutil prompt, type **roles** and press Enter. For help, type **help** and press Enter. Depending on the prompt displayed at the time, help information is shown.

3. At the fsmo maintenance prompt, type **connections** and press Enter.

4. At the server connections prompt, type **connect to server** followed by the fully qualified domain name (FQDN) of the DC that will be seizing the role. Press Enter.

5. At the server connections prompt, type **quit** and press Enter.

6. At the fsmo maintenance prompt, type one of the following commands (depending on the role you are attempting to seize):

   ➤ seize PDC

   ➤ seize RID master

   ➤ seize infrastructure master

   ➤ seize schema master

   ➤ seize domain naming master

   Press Enter.

**7.** At the fsmo maintenance prompt, type **quit** and press Enter.

**8.** At the ntdsutil prompt, type **quit** and Press Enter.

Once you have completed the command, don't forget to verify that the role has changed by using the method outlined in the "Determining Operations Master Roles" section earlier in this chapter. Don't forget that once a role has been seized, the old server playing the role must never come online again.

Ntdsutil has a host of options. Make sure you experiment with this tool. Also, don't forget to type **help** or **?** at each prompt to see a display of available options.

# Recommendations for Operations Masters

Losing an operations master does not generally have an immediate impact on your network and its users. The exception to this rule is the PDC Emulator used by down-level clients and for password changes. If the PDC Emulator goes down, you may have to seize the role fairly quickly. Protect the server playing this role as best you can.

Always transfer an operations master role rather than seize it. Only seize a role when it is unavoidable. Make sure you have a process in place that prevents the old operations master from coming back online.

Consider network traffic when deciding which servers on your network should perform each role. For instance, the PDC Emulator is contacted by all down-level clients and by each DC when a password change takes place. This can cause a lot of traffic on an enterprise network. The PDC Emulator should be in a location that allows other servers to have easy access to it. The Infrastructure Master may or may not be dependent on the Global Catalog server, depending on what functional level the domain is running in. Make sure there is a Global Catalog server in the same site as the Infrastructure Master.

It's a good idea to combine the Schema Master and Domain Naming Master roles. These roles are suited to being on the same server because these tasks are usually performed by the same group within an organization.

# Planning a Strategy for Placing Global Catalog Servers

A Global Catalog (GC) contains location information for every object created, whether it was created by default upon installation or manually with the AD. It is also responsible for several other important features, such as the following:

➤ Logon validation of universal group membership

➤ User principal name logon validation through DC location

➤ Search capabilities for every object within an entire forest

The GC retains only frequently searched for attributes of an object. There is no need, nor would it be very practical from a replication standpoint, for the GC to retain every single detail of every single object. Then the GC would be, in fact, no different from a regular DC. Instead, the GC is a DC that performs this additional functionality.

Several factors need to be considered with regard to the GC and how it functions to enhance logon validation under a Windows 2000 native mode or Windows Server 2003 functional level situation.

## GC and Logon Validation

Universal groups (discussed in Chapter 4) are centrally located within the GC. The universal groups a user belongs to are quite important in the creation of an access token, which is attached to that user and is needed to access any object, to run any application, and to use system resources. The access token is what literally holds the SID and the group IDs, which indicate what groups the user belongs to. Those access tokens are necessary for logon validation as well as resource access, so each token must include a user's universal group membership.

When a user logs on to a Windows 2000 native mode or Windows Server 2003 functional level domain (these are the only ones to include universal groups), the GC updates the DC as to the universal group information for that particular user's access token. But what if a GC is unavailable for some reason? Then the DC will use "cached credentials" to log the user on to the local computer. This cached logon provides the same level of access to network resources as the user had the last time they logged in. Furthermore, those credentials would exist only if the user had logged on prior to this point. What if the user had never logged on and the GC is not available for the first logon? If no GC server could be contacted either locally or at another site, the user would not be able to log on to the domain and could either log on locally to the machine itself or wait for a GC to become available again.

# Evaluating Network Traffic Considerations When Placing Global Catalog Servers

Because GC servers are prominent in logon validation and in locating AD resources, it is important to plan for their placement on a complex LAN. Ideally you would have at least one GC server at each AD site, though this isn't always practical, especially for small branch offices. GC traffic increases the burden on WAN links, so there is a tradeoff between having remote sites needing to contact a GC across a WAN link versus the additional replication traffic that a GC server will generate across the WAN link. Microsoft recommends having a GC server at each site, though, if your server hardware will support it.

# Evaluating the Need to Enable Universal Group Membership Caching

With the Windows 2000 native mode, a GC server must be available at all times to verify universal group membership. If you have sites separated by slow or unreliable WAN links, the practice is to place a GC server at each local site. The downside to this is that replication traffic is increased. If the domain is operating at the Windows Server 2003 functional level, you can enable the caching of universal group membership so users can log in even if no GC server is available.

Universal Group Membership Caching is most practical for smaller branch offices with lower-end servers, where it might be problematic to add the additional load of hosting a GC, or locations that have slower WAN connections. To enable caching, use the Active Directory Sites and Services utility. Navigate down the left side of the console and click the site at which you want to enable caching. On the right side (the contents pane), you'll see NTDS Site Settings, as shown in Figure 3.6. Right-click this and choose Properties, which brings up the dialog box shown in Figure 3.7.

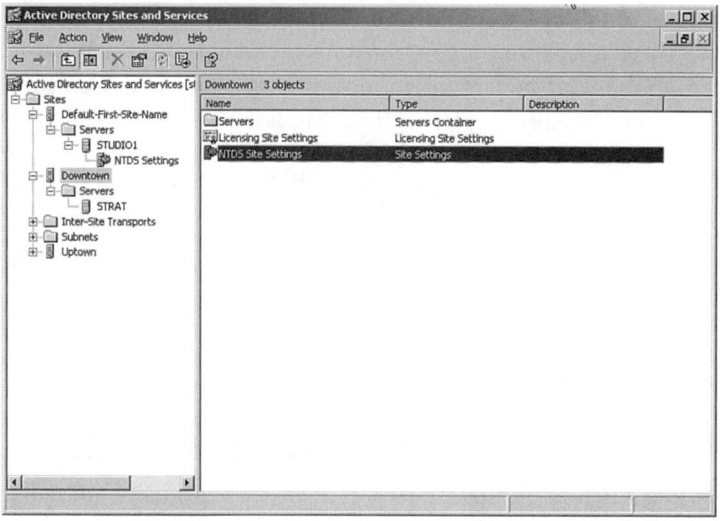

**Figure 3.6**  Configuring Universal Group Membership Caching through NTDS Site Settings in Active Directory Sites and Services.

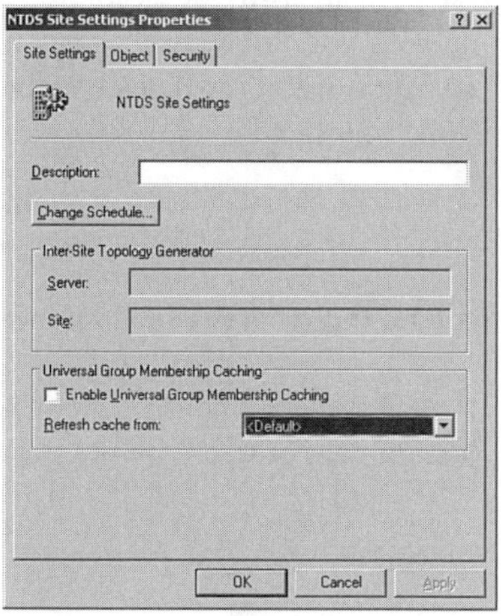

**Figure 3.7**  Check the box to enable Universal Group Membership Caching and select a cache server if desired.

To enable Universal Group Membership Caching, simply check the box on the property sheet. You have the option of choosing a specific server to refresh the cache from or leaving it as default, which will cause Windows Server 2003 to attempt to refresh the cache from the nearest GC server it can contact. By default, Windows Server 2003 will attempt to refresh the cache every 8 hours.

Once caching has been enabled, a user must log in once for his information to be cached. Upon the initial logon, a GC server must be contacted to obtain the group membership information, but after the initial logon the information is cached. As a result, logon times are faster because a GC server doesn't need to be contacted, and network bandwidth utilization is improved without GC replication taking place.

Pay keen attention to the functionality of a GC. Your knowledge of GCs will enable you to determine whether possible solutions will resolve defined problems.

## User Principal Names and Logon Validation

Normally, an individual might log on to a domain with her common name and password. For example, suppose the user's common name is DonnaD and her password is Duncan1968. Now suppose Donna attempts to log on to the system using her principal name—for example, donna@virtual-realm.com. If Donna is attempting to log on from a system that is in the accounting domain, the DC in acct.virtual-realm.com will not know her account. However, the DC will check with the GC, and that will, in turn, lead to the DC for the virtual-realm.com domain. The user will then be validated.

## Adding GC Servers

Not all DCs are GC servers. Following are several thoughts to keep in mind:

➤ The first DC in a forest is a GC server.

➤ Any DC can be a GC server if set up to assume that function by the system administrator.

➤ Usually one GC is helpful in each site.

➤ You can create additional GCs if necessary.

To add another GC, perform the following tasks from AD Sites and Services:

**1.** Within the tree structure in the left pane, expand the DC that will be the new GC.

**2.** Right-click NTDS Settings and select Properties.

**3.** In the NTDS Settings Properties dialog box, under the General Tab, select the Global Catalog check box, as shown in Figure 3.8.

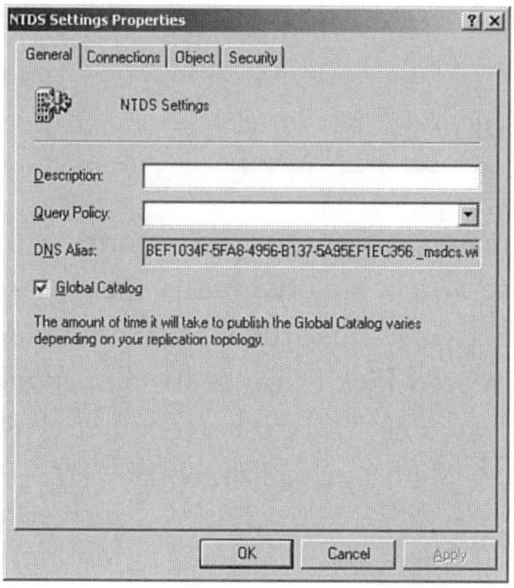

**Figure 3.8**   Adding a Global Catalog server.

# Exam Prep Questions

## Question 1

There are five operations master roles on a Windows Server 2003 network. Where is the data regarding which servers are playing which roles stored?

- ○ A.  It is stored in the Registry of the server performing the role.
- ○ B.  It is stored within Active Directory.
- ○ C.  It is stored in the Registry of the clients.
- ○ D.  It is stored in a database separate from Active Directory.

Answer B is correct. This data must be in Active Directory so clients and down-level servers can query the database when an operations master is required. Answers A and C wouldn't be effective because the Registry is used only by a local machine, and if the data is stored locally, other machines on the network won't be able to access it. Answer D is incorrect because Windows Server 2003 uses no other database than Active Directory.

## Question 2

Which of the following are names of the operations master roles? [Check all correct answers.]

- ❑ A.  Schema Master
- ❑ B.  Infrastructure Master
- ❑ C.  SID Master
- ❑ D.  Domain Naming Master

Answers A, B, and D are correct. The operations master roles that are missing are RID Master and PDC Emulator. Answer C is incorrect because there is no such role as the SID Master. The SID is the common domain portion that identifies a client's membership, and with the RID (relative identifier) it uniquely identifies an AD object such as a user account.

# Question 3

James Pyles is attempting to create a universal group in a child domain, but the option is unavailable. There are several child domains under a single parent domain that all have the ability to create universal groups, with the exception of this one. What would be a valid reason for James having such a dilemma?

- O  A.  The domain is still residing in Windows 2000 mixed mode.
- O  B.  The domain is not running at the Windows Server 2003 functional level.
- O  C.  The domain is still in Windows 2000 native mode and needs its functional level raised.
- O  D.  James is attempting to create the group on a backup domain controller (BDC).

Answer A is correct. If James is still residing in a Windows 2000 mixed-mode scenario, his groups will be only domain local and global. Universal groups exist only in Windows 2000 native mode and at the Windows Server 2003 functional level. It is perfectly legitimate for one domain in a tree to be at the default Windows 2000 mixed mode while other child domains in the tree have had their functional levels raised. Answer B is incorrect because universal groups are also available at the Windows 2000 native mode functional level. Answer C is incorrect because Windows 2000 native mode supports universal groups, so James would not need to raise the functional level. Answer D is incorrect because domains in Windows Server 2003 do not use BDCs, nor would it matter which DC James tried to implement a security group on if the domain is not in native mode.

# Question 4

Ayman Mohareb ("Mo") is a system administrator for a large company. Mo has noticed that he is getting a lot of errors in the system log of Event Viewer. The errors relate to time synchronization on his network. Mo knows that this is related to an operations master role. Which role performs time-synchronization duties?

- O  A.  The Infrastructure Master
- O  B.  The Schema Master
- O  C.  The Domain Naming Master
- O  D.  The PDC Emulator

Answer D is correct. The PDC Emulator performs time-synchronization duties within its domain. It, in turn, synchronizes with the PDC Emulator in the root domain. The PDC Emulator in the root domain should be synchronized with an external source. Answer A is incorrect because the Infrastructure Master is responsible for updating cross-domain references of objects. Answer B is incorrect because the Schema Master role is to operate as the single location where changes to the schema can be made. Answer C is incorrect because the Domain Naming Master is used to add or remove domains from the forest.

# Question 5

Robyn Hitchcock is a member of the Domain Admins group in a Windows Server 2003 network. He has been asked to add a new object type to AD. However, whenever he tries to access the schema, he is denied access. A new Windows Server 2003 MCSE named Jaime Rodriguez says this is because of insufficient permissions. However, because Robyn is a member of the Domain Admins group, Robyn doubts this is true. Instead, Robyn thinks it is a network problem. Who is right?

- ○ A. Jaime is right. Domain Admins do not have sufficient permissions to make changes to the Active Directory schema. One must be at least a Schema Admin to do this.
- ○ B. Robyn is right. Domain Admins have all permissions on a Windows Server 2003 network; therefore, he should be able to change the schema.
- ○ C. Neither is correct. Domain Admins can change a schema; therefore, Jaime is incorrect. However, receiving an "access denied message" indicates a server problem, not a network problem.
- ○ D. Jaime is right. Domain Admins do not have sufficient permissions to make changes to the Active Directory schema. One must be at least an Enterprise Admin to do this.

Answer A is correct. Only members of the Schema Admins group can make changes to the schema. Therefore, answers B, C, and D are all incorrect.

# Question 6

Pete Umlandt is attempting to log on to a domain called research.corp.com, although his user account is located in corp.com. Pete is using his user principal name, pete@corp.com. What feature of an Active Directory network will most assist him in logging on to the system?

- ○ A. Universal groups
- ○ B. Global Catalog servers
- ○ C. Additional domain controllers
- ○ D. Kerberos authentication

Answer B is correct. Global Catalog servers search for the domain information necessary during logon when an individual uses his user principal name. Answer A is incorrect because although universal groups can ease administration in domains that have had their functional levels raised, they won't help with logging in through a child domain. Answer C is incorrect because although additional domain controllers will add fault tolerance, they are not necessarily GC servers and will not assist in logon validation. Answer D is incorrect because although Kerberos is used to verify authentication to the resources, it doesn't assist in the location of the GC domain controller that will validate a user.

# Question 7

The Domain Naming Master server has crashed. The word from the hardware techs onsite is that it will take a week to order the parts to get it back up and running. Matt Thomson is the system administrator, and this could not have happened at a worse time. Matt was due to work all weekend creating two new domains. He knows that not having a functioning Domain Naming Master will prevent him from creating new domains. Therefore, Matt decides to seize the role of Domain Naming Master. Which tool will he use to perform this task?

- O  A.  Matt will use the Ntdsutil command-line utility.
- O  B.  Matt will use Active Directory Domains and Trusts to seize the role, because this is a forestwide operations master.
- O  C.  Matt will use the Active Directory Users and Computers tool. This tool is used to seize all roles except that of the Schema Master.
- O  D.  Matt will deactivate the current Domain Naming Master with Ntdsutil. He will then use Active Directory Domains and Trusts to assign the role to another server.

Answer A is correct. There is no need to use two tools to perform this task. Matt simply needs to use Ntdsutil, a command-line utility with many different options, to seize the role. Answer B is incorrect because Active Directory Domains and Trusts is not used to seize roles. Answer C is incorrect because one cannot use Active Directory Users and Computers to seize forestwide roles. Answer D is incorrect because Active Directory Domains and Trusts is not used to seize roles.

# Question 8

Marty Bouillon has just been added to the Schema Admins group, so he can make some additions to the schema of Active Directory. Marty knows that this task is very important and that he must be careful when editing the schema. Fortunately, his development background has prepared him for the task. Marty knows that he must create a custom MMC in order to edit the schema using the Schema MMC snap-in. However, when he tries to add the snap-in, it is not available on his system. He calls his help desk and asks to be added to all the necessary groups to enable this function, but the help desk tells him that it is not a permissions issue. What must Marty do to fix this problem?

- O A. Marty must contact the help desk manager because the help desk is incorrect; this *is* a permissions issue. One must be both a member of Schema Admins and Enterprise Admins to edit the schema.

- O B. Marty is obviously using a Windows 98 computer. The MMC does not work on a Windows 98 box. Marty must upgrade his system to Windows 2000 or XP.

- O C. Marty must first register **schmmgmt** with the **regsvr32** command. He will not be able to use the Schema MMC snap-in until this is done.

- O D. Marty should call the help desk and ask its staff to seize the role of Schema Master. The snap-in not showing on the system is indicative of the server being unavailable.

Answers C is correct. Marty cannot use the Schema MMC snap-in until he registers schmmgmt with the regsvr32 command. Answer A is incorrect because the help desk was correct; this is *not* a permissions issue. Answer B is incorrect because the MMC does work on a Windows 98 box. Answer D is incorrect because Marty would not know that the Schema Master is not available until he tried to make a change to the schema. Because he cannot even find the snap-in, this is not the case.

# Question 9

Miriam Haber is performing a review of the installation plan for her new Windows Server 2003 network. Her staff has detailed the placement of all DCs and operations masters. The administrators are in a small building on a single subnet. There are 10 administrators. The network design team proposes that two DCs be placed in its site. Because there are only 10 people, one server would be fairly slow. A more powerful server would be a Global Catalog server and the Infrastructure Master. Miriam rejects this plan and asks the network design team to reconsider. What was it about this design that she did not like?

○ A. Although two DCs are reasonable in other circumstances, the role of the administrators is too important not to have at least three.

○ B. The Infrastructure Master will not operate on a server that is functioning as a Global Catalog server. Either one of these tasks should be moved to the second DC.

○ C. The Infrastructure Master role does not need to be close to the administrators. Because this role is used only for schema updates, it would be better to move this elsewhere and to replace the role with something more pertinent to the administrators' jobs.

○ D. Miriam wants the help desk team to be moved to another site. Having it in a separate site will cause performance issues.

Answer B is correct. Although some of the other answers sound good, only answer B has it right. Two DCs should give enough redundancy, but three would not be going overboard either. However, answer A is incorrect because not having three would not cause the plan to be rejected. Answer C is incorrect because there are other roles that could be close to the administrators, too, but depending on what type of tasks are performed most commonly, it might make sense to make the Infrastructure Master closest. Answer D is incorrect because although the administrators are in a different site, that does not necessarily mean they have a slow connection to the rest of the network. Sites are also sometimes used to manage replication. Regardless of any of this, the Infrastructure Master will not operate correctly on a server that is also a Global Catalog server.

# Question 10

Sandy Garrity is the design analyst who determines the AD structure for W&W, Inc. The structure takes into account the physical distribution of the company, with its headquarters in Lewisville, TX and three branch offices located in Omaha, Seoul, and Barcelona. She determines a need to create a headquarters domain root called w-w.com with three child domains beneath. By default, how many Global Catalog servers will there be for this widely dispersed solution?

○ A. One

○ B. Three

○ C. Four

○ D. Zero

Answer A is correct. The first DC for the entire forest will contain the role of Global Catalog. By default, this is the only GC in the entire forest. It is recommended that the administrator manually create additional GCs in remote locations and do so at a time when it will be the most convenient for network traffic between the GCs. GCs hold a copy of every object in the entire forest and a subset of attributes for each of those objects. Answers B and C are incorrect because they provide for too many. Answer D is also incorrect because there is always at least one GC for the forest.

# Need to Know More?

 Honeycutt, Jerry. *Introducing Microsoft Windows Server 2003*. Microsoft Press. Redmond, WA, 2003. ISBN 0-7356-1570-5.

 Microsoft Corporation. *Microsoft Windows Server 2003 Resource Kit*. Microsoft Press. Redmond, WA, 2003. ISBN 0-7356-1471-7.

 Mulcare, Mike and Stan Reimer. *Active Directory for Microsoft Windows Server 2003 Technical Reference*. Microsoft Press. Redmond, WA, 2003. ISBN 0-7356-1577-2.

4

# User and Group Administration

## Terms you'll need to understand:

✓ Single sign-on
✓ Domain user account
✓ Local user account
✓ Built-in account
✓ User logon name
✓ User principal name
✓ User principal suffix
✓ Enrollment station
✓ Certificate Authority (CA)
✓ Smartcard
✓ Enrollment Agent certificate
✓ Universal groups
✓ AGDLP

## Techniques/concepts you'll need to master:

✓ Planning a user authentication strategy
✓ Creating a password policy for domain users
✓ Planning a smartcard authentication strategy
✓ Planning a security group strategy
✓ Planning a security group hierarchy based on delegation
  requirements

Active Directory (AD) is essentially a database that stores data about network resources and other objects. Two of the most common types of objects stored within AD are *users* and *groups*. Having these objects stored within AD allows people to log on to the network and gain access to a range of network resources. Because all objects are stored within AD along with access permissions, you can achieve a *single sign-on*, which is a feature in Windows Server 2003 that allows users to log in to the network with a single username and password and receive access to a host of network resources. The user does not need to enter any additional usernames or passwords to gain access to network shares, printers, or other network resources.

Generally, *groups* are collections of user accounts (although they can also include computers) that are used to ease administration. Because you can create a group and assign permissions for a resource to this single entity, using groups is far easier than assigning permissions to individual user accounts. In Windows Server 2003, you can also nest groups, which allows groups themselves to contain other groups, further simplifying network administration. In this chapter, we examine users and groups and how they can be used in a Windows Server 2003 environment.

# Introducing Users and Groups

Obviously, if a user cannot log on to a Windows Server 2003 network, he cannot gain access to the data and resources—such as files and folders, email accounts, and printers—that are stored there. User accounts are the fundamental building blocks of your network. Because they are so important, you will likely spend a lot of time working with user accounts in your environment.

A Windows Server 2003 network has three different types of user accounts:

➤ *Domain user account*—This account is used to gain access to a Windows Server 2003 domain and all its associated resources. This is the most common type of logon you will experience on a Windows Server 2003 network. A logon that exists on one domain can be given permissions in other Windows Server 2003 domains.

➤ *Local user account*—This account exists on a standalone or member server, or a Windows 2000 or XP Professional system. It enables a user to log on to a specific computer and gain access to the local resources that it offers. By definition, a standalone computer is not acting as part of a Windows Server 2003 network. Therefore, a local user account cannot grant access to resources in a domain.

➤ *Built-in user accounts*—These accounts have been created for specific administrative tasks to ease the burden of administration. They define special accounts up front that have permissions to both resources and AD itself.

The most commonly used network resources include files, folders, and printers. Given that you might have to deal with several hundred or thousand user accounts, granting access to resources based solely on user accounts would be time-consuming and hugely repetitive. So, instead, we use groups. The concept of *groups* is very simple: You create a single group object within AD and grant access permissions (or deny access) to this single entity. User accounts are then added as members of the group. By being members of a group, the user accounts inherit the permissions assigned to the group. If these permissions must be changed, you can then simply modify them on the group object a single time. Any changes to the group permissions are applied to the user accounts that are members of the group.

In addition, Windows Server 2003 allows you to build a hierarchy of groups and assign different permissions to each level of the hierarchy. This is achieved through the nesting of groups. Nesting groups further simplifies your security model.

# Planning a User Authentication Strategy

User logon names are also known as *user account names*. However, be careful with your use of terminology in Windows Server 2003; a user can have more than one type of account, because Microsoft has provided the ability to use older-style usernames in a Windows Server 2003 network along with a new type of logon name. These types of account names, called *user principle names* and *user logon names*, are discussed next.

## Types of Logon Names

When logging in to a Windows Server 2003 network, users can use either one of the two types of names they have been assigned: their *user principal name* or their *user logon name*. The end result will be the same, although the older-style logon names should slowly be phased out. Domain controllers (DCs) are able to authenticate the users regardless of what method they use. Let's look at these two types of usernames.

## User Principal Name

The *user principal name* is the new-style logon name on Windows Server 2003 networks. A user principal name is made up of two parts. One part uniquely identifies the user object in AD; the second part identifies the domain where the user object was created. A user principal name looks like this:

```
WWillis@Inside-Corner.com
```

As you can see, the two parts of the user principal name are divided by the "at" sign (@). This tells Windows Server 2003 which part of the name is the user object name and which is the domain name. These two parts can further be defined as the following:

➤ *User principal name prefix*—In the preceding example, this is WWillis.

➤ *User principal name suffix*—By default, the suffix is derived from the root domain name on your Windows Server 2003 network. You can also create additional user principal names by using other domains on your network, although doing so increases the administrative overhead of your network. Windows Server 2003 administrators who have deployed Exchange Server commonly use the email address as the user principal name. In the preceding example, the user principal name suffix would be Inside-Corner.com.

Because user principal names are by default tied to the root domain's name, moving a user object from one domain to another on a Windows Server 2003 network does not require a username change. This effectively makes the change invisible for the users. They need not be concerned that their user account has been moved from one domain to another. Also, because a user principal name can be the same as a user's email account, the name is easy to remember.

## User Logon Name

User logon names are used to describe backward-compatible usernames. They are used by clients logging on to a Windows Server 2003 network from an older operating system, such as Windows 9x or Microsoft Windows NT 4.

Logging on to a Windows Server 2003 domain using their user logon name means that users must provide two distinct pieces of information. First, they must enter their username; second, they must enter the name of the domain where their account exists. This can be confusing to users who sometimes have trouble remembering all the details of the logon process. Because a user account is also only unique within a domain (see the next section on rules for logon names), accessing resources outside of the domain can be more difficult than necessary. In this case, the user may have to enter an additional username and password. In our example, the user logon name would simply be WWillis.

# Rules for Logon Names

Because user accounts are used to gain access to a Windows Server 2003 network, each username must be unique. The scope of this uniqueness varies depending on the type of logon name you intend to use. This enables single sign-on. The administrator must ensure that user accounts follow a set of rules so that they are unique within a Windows Server 2003 forest.

User principal names must be unique within a forest. This can make coming up with a naming strategy more difficult, especially when you have tens of thousands of users. The benefits outweigh the difficulties; however, you should come up with a naming strategy that allows for usernames that are easy to remember yet at the same time are easily distinguishable.

User logon names must be unique within the domain in which they are created. If you think you will use these account types exclusively, you have a little more flexibility in naming conventions because, in effect, you can share a single username across multiple domains. However, using a single name exclusively is discouraged. Over time, this will undoubtedly cause additional administrative overhead.

The username suffix (in our case, Inside-Corner.com) is derived from the root domain by default. However, this can be changed. By adding additional suffixes, you ensure that users have a standard and easy-to-understand user principal name. Before an additional suffix can be used, it must be added to AD. We discussed adding UPN suffixes in Chapter 1, "Planning and Implementing Forests and Domains."

# Administering User Accounts

Many of the ongoing administrative tasks performed on a Windows Server 2003 network are based around user accounts. This includes the creation and maintenance of these accounts. In this section, we look at the common administrative tools you will use as well as how to search AD for specific data.

The most common administrative tool is Active Directory Users and Computers. To access this utility, select Start, Programs, Administrative Tools, Active Directory Users and Computers.

Active Directory Users and Computers provides you with all the day-to-day functionality you need. In this section, we look at some of the most common functions you are likely to perform. Being familiar with the interface of Active Directory Users and Computers helps you be more efficient at administering user accounts in your environment. The common administrative tasks we will look at include the following:

➤ Creating user accounts

➤ Resetting passwords

➤ Unlocking user accounts

➤ Deleting user accounts

➤ Renaming user accounts

➤ Copying user accounts

➤ Disabling and enabling user accounts

Because these are common tasks, Microsoft has provided an easy method to access them. To access each of these tasks, simply select the Users container in the left panel of Active Directory Users and Computers and then right-click the user object you want to change in the panel on the right. When you do this, you are presented with the context-sensitive menu shown in Figure 4.1.

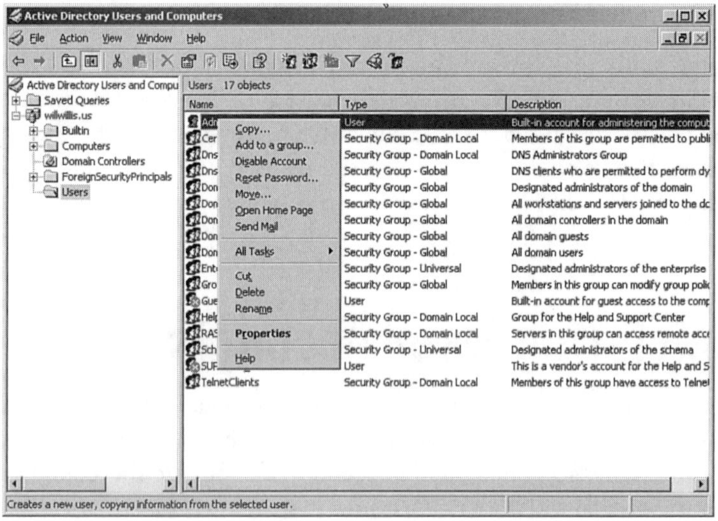

**Figure 4.1**  AD Users and Computers context-sensitive menu.

As you can see, this menu offers you a wealth of functionality. Note that it is possible to perform some tasks on multiple user accounts. For instance, if you highlight five user accounts and then right-click them, you will see a context-sensitive menu with a subset of functions. One of these functions is the ability to disable an account, which in this case lets you disable several accounts simultaneously.

# Creating User Accounts

One of the basic tasks of administering users is creating user accounts, which is done through the Active Directory Users and Computers management console. When you open Active Directory Users and Computers, you can navigate through the list of containers in your domain down the left side of the windows. User accounts are typically created in the Users container, although they can be created in other folders as well.

To create a new user, right-click the Users container, select New, and then click User. This brings up the New Object – User window, where you are prompted to supply account details. You would type in the user's first and last name (you are required to enter one or the other at minimum) and assign a user logon name. Note that when you type the user logon name, a pre–Windows 2000–compatible name is automatically generated. The field is pre–Windows 2000 because it was with the introduction of Windows 2000 that user principle names were used rather than the older style NetBIOS names.

After clicking Next, you are prompted to enter a password for the user and to confirm it and then configure any account settings, such as requiring the user to change the password at next logon, whether the user can change his own password, whether the password should never expire, and whether the account should be disabled. Once you've configured the desired settings, click Next and then Finish to complete the process.

 If the Windows Server 2003 on which you create a user account is running Exchange 2000 Server or Exchange Server 2003, or has had the Exchange management tools installed, you will be prompted to create a mailbox for the user after configuring the password settings.

# Resetting Passwords

Passwords are at the heart of the security of your network. They should be secure, changed often, and hard to crack (for instance, users should not use the name of their spouse or family pet).

You may also find that users sometimes forget their password and request that you change it for them. As an administrator, you do not need to know the user's old password to change it. If you do make a change to a user's password, don't forget to check the User Must Change Password at Next Logon check box. This is a "best practice" that allows the user to log on once with the password you set for him, and then he has to create a new one on his own.

You access this function by selecting Reset Password from the context-sensitive menu.

# Unlocking User Accounts

User accounts are subject to the security settings that have been defined in Group Policy. One of the most common settings is for an account to be locked out after three failed login attempts. This occurs when a user has forgotten her password and makes several consecutive attempts, guessing wrong each time. We'll discuss creating a password policy later in this chapter.

To unlock an account, select Properties on the context-sensitive menu. You are then presented with the User Properties dialog box. Click the Account tab and uncheck the Account Is Locked Out check box, as shown in Figure 4.2.

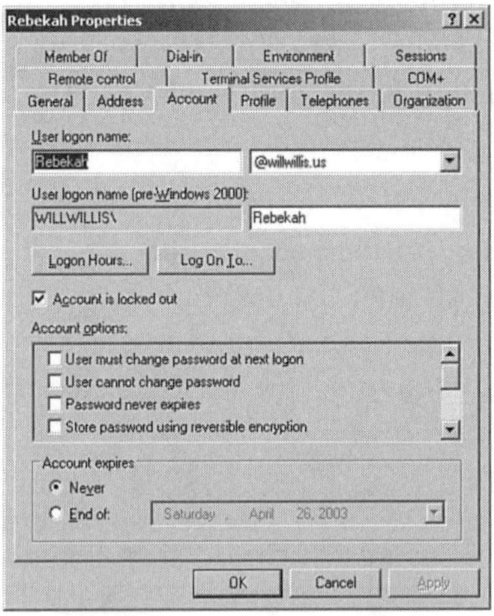

**Figure 4.2**   The User Properties dialog box.

# Deleting User Accounts

If a user leaves your organization, you have two choices. If the user is being replaced, you can simply rename the account for use by someone else,

Otherwise, you can just delete it. The choice here should be based on security, not just convenience. If the user is being replaced immediately, it is easier to rename the account. Otherwise, you should delete the account to maintain the integrity of security on your network. However, don't be too hasty in deleting a user account. Even if you don't need the account for the possibility of the employee returning to the company, there may be circumstances where that user account has exclusive rights to a particular resource. It is better to simply disable the account for a period of time prior to deleting it—90 days is usually a sufficient length of time to determine whether the account will be needed in order to transfer permissions to another account.

To delete a user account, select Delete from the context-sensitive menu. When prompted with the message "Are you sure you want to delete this object?", click Yes to delete the object or No to abort the deletion.

# Renaming User Accounts

Renaming a user account is convenient when a user's function is being taken over by someone else. A user account is not simply a name and password; it is also a set of permissions and group memberships. Sometimes it is easier to rename a user account so that this data is maintained rather than having to re-create it from scratch.

When renaming a user account, remember to take every object property into account. As a minimum, you should change the first name, last name, and logon name fields. However, several optional attributes will likely need to be changed, such as telephone number and description.

To rename an account, select Rename from the context-sensitive menu. Simply type the new name and press Enter when you are done.

# Copying User Accounts

You can also create an account and use it as a template for other accounts. For instance, you might have a standard set of permissions and group memberships that all users are assigned upon creation of the account. Say, for example, you have a member of the Finance group who has already been configured with all necessary group memberships. When a new employee joins the finance department, you can just copy a current account rather than create one from scratch.

When copying an account, you are prompted to enter a new first name, last name, and user logon name. You are also prompted to assign a new password. To copy a user account, simply select Copy from the context-sensitive menu.

You are then presented with the Copy Object-User Wizard. The settings that are copied in the process are group memberships and the account options (user must change password on next logon, user cannot change password, password never expires, and so on). The full list of account options can be seen by editing the properties of the user account being copied and then clicking the Account tab.

## Disabling and Enabling User Accounts

A variation on locking out an account, disabling an account temporarily prevents a user from logging in to the network. This is commonly performed when the user is going on an extended absence. For the account to become active again, you must then enable the account.

To disable an account, select the account in Active Directory Users and Computers and then select Disable Account from the context-sensitive menu. The account is immediately disabled, and the username is displayed with a red X through it. To enable the account, select Enable Account from the context-sensitive menu (the Disable Account option will be grayed out).

# Creating a Password Policy for Domain Users

Although we have talked about general guidelines for setting up password policies, we have yet to discuss how to actually do it. As shown in Figure 4.3, configuring password options is done through the Group Policy Object Editor.

You have several ways to start the Group Policy Object Editor snap-in. You can start an empty MMC and add the Group Policy snap-in to the console. However, for our purposes we will start the Group Policy Object Editor as follows:

1. Click Start and then go to Programs, Administrative Tools, Active Directory Users and Computers.

2. The Active Directory Users and Computers console will appear. When it appears, right-click on your domain and click Properties. Figure 4.4 illustrates this.

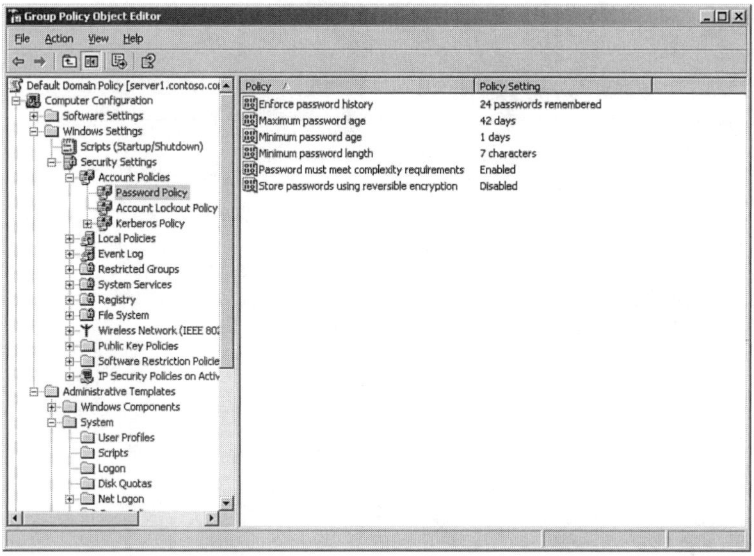

**Figure 4.3**    The Group Policy Object Editor allows you to configure your password options for all user accounts in the Active Directory.

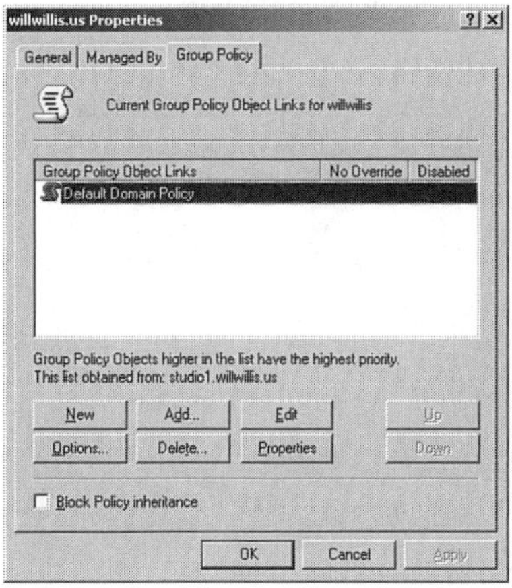

**Figure 4.4**    Opening the Domain property sheet.

**3.** Click the Group Policy tab, where you will see the Default Domain Policy link. This is the only option by default, though you could add additional group policy links or create new ones. With Default Domain Policy highlighted, click Edit. The resulting page is as shown in Figure 4.5.

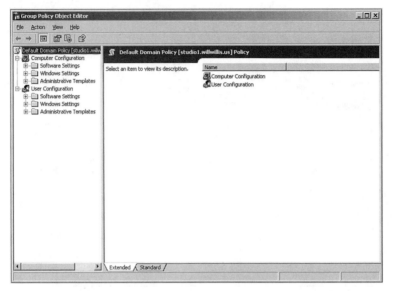

**Figure 4.5**   Editing the Default Domain Policy within the domain properties.

4. You are now in the Group Policy MMC, shown previously. Password options are located under Computer Configuration, Windows Settings, Security Settings, Account Policies, Password Policies. Here you find the options previously discussed. When you double-click a security attribute, you are presented with a security configuration window. Figures 4.6 and 4.7 show the configuration options for Enforce Password History and Minimum Password Length, respectively.

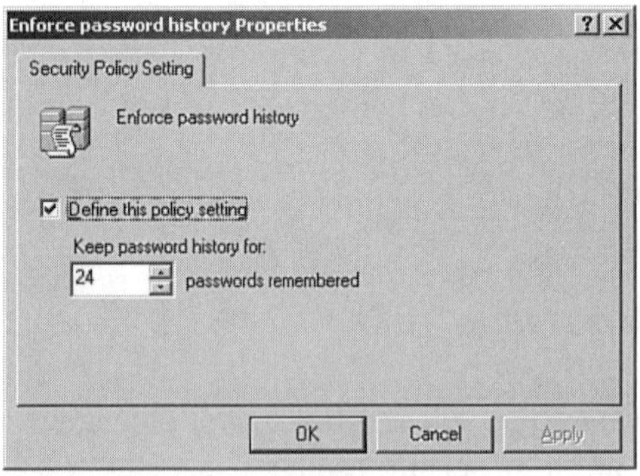

**Figure 4.6**   The Enforce Password History security attribute configuration.

With Windows 2000, these options were not configured, so when you opened the security attributes you would see a check in the Exclude This Setting from Configuration check box. This was not very conducive to a secure network, so Microsoft has changed the default settings with Windows Server 2003. By default, Windows Server 2003 has password policy settings preconfigured. For example, the Enforce Password History setting is set to remember 24 passwords, and Minimum Password Length is set to seven characters. You can change these default settings, and the changes you make here will affect all user accounts in the Active Directory domain.

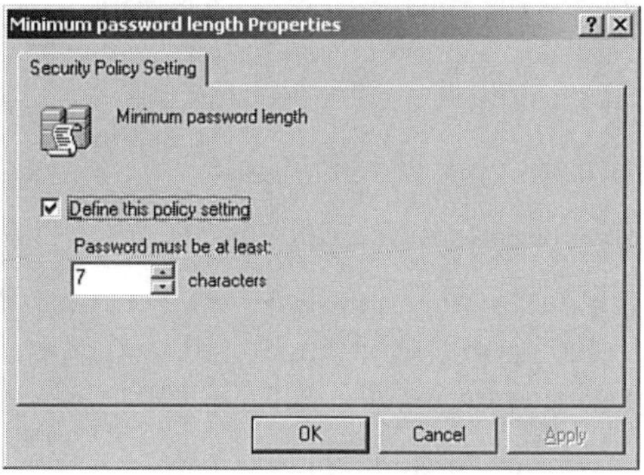

| Minimum password length Properties | ? X |
| --- | --- |
| Security Policy Setting | |

Minimum password length

☑ Define this policy setting

Password must be at least:

7 ⇅ characters

| OK | Cancel | Apply |

**Figure 4.7**   The Minimum Password Length security attribute configuration.

How strict you are with these password policy settings depends on the environment you are in. In a typical corporate environment, having passwords expire every 90–120 days is appropriate, with the default minimum password length and password history being appropriate. In an environment with high employee turnover or a lot of contractors going in and out, you would want to configure passwords to expire more frequently.

# Planning a Smartcard Authentication Strategy

To combat the hassle and lack of security of passwords, organizations are increasingly turning toward alternative methods for user authentication. One such method natively supported in Windows Server 2003 is smartcard authentication.

 It isn't within the scope of this particular exam to know all the intricacies of deploying smartcards, but you will be expected to know the fundamentals of planning an authentication strategy for smartcards. As a result, we will simply give a brief overview of what is involved in deploying smartcards without supplying much detail, then we'll use that as a lead-in to a discussion on strategy planning.

Setting up Windows Server 2003 to use smartcards involves a series of steps, some of which you may or may not have to complete depending on if you are already running Certificate Services on your network. Here are the required steps you must complete in order for users to log on using smartcards:

1. Install and configure at least one Certificate Authority (CA) on your Windows Server 2003 network. Alternatively, you could use an external CA such as VeriSign.

2. Configure the permissions in each domain that will contain smartcard users with the enroll permission for the smartcard user, smartcard logon, and Enrollment Agent certificate templates. This way, smartcard users will be able to enroll for the required certificates.

3. Configure the CA to issue smartcard certificates.

4. Configure the CA to issue Enrollment Agent certificates.

5. Install smartcard readers at each workstation and server that will be used with smartcard logons, including the workstation used by the person who will be setting up smartcards for users.

6. Prepare a smartcard enrollment station, including getting an Enrollment Agent certificate for the person who will be setting up smartcards for users.

7. Set up each required smartcard to be used for user logon.

8. Distribute the smartcards and train users on how to log on with them.

 It is important to note that Windows Server 2003 smartcard support requires that the workstation or server being logged in to be a member of a domain. Smartcards are not supported on standalone computers.

When you are planning to deploy smartcards for logon use on your Windows Server 2003 network, a few considerations must be taken into account. One of the first considerations is with respect to how smartcards will be issued. The Enrollment Agent certificate is very powerful, and whoever has one can issue smartcards on behalf of anyone in the domain. By default, only members of the Domain Admins group can request a certificate, but this permission can be delegated in Active Directory Sites and Services if a specific non-administrator is chosen to issue the smartcards. Microsoft recommends that once you have issued the necessary Enrollment Agent certificates to the people who will be enrolling users, you administer the CA and disable the issuance of Enrollment Agent certificates until they are needed. This will prevent someone from being able to get an Enrollment Agent certificate and create fraudulent smartcards on behalf of legitimate users.

If you have a mixed environment of Windows 2000 and Windows XP workstations, or Windows 2000 and Windows Server 2003 servers, you have another planning consideration. Windows 2000 systems can only use smart-cards that were enrolled on a Windows 2000 enrollment station. Windows XP and Windows Server 2003 computers can log on with smartcards that were enrolled on Windows 2000 Professional or Server, Windows XP Professional, or Windows Server 2003.

# From Passwords to Smartcards, and Back Again

When you issue smartcards to users, you will need to set up their user accounts to use these smartcards. To do this, use the Active Directory Users and Computers utility. Navigate to the user account you want to configure, right-click it, and click Properties. As you can see in Figure 4.8, when you navigate to the Account tab, you have a number of configuration options, including Smartcard Is Required for Interactive Logon. By selecting this you are disabling password logon and forcing the user to use her smartcard.

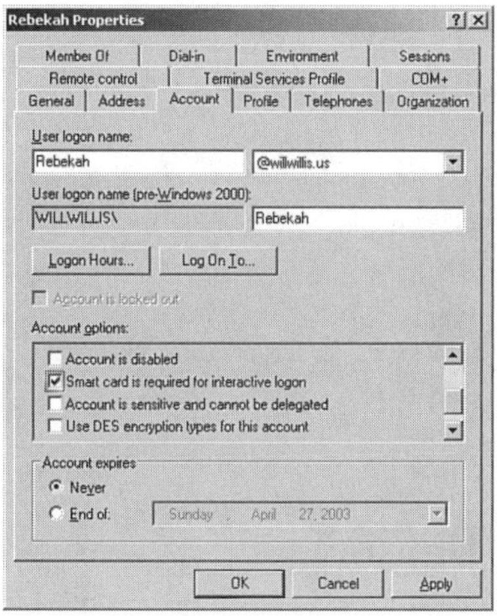

**Figure 4.8**   Forcing the user account to log on with a smartcard rather than a password.

If you have a situation come up where the user loses her smartcard, or the card or reader becomes defective for whatever reason, you can easily revert the user back to password logon by removing the check mark from the Smartcard box in the user's account properties. If you do that, you should assign the user account a temporary password and require the user to change her password at the next logon. Once the problem with logging on with the smartcard is resolved, you can disable password logon again.

What if you need to configure hundreds or thousands of user accounts to use smartcards? Fortunately, you do not have to open each individual account and check the box to require smartcard logon. Active Directory Users and Computers allows you to perform certain tasks on multiple accounts simultaneously. One of these tasks is configuring smartcard usage. Simply select as many user accounts as desired in the console, right-click, and select Properties. Go to the Accounts tab, where you see a number of options, such as those shown in Figure 4.9. Scroll down to Smartcard Is Required for Interactive Logon and select the left check box to enable the option; then select the right check box to set the option itself. Likewise, you could also uncheck the box for multiple users, if necessary.

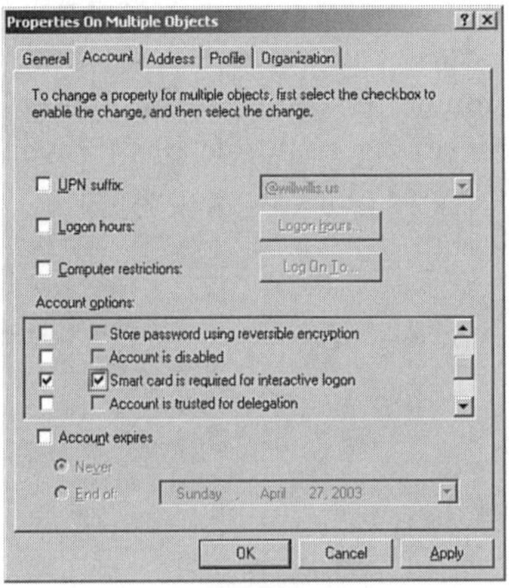

**Figure 4.9** Active Directory Users and Computers allows you to enable the smartcard requirement for user logon for multiple accounts at once.

# Smartcards and Remote Access

As an administrator, you very likely have to support remote users on your network. With Windows Server 2003, if you are using smartcards, you can extend this functionality to your remote users as well. For instance, if you have mobile sales people who log on through VPN or dialup connections across the Internet, you can support them as smartcard users just like regular domain users. Issue them their smartcards and readers as normal, and set up their VPN or dialup connection as normal to log on to the network. Once you're done, go into the properties of the connection and then to the Security tab, as shown in Figure 4.10.

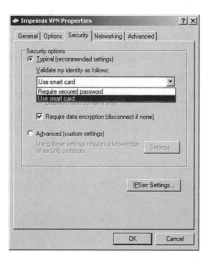

**Figure 4.10**  Configuring a remote access connection to use a smartcard.

By default, the connection is set up to require a secure password. Simply click the drop-down list under Validate My Identity as Follows and choose Use Smartcard. Once you've done that, click OK to return to the logon dialog box. You'll notice, as shown in Figure 4.11, that the password entry has been removed. Insert the user's smartcard into its reader and click Connect. The account should be able to log on to the remote access server.

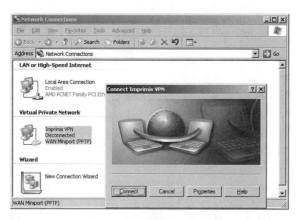

**Figure 4.11**  Once you configure the connection security to use a smartcard, the option to enter a password is removed.

Using smartcards is an effective way to overcome the limitations and inherent weaknesses of passwords.

# Planning a Security Group Strategy

Groups exist to ease the administrative burden of the system administrator. Groups are used to collect users together, either to assign them permissions to a set of files, folders, or network resources or for the purposes of distribution in email applications. There are two types of groups:

➤ Security groups

➤ Distribution groups

In addition, three different scopes define where the groups can be used on the network:

➤ Local groups

➤ Global groups

➤ Universal groups

Combining the group type and scope determines how a group can be used (in a single domain or in multiple domains within a forest).

**NOTE** Microsoft has published some conflicting documents regarding universal groups. A Windows Server 2003 domain can be in one of four functional levels: Windows 2000 mixed mode, Windows 2000 native mode, Windows Server 2003 Interim, and Windows Server 2003. Mixed mode generally means you are still using Windows NT 4 computers as DCs alongside your Windows 2000 and/or Windows Server 2003 DCs. You might read that universal groups are only available if the domain is in Windows 2000 native mode or at the Windows Server 2003 functional level. This is only partially correct. In fact, you *can* create universal groups in mixed mode—but only for distribution lists. However, distribution lists *cannot* be used for security purposes.

Security groups differ from distribution groups in that they can be used to assign security rights—that is, if you want to collect a group of user accounts together so that you can more easily assign them access to a shared folder, you must create a security group. You cannot use distribution groups for this purpose. Although theoretically you could simply use security groups for all your messaging needs rather than using distribution groups, the design of Windows Server 2003 is to evaluate a user's membership in each security group it belongs to during login. Membership in many security groups could therefore result in slow logon performance, so distribution groups should be used whenever possible.

A feature of Windows Server 2003 is the ability to *nest* groups with a level of flexibility not available in previous versions of Windows. Nesting groups is used to further simplify the management of users when assigning security permissions. When a group is nested within another group, it inherits all the security permissions from its parent. The extra nesting capabilities of Windows Server 2003 come into play when the domain has been converted from Windows 2000 mixed mode to Windows 2000 native mode or the Windows Server 2003 functional level. At these levels you can nest global groups in other global groups, nest domain local groups in other domain local groups, and utilize universal groups in general (as well as nesting).

A user can be a member of many different groups, thereby inheriting all the security permissions that have been assigned to them. This is far simpler than assigning permissions on a user-by-user basis.

# Defining Group Types

All group types are used to gather together a set of users who are going to share a particular set of permissions to a file, folder, or network resource. However, the scope of each group and the possible membership lists differ. Table 4.1 lists the differences among the three group types. For the sake of this table, we'll refer to Windows 2000 mixed mode as simply *mixed mode*, and Windows 2000 native mode and the Windows Server 2003 functional level (equivalent for our purposes here) as simply *native mode*.

| Table 4.1 | Group Comparison | | |
|---|---|---|---|
| | **Global** | **Local** | **Universal** |
| **Member List** | Mixed mode: Accounts from same domain. Native mode: Accounts and other global groups. | Mixed mode: User accounts and global groups from any domain in the forest. Native mode: User accounts, local groups from the same domain, global groups, and universal groups from any domain in the forest. | Mixed mode: Distribution lists only. Native mode: User accounts, global groups, and other universal groups in any domain in the forest. |
| **Nesting** | Mixed mode: Local groups. Native mode: Universal and local groups in any domain and global groups in the same domain. | Mixed mode: Cannot be a member of another group. Native mode: Local groups in the same domain. | Mixed mode: None. Native mode: Local and universal groups in any domain. |
| **Scope** | Can be used in its own domain and any trusted domains. | Can be used only in its own domain. | Can be used in any domain in the forest. |

| Table 4.1 Group Comparison *(continued)* | | | |
|---|---|---|---|
| | **Global** | **Local** | **Universal** |
| **Permissions To** | All domains in a forest. | Resources in the domain in which the local group exists only. | Resources in any domain in the forest. |

# Planning a Security Group Hierarchy Based on Delegation Requirements

For groups to be effective, you must use them in a structured way. This helps ensure that you get the maximum benefit from using them. The group scope determines when the best time to use a particular group type is. For instance, if you have a resource that will be available across an entire forest, you will likely start by adding users to global groups and then nesting them within a universal group.

The mere mention of universal groups implies that you are in Windows 2000 native mode or at the Windows Server 2003 functional level (because you cannot use universal groups for security purposes in mixed mode). Be sure to remember what can and cannot be achieved in both modes. If a scenario mentions a single domain, there is no use for universal groups.

The method of assigning permissions within a single domain has been used for a long time, and it still holds true for a Windows Server 2003 network. Let's now look at using groups in both a single domain and in a forest.

## Groups in a Single Domain

As mentioned previously, in a single domain there is no need to be concerned about universal groups. With a single domain, you can achieve all the simplification you need using only local and global groups. In this section, we'll use Microsoft's acronym *AGDLP* to describe the use of both local and global groups. This acronym stands for the following:

➤ *A*—Accounts (user)

➤ *G*—Global group

➤ *DL*—Domain local group

➤ *P*—Permissions

By using this acronym, you can easily recall the order in which permissions should be granted. Although this is only a suggested method, it's designed to make sure you enjoy maximum flexibility and ease of use when assigning permissions to resources.

In the following example, we use this strategy to organize access to a network resource (in this case, a folder share). This illustrates how the AGDLP strategy can work for you. This example assumes a single domain.

A publishing company has an author team. Members of this team need access to files in a folder on the network that contains the text of a book the authors are writing. To achieve this, the system administrator creates a global group called Author Team. The names of the authors are added as members of this global group.

 The practical limit on the number of users a group can contain in a Windows Server 2003 network is 5,000 members.

Next, the administrator creates a local group called Windows Server 2003 Cram. The Author Team global group is then nested within the Windows Server 2003 Cram local group. Permissions to the file share are granted to the local group. This offers the flexibility and manageability the administrator is looking for. If additional authors need access to the folder, the administrator simply has to add them to the global group.

Let's take this example one step further. Once the book is halfway complete, the publishing company needs to give access to the editorial team. The system administrator simply creates a second global group called Editors and adds the editorial team as members of the group. This group is then nested within the Windows Server 2003 Cram local group. This task is now complete. As you can see, because the AGDLP strategy was followed, it was very simple to grant permissions to an additional set of users. If the Windows Server 2003 network had included multiple domains, the method of applying permissions would have changed slightly. In this case, the administrator would use the acronym AGUDLP (where *U* stands for *universal*), creating global groups first and then nesting them within universal groups. The universal group is then nested within the local group.

Universal groups are unique because AD treats them slightly differently. Although all group names are listed in a Global Catalog server, their membership list is generally not. The exception to this rule is the universal group. Both the universal group name and the membership list is replicated to every Global Catalog server. If you add a single user to a universal group, the *entire* membership list must be replicated. Therefore, it is a good idea to keep your universal group usage to a minimum, and when you do use this type of group, keep the membership lists fairly static. Nesting universal groups is far better than adding members to a single group. Typically you would add users to global groups and then add global groups to universal groups, rather than adding users directly to universal groups.

# User and Group Recommendations

Users can log on to a Windows Server 2003 domain using either their principal names or their down-level logon names. From a user perspective, this might not seem to make any difference. However, from an administrative point of view, it is better for users to use principal names. Because using a principal name means users don't have to enter domain names for their accounts, using this type of name exclusively gives administrators the ability to move user objects from one domain to another without any user education. Therefore, it is always best to use the principal name.

Because you can create a suffix for the principal name, you should consider making it as easy on the user community as possible by making the suffix match the users' email accounts. This will make remembering their logon names easier.

You will likely be creating a lot of global groups in your domains. It is best to come up with a naming scheme for your groups so they are easily recognizable. In addition, you should create them based on job function. Doing this makes it easy to add users based on their responsibilities within the organization.

Universal groups cause additional replication on your network. Because the group name and the group membership have to be replicated to each Global Catalog server, be careful when using universal groups. Try to make them static. It is far better to nest universal groups than to create a lot of them.

Also, be sure not to enable accounts until they are ready to be used. Doing so prematurely can open your network to hackers.

# Exam Prep Questions

## Question 1

> You have issued smartcards to a small number of users as part of a pilot pro-
> gram leading up to a full-scale deployment of smartcards. You configure your-
> self as an enrollment agent, enroll the users, and configure the smartcards as
> required. You install smartcard readers on the user workstations, and have the
> users to stop by and pick up their cards so you can explain how they work. The
> first user you give a card to, Tina Rowe, calls you shortly after leaving your
> office to tell you that she can't log on with her smartcard, though she is still able
> to logon with her password. Why isn't the smartcard working? [Choose the best
> answer.]
>
> ○ A. You need to reinstall the smartcard reader drivers on the workstation.
>
> ○ B. You need to configure her user account to use the smartcard.
>
> ○ C. You need to grant Tina the necessary permissions to use the smart-
> card.
>
> ○ D. You need to configure the LAN connection on the workstation for
> smartcard logon rather than password.

Answer B is correct. A required step is to use Active Directory Users and
Computers to edit the properties of the user accounts that will use smartcards and check the box Smartcard Is Required for Interactive Logon. Unless
this is done, password logon will still be in effect. Answers A and C are incorrect because since password logon is still working, you know smartcard logon
has not been configured. Answer D is incorrect because you do not have to
configure a LAN connection to use smartcard authentication in order for
users to log in to a domain.

## Question 2

> Lisa Arase is in the process of putting together a network security plan. Because
> she will be granting many users access to shared folders and printers, she
> wants to use groups extensively. Lisa's company also has several kiosks in the
> foyer of company headquarters that visitors can use to browse the Web and
> access email. Lisa is not sure how she is going to limit the access of users.
> What method would be the easiest from an administrative standpoint? [Choose
> the best answer.]
>
> ○ A. Because groups can only contain user accounts, Lisa should create
> groups for her user community and put a firewall between the kiosk
> machines and her network.

O B. Lisa should create groups for the employees of her company. For the kiosk machines, Lisa can create a single logon and apply permissions to this group so users can access the resources they need. Because this can be a single group, this task would not involve a lot of work.

O C. Because groups can contain both user accounts and computer accounts, Lisa can go ahead and create a single group that includes both users from her company and the computers that operate as kiosks.

O D. Lisa should create a single logon for the kiosk machines. She should create a group for her employees and assign them permissions, and she should grant the user who is going to be used in the kiosks specific permissions to network resources.

Answer C is correct. Groups can contain both user accounts and computer accounts. Although answers A, B, and D are all feasible, they increase the administrative burden for the administrator. Specifically, answer A is incorrect because a firewall would be more difficult to administer than the solution in answer C. Answers B and D are incorrect because adding specific user accounts to permission lists is also administratively intensive.

# Question 3

Greg Smith has been called to troubleshoot a problem on a member server in his domain. A user named Jon Brock says he is logging in to the domain, and although he is being granted access (he is able to get to the desktop of the server), he is not able to access any network resources. Greg checks Jon's account and finds everything is normal. He has been granted access to resources and is a member of several groups that should enable him to access file shares. No one else has reported a problem with the network. Greg goes to visit Jon's office. What is a possible cause for this problem?

O A. Jon is typing the wrong password. He is being granted access to the network, but because he used the wrong password, he is being denied access to network resources.

O B. Jon is logging in to the member server using a local user account. This means he has not yet been validated by the domain and is therefore not allowed access to network resources.

O C. Jon's password must be changed. The system is giving him sufficient access to do this, but it will not let him access network resources until the change is confirmed.

O D. Jon has to wait for the logon process to complete. AD is complex, and it can take a long time for the security token to be created for a user the first time he logs on.

Answer B is correct. There are three types of user accounts: domain user accounts, local user accounts, and built-in accounts. Domain accounts are designed to allow users to log in to a network and gain access to resources. Local user accounts are used on member server and Windows Server 2003 Professional systems to allow users to log on to the local computer without network access (as in this instance). Built-in accounts are created by default for administrative purposes. Answer A is incorrect because typing in a bad password would result in the user being unable to see the desktop. Answer C is incorrect because the user would have had to type the correct password in order to access the system. Answer D is incorrect because there should be no lag when the user logs on. When a user logs on, the security token for the user is created. If there is a delay in the creation of the token, the entire logon process is delayed.

# Question 4

---

Ian McLean is the network manager for a large Windows Server 2003 environment. He delegates the task of setting a password policy for a child domain to his junior administrator, Leo Kolbeinsson. Leo opens up Active Directory Users and Computers on his Windows XP Professional workstation and navigates to the Users container, right-clicking it, and going into its properties. He soon calls Ian up and tells him that he doesn't have the Group Policy tab in his property sheet. What should Ian tell him? [Choose the best answer.]

- O  A.  Leo needs to perform the task on a Windows Server 2003 server in the domain.
- O  B.  Leo needs to go into the properties of the Domain Controllers container rather than the Users container.
- O  C.  Leo needs to go into the properties of the domain, not the Users container.
- O  D.  Leo doesn't have the required permissions, and Ian needs to grant them.

---

Answer C is correct. To configure the password policy for a domain, Leo would need to right-click the domain in question and go into its properties. Then he would click the Group Policy tab and edit the default domain policy to launch the Group Policy Editor. From there he could configure the password policy. Answer A is incorrect because the task could be performed from a Windows XP Professional workstation that has the Administrative Tools installed. Answer C is incorrect because although the property page of the Domain Controllers container does have a Group Policy tab, Leo would be editing the default domain controller's policy and not the policy for the domain itself. Answer D is incorrect because the Group Policy tab's absence is not related to permissions but rather due to Leo being in the wrong place.

# Question 5

Orin Thomas is a system administrator for a Windows Server 2003 network. He is trying to make a decision about which method users should use to log on to his network. There are four domains in his forest, and he wants to make the logon method as simple for the users as possible. The company is owned by the Smith family. Three generations of Smiths work in his organization, and he has 25 members of the Smith family working in one context or another. Family members include David Smith, David Smith II, Darrell Smith, John Smith, John Smith II, and John Smith III. After careful consideration, Orin decides to stick with using the logon method that requires users to know which domains they belong to. Why did Orin make this decision?

- ○ A. Orin knows that he has some duplicate names on his network. Because a principal name must be unique in a forest, he cannot guarantee he won't run into problems. To avoid this, he is stuck with forcing the users to enter their domain name.

- ○ B. Orin has decided that user education is going to be a problem. His user community has been migrated from a Windows NT 4 environment and is used to entering the domain name. Also, the benefits of using principal names is not great.

- ○ C. Orin eventually wants to collapse two of his domains. By forcing the users to use a domain name, he can more easily identify those who are going to be affected by such a move and perform a smoother transition.

- ○ D. It really doesn't make much difference to Orin which method is used. Because, administratively, it does not gain him anything, he decides to make sure users enter the domain name.

Answer A is correct. Because Orin has a lot of duplicate names, using principal names won't work. Orin would need to come up with a new user-naming strategy to use principal names. Therefore, answers B, C, and D are all incorrect.

# Question 6

Melissa Wise is a network administrator for a company that uses smartcard technology extensively for user logon. The company has recently closed one of its branch offices, and at the same time is offering a new kiosk service to its clients. Because of the office closing, Melissa decides to utilize those computers for the new kiosk setup, which will include the smartcard readers that have been in use for some time at the branch office. To enhance security, Melissa removes the workstations from the domain and puts them in their own workgroup. When she tests the computers after they've been hooked up at the kiosk, she finds they are unable to log on to the network, with her user account or others, even though she is able to hook up her own laptop and log on with her smartcard. What might be happening?

○ A. She needs to rejoin the workstations to the domain.

○ B. She needs to configure the user accounts the kiosk computers will use to log in with smartcards.

○ C. She needs to grant "logon locally" permissions to the user accounts.

○ D. She needs to open up the corporate firewall to allow the kiosk computers' traffic to pass.

Answer A is correct. In order to use smartcard logons, a workstation must belong to a domain. Melissa needs to rejoin the workstations to the domain in order for the smartcard logons to work. Answer B is incorrect because even though user accounts must be configured to log on with smartcards, the scenario states that Melissa's account isn't able to log on to those computers either, although she can log on with her laptop from the kiosk network (thus making answer D incorrect as well). Answer C is incorrect because this right is already given on a workstation by default.

# Question 7

Jeff Smith has been asked to secure some shared folders. He knows he should not grant access to network resources at the user level, because this increases the amount of system administration the network requires. He decides to use groups. Rather than having to manage different kinds of groups and worry about their scope, he decides to use universal groups extensively. He creates a lot of groups early Monday morning, but before he can finish, users call in and complain that the network is slow. What would cause this?

○ A. Adding large amounts of data to AD causes a lot of network traffic, and this traffic has caused the network to be slow. Administration of AD should be performed after hours.

○ B. Creating groups is processor intensive because the DC has to gather data about all user accounts in the domain. This should be done after hours.

○ C. As Jeff is adding users to groups, the user accounts logging in are trying to find their settings and permissions in AD. This is causing the traffic.

○ D. Universal groups cause more network traffic than other group types. If Jeff had used another group type, he would not have had this problem.

Answer D is correct. Because the membership of a universal group is replicated to all Global Catalog servers in a domain, more network traffic is generated. Jeff should be careful about creating a large number of universal groups. Answers A and B are incorrect because although replication of new AD data would take place, there's nothing processor intensive about it, nor is it necessary to wait to create groups until after hours. Answer C is incorrect because changing group membership or permissions would not result in additional logon traffic.

# Question 8

Chris Meyer has been migrating his Windows NT 4 network to Windows Server 2003. He is currently running in the default Windows 2000 mixed mode. Because Chris has multiple domains, he wants to use local groups, global groups, and universal groups. A consultant tells Chris that he must be running at the Windows Server 2003 functional level or in Windows 2000 native mode to create universal groups. However, Chris has already created a universal group, and he doubts the consultant knows what he is doing. Who is right?

- ○ A. Chris is correct. Universal groups can be used in either Windows 2000 mixed mode or Windows 2000 native mode, or at the Windows Server 2003 functional level.

- ○ B. Both are correct. Universal groups can be created at any functional level, but they can only be used as distribution groups in Windows 2000 mixed mode.

- ○ C. Both are correct. Universal groups can be created at any functional level, but they can only be used as security groups in Windows 2000 mixed mode.

- ○ D. The consultant is correct. Universal groups can only be used in Windows 2000 native mode and at the Windows Server 2003 functional level.

Answer B is correct. Although universal groups can be used in Windows 2000 mixed mode, their function is limited to distribution groups. You must be at the Windows 2000 native mode or Windows Server 2003 functional level to use them as security groups to grant access to network resources. Therefore, answers A, C, and D are incorrect.

# Question 9

Darren Sargent is a system administrator of a Windows Server 2003 network that has a single domain. He needs to come up with a group strategy. Darren decides to use domain local groups and global groups. His manager asks him to go back to the drawing board and come up with a strategy that uses universal groups, unless Darren has good reason not to. Why does Darren choose not to use universal groups?

- ○ A. Darren wants to minimize the replication traffic on his network.

- ○ B. Universal groups simply add another layer of global groups. Darren has a "keep it simple" philosophy.

- ○ C. Universal groups cannot be used for security purposes. They are used for distribution groups. Using universal groups would not help in assigning permissions to network resources.

- ○ D. Universal groups could be used, but in a single-domain environment, they simply add an extra level of complexity. Universal groups are really only useful in multidomain environments.

Answer D is correct. Don't forget, in a single domain, there is no need to use universal groups. They cause additional replication, and in a single-domain environment, you gain nothing by using them. Therefore, answers A, B, and C are incorrect.

# Question 10

Bob Muir has been asked to change the password for a user account. Bob is a domain administrator. However, he has tried to contact the user to get her current password but has been unable to. His boss is worried that someone might have the password for this account. What is the best course of action for Bob to take?

- O A. Bob should delete the user account and re-create it with the new password. The user will call as soon as she is unable to log on.
- O B. Because Bob is a domain administrator, he does not need the user's current password to make the change.
- O C. Bob should disable the account. This will force the user to call in with the information Bob needs.
- O D. Bob should lock the account out. This will force the user to call in with the information Bob needs.

Answer B is correct. Bob does not need the user's password. It is not advisable to change users' passwords without them knowing, but there might be times when it is necessary. Using Active Directory Users and Computers, Bob could right-click the user account and choose Reset Password. Answer A is unadvisable because each user account is associated with a unique SID. Simply deleting and re-creating a user account with the same name will not create an identical account, and all group memberships and permission would have to be re-created. Answer C would work, but this is unnecessary to accomplish the task of changing the user password. Answer D is incorrect because an account can only be locked through failed password attempts (if a lockout policy had been configured).

# Need to Know More?

 Honeycutt, Jerry. *Introducing Microsoft Windows Server 2003*. Microsoft Press. Redmond, WA, 2003. ISBN 0-7356-1570-5.

Microsoft Corporation. *Microsoft Windows Server 2003 Resource Kit*. Microsoft Press. Redmond, WA, 2003. ISBN 0-7356-1471-7.

Mulcare, Mike and Stan Reimer. *Active Directory for Microsoft Windows Server 2003 Technical Reference*. Microsoft Press. Redmond, WA, 2003. ISBN 0-7356-1577-2.

# Planning and Implementing an OU Structure

. . . . . . . . . . . . . . . . . . . . . . . . . . . . . . . . . . . . . . . . . . . . . . .

### Terms you'll need to understand:

✓ Organizational Unit (OU)
✓ Delegation of control
✓ Group Policy
✓ Security group
✓ Linked policies

### Techniques/concepts you'll need to master:

✓ Implementing an OU structure
✓ Analyzing administrative requirements for an OU
✓ Creating an OU
✓ Moving objects within an OU hierarchy
✓ Delegating permissions for an OU to a user or to a security group
✓ Planning an Organizational Unit (OU) structure based on delegation requirements
✓ Analyzing the Group Policy requirements for an OU structure

# Implementing an Organizational Unit (OU) Structure

One of the primary advantages of Windows Server 2003 and the Active Directory service over Windows NT is the ability to control administrative powers more discretely. Under Windows NT, the base unit of administrative power was the *domain*. There was no way to grant someone administrative power over a subsection of the domain, such as a sales division or geographical office. This limitation meant that either the administrator was forced to make every required change to user access rights or that administrative power was granted to a larger circle of people.

There were some workarounds to this problem, including the use of master domain/resource domain structures, but even these required careful planning and additional infrastructure to function correctly. Particularly annoying was the fact that competing network operating systems did offer the ability to segregate administrative roles to a particular element of the network.

Fortunately, Active Directory introduces the *Organizational Unit*, or *OU*, to the Windows networking environment. An OU is essentially a subset of a domain that can contain any AD object. The network administrator can designate control of and access to each OU and the objects it contains. In addition, policies can be designated on the OUs in order to manage user policies and rights.

Essentially, OUs have two main uses:

➤ *To allow sub-administrators control over a selection of users, computers, or other objects*—These are typically non–domain administrators who have been delegated administrative rights for a specific OU without being granted permissions over the whole domain.

➤ *To control desktop systems through the use of Group Policy objects (GPOs) associated with an OU*—Although we give an overview of using Group Policy with OUs, this topic is covered in more depth in Chapter 7, "Configuring the User Environment with Group Policy," and Chapter 8, "Deploying a Computer Environment with Group Policy."

We will look at each of these uses in the following sections.

# Analyzing the Administrative Requirements for an OU

One of the most common needs for an administrator is the ability to allow others to manage user accounts. There's always a fine line between maintaining security and delegating power to others. Windows NT offered the ability to grant others the right to change passwords and other limited administrative control, but these rights were applied on a domainwide basis. As a result, organizations were often forced to create complex multidomain environments to handle the varying administration requirements of different divisions.

For example, say your company has a division of software developers that needs to administer itself. The individual developers require administrative-level permissions to the division's servers. Your company also has a human resources group that must retain its own individual administration because of the confidential nature of the information it possesses, as well as a legal division that also has to administer itself for similar reasons. Plus, you have the main corporate domain that encompasses most everyone else. In the past, with Windows NT, you would be required to have four distinct domains for this scenario, with carefully managed trust relationships in place so everyone could access the corporate domain. But at the same time, you would have to ensure that the corporate domain could not access the other domains, except for some specific exceptions. Sounds like an administrative headache, doesn't it? Well, consider that as the size of the company grew, often so did its domain structure. The result often wasn't pretty.

Windows Server 2003, though, offers the capability to delegate various levels of control on only parts of a domain. This is accomplished through the use of Organization Units. As discussed earlier, an OU is a container that can hold various Active Directory objects, including user accounts, computers, printers, shares, services, and much more. An OU can be thought of as a subdomain for conceptual purposes: Administrators of a domain retain control of the OU, but specific rights can also be granted to other users or groups. It is important to note though that unlike a real domain, an OU is not a true security boundary and doesn't function in AD like a domain. The OU is the smallest level of organization that can be administered in Active Directory. Using OUs in Windows Server 2003 with our previous scenario, you would be able to use a single domain for your organization and create OUs for developers, human resources, and legal to delegate administration of their groups to the appropriate personnel. Because the delegation is within a single domain, the administrative burden of managing trust relationships and duplicating resources is reduced.

The preferred administrative model in Windows Server 2003 is to use OUs whenever possible to delegate administrative authority rather than using additional domains. Administratively, OUs are easier to manage and are a better choice, unless the scenario has specific circumstances why you should use multiple domains.

In the next few sections we will go through implementing an OU structure on your network, including creating an OU and delegating control of it. The scenario you will be following has the marketing department as somewhat of a separate organization, and it has been decided that the marketing department needs the right to change passwords for the division. Tired of changing passwords for marketing people at 2:00 a.m., the IS department agrees. So, IS will create an OU for marketing and also give someone in marketing the right to change passwords within this OU.

# Creating an OU

To give the marketing department the functionality it is asking for, first, the IS department must create an OU to contain the user accounts and other objects for the marketing department. All OU implementation and administration is accomplished through the AD Users and Computers snap-in. Once the console is started, navigate to the domain that the OU should be located within. From the context menu, choose New, Organizational Unit, as shown in Figure 5.1.

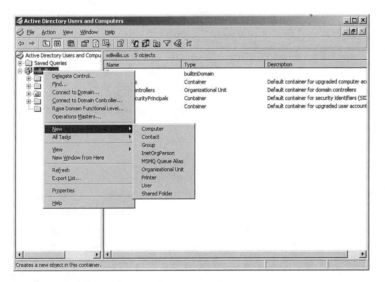

**Figure 5.1** Creating a new OU.

The first property screen for the new OU will ask for a name. This should be something that is descriptive and clearly shows the role of the OU. Enter the name in the field, as shown in Figure 5.2.

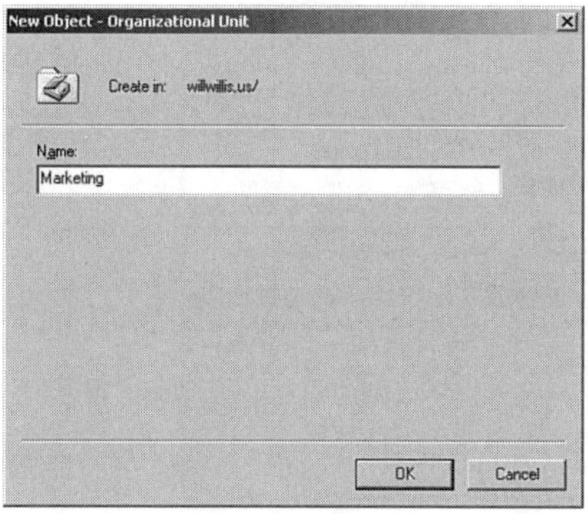

**Figure 5.2**   Enter the name for the OU.

# Moving Objects Within an OU Hierarchy

Once the OU is created, it must be populated. To move users, computers, or other objects to an OU, simply open the proper folder and highlight the desired objects. From the context menu, select Move, as shown in Figure 5.3. In addition to users, groups, computers, and printers, you can also move one OU into another to create a hierarchy. We'll discuss this a bit later in the chapter.

You can also move objects between OUs by dragging and dropping them in Active Directory Users and Computers, but you should use this functionality with great care. It is all too easy to have a slip of the mouse and inadvertently drop objects in the wrong container.

The next step is to select the destination OU for the objects, as shown in Figure 5.4.

After the various objects are moved into the OU, the contents of that OU can be viewed through the AD Users and Computers console. In Figure 5.5, you see that we placed both the marketing group and the computers the marketing group uses into the OU. As a result of this action, the Marketing OU now contains the marketing department objects.

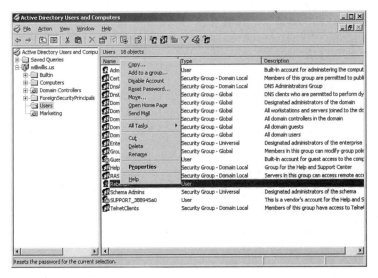

**Figure 5.3** Moving objects to an OU.

**Figure 5.4** Selecting the destination OU.

# Delegating Permissions for an OU to a User or to a Security Group

Once the OU is created, it is time to delegate control of the OU to a selected few marketing users. Begin by opening the AD Users and Computers console and selecting the desired OU, as shown in Figure 5.6. From the context menu, select Delegate Control.

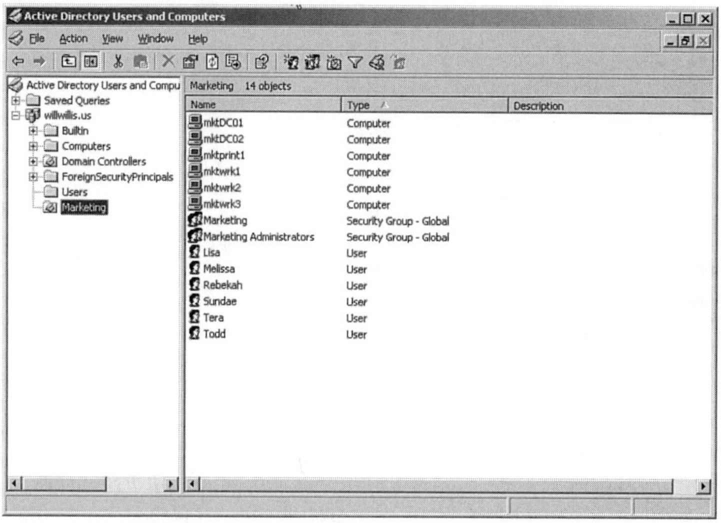

**Figure 5.5**   Viewing the contents of an OU.

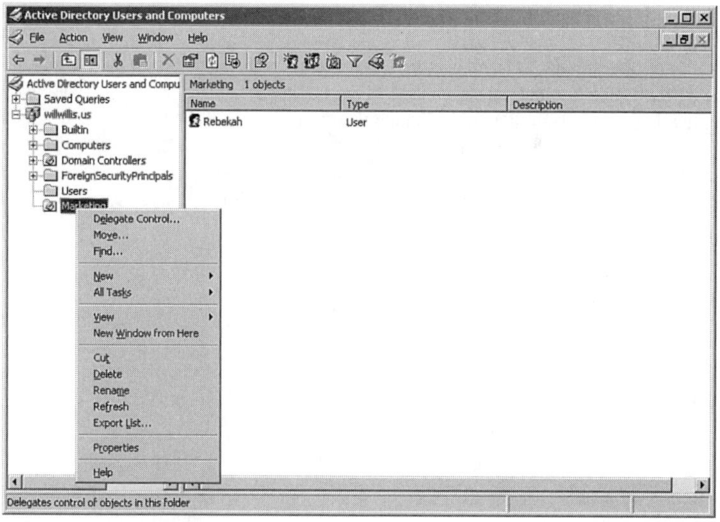

**Figure 5.6**   Delegating control of an OU.

This will launch the Delegation of Control Wizard, as shown in Figure 5.7. As with most wizards, just click Next to pass the startup screen.

**Figure 5.7** The Delegation of Control Wizard.

The next step, shown in Figure 5.8, is to choose the group and/or users to whom the control is being delegated. In this case, we'll choose a group called Marketing Administrators. This group, which was created earlier, contains the user accounts of the two people trusted to change the passwords.

 Permissions should rarely if ever be granted to individual user accounts. It is standard practice to grant permissions to groups rather than users, because it simplifies future administration in preventing you from having to change the delegation later if a user leaves the company or if a new employee is added who also needs those permissions. By using groups to delegate permissions, you delegate once and then control who has permission through their group membership.

**Figure 5.8** Select the group or user to whom control will be delegated.

After this selection, choose the rights that the delegates should exercise over the OU. The options you choose here determine the abilities of the delegated administrators. Selecting the option Reset Passwords on User Accounts will allow the administrators for the OU to reset user passwords. As you can see in Figure 5.9, several other options are available.

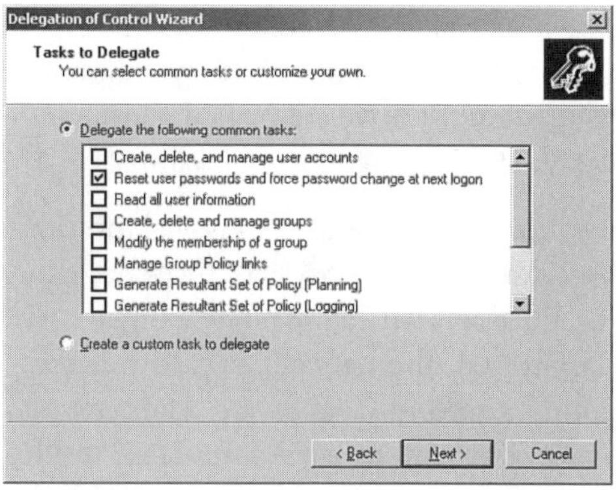

**Figure 5.9**   Assigning permissions.

The last step is merely to confirm the rights granted to the delegates. You should always double-check and verify that the rights granted actually match the intended purpose. Remember, the rights are inherited throughout the OU. If the rights granted are correct, select Finish, as shown in Figure 5.10. Note that if you need to modify the assigned permissions later, you can do so by going to the Security tab in the OU's properties.

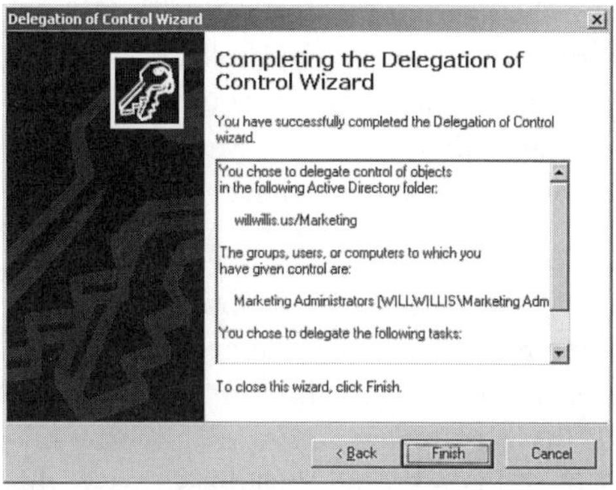

**Figure 5.10**   Verifying the delegated rights.

# Planning an OU Structure Based on Delegation Requirements

OUs provide a powerful, yet flexible mechanism for administering a Windows Server 2003 domain. As an administrator, when you look to implement an OU structure, you need to analyze your organization for its requirements prior to putting an OU structure in place. One important consideration is with respect to the OU hierarchy. Because you can nest OUs inside of OUs, you have the ability to create a very granular level of administrative control on a group-by-group basis within your organization. Consider the following example.

Your organization consists of 10 sites, corresponding to 10 physical locations in North America, Europe, and Asia. The network consists of three domains: na.wwinc.com, europe.wwinc.com, and asia.wwinc.com. The domains are part of the same forest, so they are connected automatically by two-way transitive trusts (trust relationships were discussed in Chapter 1, "Planning and Implementing Forests and Domains"). The Enterprise Admin team resides at your company's headquarters in Dallas, and each member of the Enterprise Admins group also belongs to the Domain Admins group in each domain. The office in Barcelona is the headquarters for Europe, and that's where the Domain Admins team for europe.wwinc.com resides. The office in Seoul is the headquarters for Asia, and it houses the Domain Admins team for Asia. Each of the seven non-headquarters physical locations has its own local IT department responsible for its own site.

In this scenario, you want the local IT departments to have administrative permissions for their local offices without granting them permissions at the domain level. In other words, giving them administrative rights should not allow them to administer sites other than their own. This holds true as well for the Domain Admins teams in each country. They should be able to administer their own domains but not other domains. And, finally, the Enterprise Admins team in Dallas should have administrative rights over the entire forest.

In the Windows NT days, this type of complex administrative structure would require creating a multi-master/resource domain model consisting of at least 13 domains (three master accounts domains and 10 resource domains). Furthermore, you would have to manage a lot of one-way and two-way trust relationships, all manually configured. Needless to say, this would be a messy administrative situation.

Fortunately, with Windows Server 2003 you can use OUs to accomplish your goals. You would start by creating security groups for each IT department. Then you would create OUs for each local site. After that you would delegate administrative permissions for the OUs to the desired security groups (the local IT departments plus higher-up IT departments). For example, you create an OU for the Omaha site. You also create all the relevant security groups, including OmahaIT and DallasIT (for North American administration). DallasIT includes the entire Dallas IT department, which has authority over any other site, yet only a subset of DallasIT is in Domain

Admins, and only a subset of the na.wwinc.com Domain Admins group is a member of the Enterprise Admins group. Once you had done that, you would delegate administrative control of the Omaha OU to OmahaIT and DallasIT (Domain Admins and Enterprise Admins by default have permissions).

Because the Dallas IT group is the highest level of IT in North America, above all the other site-administration groups, you would want to reflect that in your OU structure. Continuing with our example, you can use the nesting ability of Windows Server 2003 OUs to further define the structure. You could then create an OmahaIT OU and nest it inside the Omaha OU. By default, permissions in child objects are inherited from parent objects, so you wouldn't have to explicitly delegate authority to OmahaIT and DallasIT again unless you had disabled propagating permissions. If you had, you would simply delegate control of that OU to the OmahaIT and DallasIT security groups.

Inheritance is a double-edged sword. Although it can simplify administration in most cases, it can also be troublesome when you have situations where you do not want permissions to cascade down from higher levels to lower levels. You can turn off inheritance on an OU-by-OU basis, but if you do you will need to manually specify all permissions.

Continuing, you could create further child OUs in the Omaha OU, one for each department that requires separate administration (or even just for categorizing users and groups). Using a hierarchy of OUs, you could even effectively deal with a situation where a local IT department shouldn't have administrative rights to a certain OU, but the Enterprise Admins group should. For instance, if you had a human resources group in Omaha, you could create an HR OU and remove OmahaIT from having propagated administrative rights (from the Omaha OU), remove DallasIT, remove Domain Admins as well, and delegate administrative control to the HR Administrators security group. The HR Administrators group would have administrative rights to its OU but not to any higher-level OUs (such as Omaha OU), and only the Enterprise Admins security group would still have access.

You could move this philosophy of creating an OU hierarchy across domains as well, resulting in a well-structured administrative hierarchy throughout the organization, encompassing all domains and sites.

# Analyzing the Group Policy Requirements for an OU

A second major use of OUs is to assign Group Policies to particular computers and users. Group Policies are used to define default settings for computers and users, such as folder locations, what software can be installed, desktop appearance, and much more. Although Group Policies can be applied at a domain or site level, they are more commonly applied at an OU level in order to generate a specific combination of user and computer environmental factors.

Although the many details of Group Policies are beyond the scope of this chapter, we will discuss how to associate a new or existing Group Policy with an OU.

> Although using OUs allows you to control policy settings at a more granular level than the domain level, there is one important limitation. Password policies can only be configured at the domain level, even though the password policy settings still exist in the Group Policy Object Editor for the OU. Any settings you configure will simply be ignored.

First, open the AD Users and Computers management console and navigate to the desired OU. After highlighting the OU, select Properties from the context menu. This will bring up a property sheet like the one shown in Figure 5.11. Select Group Policy to view and modify Group Policies relating to the OU.

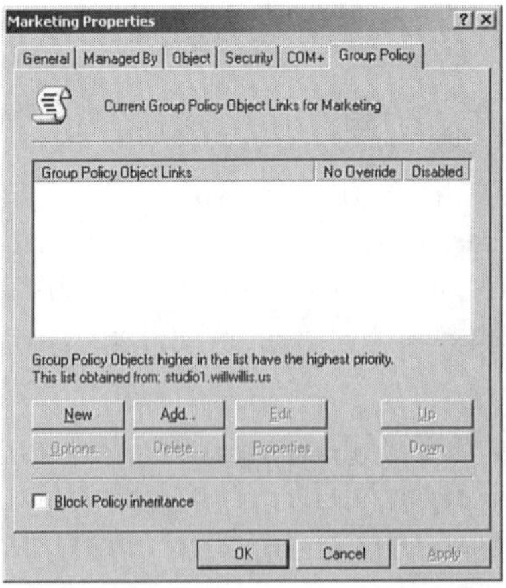

**Figure 5.11** Property sheet for the Marketing OU.

To define a new group policy for this OU, begin by selecting New from the options at the bottom of the sheet. A policy called "New Group Policy Object" will appear. Rename this policy to something memorable and descriptive. In Figure 5.12, the new policy is named Service.

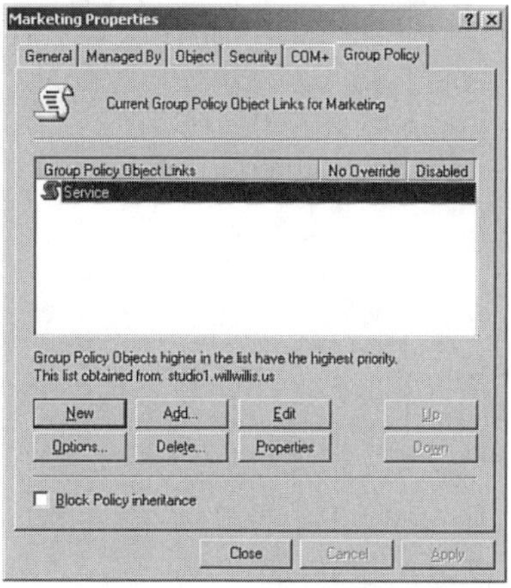

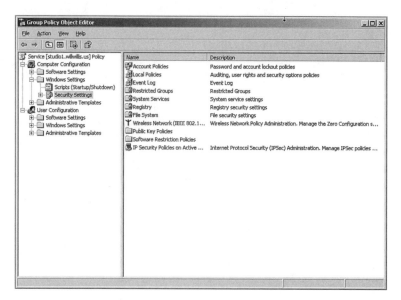

**Figure 5.12**  The first step in creating a new Group Policy.

After the new Group Policy is named, it must be defined. Choose the Edit option to bring up the Group Policy editor, shown in Figure 5.13. After the policy is modified and saved, selecting OK on the OU property sheet will finish linking that OU to the policy.

**Figure 5.13**  The Group Policy editor.

OUs can also be linked to Group Policies that have been previously defined. To link to an existing policy, choose the Add button from the OU Group Policy properties. This will bring up the screen shown in Figure 5.14. Navigate to the desired policy and select it. Choosing OK will link the policy to the OU.

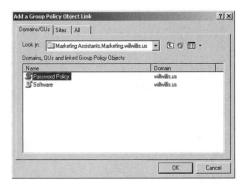

**Figure 5.14**   Selecting an existing Group Policy.

Naturally, OUs can be unlinked from Group Policies as well. To remove a Group Policy from an Organizational Unit, open the properties of the OU within the AD Users and Computers console. Select the Group Policy tab, highlight the policy, and choose Delete. AD will offer two options: The first will unlink the Group Policy from the OU, and the second will delete the Group Policy from the AD environment.

# Exam Prep Questions

## Question 1

> Jon Bischke is the network administrator for a company that is looking to migrate from Windows NT 4 to Windows Server 2003 and Active Directory. The company currently has four domains to support one location because of varying administrative requirements. The CIO has asked Jon for a proposal for the new Windows Server 2003 deployment. What type of structure would be best for him to recommend? [Choose the best answer.]
>
> ○ A. Jon should recommend just upgrading each of the four domains in order to maintain their existing structure.
>
> ○ B. Jon should recommend collapsing the four domains into a single domain and using OUs to create the organizational structure.
>
> ○ C. Jon should recommend moving all the user accounts into a single accounts domain for administrative purposes, leaving the other three domains as resource domains.
>
> ○ D. Jon should recommend upgrading each domain to Windows Server 2003 and using OUs within each domain to define the administrative structure.

Answer B is correct. Ideally, Jon will simplify the domain structure and utilize OUs to give himself the benefit of delegated administration that wasn't available in Windows NT 4 (which forced the use of multiple domains). Answer A is incorrect because a new deployment is a perfect time to analyze existing structure and make changes that will be beneficial. Windows NT 4 had limitations that forced the organization into a multidomain environment, but these limitations aren't present in Windows Server 2003. Answer C is incorrect because this is the Windows NT way of structuring things. Answer D is incorrect because although using OUs is desirable, maintaining the four domains adds unnecessary administrative burden.

## Question 2

> Which of the following are benefits of using OUs in Windows Server 2003? [Choose all correct answers.]
>
> ❑ A. Simplified domain structures
>
> ❑ B. Faster domain logons
>
> ❑ C. More granular permission delegation
>
> ❑ D. The ability to link specific Group Policies to subsets of a domain

Answers A, C, and D are correct. By using OUs, you can simplify your domain structure because you can effectively delegate administrative permissions at the OU level without granting them at the domain level. As a result, you can also apply permissions and policies through Group Policy only to specific OUs without this affecting other OUs or the rest of the domain. Answer B is incorrect because the use of OUs has no impact on logon times.

# Question 3

Gary Zimmerman is a network administrator of a Windows Server 2003 network. He has been asked to configure the marketing staff to have the same policy enforced desktop settings as the sales staff, which is different from the domain password policy. What would be the best way for Gary to go about configuring this? [Choose the best answer.]

- ○ A. Gary should link the marketing GPO to the Sales OU.
- ○ B. Gary should edit the Sales OU and create a GPO for the desired desktop configuration policy.
- ○ C. Gary should edit the domain GPO to reflect the desktop configuration policy changes.
- ○ D. Gary should add the sales staff to the marketing OU.

Answer A is correct. The most efficient way to administer this is to link the existing Group Policy Object (GPO) from the Marketing OU to the Sales OU. By linking policies, an administrator can keep from having to create duplicate GPOs to generate the same settings for multiple OUs. This is especially useful when changes need to be made. Because the sales and marketing staffs are required to have the same policies for desktop settings, it would be much easier in the future to only have one GPO to edit to make changes to both sales and marketing. As a result, answer B is incorrect because although it would work, it isn't the best answer. It would create unnecessary administrative inefficiency. Answer C is incorrect because editing the domain GPO would result in a desktop policy change for everyone in the domain, not just sales and marketing. Answer D is incorrect because there are likely specific reasons why marketing and sales have their own separate OUs, and the task at hand can be easily completed without merging the two groups in Active Directory.

# Question 4

Brian Fink is teaching a class on Windows Server 2003 administration. A student coming from a Windows NT 4 background just isn't getting the concept of OUs, and he asks Brian why one wouldn't just create the forests and domains necessary to support an organization's administration requirements. What should Brian tell the student? [Choose all correct answers.]

- ❑ A. OUs provide easier access to network resources than using multiple domains.
- ❑ B. Group Policies are easier to manage using OUs than domains.
- ❑ C. Complex multidomain models increase the chances of security problems.
- ❑ D. The multidomain model is less efficient to administer than OUs.

Answers B, C, and D are correct. As the number of domains in your organization increases, so does the amount of trust relationships that have to be managed between domains and potentially between forests. The more complex the trust relationship structure, the more likely it is that one domain will be able to connect to another domain that it shouldn't have access to. Also, the use of domains often requires a duplication of administrative effort in order to configure policies and settings, making it less efficient than using OUs within a smaller number of domains. Group Policies are easier to manage with OUs because you can easily apply different policies to different OUs without this affecting other OUs or the domain. To create domains for every business unit that needs separate permissions or needs to administer itself would be an administrative headache. Answer A is incorrect because access to resources is a permissions issue, and permissions can be granted and managed across domains. From an end-user standpoint, it is no easier or harder to access resources from one domain to another if trusts are in place.

# Question 5

John Ferguson is a junior network administrator who has been asked by his senior administrator, Vireya Jacquard, to link the GPO that restricts the Control Panel settings of the engineering group to the developers group. John uses Active Directory Users and Computers to complete the task. Later, Vireya edits the GPO in the Engineering OU to remove access to the Add/Remove Programs applet. She's working on a computer in the engineering group several days later and notices that she can run Add/Remove Programs, even though she shouldn't be able to. Why might this be happening? [Choose all correct answers.]

❑ A. John created a new GPO for the developers rather than linking the existing GPO.

❑ B. Active Directory replication isn't working properly, and the changes John made haven't replicated.

❑ C. Vireya needs to make the change to the GPO for the Developers OU as well as Engineering.

❑ D. John forgot to save his changes after linking the account GPO to the Developers OU.

Answers A and C are correct. When you link an existing GPO from an existing OU to another OU, any changes you make to the original GPO automatically apply to all OUs that link to that GPO. In this case, John must have created a new GPO in the Developers OU and configured duplicate settings. As a result, changes Vireya made to the GPO in the Engineering OU did not apply to the Developers OU. In order for the changes to apply to the Developers OU, in the current situation, Vireya would need to also edit the GPO in the Developers OU and make the desired changes. To avoid this duplication of administrative effort though, she would be better off simply going into the Developer OU, removing the GPO John configured, and linking the OU to the GPO in the Engineering OU. Answer B is incorrect because the issue isn't related to replication but rather to the way the GPO for the Developers OU was configured. Answer D is incorrect because it is unnecessary to manually save changes when creating and editing a GPO.

# Question 6

Louise is the senior network administrator and has been asked by her CIO to create an OU structure where the human resources department can administer its own user accounts, and the IT department personnel other than Louise don't have permissions to their OU. Louise is the only member of the Enterprise Admins group, other than the domain's administrator account, whose password is known only by Louise and the CIO. Louise creates a HR Admins security group and HR OU, delegates administrative permissions to HR Admins, and removes the IT security group from the permissions list. Later she finds out that another network admin has been resetting user accounts for HR personnel. What has she missed? [Choose the best answer.]

○ A.  She needs to change the password on the domain administrator account because obviously the other network administrator is using that account.

○ B.  She needs to remove the Domain Admins group from the permissions list.

○ C.  She needs to create a separate domain for HR to isolate it from the main domain.

○ D.  She needs to remove the Enterprise Admins group from having permissions to the HR OU.

Answer B is correct. By default, the Enterprise Admins and Domain Admins groups will have administrative rights over any OU that is created in the domain. In this case, another network administrator, who is a member of Domain Admins but not Enterprise Admins, is able to perform account-management tasks on the OU. By removing Domain Admins, Louise will ensure that only Enterprise Admins and HR Admins can perform these tasks. As a result, answer D is incorrect because the scenario states that Enterprise Admins should have rights to the OU. Answer A is incorrect because it isn't necessarily the domain administrator account being used; rather, any member of Domain Admins would currently have administrative rights to the OU. Answer C is incorrect because using an OU is a better choice than using a domain, which is unnecessary to accomplish the goal of the scenario.

# Question 7

Bill Eisenhamer is studying for Windows Server 2003 certification and is practicing on his home lab. He creates an OU using Active Directory Users and Computers and now needs to move his user accounts from the Users container to his new OU. What can he do to get the desired user accounts into the new OU? [Choose all correct answers.]

- ❑ A. Bill can drag and drop the users between containers.
- ❑ B. Bill needs to grant his user account the necessary permissions to move user accounts from one container to another.
- ❑ C. Bill needs to select all the desired user accounts and use the Move command from the context menu.
- ❑ D. Bill needs to move the desired user account while he is creating the OU.

Answers A and C are correct. Active Directory Users and Computers supports dragging and dropping objects from one container to another in Windows Server 2003. Bill could also select all the objects he wants to move (he could do this one at a time as well, but it's less efficient), right-click and choose Move from the context menu, and then select the destination OU when prompted. Answer B is incorrect because this isn't a permissions issue. The console simply doesn't support the method Bill is trying to use. Answer D is incorrect because there is no option to populate an OU during the process of creating it.

# Question 8

Holly Shepherd is a network administrator for a Windows Server 2003 network. She wants to configure an HR Admins group to manage the user accounts for the HR department. She creates an HR Admins OU in the HR OU and moves the user accounts for the HR administrators into the OU. Then she delegates control of the HR Admins OU to the individual HR administrators' user accounts. She receives a call a few days later, though, from Jeff Mayfield, one of the HR admins, who complains that he can't reset a user's password. What might be wrong? [Choose the best answer.]

- ○ A. Holly should have added the HR admins user accounts to the HR OU, not its own OU.
- ○ B. Jeff hasn't logged off and logged back in since the change. He needs to do so to gain his new permissions.
- ○ C. Holly did not delegate permission to the correct OU.
- ○ D. Holly should have delegated permissions to a security group and not individual user accounts.

Answers C is correct. Permissions, by default, propagate downward, but they do not propagate upward. As a result, the HR administrators would have administrative permissions to the HR Admins OU, but not to the HR OU. By default, if Holly had delegated control of the HR OU, the HR administrators would also have permissions to the HR Admins OU. Answer A is incorrect because it doesn't matter where the physical accounts are located. Answer B is incorrect because Jeff would not need to log off and on before being able to administer the OU he was delegated control of. Answer D is true in the sense that it is better to apply permissions to groups rather than individual user accounts, but it is incorrect in that there is no requirement to delegate control to a security group.

# Question 9

Charles has been asked to give an executive presentation on restructuring his company's Windows NT domains into a single Windows Server 2003 Active Directory domain utilizing OUs. During the presentation, the CEO asks Charles how having a hierarchy of OUs will affect people logging in to the domain and accessing resources compared to the current system. What should Charles tell the CEO? [Choose the best answer.]

O  A.  User accounts will be assigned to the OUs that they need to logon to.

O  B.  OUs have nothing to do with logging in to the domain.

O  C.  Because all the OUs will be in the same domain, users will have access to any domain resources.

O  D.  OUs can trust each other just like domains currently do.

Answer B is correct. OUs are a means of organizing Active Directory objects, such as user accounts, for the purpose of delegating administrative control or applying differing policies. The user login process is irrelevant to the use of OUs because users will simply log in to the domain and access resources that they have been given permission to through security groups. In that respect it is no different than what users currently do. Answer A is incorrect because users don't log on to OUs. Answer C is incorrect because domain resources are still subject to permissions granted to security groups and individual accounts. Answer D is incorrect because OUs are not entities like domains that have trusts between them. An OU in and of itself is simply a container of Active Directory objects, and membership in an OU doesn't by itself grant any type of access to network resources.

# Question 10

> Robert Gregg is the network administrator for a Windows Server 2003 network. He has delegated the control of the Developers OU to the Developer Admins security group, but after he completes the wizard he realizes he only gave permission to reset passwords and not to create and delete user accounts. What does Robert need to do to fix the problem? [Choose the best answer.]
>
> ○ A.  Robert needs to open the properties of the OU and go to the Security tab.
>
> ○ B.  Robert needs to run the Delegation of Control Wizard a second time to grant the desired permissions.
>
> ○ C.  Robert needs to edit the properties of the Developer Admins security group and change the permissions.
>
> ○ D.  Robert needs to remove the Developer Admins security group and re-create it, then run the Delegation of Control Wizard to set the permissions back up.

Answer A is correct. In order to make the required changes to the permissions currently granted, it would be best to edit the properties of the OU and go to the Security tab. From there Robert could review the currently assigned permissions and configure new ones as necessary. Answer B would technically work but wouldn't be the best answer, because when Robert reruns the Delegation of Control Wizard he would be unable to see what security groups and users currently have any privileges on the OU, and furthermore he couldn't see what permissions had been granted. As a result, it would be difficult to know what permissions he had already granted and needed to grant, which can only be done through the Security tab of the object's properties. Answer C is incorrect because the security is set on the object itself (in this case, the Developers OU), not on the security group. Answer D is incorrect because there is no need to remove and re-create the Developer Admins security group; in fact, this would likely cause more problems than it would solve because the SID associated with the security group would be lost in the process.

# Need to Know More?

 Honeycutt, Jerry. *Introducing Microsoft Windows Server 2003*. Microsoft Press. Redmond, WA, 2003. ISBN 0-7356-1570-5.

 Microsoft Corporation. *Microsoft Windows Server 2003 Resource Kit*. Microsoft Press. Redmond, WA, 2003. ISBN 0-7356-1471-7.

 Mulcare, Mike and Stan Reimer. *Active Directory for Microsoft Windows Server 2003 Technical Reference*. Microsoft Press. Redmond, WA, 2003. ISBN 0-7356-1577-2.

# Planning a Group Policy Implementation

. . . . . . . . . . . . . . . . . . . . . . . . . . . . . . . . . . . . . . . . . . . . . . . . . . . . . . . . . . . . .

## Terms you'll need to understand:

✓ Resultant Set of Policy (RSoP)
✓ Group Policy Object (GPO)
✓ Site
✓ Domain
✓ Organizational Unit (OU)
✓ Linking
✓ Storage domain
✓ Inheritance
✓ No Override
✓ Intellimirror
✓ Filtering
✓ Delegation of Control

## Techniques you'll need to master:

✓ Creating a Group Policy Object (GPO)
✓ Linking an existing GPO
✓ Modifying Group Policy
✓ Delegating administrative control of Group Policy
✓ Modifying Group Policy inheritance
✓ Filtering Group Policy settings by associating security groups
  to GPOs
✓ Using the Resultant Set of Policy MMC snap-in

Microsoft realizes that consumers today, especially those in the business world, are paying far closer attention to the total cost of ownership (TCO) of their systems. TCO can be reduced if there is a uniform way of managing systems on a network. This is the purpose of *Group Policy*, which fits into the "Change and Configuration Management" space of Microsoft technologies. As you will soon see, Group Policy sits at the heart of Microsoft's TCO and security infrastructures.

# Change and Configuration Basics

The term *Change and Configuration Management* encompasses a lot of different things. Microsoft also uses terms within Change and Configuration to describe groups of technologies, such as Intellimirror. Intellimirror is actually a catchall term that can be used when discussing Change and Configuration Management in general terms.

Group Policy is one of the technologies that makes up Microsoft's total Change and Configuration Management strategy. Group Policy is actually one element of Intellimirror.

Change and Configuration Management is actually a technology solution to a business problem. It forms the foundation for *Systems Management*, which is the old term used to describe the various issues that Change and Configuration Management tries to deal with. Change and Configuration Management includes everything from the installation of the base operating system, to applying security settings, to configuring Internet Explorer. Some of these items are in the realm of Group Policy, whereas others require additional technologies, such as operating system installation, which requires Remote Installation Services (RIS).

Microsoft includes several technologies in Windows Server 2003 that are dependent on Active Directory and make up its Change and Configuration Management initiative. This collection of technologies is commonly referred to as *Intellimirror*. Here's a quick summary of the benefits of Intellimirror:

➤ Enables administrators to define environment settings for users, groups, and computers. Windows Server 2003 then enforces the settings.

➤ Allows Windows 2000 clients and servers as well as the Windows XP Professional and Windows Server 2003 operating systems to be installed remotely onto compatible computers.

➤ Enables users' local folders to be redirected to a shared server location, and files to be synchronized automatically between the server and local hard drive for working offline.

➤ Enables users' desktop settings and applications to roam with them no matter what computer they log on from.

➤ Enables administrators to centrally manage software installation, updating, and removal. Self-healing applications replace missing or corrupted files automatically, without user intervention.

➤ Makes the computer a commodity. A system can simply be replaced with a new one, and settings, applications, and policies are quickly regenerated on the new system with a minimum amount of downtime.

One of the key features of a Windows Server 2003 Change And Configuration Management strategy involves Group Policy, which is the focus of this chapter. After a quick overview of Group Policy, we will show you the skills you will need to be successful on the exam.

# Group Policy Overview

Group Policy is at the heart of a Microsoft network that utilizes Active Directory. Even without configuration by an administrator, every user and computer has Group Policy applied to it.

If we go back through the history of Group Policy, we would need to start with early versions of the Microsoft network operating system. In earlier versions it went by the name *System Policies*. Group Policy, as it is today, first appeared with Windows 2000 family. It is dependent on Active Directory to function. Having said that, a scaled-down version of Group Policy, known as *Local Policy*, has been installed on every client and server since Windows 2000.

Group Policy is an integrated solution that solves configuration problems on a large scale. One of the beauties of it is that it is entirely invisible to the end user. Group Policy can be used to configure desktop settings (such as wallpaper), to install applications, and to apply security settings. Its broad range of possibilities is what gives it its power and, of course, what adds to its complexity.

With the release of Windows Server 2003, Microsoft has introduced over 200 new Group Policy settings that can be used to configure settings on Windows XP Professional and Windows Server 2003 machines. The new Windows Server 2003 policy settings allow administrators to control the behavior of the following items:

➤ System restore, error reporting, and PC Health

➤ Terminal server

➤ DNS and net logon

➤ Roaming user profiles and Group Policy

➤ Control Panel

➤ Windows Media Player

➤ Wireless configuration

➤ Software restriction policy

➤ Networking, such as SNMP, Quality of Service (QoS), personal firewall, and dial-up connections

Group Policy supports Windows 2000 clients and up, so Windows 9x and Windows NT 4 and earlier systems cannot realize the benefits of a Group Policy implementation. As we've alluded to, System Policies are available for use with these legacy clients.

# Group Policy Objects

The basic unit of Group Policy is the *Group Policy Object (GPO)*. A GPO is a collection of policies that can be applied at the site, domain, or Organizational Unit (OU). Additionally, GPO settings are passed along from a parent object to all child objects—a process known as *inheritance*.

Group Policy is processed by Windows Server 2003 in the following order:

➤ Site

➤ Domain

➤ OU

Don't forget, a version of Group Policy, known as *Local Policy*, exists on all installations of Windows 2000 Professional and Windows XP. The Local Policies are, in fact, applied when a machine starts up—that is, before a user has even logged in to the network. In the grand scheme of things, our acronym should be SDOU. This means that Local Policies are applied first and are then overwritten by those applied at the Site, Domain, and Organizational Unit if there are conflicts; otherwise, the settings will apply.

Group Policies are stored both within the Active Directory database and in the SYSVOL volume on each domain controller. Later in this chapter we will look at filtering the effects of Group Policy through security groups, but for now we will consider a GPO that has not been filtered. Here are some points to keep in mind:

➤ A GPO that is linked to a site will apply to all objects in the site.

➤ A GPO that is linked to a domain will apply to all objects in the domain.

➤ A GPO that is linked to an OU will apply to all objects in the OU.

Although this sounds fairly obvious, it is essential to understand the scope that Group Policy has. As an organizational structure becomes more complex and the number of GPOs grows, it becomes harder to keep track of the effects of individual GPOs and the combined effects multiple GPOs might have. Fortunately, Microsoft has introduced the Resultant Set of Policy snap-in to help with this. This is discussed later in the chapter.

By default, conflicting GPO settings applied later will override settings applied earlier. An easy way to remember what happens when there are conflicts would be "the last one in wins." Therefore, if a domain GPO has a conflicting setting with a site GPO, the domain GPO will win because it was the last one in. This provides an administrator with highly granular control over the policy behavior on a network. As you will see later, this default behavior can be modified if so desired.

If there are multiple Group Policies linked to the same object, they are processed from the bottom up. So the GPO that is shown higher will be processed after the ones below it, and it will have the ability to override conflicting settings.

## Non-Local GPOs

Non-local GPOs are stored within Active Directory. Two locations within the Active Directory database are used to store non-local GPOs: a Group Policy Container and a Group Policy Template. A globally unique identifier (GUID) is used in naming the GPOs to keep the two locations synchronized.

A Group Policy Container (GPC) is an Active Directory storage area for GPO settings for both computer and user Group Policy information. In addition to the GPC, Active Directory stores information in a Group Policy Template (GPT), which is contained in a folder structure in the System Volume (SYSVOL) folder of domain controllers, located under \winnt\ SYSVOL\sysvol\\*domain_name*\Policies.

When a GPO is created, the Group Policy Template is created, and the folder name given to the Group Policy Template is the globally unique identifier of the GPO. A GUID is a hexadecimal number supplied by the manufacturer of a product that uniquely identifies the hardware or software. A GUID is composed of 8 characters followed by 4 characters, followed by 4, followed by 4, and finally by 12. For example, {15DEF489-AE24-10BF-C11A-00BB844CE636} is a valid format for a GUID (braces included).

The GPC contains definitions of the Group Policy, including the version number of the GPO. The GPT stores the physical aspects of the GPO. For instance, a .reg file is required to store any Registry-based changes that need to be made to clients. Because this is a physical file the clients need access to, it is created and stored in the GPT for replication to all domain controllers.

## Local GPOs

So far, we've mentioned local GPOs twice but have not defined them. Local GPOs apply on every machine since Windows 2000; this goes for clients and servers alike. These are *not* domain objects because the GPO is not stored within the Active Directory database. Local GPOs are stored on the local hard drive of the local system, in the \winnt\system32\GroupPolicy directory. Non-local GPO settings will override any local GPO settings applied from the site, domain, or OU level and are only recommended for use on standalone clients and servers that are not part of an Active Directory domain or have a special purpose in the domain.

Because the local GPO does not utilize Active Directory, some AD features that are normally configurable in the Group Policy Editor, such as Folder Redirection and Software Installation, are unavailable.

A Windows computer can only have one local GPO linked to it at one time.

# Group Policy Versus System Policies

As we've said, Group Policy is not the same as Windows NT 4's System Policies. The following is a summary of the differences. As for the exam, you will need to know under which circumstance you would use one or the other.

## Windows NT 4.0 and Windows 9x System Policies

System Policies have been around for a long time and provide the only way we can configure our Windows NT and 9x machines in a consistent manner in a domain environment. With System Policies you not only have the ability to configure settings for users and computers, but you also have the ability to configure settings based on group membership. Although this sounds tempting, it can lead to major problems when trying to diagnose System Policy problems.

System Policies:

➤ Are applied only to domains.

➤ Are limited to Registry-based settings an administrator configures.

➤ Are not written to a secure location of the Registry. Hence, any user with the ability to edit the Registry can disable the policy settings.

➤ Often last beyond their useful life spans. System Policies remain in effect until another policy explicitly reverses an existing policy or a user edits the Registry to remove a policy.

➤ Can be applied through Windows NT domain security groups.

## Windows Server 2003 Group Policy

Group Policies evolved from System Policies but they are very different. Group Policies can only be applied to Users and Computers and also take advantage of Active Directory's logical structure. This gives you granular control over where you want to place these policies.

Group Policy:

➤ Can be applied to sites, domains, or OUs.

➤ Can be applied through domain security groups and can apply to all or some of the computers and users in a site, domain, or OU.

➤ Is written to a secure section of the Registry, which prevents users from being able to remove the policy through the `regedit.exe` or `regedt32.exe` utility.

➤ Is removed and rewritten whenever a policy change takes place. Administrators can set the length of time between policy refreshes, ensuring that only the current policies are in place.

➤ Provides a more granular level of administrative control over a user's environment.

That should provide enough of an overview to lead in to the rest of this chapter. Although you may not think that the theory behind Group Policy will be directly applicable to the exam, without an understanding of what Group Policy is and what it is used for, you'll find answering scenario questions involving Group Policy implementation very difficult.

# Creating a Group Policy Object

Creating a GPO is done primarily through the Active Directory Users and Computers management console, which is accessed through Start, Administrative Tools. From within the console, right-click a domain or OU and select Properties; then click the Group Policy tab. You will notice options such as Add, New, Edit, and Delete. These are the major commands, and they perform the following functions:

➤ *Add*—Add a Group Policy Object link

➤ *New*—Create a new GPO

➤ *Edit*—Modify an existing GPO

➤ *Delete*—Remove a GPO, a GPO link, or both

From Active Directory Users and Computers, right-click the domain name and click Properties. Then click the Group Policy tab, which will bring up the sheet shown in Figure 6.1.

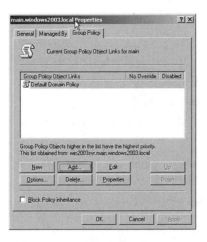

**Figure 6.1**   The Group Policy tab of a site, domain, or OU's property sheet supplies the options for creating, linking, and modifying GPOs.

Creating a new GPO is as simple as clicking the New button. As shown in Figure 6.2, clicking New will create a new GPO with a generic name, *New Group Policy Object*. You will probably want to rename it something more descriptive. For our purposes in this chapter, we have just left it with the default name supplied by Windows Server 2003.

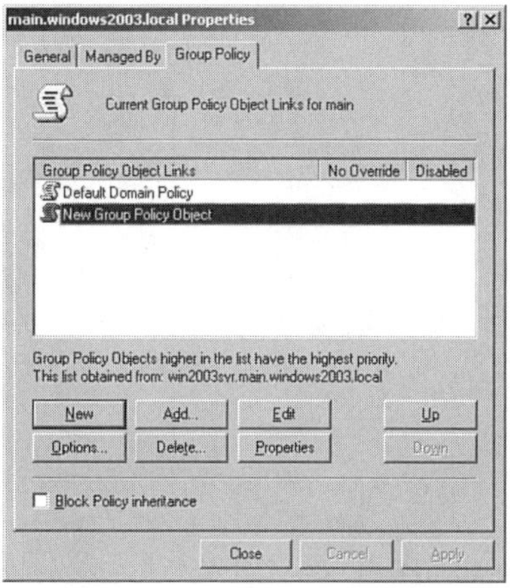

**Figure 6.2**    Creating a new GPO is as simple as clicking the New button.

# Modifying Group Policy Objects

When you create a GPO, the default settings that are created do not really accomplish anything. You will need to edit the GPO in order to define the settings that will affect the behavior of objects linked to the GPO. To edit a Group Policy Object, you use the Group Policy Editor. There is no administrative utility for the Group Policy Editor, though there are a couple different ways it can be invoked:

➤ As a standalone console

➤ Through editing a GPO

# Group Policy Editor As a Standalone Console

The first method of accessing the Group Policy Editor is through a standalone console. First, click Start, Run and type the following:

MMC /A

This command will open a new, empty Microsoft Management Console (MMC). Next, click the File menu and select Add/Remove Snap-in. You will see a dialog box like the one shown in Figure 6.3.

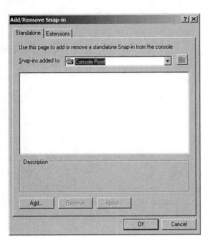

**Figure 6.3** The first step in adding a snap-in is to select the Add/Remove Snap-in Console menu option.

Figure 6.4 shows the next step of the process: to select Group Policy Object Editor from the list of available snap-ins. Click the Add button to see this dialog box. Scroll down the list until you find the snap-in shown in Figure 6.4.

**Figure 6.4** The list of snap-ins shows the available standalone snap-ins that can be added to the console.

The next step is the most important, and the reason we are stepping through this process in the first place. You must define the scope of the Group Policy Editor, which equates to what GPO you will be editing. Figure 6.5 illustrates that the Group Policy Editor defaults to the Local Computer GPO. Most likely you will want to edit a non-local GPO, so click Browse to look for the desired GPO.

**Figure 6.5** You must determine the focus of the Group Policy Editor when you add the snap-in to the console.

As you can see in Figure 6.6, you have a number of options when you browse. You can browse by Domains/OU, Sites, Computers, or all GPOs. Windows Server 2003 defaults to the current storage domain that you are logged in to, but that could be changed by dropping down the list next to the Look In window.

It is also possible to right-click in an open area and select New to create an unlinked GPO. This is very helpful for companies that may split their responsibility of creating and linking GPOs into two separate groups. Now one group can create a policy but not link it, and another group can go in and run tests to ensure that this policy is going to function the way it was intended before it is rolled out.

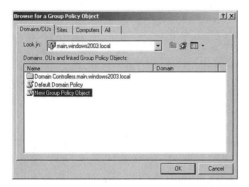

**Figure 6.6** You can browse for non-local GPOs in the current storage domain as well as other available domains.

The last option we have yet to address appears back in Figure 6.5, which you can see again once you click OK to select your choice of GPO, as was done in Figure 6.6. There is a check box titled "Allow the Focus of the Group Policy Snap-in to Be Changed When Launched from the Command Line. This Applies Only If You Save the Console." By default this is not selected, but if you plan on saving your console, you might choose to enable this option. All it does is allow you to specify a different GPO to be the focus of the console, if you choose, when entering the command line.

If you plan on editing a particular GPO frequently, it makes sense to save the console after you have opened the snap-in and returned to the console screen. Windows Server 2003 will prompt you for a filename and will save the file with an .msc extension to your Administrative Tools folder, located in the \Documents and Settings\\*username*\Start Menu\Programs folder. The name you assign to the console will be what appears in the Start menu, so choose a descriptive name that indicates the purpose of the console.

# Accessing the Group Policy Editor Through Editing a Group Policy Object

The other method of accessing the Group Policy Editor is to simply edit the GPO from the Group Policy tab of a site, domain, or OU's property sheet. This can be accessed from the Active Directory Users and Computers administrative utility.

From Active Directory Users and Computers, right-click an object that has the desired Group Policy Object linked to it. For example, if you want to edit the Default Domain Policy GPO, right-click the desired domain in Active Directory Users and Computers and click Properties; then click the Group Policy tab. Click the Edit button, which will launch the Group Policy Editor with the GPO you selected as the focus.

In the example from Figure 6.2, where we created a new GPO, if we chose to edit it at the time (before renaming it to something less generic), we would see a screen such as the one shown in Figure 6.7. In the Group Policy Editor, the new Group Policy Object is the focus of the console, and changes to the policy can happen in this editor.

In the following two chapters we will work with the Group Policy Editor to manage the user environment and to manage and deploy software. For now, let's just briefly discuss the Group Policy Editor environment.

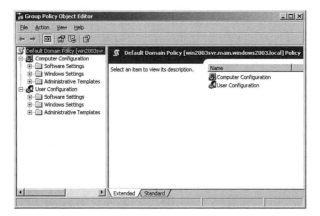

**Figure 6.7**   Editing a GPO through the Group Policy properties of an Active Directory object launches the Group Policy Editor with the selected GPO as the focus.

# Working Inside the Group Policy Editor

No matter whether you open the Group Policy Editor as a standalone console or by editing a GPO in Active Directory Users and Computers, the appearance of the console will be the same. Looking at the sample console from Figure 6.7, you'll find the following structure:

➤ *Root container*—Defines the focus of the Group Policy Editor by showing the GPO that is being edited as well as the fully qualified domain name (FQDN) of the domain controller from which you are editing the GPO. In Figure 6.7, the GPO Default Domain Policy is being edited by win2003svr.main.windows2003.local. If we were to open the GPO for editing on a domain controller named ws.main.windows2003.local, the root of the Group Policy Editor would reflect that.

➤ *Computer Configuration*—A container that holds settings specifically covering computer policies. Computer policies are processed before user policies, by default.

➤ *User Configuration*—A container that holds settings specifically covering user policies. User policies are processed after computer policies, by default.

➤ *Software Settings*—A subcontainer under both the Computer Configuration and User Configuration containers that holds Software Installation settings for computers and users.

> *Windows Settings*—A subcontainer under both the Computer Configuration and User Configuration containers that holds script and security settings as well as other policy settings that affect the behavior of the Windows environment.

> *Administrative Templates*—A subcontainer under both the Computer Configuration and User Configuration containers that provides the majority of settings for controlling the desktop environment and restricting access to applications, applets, and the appearance of the desktop. Administrative templates are discussed heavily in the next chapter.

# Linking a GPO

One important concept that should be learned is that Group Policy is simply an object created within Active Directory. Creating a new policy within the Group Policy Object Editor does not, within itself, achieve a result. For a Group Policy to be applied, it must first be linked to a container (don't forget the acronym, SDOU). The effects of a GPO are applied to the object(s) they are linked to. If you use one of the other tools to create a Group Policy, it will link that policy to the object you created it in.

The acronym SDOU (which stands for site, domain, and Organizational Unit) has long been applied to Group Policy. It is an easy way to remember the precedence of policies and how they can be overwritten. In the Windows 2003 documentation, Microsoft has begun to refer to sites, domains, domain controllers, and Organizational Units. The addition of "domain controllers" in this context is to take into account the special domain controller Organizational Unit. In normal discussions of Group Policy and precedence, this can be ignored. However, pay attention to the inclusion in special cases, such as when domain controllers, in particular, are being discussed.

As previously mentioned, by default the effects of GPOs are inherited by all child objects of a parent object, essentially creating a hierarchy of policy objects. That is, a GPO linked to a site will apply to all computers and users in that site, regardless of their domain membership. A GPO linked to a domain will apply to all computers and users within the domain. A GPO applied to an OU will apply to all users and computers within the OU. Because of the effects of inheritance and the overriding effects of policies applied later in the processing order, it is important to be careful with GPO links. Failure to account for the interaction between different sets of polices can have an adverse impact on your network by introducing undesired behavior of policy recipients.

Before you can link a GPO, you must have at least the permissions necessary to edit a GPO—that is, Read/Write or Full Control permissions. By default, administrators have this capability. As you will see later in this chapter, administrators can delegate the authority to perform certain Group Policy functions, such as linking GPOs to non-administrators.

To link a GPO, open Active Directory Users and Computers (or Active Directory Sites and Services, if you wish to link a GPO at the site level) and right-click the domain or OU to which you want to link the GPO. Choose Properties and then click the Group Policy tab. Click the Add button and navigate to select the GPO you want to link to the particular domain or OU. In Figure 6.8, we have selected an OU called *Test OU*. As you can see, there are currently no linked GPOs within Test OU. However, if you click the All tab, as shown in Figure 6.9, you'll see all the GPOs that have been created. Click OK when you are done selecting a GPO to link to. The GPO is now successfully linked to the Test OU.

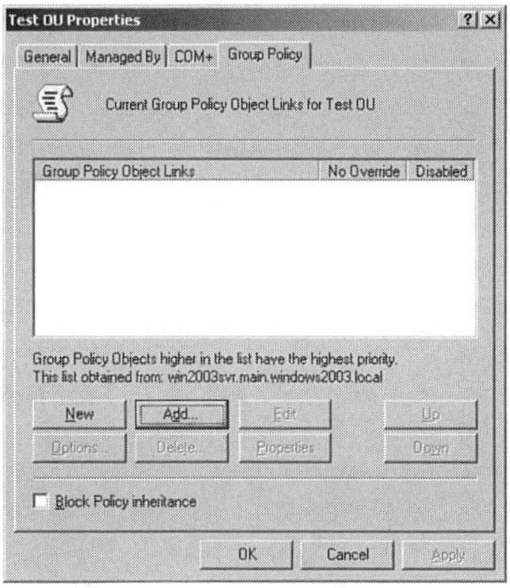

**Figure 6.8**   When adding a GPO link, you first see the domains, OUs, and linked GPOs within the object selected.

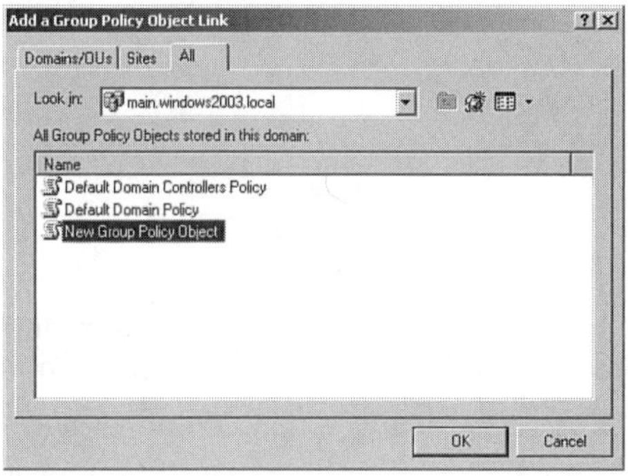

**Figure 6.9**   Clicking the All tab brings up the entire list of GPOs stored in the Active Directory database.

It is important to note that GPOs *cannot* be linked to the generic Active Directory containers. Here's a list of those generic containers:

➤ Builtin

➤ Computers

➤ Users

## Linking Multiple GPOs

Non-local GPOs are stored in the Active Directory database and are, in theory, available to all members of an Active Directory forest. We say "in theory" because in reality there are some limitations on GPO linking. First, let's look at how GPOs can and can't be linked.

Multiple GPOs can be linked to a single site, domain, or OU. As you saw in the example from Figure 6.1, a second GPO was added to the windows2003.local domain. The converse is also true—that is, multiple sites, domains, and OUs can be linked to a single GPO. Every GPO is stored within Active Directory in the domain in which it was created, which is called its *storage domain*. The storage domain is not necessarily the domain in which the GPO is linked, though that is usually the case. The reason for this is that a significant performance hit occurs when you link GPOs across domains. Therefore, Microsoft recommends that you avoid linking a GPO to an object in a different domain.

In Windows Server 2003, it is possible to have transitive trust between forests. Although this simplifies the administration of Group Policy, because it is now possible to delegate authority to administrate GPOs in other forests, it is still not a recommended practice.

 It is *not* possible to link to only a subset of a GPO's settings. This Group Policy Object is the most basic unit of Group Policy, so you can only link to an entire GPO.

## Cross-Domain GPO Links

It is possible to create GPOs in one domain and have them apply to users and computers in another domain or forest. However, as mentioned earlier, this is not recommended in most cases. The reason being is that computer start-up and user logon are slowed, sometimes dramatically, if authentication must be processed by a domain controller (DC) from another domain. To apply a

GPO, the target of the policy must be able to read the GPO and have the permission to apply Group Policy for the GPO.

There are additional authentication mechanisms to validate the computer or user account in the remote domain, so processing will not be as fast as when reading a GPO in the same domain. Because of this, normally it is better to create duplicate GPOs in multiple domains rather than to attempt to cross-link GPOs to other domains or forests.

Other than the performance issue, there's no real reason not to cross-link domain GPOs above creating multiple duplicate GPOs. In fact, cross-linking a single GPO is actually easier to manage because if you make a modification to the GPO, the change automatically applies to all users and computers in the target container. Alternatively, you would have to make the change in every GPO that you had created to perform the same function.

# Delegating Administrative Control of Group Policy

In larger enterprises, network administration is usually distributed among multiple individuals, often at multiple locations in multiple cities. It becomes necessary for more than one person to be able to complete a given task, and in some instances you might need to allow a non-administrator to have a subset of administrative authority in order to complete a task. Such would be the case at a small, remote branch office that does not have enough staff to warrant having a full-time systems administrator onsite to manage the servers. To accommodate this, Windows Server 2003 provides the ability for administrators to delegate authority of certain Group Policy tasks.

Keep in mind that the delegation applies only to non-local GPOs. Local Group Policy applies to standalone computers only, whereas non-local Group Policy requires a Windows domain controller. The rights to administer Group Policy can be found under the <GPO name>\User Configuration\ Administrative Templates\Windows Components\Microsoft Management Console\Group Policy node while the GPO is open in the Group Policy Editor.

## Managing Group Policy Links

The Delegation of Control Wizard is used to delegate control to users or groups that will manage GPO links. The wizard is accessible by right-clicking the desired domain or OU in Active Directory Users and Computers and selecting Delegate Control.

When the wizard starts, it is first necessary to select the users and/or groups to which you want to delegate control. Once the appropriate users and/or groups are selected, click Next. Then you will see a window like the one shown in Figure 6.10, which shows a list of tasks to be delegated. As you can see, there are tasks the Delegation of Control Wizard can delegate other than *Manage Group Policy Links*. For Group Policy though, only this task is applicable. Simply click Finish once you've made your settings and clicked Next, as the wizard requires no other settings.

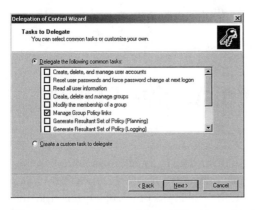

**Figure 6.10** The Delegation of Control Wizard is used to delegate control of managing Group Policy links to users and groups.

When you delegate control, you are allowing the individuals or groups to perform those functions as if they were an administrator. Therefore, it is important to be careful not to delegate control indiscriminately.

# Creating GPOs

Delegating the ability to create GPOs is accomplished through Active Directory Users and Computers as well. In order to create a GPO, a user account must belong to the Group Policy Creator Owners administrators group. Double-click the Group Policy Creator Owners group in the Users container and then click the Members tab. This is shown in Figure 6.11. Now you can add the users who should be able to create GPOs.

**Figure 6.11** In order to create a GPO, a user or group must belong to the Group Policy Creator Owners group.

# Editing GPOs

You might also want a non-administrator to be able to edit a specific GPO in the domain. The ability to edit a GPO comes from an administrator having delegated administrative control of a specific GPO. This delegation is completed by opening the GPO into the Group Policy Editor. Right-click the GPO name, choose Properties, and then click the Security tab. Add the user(s) you want to have administrative control and set the appropriate permission levels. At minimum, a user or group would need Read/Write permissions in order to edit a GPO, though you could go so far as to grant Full Control if necessary.

For the exam you will need to know how Group Policy tasks are delegated, so you should take care to know the information in Table 6.1.

| Table 6.1 Group Policy Tasks and Their Delegation Methods | |
|---|---|
| **Task** | **Method** |
| Managing Group Policy links | Delegation of Control Wizard |
| Creating GPOs | Group Policy Creator Owners membership |
| Editing GPOs | Security properties of the specific GPO (Group Policy Editor) |

# Group Policy Inheritance

From earlier in the chapter you know that Group Policy is processed in the following order:

➤ Local

➤ Site

➤ Domain

➤ Organizational Unit

Inheritance is enabled, by default, and is the process where a policy applied at one level is passed down to lower levels. Objects have parent-child relationships, and parent objects pass their settings down to child objects, forming a hierarchy. The child objects can override parent settings by explicitly defining different policy settings; however, in the absence of a specifically defined setting, the settings from the parent object apply.

To look at it from the perspective of the preceding list, an OU would automatically inherit all the settings from the domain it belongs to, while at the same time automatically inheriting settings from the site.

In some cases, it is not desirable for inheritance to take effect. Because of this, Windows Server 2003 allows for two methods of changing the default behavior of setting inheritance:

➤ Block Policy Inheritance

➤ No Override

## Block Policy Inheritance

Block Policy Inheritance prevents policies from higher up in the Active Directory structure from being automatically applied at lower levels. You would use Block Policy Inheritance to stop settings from higher-level objects from applying later in the processing order. For example, you can block a domain policy from applying settings to an OU by selecting the check box Block Policy Inheritance.

To enable Block Policy Inheritance, open the Group Policy tab of an object's properties, as discussed earlier. The check box appears in the lower-left corner of the Group Policy property sheet.

# No Override

Like Block Policy Inheritance, *No Override* is a method of altering the default behavior of policy inheritance in Windows Server 2003. Unlike Block Policy Inheritance, which is applied at the domain, OU, or local level, No Override is applied to a GPO *link*. Table 6.2 summarizes these differences.

| Table 6.2 Block Policy Inheritance Versus No Override | | |
|---|---|---|
| **Method** | **Applied To** | **Conflict Resolution** |
| Block Policy Inheritance | Domains, OUs, and local computers | Defers to No Override |
| No Override | GPO links | Takes precedence |

No Override is used to prevent policies at lower levels in the Active Directory tree from overwriting policies applied from a higher level. For example, say you have linked a GPO to a domain and set the GPO link to No Override and then configured Group Policy settings within the GPO to apply to OUs within the domain. GPOs linked to OUs would not be able to override the domain-linked GPO. This is a way to minimize the effects of multiple GPOs interacting and creating undesirable policy settings. If you want to ensure that a default domain policy is applied regardless of OU polices, use No Override.

If you want to view what objects a GPO is linked to in order to determine the effects of setting No Override, open the Group Policy property sheet for an object in Active Directory Users and Computers. Select the desired GPO, click Properties, and then click the Links tab. Click Find Now to search the default domain, or select a different domain from the drop-down list. Alternatively, you could use the Resultant Set of Policy tool covered later in this chapter.

For the exam, make sure you know that No Override will take precedence over Block Policy Inheritance when the two are in conflict.

To configure No Override, open the Group Policy property sheet for an object in Active Directory Users and Computers. Select the GPO in question and click the Options button, at which time you will see the dialog box shown in Figure 6.12.

Block Policy Inheritance and No Override can make it extremely complex to troubleshoot policy-related problems on a network, especially as the size of the network and the number of GPOs grow. For that reason, it is recommended to avoid using these options whenever possible.

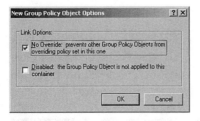

**Figure 6.12** Configuring No Override is done through the Group Policy Object's Options button.

# Disabling a GPO

One of the best things to do when troubleshooting Group Policy problems is to disable a portion of it. Although not exactly the same as the previous methods of preventing policy inheritance, Figure 6.12 shows another option that prevents the effects of a GPO from being applied to an object. By selecting the Disabled check box, an administrator can prevent the effects of a GPO from being applied to any object within the selected container, such as a domain or an OU.

# Filtering Group Policy

Security groups were mentioned previously when we discussed delegating control over editing Group Policy Objects. The other time you'll use security groups in relation to Group Policy is for the purpose of filtering the scope of a GPO. You might have a GPO that applies to an entire OU, for example, yet there are specific objects within the OU that you do not want to be affected by the policies. Through security groups you can filter out the desired object from the OU and prevent it from having policy applied to it.

When filtering the effects of a GPO by security group, you are essentially editing the discretionary access control list (DACL) on that GPO. Using the DACL, you allow or deny access for users and computers to the GPO based on their memberships in security groups. In addition to DACLs, you also have access control entries (ACEs), which are the permission entries within a DACL. ACEs are permissions such as Full Control, Read, Write, and Apply Group Policy.

Two permissions are required for an object to be able to receive policy settings from a GPO, and by default all authenticated users have these two permissions:

➤ Read

➤ Apply Group Policy

The easiest way to prevent Group Policy from applying to an object is to remove that object's Read permission. If the Read permission is taken away, an object cannot access the GPO and therefore policy settings will not be applied. Microsoft strongly recommends removing the Apply Group Policy permission as well, however, because it will speed up the time it takes to process Group Policy for an object if unused permissions do not have to be processed.

To reiterate, the security settings for a GPO are selected by going into the property sheet for a specific GPO and choosing the Security tab.

Filtering affects the entire Group Policy Object. You cannot filter only specific settings within a GPO from applying to a security group. However, you can disable an unused portion of a GPO from applying anywhere if you are not using it.

# Disabling Unused Portions of a GPO

Windows Server 2003 Group Policy gives you the option of disabling either the Computer Configuration container or the User Configuration container (or both, although that would be pointless) within a GPO if you are not using it. Doing so will speed up Group Policy processing and can be beneficial if you have targeted GPOs that apply only to computers or only to users.

To disable an unused portion, open the Group Policy property sheet for an object such as a domain, as done previously in this chapter. Select the desired GPO and click Properties. As you can see from Figure 6.13, at the bottom of the page are the options to disable Computer Configuration and User Configuration settings in order to speed up performance.

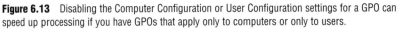

**Figure 6.13** Disabling the Computer Configuration or User Configuration settings for a GPO can speed up processing if you have GPOs that apply only to computers or only to users.

# Resultant Set of Policy (RSoP)

Group Policy is a powerful tool for configuring users and computers. However, along with its power comes complexity. In previous versions of Microsoft's operating systems, we were, at times, left to muddle through trying to determine the end result of applying a Group Policy.

As you can imagine, Group Policies can get quite complex as they are layered in sites, domains, and Organizational Units. The result of applying a policy—in other words, the ultimate effect of applying a group of settings to a user or computer—was often quite difficult to determine. Without third-party tools, it was up to administrators to document, in Microsoft Excel spreadsheets or in databases, which Group Policies had been applied and to which parts of Active Directory. Only by working through this information was it possible to troubleshoot or plan a Group Policy implementation.

In order to assist with these issues in Windows Server 2003, Microsoft has introduced a new Microsoft Management Console (MMC) snap-in called *Resultant Set of Policy (RSoP)*. RSoP is, in fact, a query engine. In effect, it can query about an object (such as a computer or user) and determine what policies have been applied to it. It does this by utilizing Windows Management Instrumentation (WMI).

NOTE

A discussion of WMI is outside the scope of this book. It was first introduced in Windows NT 4 and represents Microsoft's strategy to make the Windows platform more manageable. WMI consists of several components. Two of these components are the Common Information Management Object Model (CIMOM) database and agents that are used to both accumulate and store WMI data. The CIMOM database is also known as the *WMI repository*, because WMI uses it to store state data. This is the database that is used by RSoP; hence it is mentioned here.

You can think of WMI, in this context, as being a data store for information regarding Group Policy. It replaces the manual methods of recording this data that we had in previous versions of the operating system. You would be forgiven for assuming any data about policies being applied to an object would be queried from Active Directory itself; however, in this case, the data is coming from a local data store, WMI. RSoP is an MMC snap-in that compiles this data and then queries it for you. RSoP works in one of two modes:

➤ Planning mode

➤ Logging mode

It is important to note that RSoP can be used to determine details of Group Policies that affect administrative templates, Folder Redirection, and scripts.

# Planning Mode

Planning mode gives you the opportunity to apply Group Policies to an object, such as a user or computer, in order to see the net effect a new policy will have. This allows you to set up "what-if" scenarios.

For instance, let's say you have a computer that has several group policies applied to it through membership to sites, domains, or Organization Units. As an administrator, you want to configure a new Group Policy. Further, you would like to know the net effect should the computer object be moved from one security group to another with Active Directory. This is the purpose of planning mode.

It is possible to run RSoP in planning mode on both local and remote machines. In order to access remote machines using this utility, you must have one of these three security rights:

➤ Be a member of the Domain Admins group

➤ Be a member of the Enterprise Admins group

➤ Be delegated the Generate Resultant Set of Policy (planning) rights

In planning mode, you are able to determine what would happen if a new policy were applied to an object, or if an object is moved with the directory. Once you have determined the net effect, you can make adjustments to your Group Policy planning, if necessary. A good way to think of planning mode is as a "simulator" for new Group Policy settings.

# Logging Mode

Logging mode give you the ability to determine which policies are currently being applied to an object. In this mode you can generate a report as well as work out what each of the policies is doing to an object. This is useful for troubleshooting Group Policy problems. A good way to think about logging mode is as a report engine for Group Policy.

# Using the RSoP Snap-In

Earlier in this chapter we discussed how you could add an MMC snap-in to an empty console. In Figure 6.4, we showed you an example of how to add the Group Policy Object Editor. The process for using the RSoP console is the same. In Figure 6.14 you see an example of selecting Resultant Set of Policy from the list.

**Figure 6.14** Adding the Resultant Set of Policy snap-in.

Before you can use the RSoP snap-in, you must first generate the RSoP data. This process ensures that all data is written to the WMI database. This is achieved by clicking the Action menu and selecting Generate RSoP Data.

This will start the Resultant Set of Policy Wizard. At this time, you are asked to select whether you will be using logging mode or planning mode. This is shown in Figure 6.15.

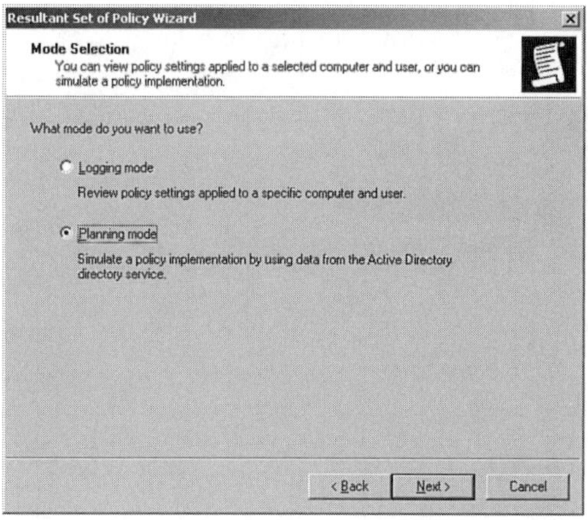

**Figure 6.15**  Using the Resultant Set of Policy snap-in.

The screens that follow vary, depending on which of the options you choose (logging mode or planning mode). Logging mode essentially allows you to select the computer and user against which you want to run the wizard. Planning mode demands that you enter the object that you want to use to simulate the application of a policy. Choosing planning mode displays the screen shown in Figure 6.16.

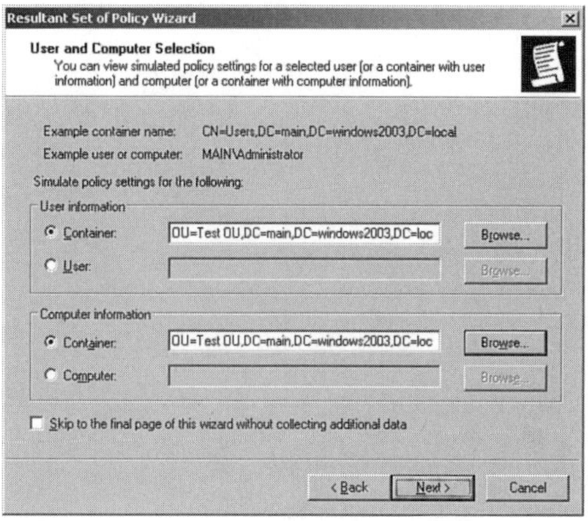

**Figure 6.16**  The User and Computer Selection screen of the Resultant Set of Policy Wizard.

In the lower-left corner of the screen is the option Skip to the Final Page of This Wizard Without Collecting Additional Data. Doing so skips wizard pages that allow you to configure data about the speed of network connections, loopback settings, and simulating changes based on user groups.

Completing the wizard displays the screen shown in Figure 6.17.

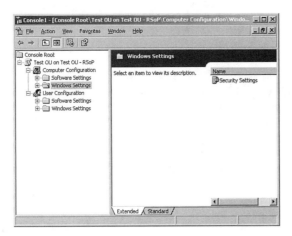

**Figure 6.17**  The completed Resultant Set of Policy snap-in.

Once the wizard is complete, it is possible to step through each of the options available in Group Policy to see what settings have been applied.

# Exam Prep Questions

## Question 1

Scott Keatinge has been asked to design and deploy a new Windows Server 2003–based network. Because the company he has contracted with wants to save money, Scott cannot upgrade each of the clients until the next financial year. This means that his client base will be Windows XP and Windows NT 4. Scott has been told that all systems must be managed in a uniform fashion. It is understood that Group Policy can be used to control user settings and to configure the desktop. Scott decides that he will use Group Policy at the domain level in order to ensure uniformity. Can Scott use a domain-based Group Policy to achieve his desired results?

- ○ A. Scott has chosen a perfect solution. Applying a policy at the domain level means that all clients will be affected by the settings in a uniform fashion.

- ○ B. Scott has the right idea, but he would be better advised to use Group Policy at the Organizational Unit level. This would ensure that while policies are applied uniformly, he would have the flexibility to make exceptions.

- ○ C. This solution will not work. User-defined Group Policy cannot be applied at the domain level. Domain-level policies are reserved for operating system use only.

- ○ D. This solution will not work. Group Policy can only be used by Windows 2000 computers and up. In this scenario, Scott would not be able to achieve his objective without upgrading all Windows NT computers to Windows 2000 or greater.

Answer D is correct. Group Policy was first introduced with Windows 2000, and only operating systems of this version, or greater, support it. Answer A is incorrect because, since all clients are not Windows 2000 or greater, Group Policy cannot be applied. Answer B is incorrect for the same reason. Answer C is incorrect because although there is a default domain-level Group Policy in place, it is indeed possible for administrators to create their own domain-level policies.

# Question 2

Bertram Rawe is working as a consultant in Landau. He has been called to a client site to troubleshoot some configuration problems with a Windows Server 2003–based network with Windows XP clients. The client wants to know why configuration settings for Internet Explorer are being applied to some of the computers on his network and not others. The client assures Bertram that he is not using Group Policy within Active Directory for anything. Bertram arrives at the site and quickly fixes the problem. What did Bertram know that the client did not?

○ A. Bertram knew that Internet Explorer is not configured through Group Policy. Instead, it is configured on a machine-by-machine basis. This was a user-education problem; Bertram simply taught the users how to use Internet Explorer.

○ B. Bertram knew that there are always two Group Policies applied to a Windows Server 2003–based network with Windows XP clients. The first of these is the Local Policy, and the second is the Default Domain Policy. Because the configuration was only taking place on certain machines, the options were most likely being configured through Local Policy—and this proved to be the case.

○ C. Bertram knew that the client was mistaken. Internet Explorer, as a part of the base operating system, will always be affected by the Default Domain Policy. However, these settings can be overridden by Local Policy.

○ D. Bertram knew that there are no settings for Internet Explorer in Group Policy. Therefore, the issues had to have been created by users on their own machines.

Answer B is correct. Note the use of the words *most likely*. It is possible through Group Policy filtering for settings to be coming from the domain, but this would be unlikely. It is far more likely that Internet Explorer settings are being configured and applied from the Local Policy on the Windows XP systems. Answer A is incorrect because it is possible for Internet Explorer to be configured via Group Policy. Answer C is incorrect because this statement violates the rules of precedence for Group Policy. Answer D is incorrect because there are indeed settings for Internet Explorer in Group Policy.

# Question 3

Volker Wiora is working on planning for the Change and Configuration policy of his Windows Server 2003–based network. He wishes to apply security settings to all Windows XP–based computers. In order to allow himself the greatest flexibility, he decides to apply policy to the security group level. A colleague tells him that this should not be done because it is too complex. Volker disagrees, saying that he prefers to use the target groups because it minimizes administrative efforts. Who is correct?

- O  A.  The colleague is correct. Although this is possible, it is very complex to manage.

- O  B.  Volker is correct. There are alternative ways of doing this, but Volker's method is the least time consuming administratively.

- O  C.  The colleague is correct. However, the reason for this does not have to do with complexity; instead it has to do with Active Directory and the overhead of creating unnecessary replication.

- O  D.  The colleague is correct. However, the reason is far simpler—it is simply not possible to target Group Policy at security groups.

Answer D is correct. Group Policy cannot be targeted at security groups. Instead, you must target sites, domains, or Organizational Units. Answer A is incorrect because complexity is simply not an issue (in this case, the option is not possible). Answer B is incorrect because you cannot directly apply Group Policy to a security group. Answer C is incorrect because assigning a Group Policy would not create a lot of replication.

# Question 4

Younes Dallol works as a system administrator for a law firm. Younes understands Group Policy very well and is asked by one of his colleagues to explain how Group Policy is stored in the network. Younes, of course, answered this correctly. What did Younes reply?

- O  A.  Younes replied that Group policy is a name given to a set of technologies. Rather than being any one thing, it is actually two different things. First, there exists a Group Policy Container (GPC) that is stored within Active Directory. Second, there is a Group Policy Template. The template contains the physical files associated with Group Policy, which are stored in the SYSVOL folder on each domain controller.

- O  B.  Younes replied that Group policy is a name given to a set of technologies. Rather than being any one thing, it is actually two different things. First, there exists a Group Policy Container (GPC) that is stored within SYSVOL. Second, there is a Group Policy Template. The template contains the physical files associated with Group Policy, which are stored in Active Directory on each domain controller.

○ C.  Younes replied that a Group Policy is actually a physical file, usually with a **.reg** extension. This is stored within Active Directory.

○ D.  Younes replied that a Group Policy is actually a physical file, usually with a **.reg** extension. This is stored within the SYSVOL volume on each domain controller.

Answers A is correct. Group Policy is actually stored in two places: in a GPC within Active Directory, with the physical files stored in the SYSVOL volume of a domain controller. Answer B is incorrect because it has these two facts reversed. Answer C is incorrect because the physical file associated with Group Policy is never stored within Active Directory. Answer D is incorrect because it only gives half the story (it does not mention the GPC).

# Question 5

As an experiment, Dennis Liebich decides to have three Group Policies. The first one he creates sets the wallpaper to the color red; this he applies to the site. The second one changes the wallpaper to blue, and he sets this at the domain level. The third one changes the wallpaper to yellow; this is attached to an Organizational Unit. He then logs on to a computer that is a member of each of these. What color is his wallpaper?

○ A.  Red.

○ B.  Blue.

○ C.  Yellow.

○ D.  The wallpaper remains at the default because there is a Group Policy conflict.

Answer C is correct. Answers A and B are incorrect because red and blue are applied before yellow. Remember to use the SDOU acronym when working through these types of questions, and also remember that by default the last one in wins. Answer D is incorrect because Group Policy has been linked and colors have been configured. This is what would happen if the client logged on locally and not into Active Directory.

# Question 6

Bertram Rawe has taken over as system administrator of a Windows 2003 network with Active Directory. One of the departments (finance) within the organization has a set of Group Policies applied that limits user access to their computers. This has been found to reduce the number of helpdesk calls the users generate. Bertram has been asked to apply the same policies to the sales organization. What is the best way to achieve this?

○ A.  Bertram should export the properties from the current Group Policy and import them into a new policy. He should then link the new policy to the Organizational Unit that contains the sales team members.

○ B.  Bertram should simply link the current policy to the Organizational Unit containing the sales team members.

○ C.  Bertram should create a new Group Policy containing the settings he requires. He should then link this to the Organizational Unit containing the sales team members.

○ D.  Bertram should simply add the sales team members to the same Organizational Unit as the finance group.

Answer B is correct. Because the Group Policy already exists, it is best to simply link it to the container in which the sales team members exist. Answer A is incorrect because it would take to much administration to export and then import this policy when Bertram could simply link it to the container. Answer C is incorrect because although this would work, it is administratively time consuming. Answer D is incorrect because adding the sales team members to the same container as the finance team might have unexpected results (other policies might be in place that would affect the sales team members).

# Question 7

Scott Keatinge works in an environment with both Windows 2003 and Windows NT clients. He wants to have a fully managed environment. Which technologies will Scott have to use in order to achieve this? [Choose all that apply.]

❑ A.  Group Policy

❑ B.  System Policies

❑ C.  Active Directory

❑ D.  A legacy Windows NT domain

Answers A, B, and C are correct. Group Policy cannot work without Active Directory. Group Policy also does not support Windows NT 4 computers—

these require System Policies for management. Because a Windows 2003 environment can deliver System Policies to down-level clients, there is no need to keep a legacy domain on this network. Therefore, answer D is incorrect.

# Question 8

Siobhan Chamberlin has been tasked with examining the effects of applying a new set of policies to the sales team members of her organization. She knows it is important that she not create problems for these users; she must be certain of the ultimate effect the new policies are going to have. Which tool should Siobhan use to determine the effect of the new policy settings?

- ○ A. Group Policy Editor
- ○ B. The Resultant Set of Policy tool, in logging mode
- ○ C. The Resultant Set of Policy tool, in planning mode
- ○ D. The Resultant Set of Policy tool, in text mode

Answer C is correct. Planning mode allows one to set up "what-if" scenarios for new policy settings. Answer A is incorrect because this allows Siobhan to create new policies, or edit the settings in policies that have already been created, but it does not allow her to determine precisely how they will affect a client. Answer B is incorrect because logging mode gives you what the resultant set of policies would be. Answer D is incorrect because the Resultant Set of Policy tool does not have a text mode.

# Question 9

Volker Wiora is an administrator for a large Windows Server 2003 network. A temporary set of developers is going to be working for his organization. They will only be with the company for six months. Volker already has a development group defined, and the members exist in an Organizational unit called Developers. He had applied Group Policy at this level to control what the developers can do to their systems. The new group of developers is to have an even stricter set of policies applied. Which of the following solutions would work in this situation?

- ○ A. Volker should create a new set of policies and link these settings to a security group defined for the new developers.
- ○ B. Volker should create a child Organizational Unit beneath the current Developers OU. He should then define a new Group Policy and link it to the parent. This policy will then, through inheritance, be passed on to the new developers.

○ C. Volker should create a new Group Policy. He should add the new developers to the current Developers OU and then link the new Group Policy to the Developers OU. He should create a security group and add the current development team members to it. Finally, he should remove Read rights from the new Group Policy Object for this security group.

○ D. This cannot be done. Because all the developers are in the same Organizational Unit, either policies applied to it affect all users, or none. One cannot have a situation where some of the users get the policy and others do not.

Answer C is correct. In this case, this is the only solution that would work (although it's rather complex). Answer A is incorrect because Group Polices cannot be applied to a security group. Answer B is incorrect because if the policy is applied to a parent in this fashion, it would affect both the members of the parent Organizational Unit and the members of the child Organizational Unit. Answer D is incorrect because it is possible to change who is affected by a policy by altering permissions at the group level.

# Question 10

Ester Helwig has been asked to troubleshoot a Group Policy issue. In this case, she has been asked to ensure that a policy is not passed down from a parent Organizational Unit to a child Organizational Unit. The current administrator has made sure that the Block Inheritance setting has been turned on, but the policy is still being applied. Why is this? [Choose the best answer.]

○ A. The policy has been set at the parent. The No Override setting has been checked at this level.

○ B. The policy has been misconfigured. The No Override option needs to set at the child Organizational Unit.

○ C. Policies applied at the parent Organizational Unit are always applied to child Organizational Units. This is by design. To prevent this would require a new design for Organizational Units.

○ D. In order to prevent a policy from being applied, Ester must set No Override in the local policies of the client computers.

Answer A is correct. There are two settings that can be made that affect inheritance: The first is Block Inheritance. This has the effect of preventing policies being inherited from a parent Organizational Unit. However, this can be overridden by the second setting, No Override. Answer B is incorrect because setting No Override at the child level would not prevent inheritance coming from above. Answer C is incorrect because inheritance can, as just described, be altered between parent and child Organizational Units. Answer D is incorrect because one cannot set No Override at the local level.

# Need to Know More?

 Morimoto, Rand, et al. *Windows Server 2003 Unleashed.* Sams Publishing. Indianapolis, IN, 2003. ISBN 0672321548.

Jones, Don and Mark Rouse. *Windows Server 2003 Delta Guide.* Sams Publishing. Indianapolis, IN, 2003. ISBN 0789728494.

# Software Distribution with Group Policy

## Terms you'll need to understand:

✓ Intellimirror
✓ Software Installation
✓ Windows Installer
✓ Assigned applications
✓ Published applications
✓ Pilot program
✓ Package

## Techniques/concepts you'll need to master:

✓ Configuring deployment options
✓ Deploying software by using Group Policy
✓ Maintaining software by using Group Policy
✓ Troubleshooting common problems that occur during software deployment

Although Group Policy is often associated with configuring security settings within a Windows Server 2003 environment, it is also common for it to be used for managing applications within corporate environments.

Application management through Group Policy encompasses the entire life-cycle of an application, including installation, maintenance (service packs and updates), and uninstallation. By leveraging the Active Directory infrastructure, software maintenance through Group Policy brings a uniform approach to the task of managing your user environment.

# Intellimirror Concepts

Before moving into more detailed discussions on software distribution, let's explore Intellimirror and its role with Group Policy functions—including software distribution. Microsoft has grouped many Group Policy concepts under the name *Intellimirror*. Intellimirror is a collection of technologies that work together in Windows Server 2003 to reduce the Total Cost of Ownership (TCO) by simplifying the management of Windows Server 2003 computers.

The features of Intellimirror include the following:

➤ *Data management*—The first feature of Intellimirror is managing user data. This is implemented in Windows Server 2003 through Folder Redirection. When Folder Redirection and Offline Folders are used, user data can be synchronized between a server copy and a local copy, ensuring that data files are accessible no matter where the user is and what computer he logs on from.

➤ *Desktop settings management*—Desktop settings can be stored in profiles that roam with a user so that they are applied whenever the user logs in to a networked computer. Group Policy is used to control what settings should be stored, and it can control a user's ability to make changes to desktop settings. Group Policy can be used to lock down desktop configurations and define a standard level of security for Windows Server 2003 computers.

➤ *Software Installation and Maintenance*—The focus of this chapter, this feature of Intellimirror allows applications to be published by an administrator for use by defined users and computers. It does this by using the infrastructure provided by Active Directory.

Specifically, the following are the available Windows Server 2003 Intellimirror technologies and their interdependencies:

➤ *Active Directory*—This is the cornerstone of Intellimirror, because without AD none of the rest would be possible. Active Directory stores the GPOs and other user, group, and computer information, and it provides centralized management for Windows Server 2003 networks.

➤ *Group Policy*—Through Group Policy you can manage desktop settings and determine what to apply and where. Group Policy is dependent on Active Directory because it stores Global Policy information in the Active Directory database. Group Policy is the primary method of managing the Intellimirror features listed previously.

➤ *Roaming user profiles*—Roaming profiles are used to enable user settings, such desktop wallpaper and customized Start menu settings, to follow a user to whichever computer he logs on from. Any changes that are made to the user environment while the user is logged in are saved to the profile, ntuser.dat, and are stored in Active Directory. Roaming profiles existed in Windows NT 4 and have largely been superceded by Group Policy.

➤ *Folder Redirection*—Folder Redirection is one of the primary components of the data management Intellimirror feature discussed previously. Folder Redirection can be used to seamlessly move the contents of certain local user folders to a network location. Combined with Offline Folders, Folder Redirection provides much greater data protection and availability than by having files stored only on local hard drives.

➤ *Offline Folders*—Offline Folders is an Intellimirror capability that allows for the synchronization of files and folders between the local hard drive and a network location. This is particularly useful for users who have laptops, because you are able to use Offline Folders in conjunction with Folder Redirection to ensure they can have full access to their files, regardless of whether they are in the office on the LAN or working offline on an airplane.

The focus of this chapter is software deployment and management, so let's discuss how these technologies work in this context.

# Software Installation and Maintenance Overview

Through Intellimirror, and specifically the Group Policy component, Microsoft has provided the Software Installation and Maintenance feature, which provides a way for administrators to deploy software so that it is always available to users, and repairs itself if necessary. Software Installation and Maintenance is implemented as a Group Policy extension called *Software Installation* and is located, as shown in Figure 7.1, under both the Computer Configuration container and the User Configuration container in a GPO, under the Software Settings nodes.

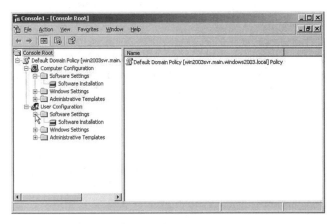

**Figure 7.1** The Software Installation extension to Group Policy is located under the Software Settings node in the Computer and User Configuration containers.

Through Software Installation, you can centrally manage the following:

➤ *Deployment of applications*—You can deploy shrink-wrapped applications as well as custom-built in-house applications. Most any type of application can be deployed through Software Installation.

➤ *Upgrades and patches*—Through Software Installation you can update existing software or even replace it in the case of a product upgrade. Deploying service packs for operating systems becomes much easier as well.

➤ *Uninstall software*—When a product is no longer in use or supported by the IT department, you can easily remove it from users' computers without their intervention or you needing to go out and physically touch each computer containing the installed software.

This technology is often referred to as *Just-In-Time (JIT)*, because deployment will occur either during user logon or when the user goes to launch a particular application. For example, say you have assigned Microsoft Word to a particular user. Even though the user has not explicitly installed Microsoft Word herself, she sees the icon for it on her desktop or in her Start menu. The first time she attempts to use the program, the system goes out and installs the application automatically, with no user intervention, and then launches the program.

Likewise, if the same user attempts to use a feature of the program that is not installed by default, the application will be smart enough to automatically install the missing feature on the fly from the network and then allow the user to use it. In the past, installing a missing feature has invariably meant manually running the program's setup utility and either reinstalling the entire product to add the missing feature or simply selecting the missing feature and choosing to update the installation. In either case, this was an interruption to the workflow of the user and very likely required a desk-side trip from a desktop support technician.

# Requirements for Software Installation

In order to use the Software Installation extension, you must first ensure a couple prerequisites are met:

➤ *Active Directory dependency*—Because Group Policy is dependent on Active Directory, it makes sense that you cannot use the Software Installation extension unless you have deployed Active Directory on your network. Software Installation relies on GPOs, which are stored in Active Directory, to determine who can access the software that it manages. As with Group Policy, Windows 9x and NT 4 computers cannot participate in Active Directory.

➤ *Group Policy dependency*—In order to use the Software Installation extension, you must be using Group Policy on your network. Because Group Policy is limited to Windows 2000 computers and upward, you will only be able to manage software in newer environments. Any legacy Windows 9x or NT 4 clients will not be able to receive applications through Group Policy and Software Installation.

The primary function of Software Installation is to deploy software, so let's discuss that next.

# Deploying Software with Group Policy and Software Installation

On the exam, you will be expected to know how to deploy software using the Software Installation extension and how to configure deployment options. In this section, we will explore the Software Installation extension and specifically cover the following topics:

➤ Configuring Software Installation properties

➤ Deploying a new package

➤ Configuring package properties

Knowledge of these topics will allow you to deploy software, from setting up the Software Installation extension's global properties to deploying a new package, and then be able to configure additional properties for the deployed software package.

# Software Deployment to Users and Computers

When deploying software, you will have to make a choice whether to deploy it to a user or a computer. Therefore, you should be aware of some of the differences between the two.

Deploying software to a user means that the deployment will follow the user as he changes computers. This works well for users who share computers. For instance, if you have a user who is part of the accounting group, he might well have some software that is specific to his task targeted to him through Group Policy. If this user does an audit of another department, he might well use hardware within that department to do his work. It is, obviously, useful if Active Directory detects that the user is on another machine and offers the same software he is used to. This is the case if software is targeted at a user—wherever that user logs on, the software remains targeted to him.

In contrast, software can also be targeted at computers. In this case, the software is installed on a specific computer (or set of computers) and only that machine. A user logging in to such a machine might well have software packages available to him that he will see nowhere else. This is useful for computers installed in booths or in reception areas.

This distinction between the two types of deployment might seem minor, but it's an important point. Software targeted at a user follows that user around. Essentially, it knows where the user is and makes sure the user's environment does not change. Software targeted at a computer essentially belongs to the machine. A user at this machine can use the software package, but only while he is logged on at that particular piece of hardware.

Other distinctions exist when it comes to assigning and publishing software, but these will be discussed later in the chapter.

# Configuring Software Installation Properties

To configure the global properties of the Software Installation extension, simply right-click the Software Installation option shown in Figure 7.1. Keep in mind that computer and user settings are independent of each other, so making changes to the computer policy for Software Installation will have no effect on the user policy, and vice versa.

The first dialog box you are presented with when you enter Software Installation properties is shown in Figure 7.2.

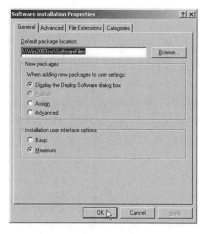

**Figure 7.2** The General tab on the Software Installation Properties dialog box contains information about the default behavior of the Software Installation extension.

The first section on the General tab allows you to define the default package location for new packages. This should be a network share rather than a local hard drive path (for example, \\Win2003svr\SoftwareFiles rather than E:\apps) and is used if you use a centralized distribution location for your software.

The General tab also contains settings that define the behavior of the extension with regard to new package creation. By default, the Deploy Software dialog box is displayed when you choose to create a new package. This dialog box contains the choice to assign or publish a package, allowing you to choose how you want Software Installation to handle a package on a per-instance basis. Unless you strictly publish or assign applications, there is probably no need to change this default setting.

Additionally, the General tab contains the option to define how much information is presented to the user during package installation. By default, only basic information about the software installation is supplied, such as the installation progress meter. Optionally you can specify that a maximum amount of information and options be shown to the user during installation, which includes all installation messages and dialog boxes being shown during the installation.

## Configuration from the Advanced Tab

The next tab on the Software Installation Properties dialog box is the Advanced tab. This tab provides advanced options that include the ability to have software uninstall if it falls out of scope. Software can only be targeted to users and computers through their membership in a site, domain, or Organizational Unit (OU). If a user has software installed because of her membership in one of these, the software can be uninstalled if she is removed by checking the Uninstall the Applications When They Fall Out of the Scope of Management option.

The Advanced tab also allows you to specify which applications will be advertised to 64-bit clients. An example of this is the ability to specify whether applications designed for 32-bit operating systems should be offered to 64-bit systems.

## The File Extensions Tab

After the Advanced tab is the File Extensions tab. In many cases, you will have more than one application installed on your computer that is capable of opening a given type of file. This property sheet allows you to pick a file type and set the order of precedence for applications that are capable of opening the file. If the first application listed isn't available for some reason, such as it was uninstalled, the second application listed will attempt to open the file.

## The Categories Tab

The last tab is Categories, which is an organizational option. You can create categories to help you keep track of where software is deployed. By default, no categories are listed, so you must create them if you want to use this feature. You might choose to create categories for your software based on department or location or some other naming convention that makes sense for your organization.

Be careful with software categories because they are domainwide settings and are not specific to any particular OU.

# Deploying a New Package

In order to deploy a new package, first you must have copied the installation files to a *distribution point*, which is simply a network share you designate as a repository for software. Right-click the Software Installation extension and click New, Package. The dialog box shown in Figure 7.3 will appear.

**Figure 7.3**  The first step in deploying a new package is to select the package to be deployed.

In this example, a Windows Installer package for the Admin Pack of Windows Server 2003 is selected, which is located in the SoftwareFiles share on the server Win2003svr. This is the distribution point. When you select the file and click Open, you are presented with the dialog box shown in Figure 7.4. This dialog box is presented because previously we left the global setting for Software Installation to show us these choices when creating a new package, rather than to default to either publishing or assigning.

It is important to note that the Published option is available only if the package is being deployed under the User Configuration container. Software deployed to computers does not support publishing. Therefore, these packages can only be *assigned*. If you've deployed the package under the Computer Configuration container, when you get to the dialog box shown in Figure 7.4, the Published option will be grayed out.

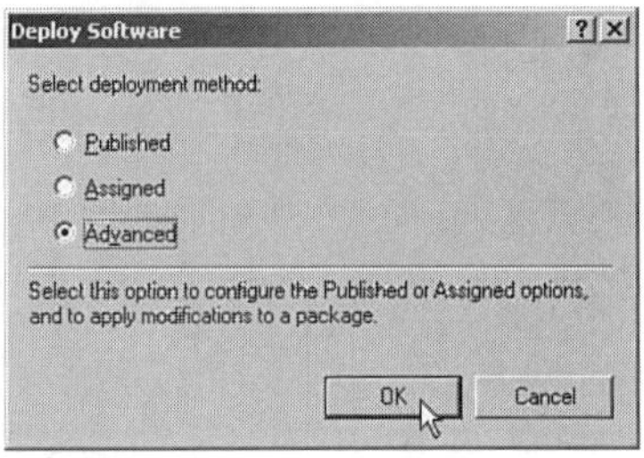

**Figure 7.4** After choosing the software package to deploy, you must decide whether to publish or assign it.

When you select either Published or Assigned and then click OK, the package is deployed without any further prompting. If you select Advanced, the package will still be deployed, but you will be prompted with a dialog box similar to the one shown in Figure 7.5. This is the same dialog box you can access later by going into the properties of a package, which is discussed next.

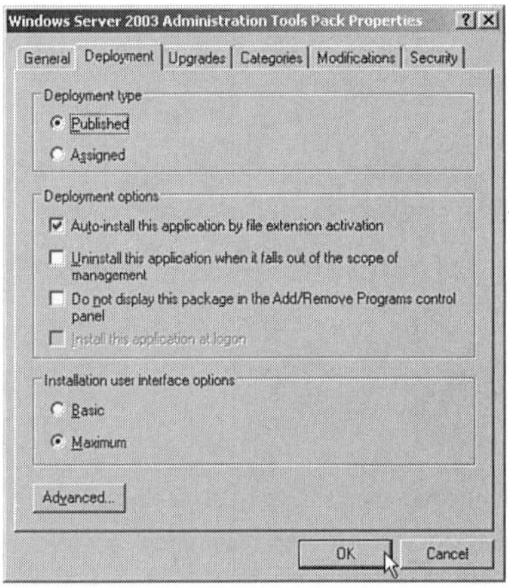

**Figure 7.5** You can configure a number of advanced settings for an application once it has been deployed.

# Configuring Package Properties

To access the properties of a package once you've deployed it, simply right-click the package and click Properties. You will see the same dialog box shown previously in Figure 7.5, when you selected Advanced during the new package deployment. A number of property sheets contain settings for the package. Here's an overview of them:

➤ *General*—Contains product information, such as the name and version number, as well as contact information.

➤ *Deployment*—Defines the deployment type (assigned or published), which can also be changed here. In addition, this property sheet contains settings for deployment options, including whether the package should be uninstalled if it falls outside the scope of management and whether it should be displayed in the Add/Remove Programs applet. Advanced deployment options determine whether the language setting should be ignored when installing the software and whether previous installations of the product should be uninstalled if they weren't installed through Group Policy.

➤ *Upgrades*—Defines the applications that are to be upgraded by this package as well as which packages can upgrade this package.

➤ *Categories*—Determines the categories that the software will be displayed under in the Add/Remove Programs applet.

➤ *Modifications*—Allows you to apply modifications or transforms to the package in order to customize the deployment.

➤ *Security*—Determines who has what level of access to the package. It is through this property sheet that you control the deployment of the software to computers, users, and groups.

We've now covered the basics of the Software Installation extension. At this point, we should take a moment to discuss assigned applications versus published applications and when to use one over the other.

# Assigned Versus Published Applications

When deploying software, you need to know whether the application will be associated with the user or computer, and whether you need the application to be assigned or published.

When it is mandatory that an application be installed, it is a good rule of thumb to *assign* the application. Assigning applications makes them resilient—they are available no matter what the user does. For example, if the user removes an application, it will automatically be reinstalled on demand.

You can assign applications to either a user or a computer using Group Policy. When you assign an application to a computer, the application is automatically installed the next time the computer is started. When you assign an application to a user through Group Policy, you can choose to have the application installed either upon document activation (when the user selects the application) or in full at the user's next logon.

If some applications are not mandatory, but you would still like to give users the option to install them on their machines through Group Policy, you can *publish* these applications to the users. Publishing applications is not an option with computers; it's only available to deploy to users.

After you publish an application, it appears in Add or Remove Programs in the Control Panel. The installation of the application can also be configured to occur automatically through document activation. With published applications, this activation method happens when a user tries to open a file whose extension is associated with this application. Published applications are not resilient, so if a user uninstalls the application, it will not automatically reinstall.

To take advantage of all the benefits of Software Deployment in Group Policies, all applications should use the Windows Installer service, which has the .msi extension. Although you can still publish non–Windows Installer service applications using ZAP files, you won't get the benefits of elevated privileges, as explained earlier, and, of course, you won't get the benefits of using Windows Installer either.

A ZAP file is a text file that provides a pointer to the setup package, which enables the application to be listed in Add or Remove Programs.

The preferred way to use Software Deployment is to follow these guidelines, assign software when it is mandatory, and publish software when it is optional.

# Phases of Software Deployment

In order to ensure success, software deployment is best done through a systematic method. Managing a documented process removes many of the variables associated with deploying new software, thus reducing support costs related to troubleshooting problems.

Microsoft recommends a software-deployment strategy similar to the one that follows:

➤ *Preparation phase*—The preparation phase of software deployment includes analyzing the requirements of your organization to determine the needs to be filled. Some of the tasks include determining licensing requirements, determining whether applications will be run from a network server or local hard drives, and determining whether the current network infrastructure will support the deployment or if you will be required to make modifications before deploying the new application to your users. You must also decide whether you will publish or assign applications in this phase.

➤ *Distribution phase*—The distribution phase includes setting up network distribution points for the new software package and copying the source installation files to your distribution points.

➤ *Targeting phase*—In the targeting phase, you use Group Policy to create and/or modify GPOs in order to effectively manage the software for users, groups, and computers. In addition, you will use the Software Installation extension in Group Policy to configure deployment options for the new software package.

➤ *Pilot program phase*—The pilot program phase is perhaps the most important phase. In this phase, you deploy your software package to a select group of users, groups, and computers that is representative of the whole that you are going to target with this package. By deploying to a select group and not everyone who will ultimately receive the package, you will be able to put the application through all possible scenarios without impacting everyone if there are problems to be worked out. Once you have thoroughly tested the application under a pilot program, you are ready to deploy it to everyone.

➤ *Installation phase*—The installation phase is where the software is actually deployed to the desktops of all the users included in the target phase. The installation phase can include installing new applications, installing modifications or updates to existing applications, repairing existing applications, or removing applications entirely.

These phases provide the best chances for a successful software deployment; however, there will probably be times when you run into problems. Therefore, it is important to know how to troubleshoot some of the common problems you might run into.

# Troubleshooting Software Deployment Problems

In a perfect world, you would follow the previous software-deployment phases and roll out an application with no problems whatsoever. Unfortunately, things don't always seem to work out in the real world the way they do in a textbook. Because of this hard reality, let's discuss some of the more common problems you might run into with software deployment and what steps you might take to resolve them.

# General Troubleshooting Guidelines

There are some general guidelines to follow in troubleshooting. In many cases, problems can be traced to a lack of necessary permissions. One of the first troubleshooting steps should be to ensure that an appropriate level of permissions exists to access the needed resource. Missing source files or corrupted Windows Installer packages are another potential source of trouble. You should check to make sure the necessary files are available as part of your troubleshooting steps.

The remaining subsections discuss some common problems and the things to look for to resolve them.

### "Active Directory Will Not Allow the Package to Be Deployed" Error Message

This error is usually the result of a corrupt Windows Installer package or the inability of the Software Installation Group Policy extension to communicate properly with Active Directory.

To resolve this problem, test for connectivity with the DNS server and domain controllers containing the Active Directory database. You can use the PING command to establish basic connectivity and then browse through My Network Places to the servers to see if you can access the required share directories. To test for a corrupted Windows Installer package, see if you can open the package on another similarly configured computer.

 DNS plays a major role in deploying Group Policies. If client machines cannot contact the appropriate domain controller, they will not have their Group Policies applied to them.

### "Cannot Prepare the Package for Deployment" Error Message

This error is similar to the preceding Active Directory error in that it can be the result of a corrupt package; but rather than the Software Installation extension not being able to communicate with Active Directory, in this case it cannot communicate with the SYSVOL share.

The troubleshooting steps are the same as with the previous error. Test for connectivity between the workstation and the SYSVOL share on the domain controllers, try from another computer if communication fails, and attempt to install the package on another system if connectivity is fine.

# Various Installation Error Messages

A number of different error messages can appear when you go to install an application on a workstation. There could be a problem with the Windows Installer packages, or there could be a permissions problem where the user or computer account attempting to install the application doesn't have the necessary level of permissions in order to complete the installation. The permissions problem could relate to not being able to execute the particular package, not being able to access the distribution point, or not being able to install the application to the target directory on the local hard drive as defined by the package.

To troubleshoot, first determine if you have permission to access the distribution point. If you do, copy the package to the local hard drive and attempt to execute it from there. If the package begins installing and fails, ensure that the user account being used has Write permissions to the target directory. If the package gives an error before attempting to install, make sure the user account has Execute permissions for the package and then test the package on another system to ensure its integrity (that is, to ensure it's not corrupted).

## "The Feature You Are Trying to Install Cannot Be Found in the Source Directory" Error Message

This type of error is most likely related to permissions or connectivity. Either the user doesn't have the necessary permissions level to access the distribution point or the distribution point is unavailable over the network. Additionally, you should check to ensure that the source files were not accidentally deleted or moved to another location on the network.

To troubleshoot this error, first make sure the required source files exist at the distribution point. If they do, make sure the user attempting to install the feature has connectivity to the server containing the distribution point. If this checks out, check the permissions on the distribution point to see if the user has the required permissions. Most likely one of these three aspects will be the cause of the error.

## Shortcuts Still Appear for Removed Applications

This isn't an error message but rather a condition that might exist after uninstalling a managed application. After either the user uninstalls an application or the Software Installation extension removes the software when an administrator removes it from the applications list, the shortcuts for the applications still appear on the Start menu and/or the desktop.

To troubleshoot, determine if the shortcuts were user created or program created. In many cases, users copy shortcuts from the Start menu to the desktop for convenience. The application's installation program would not be aware of this type of user-created shortcut and therefore would not be able to remove it during the application's uninstallation process.

Another cause might be that the shortcuts point to another installation of the same program. Perhaps the user belongs to multiple GPOs and the application has only been removed from one of them. Another possibility is that there was a locally installed copy prior to the installation of the assigned or published application, and those files were not removed.

You should check to see if the shortcuts point to valid programs. If they do, determine why the programs are installed (local install, another GPO, and so on) and if it is appropriate. If the shortcuts do not point to valid applications, simply delete them.

## An Installed Application Is Suddenly Uninstalled from a User Workstation

This condition almost always occurs when the software deployment option Uninstall This Application When It Falls Outside the Scope of Management is selected. However, it could result if a computer account was moved outside the influence of the GPO managing the software.

If the computer account was not moved, determine if a GPO that the user or computer belongs to is still managing the application.

Troubleshooting is often more of an art than a science. However, remembering to check connectivity, permissions, and the existence of source files goes a long way toward successfully troubleshooting software deployment.

# Exam Prep Questions

## Question 1

> Volker Wiora is a consultant who has been asked to make a presentation about the features and benefits of Windows Server 2003 and Active Directory. One of the things he wants to talk about is software deployment with Group Policy. Which statement would best describe this feature?
>
> ○ A. Software deployment is an integrated feature of Windows Server 2003. It is most commonly used to deploy operating systems and common applications such as Microsoft Office.
>
> ○ B. Software deployment is an integrated feature of Windows Server 2003. It can be used to deploy applications to client computers. It can also be used as part of the migration process of moving from earlier versions of Windows NT to Windows Server 2003.
>
> ○ C. Software deployment is a feature of Group Policy. It can be used to manage the entire lifecycle of an application, from deployment to uninstall.
>
> ○ D. Software deployment is a feature that can be installed either as part of Group Policy or as a standalone feature.

Answer C is correct. Software deployment with Group Policy allows the management of the full lifecycle of software maintenance. Answer A is incorrect because software deployment cannot deploy operating systems. This also explains why Answer B is incorrect. Software deployment cannot migrate operating systems. Answer D is incorrect because the software deployment features are integral to Group Policy, and they are not installed separately.

## Question 2

> Zevi Mehlman, a consultant busy designing a Windows Server 2003 Active Directory network, has been asked to explain why software deployment is important for the client's environment. He tells them that it is important because it can support the full lifecycle of an application. He is asked to explain this statement. What will he say?
>
> ○ A. Software deployment can support the entire lifecycle of a software application. This means that it can be used to install, maintain (through service packs), and uninstall an application.
>
> ○ B. Software deployment supports the entire lifecycle of an application. This includes development, deployment, and removal.

○ C. *Full lifecycle* means that a program can be both installed and maintained. Uninstallation is achieved through the Control Panel on the client computers.

○ D. *Full lifecycle* is a term associated with users. It means that software can be provided to users when they need it (Just-In-Time). However, if a user leaves the company, the software is removed.

Answer A is correct. When we talk about the full lifecycle of an application, we are talking about deploying it, maintaining it by applying service packs, and uninstalling it automatically if a user goes out of scope. Answer B is incorrect because the software deployment capabilities of Group Policy have nothing to do with the development of applications. Answer C is incorrect because the lifecycle includes the ability to automatically uninstall a program. Answer D is incorrect because the lifecycle is not user specific; instead, it is application specific.

# Question 3

Software deployment is part of the Windows Server 2003 operating system. What are the requirements for its use? [Choose all that apply.]

❏ A. Active Directory must be present.

❏ B. The software-deployment features of Group Policy must be installed and working.

❏ C. Group Policy must be utilized on the network.

❏ D. Security groups must be created to fit the deployment scenario.

Answers A and C are correct. In order for software deployment to be used, both Active Directory and Group Policy must be installed and functional on the Windows Server 2003 network. Answer B is incorrect because it suggests that the software-deployment features of Group Policy can be uninstalled, or not installed at all. The software-deployment features of Group Policy always exist on a Windows Server 2003 network with Active Directory installed. Answer D is incorrect because user groups cannot be directly targeted for software deployments.

# Question 4

Bertram Rawe has been asked to make a presentation describing software deployment. Part of this presentation is talking about how users and computers will be targeted. Bertram knows that management would really like to target security groups, and he must address this. What are the only ways software deployment can be targeted?

○ A. Software deployment can be targeted at sites, domains, or Organization Units only. It cannot target specific security groups.

○ B. Software deployment can be targeted at sites, domains, Organizational Units, and groups. It can target one or all of these at the same time.

○ C. Software deployment targets security groups and *only* security groups.

○ D. Software deployment targets sites, domains, and Organizational Units. The requirement for targeting security groups can also be achieved; however, this involves extensive use of ACLs, which can be complex to manage over an enterprise.

Answer D is correct. The requirement for targeting groups can be achieved through access control lists (ACLs). However, this is complex and should be avoided in an enterprise. Answer A is incorrect because although it is not possible to target security groups directly, it is possible to achieve the same thing by targeting sites, domains, and Organizational Units and changing the ACLs on Group Policy Objects. Answer B is incorrect because it is not possible to target groups specifically. Answer C is incorrect because software deployment targets sites, domains, and Organization Units, not groups.

# Question 5

Justin Rodino has been asked to come up with a design for software deployment for the enterprise he administrates. He knows he must have Active Directory in place along with Group Policy. Along with this, he knows he must have software distribution points for the program source files. He wants a scalable solution that utilizes the benefits of Active Directory. What is the best solution?

○ A. The best solution is to create a software installation point on the domain controller where the policy is created. Because this is where the package is created, it is the most likely place that users will connect in order to install the software.

○ B. Group Policy has a built-in replication system. It is best to use this. Group Policy examines who is being targeted and makes sure a copy of the source files are in the same site.

○ C. Group Policy and software deployment do not provide a solution within themselves. You must use a third-party solution for this issue.

○ D. Microsoft provides the Distributed File System (Dfs), which can be used for this task.

Answer D is correct. Scaling distribution points is best done through Dfs. Answer A is incorrect because forcing all clients to access a single domain controller for the source files is highly unlikely to be a scalable solution. Answer B is incorrect because although Group Policy does indeed utilize a replication system, it does not in any way auto-configure itself for software deployment. Answer C is incorrect because third-party solutions are not necessary for this purpose; Dfs ships with the operating system.

# Question 6

Scott Keatinge has been asked to deploy a software package to users on the network. The users will have the ability to install this software at their discretion. If they do not want the software, they should be able to ignore it. What is the best solution?

○ A. Scott should publish the application to the target objects.

○ B. Scott should assign the software to the target objects.

○ C. Scott should perform a mandatory publication to the target objects.

○ D. Scott should perform a mandatory assignment to the target objects.

Answer A is correct. With a published application, the software shows up in the Add/Remove Programs applet in Control Panel. The user can then choose whether to install the application. Answer B is incorrect because assigning an application causes icons to appear on the user's Start menu. Answers C and D are incorrect because there is no feature to make a mandatory distribution. This terminology is common with Systems Management Server, but not Group Policy.

# Question 7

Siobhan Chamberlin has been asked to deploy software targeting computers. The software should be available on the client machines but not necessarily installed. The concept is that users can simply go to the Add/Remove Programs option in Control Panel and install the applications they need as they want them. At a managers meeting Siobhan announces that she intends to publish applications to the computers through Group Policy. Is this a good decision?

○ A. Yes, the difference between assigning and publishing is that an assigned application appears on the Start menu, even if the application is not installed. Published applications do not. They simply appear in Add/Remove Programs.

○ B. Yes, but Siobhan could have assigned or published the software because the end result when targeting computers is the same.

○ C. No, this simply will not work. Siobhan cannot publish software to a computer. She can only assign software to computers. However, both options are available for users.

○ D. No, this is not the best solution. Siobhan should assign the software to the computers. Published packages appear on the Start menu.

Answer C is correct. When one is making distributions to a computer, the Published option is grayed out. Software can only be *assigned* to computers. Answer A is incorrect because it does not state that Siobhan cannot publish an application to a computer. Answer B is incorrect because it fails to recognize the difference between assigning and publishing an application. Answer D is incorrect because it mistakenly suggests that published applications show up on the Start menu—they do not.

# Question 8

Which of the following constitute the phases of software deployment? [Check all that apply.]

❏ A. Preparation

❏ B. Distribution

❏ C. Targeting

❏ D. Pilot Program

❏ E. Installation

Answers A, B, C, D, and E are correct. The prescribed method of performing a software deployment is to have five phases: Preparation, Distribution, Targeting, Pilot Program, and Installation.

# Question 9

How would you determine whether a user has an appropriate level of permissions to execute a managed application? [Choose the best answer.]

- ○ A. Through the Security tab in the package's properties in Software Installation
- ○ B. Through the Deployment tab in the package's properties in Software Installation
- ○ C. Through OU membership in Active Directory Users and Computers
- ○ D. Through GPO membership in Active Directory Users and Computers

Answer A is correct. The key to this question is the permission to execute a managed application. Permissions for managed applications are set through the Security tab in the package's properties in the Software Installation extension. Answer B is incorrect because the Deployment tab is used to configure other package properties, such as whether it is assigned or published. Answers C and D are incorrect because Active Directory Users and Computers is used to control security group membership as a whole rather than setting permissions on a particular resource.

# Question 10

In which software deployment phase would you create and/or modify GPOs? [Choose the best answer.]

- ○ A. Preparation
- ○ B. Distribution
- ○ C. Targeting
- ○ D. Pilot Program
- ○ E. Installation

Answer C is correct. The targeting phase is used to create and/or modify GPOs that will be the target of the software package. Answer A is incorrect because, in the preparation phase, you determine who the target will be, but you do not actually create GPOs at that point. Answer B is incorrect because the distribution phase involves setting up the source files on distribution points you have created. Answer D is incorrect because the pilot program phase involves testing the software on a limited number of users, and answer E is incorrect because the installation phase is the actual deployment.

# Need to Know More?

 Morimoto, Rand, et al. *Windows Server 2003 Unleashed.* Sams Publishing. Indianapolis, IN, 2003. ISBN 0672321548.

 Jones, Don and Mark Rouse. *Windows Server 2003 Delta Guide.* Sams Publishing. Indianapolis, IN, 2003. ISBN 0789728494.

**8**

# Understanding Security
# Settings with Group Policy

. . . . . . . . . . . . . . . . . . . . . . . . . . . . . . . . . . . . . . . . . . . .

### Terms you'll need to understand:

✓ Scripts
✓ Windows Script Host (WSH)
✓ Folder Redirection
✓ Offline Folders
✓ Templates
✓ User profiles
✓ Roaming profiles
✓ Mandatory profiles

### Techniques you'll need to master:

✓ Controlling user environments by using administrative
   templates
✓ Managing security configurations
✓ Assigning script policies to users and computers
✓ Using Folder Redirection

Group Policy is ubiquitous in a Windows Server 2003 environment. As soon as you install Active Directory, or join a Windows-based client to an Active Directory environment, Group Policy will play a role.

Group Policy is used to apply many settings that we once considered as simply being "automatically" applied in Windows NT 4.0 domains. Settings such as password complexity, expiration dates for passwords, and the number of false logins that can be tried before a user account is locked out are all, in Windows Server 2003, Group Policy settings.

These settings, and many more, can be used to make an environment more secure. Security has risen to the top of enterprise-level concerns over the years. Now, more than ever, security is a major concern. Group Policy allows a uniform, targeted application of settings to servers and clients alike. In this chapter we will be taking a look at some of the ways Group Policy can used and how Microsoft has made using Group Policy easier with standardized templates.

# Controlling User Environments with Administrative Templates

Administrative templates provide the primary means of administering the user environment and defining the end-user computing experience. As an administrator, you can use administrative templates to deny access to certain operating system functionality (for example, the ability to add or remove programs). Additionally, you can define settings such as the wallpaper and screensaver to use on a system, and you can rely on Windows Server 2003 to enforce those settings.

For the exam, you will need to know the following about the use of administrative templates:

➤ ADM files and their structure

➤ Applying Computer and User templates

## ADM Files and Their Structure

Administrative templates are stored in Windows Server 2003 as text files in one of two places. The first is <systemroot>\inf, which contains the generic templates that install with the operating system. The second is a copy stored in specific Group Policy Templates (GPTs). An example of this would be the `\WINDOWS\SYSVOL\sysvol\`*`domain`*`\Policies\`*`GUID`*`\Adm` folder. These files carry an `.adm` file extension. A real-world example of this is the following directory structure on a Windows Server 2003 domain controller in my own domain: `C:\WINDOWS\SYSVOL\sysvol\main.windows2003.local\Policies\ {31B2F340-016D-11D2-945F-00C04FB984F9}\Adm`.

*GUID* in this example is the Global Unique Identifier assigned to a specific Group Policy. If you have many Group Policies, you might have many different ADM files.

Windows Server 2003 includes four standard administrative templates. Along with these are five additional ADM files for backward compatibility. Besides this, applications such as Microsoft Office might also introduce their own sets of ADM files. Here's a list of the standard ADM files:

➤ `System.adm`—This file is installed by default in Group Policy. It contains policy settings that affect the Explorer shell.

➤ `Inetres.adm`—This file is installed by default in Group Policy. It contains Internet Explorer policies along with policies that affect the Control Panel, offline pages, browser menus, and so on.

➤ `Conf.adm`—This file contains settings to configure NetMeeting.

➤ `Wmplayer.adm`—This file contains settings for Windows Media Player.

Here are the ADM files included for backward compatibility:

➤ `Inetset.adm`—This file contains Internet Explorer settings for older clients.

➤ `Inetcorp.adm`—This file contains settings for Internet Explorer, such as languages and dial-up restrictions.

➤ `Winnt.adm`—This file contains user interface options for Windows NT 4.0 systems and is used with the System Policy Editor (`poledit.exe`).

➤ `Windows.adm`—This file contains user interface options for Windows 9x systems and is used with the System Policy Editor (`poledit.exe`).

➤ `Common.adm`—This file contains user interface options common to both Windows NT 4.0 and Windows 9x systems.

Don't forget, you might have other administrative templates on your system as well, depending on what you have installed on your system.

## ADM Structure

An ADM file is a text file, so it can be edited with a text editor such as Notepad. You can open any of the ADM files listed previously to view the settings, and you can even modify them if desired. However, it is not recommended that you modify the default administrative templates. You can create new administrative templates if you need to, though, because Windows Server 2003 is flexible enough to let you tailor Group Policy to your specific network environment.

The following is an edited sample file from the conf.adm administrative template. Following this sample file is a description of the file's structure and a definition of the variables you can use when creating an administrative template:

```
; NetMeeting policy settings
#if version <= 2
;;;;;;;;;;;;;;;;;;;;;;;;;;;;;;;
 CLASS USER   ;;;;;;;;;;;;;;;;;
;;;;;;;;;;;;;;;;;;;;;;;;;;;;;;;
CATEGORY !!WindowsComponents
CATEGORY !!NetMeeting
         ; App Sharing
            CATEGORY !!AppSharing
            POLICY !!DisableAppSharing
            KEYNAME "Software\Policies\Microsoft\Conferencing"
            EXPLAIN !!DisableAppSharing_Help
            VALUENAME "NoAppSharing"
            END POLICY
            POLICY !!PreventSharing
            KEYNAME "Software\Policies\Microsoft\Conferencing"
            EXPLAIN !!PreventSharing_Help
            VALUENAME "NoSharing"
            END POLICY
            POLICY !!PreventGrantingControl
            KEYNAME "Software\Policies\Microsoft\Conferencing"
            EXPLAIN !!PreventGrantingControl_Help
            VALUENAME "NoAllowControl"
            END POLICY
            POLICY !!PreventSharingTrueColor
            KEYNAME "Software\Policies\Microsoft\Conferencing"
            EXPLAIN !!PreventSharingTrueColor_Help
            VALUENAME "NoTrueColorSharing"
            END POLICY
END CATEGORY ; AppSharing
[strings]
WindowsComponents="Windows Components"
NetMeeting="NetMeeting"
AppSharing="Application Sharing"
DisableAppSharing="Disable application Sharing"
DisableAppSharing_Help="Disables the application sharing feature of
NetMeeting completely.  Users will not be able to host or view shared
applications."
PreventSharing="Prevent Sharing"
PreventSharing_Help="Prevents users from sharing anything themselves.
They will still be able to view shared applications/desktops from
others."
PreventGrantingControl="Prevent Control"
PreventGrantingControl_Help="Prevents users from allowing others in a
```

```
conference to control what they have shared. This enforces a
read-only mode; the other participants cannot change the data in the
shared application."
PreventSharingTrueColor="Prevent Application Sharing in true color"
PreventSharingTrueColor_Help="Prevents users from sharing applications
in true color. True color sharing uses more bandwidth in a conference."
```

The structure of the preceding sample file is fairly simple. The header at the top defines what the purpose of the file is. It is a comment, as denoted by the semicolon at the beginning of the line. The semicolon tells Windows not to process the line when parsing the file. Following the description are sections and variables defined by the following keywords:

➤ CLASS—The first entry in the administrative template file, the CLASS keyword can either be MACHINE or USER, which defines whether the section includes entries in the Computer Configuration or User Configuration containers in Group Policy.

➤ CATEGORY—The CATEGORY keyword is what's displayed in the Group Policy Editor as a node under Computer Configuration or User Configuration. Whether the category is located under the MACHINE or USER class determines which node it is located under. In the preceding example, the categories under the USER class define the Windows Components, NetMeeting, and Application Sharing subnodes under User Configuration.

➤ POLICY—The POLICY keyword defines the policies available for modification in the Group Policy Editor. In the administrative template, the POLICY keyword specifies a variable that is defined in the STRINGS section at the bottom of the file.

➤ KEYNAME—The KEYNAME keyword defines the Registry location for the policy the key name is associated with.

➤ EXPLAIN—The EXPLAIN keyword is used to supply help text for a policy setting. When viewing the properties of a policy in the Group Policy Editor, you'll see an Explain tab that contains the help text specified here. Actually, in the administrative template the EXPLAIN keyword specifies a variable that is defined with the help text in the STRINGS section at the bottom of the file.

➤ VALUENAME—The VALUENAME keyword is also associated with the POLICY keyword, and it defines the options available within a policy. It defines the values located within the Registry key specified by the KEYNAME keyword.

➤ STRINGS—The STRINGS section defines the variables used earlier in the file for the keywords POLICY and EXPLAIN.

Putting it all together, Figure 8.1 shows the results. In this figure, we have the Group Policy Editor with the previous administrative template as the focus of the editor. You can see the User Configuration container expanded to the Windows Components, NetMeeting, Application Sharing nodes, which were defined by the CATEGORY keyword. There you'll find the policies defined by the POLICY keywords in the right-side window pane, such as Disable Application Sharing and Prevent Sharing.

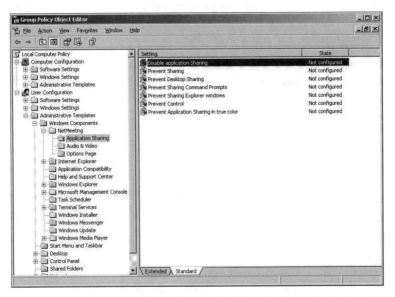

**Figure 8.1** The available entries in the Group Policy Editor reflect the contents of the administrative template.

In Figure 8.1, note the two tabs at the bottom of the screen: Standard and Extended. The former shows the console view, similar to the one we had in Windows 2000. However, by clicking the latter, you can see a new view, where a description of the policy setting is viewable. This is shown in Figure 8.2.

Creating administrative templates on your own allows you to define custom settings for your network. This is beneficial for those situations where the built-in policies are not sufficient enough. This is an easier solution than having a developer write a custom Group Policy extension with a Software Development Kit (SDK). Windows Server 2003 includes everything you need to write an administrative template, which can then be added (or later removed) from a GPO, as you'll see in the following section.

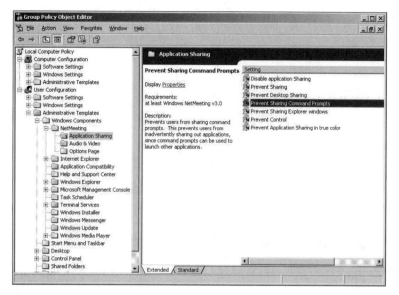

**Figure 8.2** The Extended tab shows a policy description.

# Adding and Removing Administrative Templates

After you've created a custom administrative template, it needs to be added to the GPO in order to be used. It is important to note that your custom administrative templates must be added to *each* GPO you want them to apply to.

To add or remove an administrative template, right-click the appropriate Administrative Templates folder in the Group Policy Editor (either under Computer Configuration or User Configuration) and select Add/Remove Templates. Figure 8.3 shows the resulting dialog box, which shows the currently installed administrative templates. You can remove an existing one by selecting it and clicking Remove, or you can add an administrative template by clicking the Add button. If you click Add, you will see the dialog box shown in Figure 8.4.

Once you add an administrative template, the additional nodes and policies will appear under the administrative template's node you added the template to.

Although it is important to understand how administrative templates are constructed and how to add and remove templates, the majority of your experience with administrative templates will be in using them to apply policy settings.

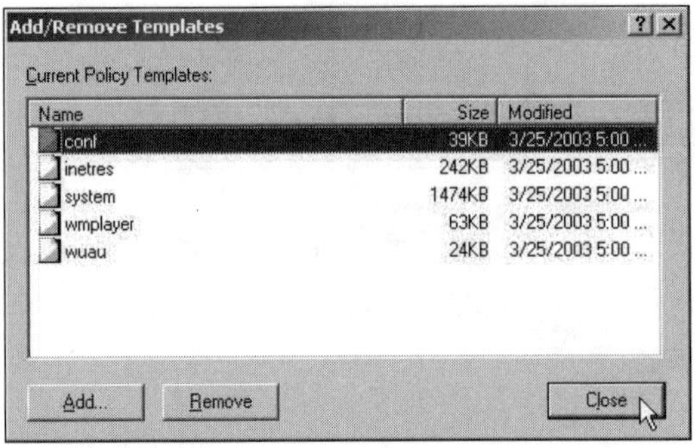

**Figure 8.3** When you choose Add/Remove Templates, you first see a listing of currently installed administrative templates.

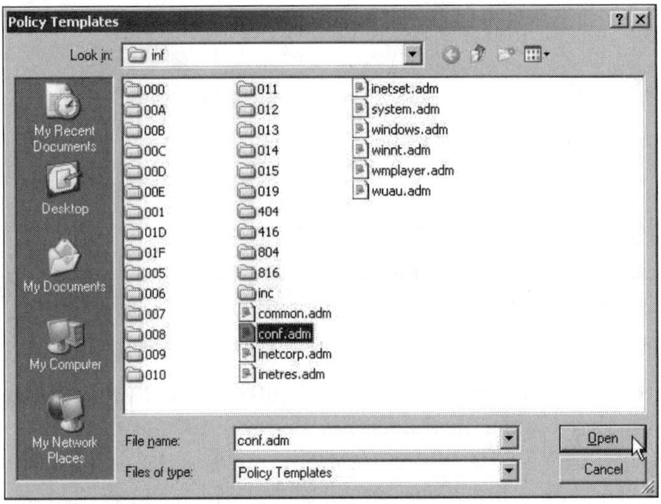

**Figure 8.4** Choosing to add an administrative template allows you to browse for an ADM file to add to the current GPO.

# Applying Computer and User Templates

Administrative templates allow an administrator to exert a measure of control over the user environment. In this section, we'll look at the types of configuration settings available with Group Policy and then examine a couple scenarios where we would use administrative templates to manage a Windows Server 2003 network.

There are two different Administrative Templates sections within a Group Policy Object. One is under the Computer Configuration container, and the other is under the User Configuration container. As you would expect, these separate nodes determine whether policies apply to computer accounts or user accounts. Let's look at the similarities between the two and then the differences.

## Common Administrative Templates Categories

Regardless of whether the Administrative Templates container is under the Computer Configuration or User Configuration container, some common categories create nodes under the Administrative Templates container:

➤ *Windows Components*—Contains configuration settings for common Windows components, such as Internet Explorer, Task Scheduler, NetMeeting, Windows Explorer, Windows Installer, and Microsoft Management Console (MMC). The policies that exist for these categories control the behavior of the programs—from what functionality is available to the user, to configuring the features of an application.

➤ *System*—Contains configuration settings that do not really fall neatly under any other category within the administrative templates. Here, policies exist for logon/logoff, disk quotas, Windows File Protection, Group Policy, DNS client, and general settings, such as whether Registry editing is allowed and whether certain applications should not be allowed to run.

➤ *Network*—Contains configuration settings for network options, such as Offline Folders and Network and Dialup Connections. Offline Folders are discussed later in this chapter. Different policy options are available depending on whether you are under the Computer Configuration or User Configuration container.

Additionally, the nodes discussed in the following subsections exist under either Computer Configuration or User Configuration, but not both.

### Computer Configuration Administrative Templates

Computer template settings are stored under the HKEY_LOCAL_MACHINE hive in the Registry.

Here's the administrative template that exists only under the Computer Configuration container:

➤ *Printers*—The Printers category contains configuration settings for printers and their properties. Through these policies you can control the publication of printers into Active Directory, allow printer browsing, and allow Web-based printing, among other policy settings.

### User Configuration Administrative Templates

User templates are stored under the HKEY_CURRENT_USER hive in the Registry.

Here are the administrative templates that exist under the User Configuration container:

➤ *Start Menu & Taskbar*—Controls the appearance and behavior of the Start menu and the Taskbar. Through this administrative template you can remove functionality such as the ability to search or remove the Run line from the Start menu. Additionally, you can alter the default behavior of the Start menu, such as clearing the Documents folder upon exiting or not allowing users to change the configuration of the Start menu.

➤ *Desktop*—The Desktop policy settings compliment the policy settings under the Start Menu & Taskbar category. You can configure the behavior of the Active Desktop, such as the wallpaper to use, filtering in Active Directory searches, controlling the appearance of desktop icons, and specifying whether any changes made by users will be saved upon exiting Windows.

➤ *Control Panel*—Contains settings that determine what level of functionality is available to users in the Control Panel. These policies can include Add/Remove Programs, Display, Printers, Regional Options, and even whether the Control Panel is available to Windows users.

➤ *Shared Folders*—Contains settings that define whether shared folders or Dfs roots can be published in Active Directory.

# Policy Application Scenarios

As an administrator, you will run into different circumstances that require different applications of Group Policy. In order to create an effective usage policy, you must first analyze your environment and determine your requirements. To that extent, let's look at a couple scenarios and how you might approach them.

# Policy Application Scenario #1

In the first scenario, you are the network administrator for a retail chain of computer superstores. Specifically, you are in charge of a customer ordering system where customers can access Windows systems to create custom computer configurations for "build to order" systems right in the store. These orders are fed into a database, and credit cards can be processed.

In this type of environment, you would have users accessing your network who are nonemployees. You would not want them to be able to alter the operating system or the user environment in any way. To reach that goal, you would want to use the Start Menu & Taskbar, Desktop, and Control Panel nodes in the User Configuration container to prevent changes from being made. These policies would include disabling the Control Panel, removing the Run line from the Start menu, hiding all icons on the desktop, and preventing changes from being saved upon exiting. Additionally, you would use settings under the System node in both Computer Configuration and User Configuration to disable Registry editing, so that a savvy customer who wanted to be malicious couldn't get around your policy settings by disabling them in the Registry, and to disable the command prompt so programs could not be executed there.

These settings essentially lock down the user environment, which is what you would want in this type of scenario. In the following scenario, however, that type of network policy would be counterproductive and inappropriate.

# Policy Application Scenario #2

Consider a scenario where you are the network administrator of a medium-sized company that has a Windows Server 2003 network. The environment is not highly secure, nor is there a real need to limit functionality. However, there are three shifts of workers who use the company computers. Therefore, you have three people using each computer in the company each day.

In this scenario, you would want to use Group Policy to define a common desktop for corporate use and to discard any user changes upon exiting. There are actually a couple ways you could approach this. One way would be to create roaming profiles that follow each user wherever he or she goes. With the high number of users accessing the computers, it would be more desirable to simply create a "corporate standard" and define the desktop appearance across all computers.

To reach this goal, you would use the Control Panel\Display policies under the User Configuration container to disable changing the wallpaper and to specify a screensaver. With the Desktop\Active Desktop policies you would specify the wallpaper to be used. With the Start Menu & Taskbar policies you would disable changes to the Start menu and the Taskbar, disable personalized menus, and remove the user's folders from the Start menu.

These settings create a computing environment that has a consistent look and feel across all corporate systems, while still allowing full operating system and application functionality to the users.

With Group Policy you can also manage security configurations for Windows Server 2003, as you will see next.

# Managing Security Configurations

Group Policy can also be used to manage security settings on a Windows Server 2003 network. Under the Windows Settings node in both the Computer Configuration and User Configuration containers is a node for security settings. The vast majority of the settings apply to computer policies, as only user security settings are related to Public Key Policies (which also exists under Computer Configuration). The security categories available and their purpose are as follows:

➤ *Account Policies*—Contains settings related to user accounts, and applies at the domain level. You can configure the password policy for a domain (minimum length, uniqueness, minimum password age, and so on), the account lockout policy (whether accounts should be locked out, how many bad password attempts are allowed before lockout, the length of time after lockout before the counter is reset), and the Kerberos policy (maximum lifetime for tickets, ticket renewal threshold, and so on).

Account Policies are the only settings applied through Group Policy that do not follow the default behavior. These policies should always be configured and linked at the domain level. These settings cannot be overridden by any other conflicting policy, even if the policy is set at an OU.

➤ *Local Policies*—Contains settings for local system policies, including audit policies, user rights assignment, and security options. Auditing can be used to log the success or failure of common events, such as logging on and logging off, accessing objects, using permissions, and directory service access, among other events. User rights assignment allows you to control user rights for users and groups, such as the ability to log on locally, log on as a service, change the system time, shut down the system, and take ownership of objects, among other settings. Security options are numerous. As you can see from Figure 8.5, there's a wealth of policy settings you can configure for local security.

➤ *Public Key Policies*—Enables you to add policy settings to manage public key–related security items, such as trusted Certificate Authorities. You can also add additional Encrypted Data Recovery Agents, if desired.

➤ *Software Restriction Policies*—With software restriction policy settings, you can protect your computing environment from nontrusted software by identifying and specifying which software is allowed to run.

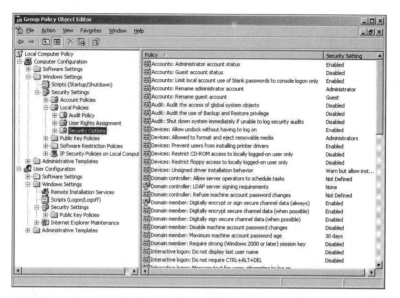

**Figure 8.5** Numerous local security policy settings can be configured with Group Policy on a Windows Server 2003 system.

➤ *IP Security Policies on Local Computer*—Contains policy settings for the IPSec security protocol. These settings allow you to tell your server or client how to respond or how to request IPSec communication requests.

The use of these security settings allows you as an administrator to provide a much tighter level of security than what is configured by default when you install Windows Server 2003. If it seems like a daunting task, though, to go through and configure security, you can use one of the security templates that Windows Server 2003 includes for use on your network.

# Security Templates

Security templates in Windows Server 2003 are sets of profiles that can be imported into a GPO, and they provide a specific level of security for Windows Server 2003 domain controllers, servers, and clients. There are two different sets of templates, stored in different locations. Let's take a look at the templates stored in <systemroot>\security\templates first:

➤ *Compatible*—Decreases security over the basic template to allow members of the local Users group to be able to run non–Windows Server 2003–compliant applications with elevated Power Users privileges. This is useful for environments where administrators do not want standard users to have to be members of the Power Users group (which grants substantial additional privileges over the Users group) in order to run legacy applications that will not run without Power User permissions.

➤ *Secure*—This template removes all members from the Power Users group and modifies security settings that pertain to the behavior of the operating system and network protocols rather than application functionality. Settings of this type include password and audit policies and Registry settings.

➤ *High Secure*—This template goes beyond the Secure template to extreme security measures. In doing so, it has no regard for functionality, performance, connectivity with computers running an operating system prior to Windows 2000, and ease of use. As an example, the Secure template might warn you if you attempt to install an unsigned driver. The High Secure template would simply block the installation of the unsigned driver without giving you the opportunity to override it.

To implement security templates, right-click the Security Settings folder under the Computer Configuration container (this will *not* work under the User Configuration container) and click Import Policy. You will be presented with the dialog box shown in Figure 8.6.

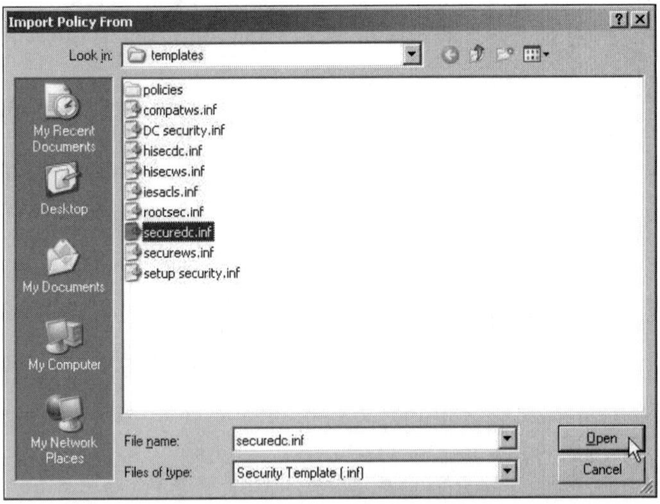

**Figure 8.6** You can import Windows Server 2003 security templates into a Group Policy Object through the Computer Configuration container's Import Policy command.

Table 8.1 defines the available security templates.

**Table 8.1  Windows Server 2003 Security Templates**

| Template Name | Definition |
|---|---|
| COMPATWS.INF | Opens up the default permissions for the Users group so that legacy applications are more likely to run |
| DC SECURITY.INF | Default settings (Updated) for domain controllers |
| HISECDC.INF | High-security settings for a domain controller |
| HISECWS.INF | High-security settings for a Windows 2000 Professional system |
| SECUREDC.INF | Secure domain controller settings |
| SECUREWS.INF | Secure Windows 2000 Professional settings |
| SETUP SECURITY.INF | Default settings applied after installation (installation defaults) |
| IESACLS.INF | Default settings for Internet Explorer |
| ROOTSEC.INF | Applies default root permissions for the OS partition |

Another way to use Group Policy to manage the user environment is through script policies, as you'll see in the next section.

The second set of security template files are stored in <systemroot>\inf. These security templates are applied during the setup process and are defined in Table 8.2.

**Table 8.2  Windows Server 2003 Setup Security Templates**

| Template Name | Definition |
|---|---|
| DEFLTSV.INF | Applied when a server is installed from scratch |
| DEFLTDC.INF | Applied when a server is promoted to a domain controller |
| DSUP.INF | Applied when a server is upgraded from Windows 2000 or NT 4.0 |
| DCUP5.INF | Applied when a DC is upgraded from a Windows 2000 DC |
| DSUPT.INF | Applied when a server is upgraded from NT 4.0 Terminal Server Edition or when a Windows 2000 Server is installed in application mode |
| DCFIRST.INF | Applied to the first server promoted to a DC in a domain |

# Assigning Script Policies to Users and Computers

Windows Server 2003 offers a significant role for scripts in managing the user environment. In previous versions of Windows NT, scripts were limited to batch files that could only be run at startup. With Windows Server 2003, however, scripts can be run at any or all of the following times:

➤ *Startup*—Computer scripts that run under the Local System account and apply settings during computer startup, before the user logon dialog box is presented.

➤ *Logon*—Traditional user login scripts that run when the user logs on to the system. The scripts run under the user account they are associated with. Logon scripts are executed only after computer startup scripts have been processed by Windows Server 2003.

➤ *Logoff*—User scripts that run when the user either chooses Start, Logoff or chooses to shut down or restart the computer. Logoff scripts are executed before computer shutdown scripts.

➤ *Shutdown*—Computer scripts that run when the computer is shut down. As with startup scripts, shutdown scripts run under the Local System account to apply settings at the computer level.

Additionally, Windows Server 2003 allows you to go beyond the limitations of DOS-based batch files into ActiveX scripting using the VBScript and JavaScript (also known as *JScript*) engines. To support these ActiveX scripting engines, Windows Server 2003 provides the Windows Script Host.

# Windows Script Host

The Windows Script Host (WSH) is a scripting host that allows you to run VBScript (.vbs) and JavaScript (.js) scripts natively on 32-bit Windows platforms. That means you can execute VBScript or JScript scripts just as you would DOS batch files. WSH is extensible, so in the future you might be able to run third-party scripts natively as well, such as Perl or Python.

Windows Server 2003 ships with Windows Script Host 5.6. WSH 5.6 replaces Windows Scripting Host 2.0, which shipped with Windows 2000. WSH 5.6 is fully backward compatible, and it's able to run any 1.0 scripts onward. It is beyond the scope this chapter to point out the differences between the 2.0 and 5.6 versions.

Windows Script Host comes with two executable files:

➤ WScript.exe

➤ CScript.exe

## WScript

WScript.exe is the graphical version of WSH, and it allows you to run VBScript and JScript scripts inside of Windows by double-clicking the filename. You can also execute WScript.exe from the Run line in the Start menu. Here's the syntax:

```
wscript <script name>
```

You must specify the path to the script in <script name> for it to execute properly if the script is not located in a directory included in the environment variable PATH statement. WScript provides the following properties that can be configured:

➤ *Stop script after specified number of seconds*—This setting specifies the maximum length of time a script can run. By default, there is not a time limit placed on script execution.

➤ *Display logo when script is executed in a command console*—This setting will display a WSH banner while running the script. This setting is turned on by default.

## CScript

CScript.exe is the command-line version of WSH, and it's useful when you need to specify parameters at runtime. CScript is great for the computer and user scripts that are executed during startup, logon, logoff, and shutdown. Here's the syntax of CScript.exe:

```
cscript <script name> <script options and parameters>
```

And here are the definitions for its options:

➤ <script name>—The full path and filename of the script to be executed by CScript.exe.

➤ <script options and parameters>—Used to enable or disable various WSH features. Options are preceded by two forward slashes, as in //logo. Table 8.3 summarizes the host options.

| Table 8.3 | Windows Script Host Options and Their Meanings |
|-----------|------------------------------------------------|
| **Option** | **Definition** |
| //B | Batch Mode. Suppresses script errors and any user prompts that might display. The Computer and User scripts we'll discuss in this chapter typically have this option specified. |
| //I | Interactive Mode. This is the opposite of Batch Mode. Interactive Mode is the default if neither is specified. |
| //Logo | Displays a logo banner during script execution, which is the default setting if not explicitly specified. |

| Table 8.3 Windows Script Host Options and Their Meanings *(continued)* | |
|---|---|
| Option | Definition |
| //Nologo | Disables the logo banner from displaying during script execution. |
| //H:WScript | Changes the default script host to WScript. This is the default setting if none is explicitly specified. |
| //H:CScript | Changes the default script to CScript. |
| //E:*engine* | Specifies which engine to use in executing the script—either the VBScript or JScript engine can be specified. |
| //T:nn | The timeout in seconds. The maximum amount of time the script is allowed to run before it is terminated by the script host. |
| //D | The debugger. This setting enables Active Debugging. |
| //X | Executes the script in the debugger. |
| //S | Save. This setting saves the current command-line options for this user. |
| //Job:*<jobID>* | Runs the specified job ID from a WSH 2.0 **.wsf** file. |
| //U | Tells WSH to use Unicode for redirected I/O from the console. |
| //? | Displays the help file for syntax and options. |

# Assigning Scripts Through Group Policy

The hardest part about implementing scripts on a Windows Server 2003 network is the actual writing of the scripts. Assigning scripts through Group Policy, though, is easily accomplished.

Startup and shutdown scripts apply to computers, and logon and logoff scripts apply to users. As you know, the Group Policy Editor divides the GPO into two main nodes: Computer Configuration and User Configuration. The Scripts node is located under the Windows Settings node in each container, and parentheses indicate the type of scripts that the node supports.

To apply a script, simply click the Scripts node under the appropriate container. Then double-click the desired script, such as the startup script. This brings up the dialog box shown in Figure 8.7.

In the script's Properties dialog box, click the Add button to add a new script. This will bring up the dialog box shown in Figure 8.8.

You can type in the name (and path, if applicable) of the script you want to use if you know it. Otherwise, you can just click Browse. Select the script you want to use, as shown in Figure 8.9, and click Open. This will return you to the dialog box shown in Figure 8.8. Enter any parameters, such as `//Nologo`, and click OK.

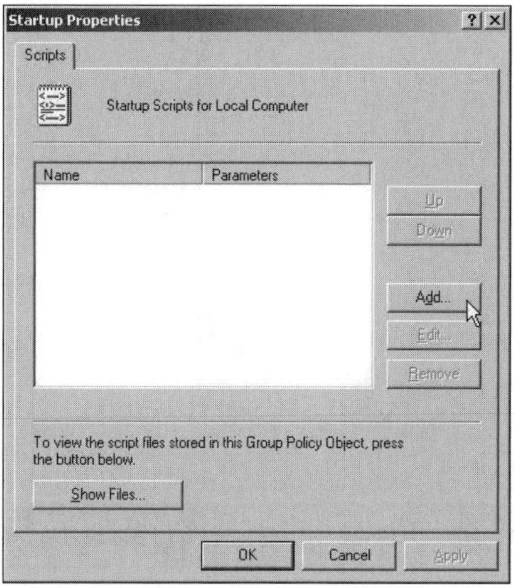

**Figure 8.7**   Double-clicking a script brings up this dialog box.

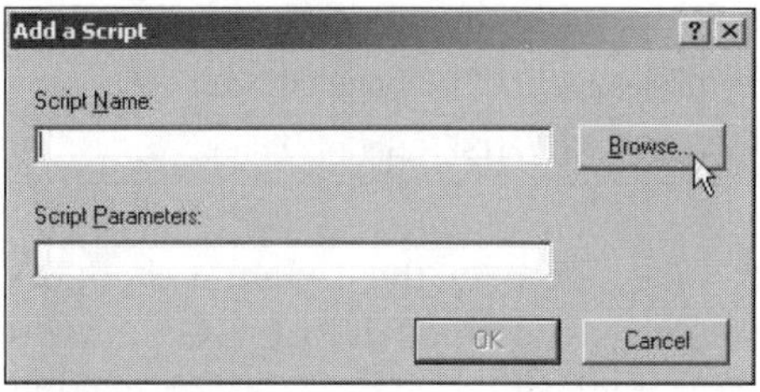

**Figure 8.8**   The Add a Script dialog box allows you to specify a script name and script parameters.

Although it is not recommended that you use other locations for the storage of scripts other than the default directories, shown in Table 8.4, it is important to note that when you're assigning a script through Group Policy, the script can be located on any drive and folder the system can read. This is in contrast to Windows NT 4.0, which required login scripts to be located in the NETLOGON share, which was located at \winnt\system32\repl\ import\scripts.

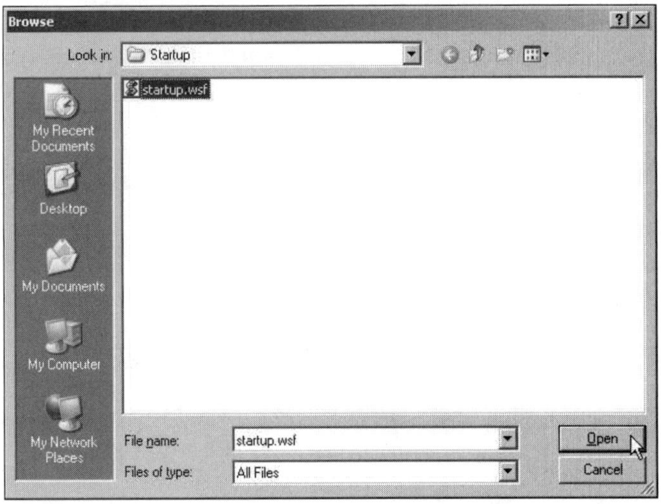

**Figure 8.9**  After selecting the script you want to assign, click Open.

| Table 8.4 The Default Directories for Windows Server 2003 Scripts When Assigned from a GPO | |
|---|---|
| **Script** | **Directory** |
| Startup | \winnt\sysvol\sysvol\\*domain*\Policies\\*GUID*\MACHINE\Scripts\Startup |
| Shutdown | \winnt\sysvol\sysvol\\*domain*\Policies\\*GUID*\MACHINE\Scripts\Shutdown |
| Logon | \winnt\sysvol\sysvol\\*domain*\Policies\\*GUID*\USER\Scripts\Logon |
| Logoff | \winnt\sysvol\sysvol\\*domain*\Policies\\*GUID*\USER\Scripts\Logoff |

In Windows NT, scripts and other files placed in the \winnt\system32\repl\export\scripts directory were replicated to the NETLOGON shares on domain controllers configured for replication. The File Replication Service (FRS) in Windows Server 2003 has replaced the NT 4.0 and earlier Directory Replication Service and now replicates the entire SYSVOL directory tree across all domain controllers (it uses the same system as Windows 2000).

The exception to the recommendation about not changing the default location for scripts is if you are supporting legacy clients on your network (Windows 9x, Windows NT 4.0). For these clients, you should copy the relevant logon scripts to the NETLOGON share, which in Windows Server 2003 is located under the \winnt\sysvol\sysvol\\*domain*\scripts directory. Legacy clients cannot use the Windows Server 2003 features of startup, shutdown, and logoff scripts, so the NETLOGON share exists for backward compatibility with their logon script capabilities.

# Use of Folder Redirection

One of the early goals for local area networks was that all user data could be stored on central servers, where mass storage was cheaper, and could be protected through stringent backup routines. This goal was never fully realized, as technology took over.

One of the issues that prevented this was that hard disks simply got cheaper and cheaper. The relative cost of storing a huge amount of user data centrally became higher, whereas the cost of local storage continued in a downward spiral. Also, easy-to-use and flexible tools to make sure data was stored on a server never existed.

This changed in Windows 2000 with the introduction of *Folder Redirection*, which is the simple concept of having data redirected from local storage to server storage, transparently for the user.

The success of this technology did not only come about with the introduction of an easy-to-use tool. You see, another problem that prevented this idea from gaining ground was that the application developers used to store data all over a hard disk. There never existed a standard location for document storage, policy storage, and so on. This changed when Microsoft changed its logo standards for application developers, which stated that the default location for data storage should be *My Documents*. Having an existing default meant it was much easier to design a technology to enforce it.

Although the general concept of Folder Redirection has not changed very much in the move from Windows 2000 to Windows Server 2003, some significant changes will be outlined here.

First of all, you should note that not all folders can be redirected. Microsoft has included those folders that are defined in logo-compliant applications:

➤ *Application Data*—Contains user-configuration files, and user-specific data used by applications

➤ *Desktop*—Contains the icons and documents displayed on the user's desktop

➤ *My Documents*—Contains user documents and pictures

➤ *Start Menu*—Contains the files and shortcuts displayed on the Start menu

Folder Redirection is useful from an administrative standpoint for backups. In most environments, user workstations are not backed up. By having folders redirected to a server share, the files are usually backed up. That provides an extra measure of protection against potential data loss.

Folder Redirection is part of Group Policies and is configurable from within the Group Policy Editor. You will find it under User Configuration, Windows Settings, Folder Redirection.

When you right-click one of the special folders in the Group Policy Editor and choose Properties, the first dialog box you see contains the target setting. By default, this is Not Configured. You can change this to either of the following settings:

➤ *Basic - Redirect Everyone's Folder to the Same Location*—This policy will redirect all folders to the same network share.

➤ *Advanced - Specify Locations for Various Groups*—The Advanced policy allows you to redirect folders based on security group memberships. Members of one group can have folders directed to one share, and members of another group can have folders redirected to a different share.

Once you have chosen one of these options, you are then presented with an option to define the location and name for the redirected folders. This is shown in Figure 8.10.

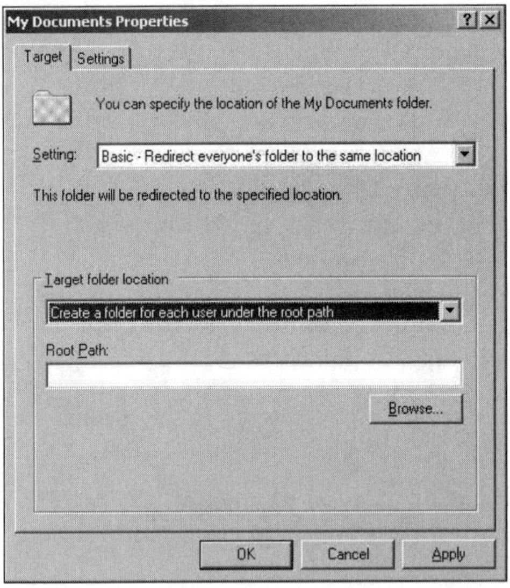

**Figure 8.10** The Target tab of the My Documents Properties dialog box.

Four options are available under Target Folder Location:

➤ *Redirect to the user's home directory*—This option is new in Windows Server 2003 and allows you to leverage a traditional home folder structure on a server.

**NOTE**

This setting is only available to Windows Server 2003 and Windows XP clients!

➤ *Create a folder for each user under the root path*—This feature is new to Windows Server 2003. If you select this option, you must enter a Universal Naming Convention (UNC) path. The system then uses the %username% variable and appends this data to the folder name, followed by a folder called My Documents.

➤ *Redirect to the following location*—With this option you specify an UNC path, with the %username% variable, followed by My Documents. This choice has the benefit of being backward compatible with Windows 2000 and down-level clients.

➤ *Redirect to the local user profile location*—This essentially is an "undo" function that works to put any folders that have previously been redirected back to the user's local systems.

Once you have decided on the location, you should make some selections that affect permissions. These are done from the Settings tab of the Properties dialog box shown in Figure 8.11.

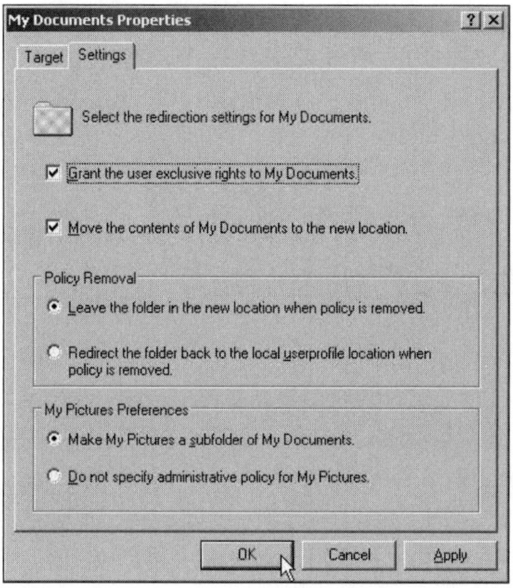

**Figure 8.11** The Settings tab of the My Documents Properties dialog box.

These settings allow you to define how the clients will react if the policy is removed and what permissions the clients will receive for their newly redirected folders. These options are self-explanatory and will not be covered further.

# Automatically Enrolling Certificates with Group Policy

If I said that privacy and protection are important in today's networks, you'd probably start thinking I was a little behind the times. In this day and age, security is high on everyone's priority list (or should be).

Like all good ideas, the acceptance of a given technology has a relation to its complexity, cost, and ease of deployment. Sadly, we can't do much about the complexity of understanding the details of a Public Key Infrastructure (PKI). In fact, entire books have been written about this subject, so we will not be able to go into too many details here.

However, you should know that PKI is all about giving users confidentiality when transmitting or receiving data. It also covers authentication and integrity.

PKI does its work by using various components. One of these components is the *certificate*, which provides a client and server the ability to exchange cipher keys used by encryption algorithms. Although this is all beyond the scope of this book, you will need to know how to automatically enroll users and computers to get their certificates.

 NOTE | Windows Server 2003 has two new features you should know about. The first is that computers and users can be "autoenrolled" for user certificates using Group Policy, which is the subject of this section. The second is the ability to recover keys if they are lost or erased. Although this is not a topic for this section, it is worth noting as a point of interest.

The method used for autoenrollment is similar to what you saw earlier with security templates. In this case, there are certificate templates stored within Active Directory. These templates are applied if a computer or user has been targeted.

To confuse matters, Windows Server 2003 uses "Version 2" templates (Windows 2000 used Version 1 templates). It goes without saying that these two are not completely interchangeable—Windows 2000 Active Directory cannot use Version 2 certificates because some schema components are missing.

It gets even more complex, because not all versions of the Windows Server 2003 operating system can support this feature. The Windows Server 2003 Standard Edition lacks the necessary features to support Version 2 templates. To use them, you must have Windows Server 2003 Enterprise or Datacenter Edition.

# Implementing Autoenrollment

Like many of the new features found in Windows Server 2003, autoenrollment with Version 2 templates is only available to Windows Server 2003 and Windows XP clients. In Windows 2000, computers could be configured to autoenroll, but users could not. In other words, even with a full Windows Server 2003 environment, user enrollment is only available to Windows XP clients (computer enrollment is available in both, but they have different versions of templates).

You will find the autoenrollment feature settings in Group Policies under Computer Configuration, Windows Settings, Security Settings, Public Key Policies. This is shown in Figure 8.12.

Either the Enterprise Edition or the Datacenter Edition of Windows Server 2003 is required to configure version 2 certificate templates for autoenrollment requests. However, autoenrollment manages certificates or pending certificate requests based on any version of the certificate template.

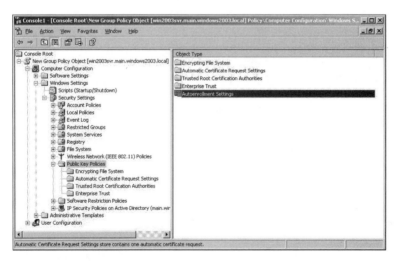

**Figure 8.12** Autoenrollment settings in the Group Policy Editor.

To configure this setting, right-click Autoenrollment Settings in the right panel and then choose Properties. You will see the Autoenrollment Settings Properties dialog box appear, as shown in Figure 8.13.

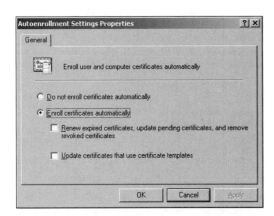

**Figure 8.13** The Autoenrollment Settings Properties dialog box.

The options in this dialog box allow you to turn on or turn off this feature, along with actions that should be taken for expired certificates.

Of course, PKI and certificates are very complex subjects. For the purposes of this exam, the preceding information is all you will need to know. However, if you are going to be designing Windows Server 2003 environments, you would be well advised to study this topic in detail.

# Exam Prep Questions

## Question 1

From the following list, choose the security templates that can be used in configuring computer and user settings.

**COMPATWS.INF**

**COMPAT2K.INF**

**COMPATNT.INF**

**HISECDC.INF**

**SECUREDC.INF**

**LOWSECDC.INF**

The correct answer is:

```
COMPATWS.INF

HISECDC.INF

SECUREDC.INF
```

## Question 2

Ron Porter has been given a script that he needs to execute on his users' workstations. He has been asked to ensure that the script runs from the command line. What is the name of the Windows Scripting Host tool he should use?

- ○ A. **WScript.exe**
- ○ B. **CScript.exe**
- ○ C. **WSH.exe**
- ○ D. **CMD.exe**

Answer B is correct. CScript is the WSH tool that runs scripts from the command line. WScript is the Windows GUI version of Windows Script Host. Therefore, answer A is incorrect. WSH is the abbreviation for Windows Script Host; returns and error are run alone. Therefore, answer C is incorrect. CMD.exe is the command interpreter for Windows Server 2003 and simply opens a Command Prompt window. Therefore, answer D is incorrect.

# Question 3

Siobhan Chamberlin knows that administrative templates contain settings that can be applied to clients through Group Policy. Siobhan wants to make sure she never makes the mistake of applying one of the legacy templates on her all Windows Server 2003 and Windows XP clients. She decides to delete the template files she does not need. Of the following, which templates should she delete? [Check all correct answers.]

- ❏ A. **System.adm**
- ❏ B. **Windows.adm**
- ❏ C. **Inetres.adm**
- ❏ D. **Default.adm**
- ❏ E. **Common.adm**
- ❏ F. **Winnt.adm**
- ❏ G. **Conf.adm**

Answers B, E, and F are correct. Windows.adm contains settings for Windows 9x machines. Common.adm contains system settings for both Windows 9x and Windows NT 4.0. Winnt.adm contains settings specific to Windows NT 4.0. Answers A, C, D, and G are incorrect because System.adm contains settings for the Explorer shell, Inetres.adm contains policies for Internet Explorer, Default.adm does not exist on a Windows Server 2003 installation, and Conf.adm exists in both Windows 2000 and Windows Server 2003 and contains settings for NetMeeting.

# Question 4

Windows Server 2003 ships with many templates that can be used to configure clients. The following are administrative template categories:

Desktop

Printers

Control Panel

Start Menu & Taskbar

Identify how each of the preceding administrative templates fits into the following Group Policy configuration containers:

Computer Configuration

User Configuration

The correct answer is:

Computer Configuration

Printers

User Configuration

Desktop
Control Panel
Start Menu & Taskbar

# Question 5

Zevi Mehlman has been studying Windows Server 2003 security templates. He
knows that security templates are groups of security settings that can be applied
to machines of a specific type. During a conversation with a new administrator
who is not familiar with Windows Server 2003, he is asked what levels of security are available with these templates in Windows Server 2003. Because Zevi
had just studied the topic, of course he knew the answer. Which of the following did he mention? [Check all correct answers.]

❑  A.  Basic

❑  B.  High

❑  C.  Secure

❑  D.  DC Secure

Answers B, C, and D are correct. There are several templates available, and
they are indeed aimed at different types of machines (workstations, domain
controllers, and even Windows 2000 Professional machines). However,
although a "basic" template shipped with Windows 2000 Server, it does not
exist in Windows Server 2003. Therefore, answer A is incorrect.

# Question 6

Bertram Rawe needs a script to run to every workstation. This script will add a
new folder structure to each drive. Every machine in his environment must be
affected by this change. He is very much aware that putting any delay on the
users' logon times is best avoided. Which one of the following types of scripts
would ensure that every machine is affected by the change?

○  A.  Startup

○  B.  Logon

○  C.  Logoff

○  D.  Shutoff

Answer A is correct. In this circumstance, it is best if the script is added to the startup. This affects the computers as they are turned on, and although the script will indeed run prior to users logging on, it will not directly impact the users themselves. The logon script could have been used, but this is part of the user logon experience. Therefore, answer B is incorrect. The logoff script would also affect the user. Therefore, answer C is incorrect. There is no Shutoff script option. Therefore, answer D is incorrect.

# Question 7

Leonard has been asked to work on making his users' data more secure. One of the concerns is that no system currently exists to back up user data on their workstations. It is decided that it would be much better to store all user data on a server. Leonard draws up a list of the items he wants redirected. He then asks one of his assistants to set the Group Policy. However, the assistant, Kit, tells him that he can't redirect all the folders as required. Which of the following can't Kit redirect?

- ○ A. My Documents
- ○ B. Favorites
- ○ C. Application Data
- ○ D. Desktop
- ○ E. Start Menu

Answer B is correct. Windows 2030 Folder Redirection can be used to redirect any of the listed user folders, with the exception of a user's Favorites folder. Therefore, answers A, C, D, and E are incorrect.

# Question 8

Ester Helwig wants to turn on autoregistration of certificates through Group Policy. However, despite having a Windows Server 2003 environment based on Windows Server 2003 Standard Edition and Active Directory, she is unable to do so. Why?

- ○ A. Ester has a Windows 2000 server still in the environment. This feature will not work if there is any Windows 2000 server or client on the network.
- ○ B. This feature is not supported by Windows Server 2003 Standard Edition. She must upgrade her servers to the Enterprise Edition first.
- ○ C. Although this option is available, it's position in the Group Policy Editor is different. Ester simply cannot find it.
- ○ D. This feature requires a schema change. Ester must first run **/forestprep** to use this feature.

Answer B is correct. Only certain versions of Windows Server 2003 support this feature. Answer A is incorrect because it is already stated that Ester only has Windows Server 2003 machines in her environment. Answer C is incorrect because, although there are expanded features in Windows Server 2003, the console to control them remains the same. Answer D is incorrect because this feature does not require the use of /forestprep.

# Question 9

Siobhan is a new system administrator for a banking company. She had spent her first few weeks creating an inventory of machines and mapping out her network. She has found a server that does not comply with the standards her organization has set. This is because the default root permissions for the OS partition have been changed. Siobhan decides the best way to deal with this is to apply a security template to the server. Which template should she use?

- A. **IESACLS.INF**
- B. **SECUREDC.INF**
- C. **SETUP SECURITY.INF**
- D. **ROOTSEC.INF**

Answer D is correct. ROOTSEC.INF is used to reapply the default permissions to the partition containing the OS. Answers A, B, and C are incorrect because IESACLS.INF contains the default settings for IE, SECUREDC.INF contains the default settings for domain controllers, and SETUP SECURITY.INF contains default settings to be applied after setup that are not specific to the root partition permissions.

# Question 10

Volker Wiora knows that autoenrollment is a key feature for his Windows Server 2003 environment. Having just come from a Windows 2000 environment and seeing it at work, he knows he wants to implement this feature as soon as possible. However, Volker is considering a third-party solution because he wants to have the most secure environment possible, and he wants to assign certificates to both users and computers. What should Volker do?

- A. Certificates are more important for computers. Although in theory it is possible to use a third-party tool to assign certificates to users, assigning them to computers gives one better control and is actually more secure.
- B. In Windows Server 2003, it is possible to assign certificates to both users and computers. There is no need to use a third-party tool.

○ C. Volker's instincts are correct. Because Group Policy can only assign certificates to computers, he should find a third-party tool to do the task.

○ D. Windows Server 2003 offers autoenrollment to users, not computers. Therefore, he should look for a third-party tool that assigns to computers only.

Answer B is correct. The ability to assign to both computers and users is new in Windows Server 2003. Answer A is incorrect because for a fully secure environment, certificates should be assigned to both the computers and the users. Answer C is incorrect because this defines the restrictions we had in Windows 2000; it does not apply to Windows Server 2003. Answer D is incorrect because Windows Server 2003 can assign to both users and computers.

# Need to Know More?

 Jones, Don and Mark Rouse. *Windows Server 2003 Delta Guide.* Sams Publishing. Indianapolis, IN, 2003. ISBN 0789728494.

 Morimoto, Rand, et al. *Windows Server 2003 Unleashed.* Sams Publishing. Indianapolis, IN. 2003, ISBN 0672321548.

# Troubleshooting Group Policy

## Terms you'll need to understand:

✓ DNS
✓ FRS
✓ GPUpdate
✓ Loopback processing
✓ Resultant Set of Policy (RSoP)
✓ GPResult

## Techniques you'll need to master:

✓ Using the GPUpdate tool and its command-line switches
✓ Using the GPResult tool and its command-line switches

Although this chapter is not very long, it is an important one, both for the Microsoft Certified System Engineer (MCSE) exams and for the real world. You should make sure you are familiar with the tools that can be used to troubleshoot Group Policy problems as they arise. However, it is worth noting that Microsoft tests are based on core operating systems and do not contain questions concerning resource kit utilities and add-ons. Therefore, this chapter is not intended to be exhaustive on the task of troubleshooting Group Policy.

Troubleshooting is always a tricky task (that is why those who are good at it are much prized). Trying to figure out why Group Policy is not doing everything you thought it would is no exception. Like all good specialists, knowing which tools work in which circumstances is more than half the battle.

# Introducing Group Policy Troubleshooting

We will spend some time looking at the tools available to troubleshoot Group Policy in a moment. However, before doing that, it is a good idea to make a very valuable point. Group Policy is actually made up of many different technologies, and there is plenty of room for errors, or just flat out misunderstandings.

In case you're wondering what technologies I am talking about, I'll list just a few of them:

➤ Active Directory (AD)

➤ Domain name system (DNS)

➤ File Replication Service (FRS)

➤ Windows Server 2003 Security Groups

➤ Organizational Units (OUs)

This list is not an exhaustive one, but it does offer some insight into where problems could exist. Clearly, we are not going to be able to go into detail about all these technologies and features. Instead, we will concentrate on the tools specific to Group Policy. However, forewarned is forearmed. As long as you know that issues with Group Policy can come from many different places, you are better prepared for in-depth troubleshooting.

# Active Directory and Group Policy

When you get under the hood of Group Policy, you'll see that there are actually two components: the Group Policy Container (GPC) and Group Policy Template (GPT). We will be talking about GPTs in a moment because they are stored outside of AD.

GPCs are objects created within AD. They define what a Group Policy is supposed to do, and they can have permissions assigned to them. Without GPCs, Group Policy would not work. A GPC for a Group Policy exists on every domain controller within a domain (it's actually stored as part of the Domain partition in AD). Therefore, it must be replicated. Normal AD replication processes take care of this. If AD replication is failing, it is highly likely that Group Policy will have problems.

# Domain Name System (DNS)

As you already know, the domain name system exists to aid clients and servers in finding things on the network, such as client computers, shares, printers, and the services offered by these objects. A Windows Server 2003 network without a fully functional DNS infrastructure is an environment in a world of hurt.

Clients must be able to read their Group Policy data. They read this data from domain controllers (DCs). If a client cannot find a DC, Group Policy will appear to fail. In fact, the error is not caused by Group Policy, but a Group Policy failure in this case would be a symptom of a larger problem.

# File Replication Service (FRS)

A little earlier I mentioned GPCs and GPTs. The GPT represents the physical files that make up a Group Policy (for instance, a REG file that contains Registry settings that must be applied to a target machine). These must be replicated to all DCs in a domain. You might think this process is taken care of by AD replication—but you'd be wrong!

FRS is, in fact, a simple file-replication process that runs outside of AD replication. By default, it follows the same replication topology, but it does not rely on the same change-notification process. Don't forget, in Windows Server 2003, FRS can be configured to have a unique replication topology. If FRS is broken, Group Policy cannot replicate correctly.

# Security Groups

Group Policy can target users and computers through their memberships to Sites, Domains, or Organizational Units (SDOUs). Take OUs as an example: A Group Policy Object (GPO) can be linked to an OU so that all objects within it have the policy applied. However, this does not tell the whole story.

On the face of it, the granularity of applying Group Policy seems rather sparse. What if you want to apply a policy to only half the members of an OU? This is possible, if you do filtering with security groups. In simple terms, if you do not have permissions to read something (in this case, the GPO), then it can't apply to you.

Using this feature can make troubleshooting quite complex. If you've used it extensively, you will have to keep in mind which groups are, and which are not, allowed to access a GPO.

As you can see, some things outside of specific Group Policies can affect their application. Let's now take a look at some issues you might run into while working with Group Policy.

# General Troubleshooting

Given some of the preceding information, it should be clear that when troubleshooting Group Policy, you should check the simple things first. Participation on a network starts with logging on and being authenticated. This means that TCP/IP connectivity must be present and working.

Simple tasks you should consider include using the ping command-line utility to establish that a client has connectivity to a Domain Controller. Don't forget that in a Windows Server 2003 environment it is possible for things to appear to be working, when in fact problems exist. More specifically, you can log on to a workstation using cached credentials, and it will appear you are on the network without problems, when in fact, you are not.

There are also times when Group Policy will not be applied, even when logging on to a network works as designed. This is the case with VPN connections. A user might well be working from home with his corporate laptop, but because he has logged on to his machines before, establishing the VPN connection, Group Policy will not be applied.

A common tool for troubleshooting is the Event Viewer. Event Viewer contains log files for many different services. You should always check the Event Viewer logs before digging deeper with other tools. These log files can alert you to unrelated issues, such as DNS problems, network connectivity, and corrupt files on the local system.

Always keep in mind that Group Policy is replicated on two different schedules. The GPC is contained with AD; therefore, normal AD replication must take place before a policy will work or can be updated. At the same time, FRS must do its job, too. Not until these two replication topologies reach convergence will a policy function correctly.

# Group Policy Application

Group Policy has many uses, and it can sometimes be confusing to think about how exactly it is applied. You should note that Group Policies are applied during the computer startup, and when a user logs on. However, because Group Policy is used to assign scripts to a client, it might also have effects during logging off or when a computer is shut down.

At the same time, Group Policy is also refreshed at intervals. For a workstation, this interval is 90 minutes. However, this is not hard-coded. In fact, a 30-minute random factor is thrown in to stop all clients refreshing at the same time. This is important when you have changed a Group Policy and are waiting for it to affect a targeted workstation. First, you would have to wait for AD and FRS replication to take place; then you would have to wait for the refresh period to take effect. As always, there is an exception: Domain controllers update their Group Policies every 5 minutes.

Always remember the acronym SDOU, which stands for *Site, Domain*, and *Organizational Unit (OU)*. Users and computers can be targeted to receive Group Policies through their logical placement in Active Directory. The order is also important, and it tells you the precedence. Group Policies set at a site are applied first, then those at the domain, then those at the OU. When there are conflicts between Group Policies within this hierarchy, the last one applied takes precedence. There is one exception to this rule, however: Account Policies should always be configured at the domain level. By default, they will override any other Account Policy settings configured.

# GPUpdate

GPUpdate is a command-line tool that ships with Windows Server 2003. Its purpose is to allow you to manually trigger the refreshing of Group Policies from a client machine (be it a server or workstation). This is useful when you have changed a Group Policy and want to see the effects immediately.

Table 9.1 shows the command-line switches for GPUpdate. Always remember that you can get these options simply by typing GPUpdate /? from the command prompt.

| Table 9.1 GPUpdate Command Switches | |
|---|---|
| **Switch** | **Definition** |
| **/Target:{Computer \| User}** | Specifies that only user or only computer policy settings are refreshed. By default, both user and computer policy settings are refreshed. |
| **/Force** | Reapplies all policy settings. By default, only policy settings that have changed are applied. |
| **/Wait:{value** | Sets the number of seconds to wait for policy processing to finish. The default is 600 seconds. The value **0** means not to wait. The value **1** means to wait indefinitely. When the time limit is exceeded, the command prompt returns, but policy processing continues. |
| **/Logoff** | Causes a logoff after the Group Policy settings have been refreshed. This is required for those Group Policy client-side extensions that do not process policy on a background refresh cycle but do process policy when a user logs on. Examples include user-targeted Software Installation and Folder Redirection. This option has no effect if there are no extensions called that require a logoff. |
| **/Boot** | Causes a reboot after the Group Policy settings are refreshed. This is required for those Group Policy client-side extensions that do not process policy on a background refresh cycle but do process policy at computer startup. Examples include computer-targeted Software Installation. This option has no effect if there are no extensions called that require a reboot. |
| **/Sync** | Causes the next foreground policy application to be done synchronously. Foreground policy applications occur at computer boot time and user logon. You can specify this for the user, computer, or both using the **/Target** parameter. The **/Force** and **/Wait** parameters will be ignored if specified. |

GPUpdate is a useful tool, but it won't apply settings that occur only during logon. For instance, Folder Redirection and Software Installation only take place during logon, and running GPUpdate will not force these to occur after the fact. Only the logoff and logon process will trigger these events.

# Group Policy and Precedence

When troubleshooting Group Policies, it is important that you know the order in which the Group Policies are applied, because settings higher in the hierarchy can be overwritten as other policies are applied.

Earlier I mentioned the SDOU rule; this should be foremost in your mind. At the same time, keep in mind that some settings can only be applied at the domain level. The most common example of this is password settings for complexity and so on. While settings within Group Policy can be made for these options, they can only be applied to local accounts on a machine, not for anything domain related (such as a user's own logon).

Group Policy forms a hierarchy, so settings for a child OU are a combination of those linked to the OU itself and those settings inherited from the OU above it (the parent) in the hierarchy. There are, of course, exceptions. Exceptions occur when Block Inheritance is set at an OU. Block Inheritance prevents usual rules of inheritance from taking place, and settings are not passed down. Of course, this can be defeated by using the No Override feature (known in the GPMC as *Enforce*). Make you sure you understand that these options apply to an entire Group Policy. You cannot choose a single setting within a Group Policy and enforce it, while the rest of the policy follows the usual inheritance rules.

As Group Policies are linked to a container (SDOU), they are ordered. You can change this link order as often as you like. Policies are applied as per the rules of SDOU, and within a container, they are applied in the link order. There will be times when you will need several policies to be linked to the same container object in Active Directory. Group Policies linked to the same object are processed from the bottom up, so if conflicts arise between the policies linked to the object, the one that appears higher has the higher value.

# Loopback Processing

One more wrinkle in the processing of Group Policies is loopback, which is designed to reverse the usual processing rules. If you think about it, user settings usually override computer settings. In other words, policies that affect a computer are applied when that computer starts up, before a user has even logged on to the machine. When the user logs on, his policies get applied, and it is possible for that user's settings to override those already applied to the computer. Further, user-configuration settings made in policies targeting the machine are not applied at all.

What if this is not the way you want things to work? What if you have a computer running in a kiosk in your reception area, and you want anyone to be able to log on, but you do not want users from your community logging on, forgetting they have done so, and then giving any stranger that wanders up access to your corporate LAN? For these types of situations, we have loopback processing.

Loopback basically allows you to make sure that policies set for a computer take priority. Further, it allows user-configuration settings set at a policy targeting computers to be applied. Loopback has two settings: Loopback with Replace and Loopback with Merge. The Replace option basically gives the user settings applied to the computer precedence over the user-configuration settings targeting the logged-on user. The Merge option applies those settings aimed at the computer and then combines them with those targeting the user.

To be clear, let me put it another way: Every Group Policy can be made up of settings configured in the User Configuration section or the Computer Configuration section. In normal practice, the computer settings are applied first, followed by the user settings. Any settings made in the User Configuration section of a policy designed to target computers are ignored.

Now, if you want to change this to have the user-configuration settings targeting the computer to override those targeting the user, you need Loopback with Replace. If you want a combination of the two, use Loopback with Merge.

# Tools for Troubleshooting

So far in this chapter, we have mentioned several tools. In this section I'll highlight two that are of particular interest for the exam. For completeness, I will also outline several other tools that are available, either for free download from Microsoft's Web site or shipped with the resource and deployment kits. You should note that Microsoft exam 70-294 should only contain questions based on the first two tools listed—Resultant Set of Policy (RSoP) and GPResult—because they ship with the operating system and are not add-ons.

## Resultant Set of Policy (RSoP)

We discussed this Microsoft Management Console (MMC) snap-in in Chapter 6, "Planning a Group Policy Strategy." The Resultant Set of Policy (RSoP) snap-in works with Windows Management Instrumentation (WMI) to allow you to work out which policies are currently being applied to a given environment.

Once you have created what is essentially a snapshot of a system and the policies that are being applied to it, you can simulate applying additional policies to a certain target to see what effect they will ultimately have. It should be clear that with hierarchies of containers that can have Group Policies linked to them, working out what was actually applied can be quite a headache. This is the very problem RSoP was designed to address.

RSoP is a good tool that's new to Windows Server 2003, and it should be part of your arsenal when encountering Group Policy issues.

# GPResult

GPResult (obviously short for *Group Policy Result*) is a precursor to RSoP. It has the benefit (depending on how you look at it) of being command-line driven.

Originally, this tool formed part of the Windows 2000 Resource Kit. In Windows Server 2003, it ships as part of the core operating system. GPResult gives you data similar to that found in RSoP, but it can more easily be piped to a file for later analysis.

Table 9.2 shows the command-line switches for GPResult. Always remember that you can get these options simply by typing GPResult /? from the command prompt.

| Table 9.2 | GPResult Command Switches | |
|-----------|---------------------------|---|
| **Parameter** | **Switch** | **Description** |
| /S | system | Specifies the remote system to connect to. |
| /U | [domain\]user | Specifies the user context under which the command should execute. |
| /P | [password] | Specifies the password for the given user context. Prompts for input if omitted. |
| /SCOPE | scope | Specifies whether the user or the computer settings need to be displayed. Valid values are "**USER**" and "**COMPUTER**". |
| /USER | [domain\]user | Specifies the username for which the RSoP data is to be displayed. |
| /V | | Specifies that verbose information should be displayed. Verbose information provides additional detailed settings that have been applied with a precedence of 1. |

| Table 9.2 GPResult Command Switches *(continued)* | | |
|---|---|---|
| **Parameter** | **Switch** | **Description** |
| /Z | | Specifies that super-verbose information should be displayed. Super-verbose information provides additional detailed settings that have been applied with a precedence of 1 and higher. This allows you to see if a setting has been set in multiple places. See the Group Policy online help topic for more information. |
| /? | | Displays this help message. |

Running GPResult without a command-line parameter gives you an RSoP for the currently logged-on user. The following text is the output from a standard installation of Windows Server 2003:

```
RSOP data for MAIN\Administrator on WIN2003SVR : Logging Mode
----------------------------------------------------------------

OS Type:                Microsoft(R) Windows(R) Server 2003,
↪ Enterprise Edition
OS Configuration:       Primary Domain Controller
OS Version:             5.2.3790
Terminal Server Mode:   Remote Administration
Site Name:              Default-First-Site-Name
Roaming Profile:
Local Profile:          C:\Documents and Settings\Administrator
Connected over a slow link?: No


COMPUTER SETTINGS
------------------
    CN=WIN2003SVR,OU=Domain Controllers,DC=main,DC=windows2003,DC=local
    Last time Group Policy was applied: 6/24/2003 at 7:36:12 AM
    Group Policy was applied from:     win2003svr.main.windows2003.local
    Group Policy slow link threshold:  500 kbps
    Domain Name:                       MAIN
    Domain Type:                       Windows 2000

    Applied Group Policy Objects
    ----------------------------
        Default Domain Controllers Policy
        Default Domain Policy
        New Group Policy Object
        Local Group Policy

    The computer is a part of the following security groups
    -------------------------------------------------------
        BUILTIN\Administrators
        Everyone
        BUILTIN\Users
        BUILTIN\Pre-Windows 2000 Compatible Access
        Windows Authorization Access Group
        NT AUTHORITY\NETWORK
        NT AUTHORITY\Authenticated Users
        This Organization
```

```
WIN2003SVR$
Domain Controllers
NT AUTHORITY\ENTERPRISE DOMAIN CONTROLLERS


USER SETTINGS
--------------
    CN=Administrator,CN=Users,DC=main,DC=windows2003,DC=local
    Last time Group Policy was applied: 6/24/2003 at 6:43:52 AM
    Group Policy was applied from:      win2003svr.main.windows2003.local
    Group Policy slow link threshold:   500 kbps
    Domain Name:                        MAIN
    Domain Type:                        Windows 2000

    Applied Group Policy Objects
    ----------------------------
        Default Domain Policy

    The following GPOs were not applied because they were filtered out
    ----------------------------------------------------------------------
        New Group Policy Object
            Filtering:  Not Applied (Empty)

        Local Group Policy
            Filtering:  Not Applied (Empty)

    The user is a part of the following security groups
    ----------------------------------------------------
        Domain Users
        Everyone
        BUILTIN\Administrators
        BUILTIN\Users
        BUILTIN\Pre-Windows 2000 Compatible Access
        NT AUTHORITY\INTERACTIVE
        NT AUTHORITY\Authenticated Users
        This Organization
        LOCAL
        Enterprise Admins
        Group Policy Creator Owners
        Schema Admins
        Domain Admins
```

As you can see, this offers a lot of data, including which policies are being applied, which security groups the user is a member of, and a list of which policies were filtered.

# Other Tools

This section exists only for completeness. It lists a few tools you might want to be aware of as you work with Group Policies. However, these tools should not appear on the exam.

## Group Policy Management Console (GPMC)

On the face of it, this tool could revolutionize the management of Group Policy. It is a free download, and one wonders why it did not ship with the operating system. You can get it from the following URL:

```
http://www.microsoft.com/windowsserver2003/gpmc/default.mspx
```

GPMC offers a plethora of features, such as the ability to administer policies across domains and forests, to perform backups, and to restore policy data, and to import or copy policy data. Not only that, it's all scriptable for ease of use.

The aforementioned link also offers a good deal of technical documents on this new add-on. It is highly recommended that you look into the Group Policy Management Console.

## GPMonitor

This utility is part of the Windows Server 2003 Deployment Kit. This kit is available for download from the following URL:

```
http://www.microsoft.com/windowsserver2003/techinfo/reskit/deploykit.mspx
```

GPMonitor actually comes in two parts. The first is a service that runs on client computers. This service collects policy data from the client and forwards it to a central repository. The second part is a viewer tool. The help file with the deployment kit can provide you with more details.

## GPOTool

This utility is available as part of the Windows Server 2003 Resource Kit. For details about the contents of this kit, and for a free download of the tools, use the following URL:

```
http://www.microsoft.com/windowsserver2003/techinfo/reskit/resourcekit.mspx
```

GPOTool allows you to check the consistency, within a domain or across domains, of the Group Policy Container (GPC) and Group Policy Template (GPT) data. This can be used to determine whether you have replication issues.

# Exam Prep Questions

## Question 1

Ron Porter is a consultant working for a systems management company. He has been onsite for several months and has run into a Group Policy issue. In this case, he has updated a Group Policy, but it is not being refreshed for some clients. Ron decides to call his partner, Dave, to see if he has any ideas of why this might be. Dave explains how group replication works, and Ron soon understands the issue and resolves it. What did Dave tell Ron?

○ A. Dave told Ron that Group Policy is replicated on two different technologies. One is Active Directory replication, and the other is handled by the File Replication Service. These two replication infrastructures have to reach convergence if Group policy is to work.

○ B. Dave told Ron that Group Policy updates can take up to 48 hours to fully replicate (depending on whether they are applied to a site, domain, or OU). Ron simply has to wait.

○ C. Dave told Ron to log off and log back on with a different username. This causes a refresh on the client, thereby making the policy work.

○ D. Dave told Ron that Group Policy is replicated by Active Directory. This takes time to converge on the network. Patience is a virtue, and Ron simply has to wait 15 minutes.

Answer A is correct. The two replication technologies simply have to reach convergence in this case. Answer B is incorrect because although there is no defined window for a policy to replicate, 48 hours is far longer than convergence should take. Answer C is incorrect because logging on and off with a different username is not required. If the policy exists, logging on and off might well resolve it by causing a refresh, but a different username is not required. Answer D is incorrect because policies are replicated by both Active Directory and the File Replication Service.

## Question 2

Dwain Kinghorn is a new system administrator. He has been analyzing policies on his Windows Server 2003 network and is confused by a particular policy. The policy is linked to an OU, and a user is a member of that OU. However, the policy is never applied. Everyone else in the OU gets the policy as intended. Dwain calls Poul Neilsen, a friend, and asks if he has any ideas of why this might be. Poul does indeed offer the solution. What did Poul say?

- ○ A. Poul told Dwain that this user must have overridden the settings in this OU with a local policy. Because local policies are applied last, if a setting conflicts, it wins.

- ○ B. Poul told Dwain that the user has obviously not logged off since the policy was created. Because policies are only ever refreshed during logon, this policy had been missed.

- ○ C. Poul told Dwain that it is likely that security group filtering was taking place and that the user does not have permissions to this Group Policy Object.

- ○ D. Poul told Dwain that the policy replication was probably not complete. Dwain should wait for convergence before worrying about it.

Answer C is correct. Although policies are usually applied to sites, domains, and Organizational Units, it is possible to filter their application by denying security groups read access to the object. Answer A is incorrect because local policies never override those coming from Active Directory. Answer B is incorrect because it is not accurate to suggest that policies are only refreshed during logon. Some policies are refreshed in the background. Answer D is incorrect because other users were getting this policy.

# Question 3

Bertram Rawe wants to know which policies have been applied to him. He is using a Windows XP client. He would rather not install additional tools because he shares the system with someone else. Which tool should he use?

- ○ A. Group Policy Management Console
- ○ B. GPResult
- ○ C. Resultant Set of Policy
- ○ D. Active Directory Sites and Domains

Answer B is correct. Although answers A, B, and C will all provide the answer Bertram requires, the Group Policy Management Console and the Resultant Set of Policy console require the installation of software, thus making answers A and C incorrect. Answer D is incorrect because Active Directory Sites and Domains also requires a software installation.

# Question 4

Lorena Lardon is trying to find out why a Group Policy targeted at users is not being applied to her computer. She has logged on to her machine but cannot figure out what is wrong. When she logs on to another machine, the policy works. Everyone else is also getting the policy. What is a likely reason for this?

O A. Group Policy refreshes every 90 minutes on a client machine. At log on, the machine uses cached policies, which are updated at this interval. Lorena should simply wait 90 minutes.

O B. FRS has failed on her network. Lorena should address this problem first.

O C. When Lorena logs in to different machines, her position in the OU infrastructure changes. On the problem machine, it simply is not targeted at her.

O D. The problem machine has network connectivity issues. Lorena should use **ping** to make sure she can contact a DC.

Answer D is correct. Lorena is logging on with cached credentials, and the policies are never being read. Answer A is incorrect because policies are always read at log on. Answer B is incorrect because others are getting the policy, and even Lorena does when she logs on to a different machine. Answer C is incorrect because logging on to different machines does not change Lorena's position in the OU structure.

# Question 5

Zevi Mehlman is troubleshooting a new Group Policy remotely. He has created a batch file that will be run on the remote clients and will cause them to refresh their policies. The policy he is testing is a software installation targeting computers. Which command-line tool did Zevi use, and with which switch?

O A. GPUpdate with the **/Reboot** switch

O B. GPResult with the **/Reboot** switch

O C. GPUpdate with the **/Boot** switch

O D. GPResult with the **/Boot** switch

Answer C is correct. GPUpdate is used to refresh policies. Some policies can be applied on the standard refresh (every 90 minutes) or simply by running GPUpdate. However, certain settings, such as software installation with computers, only occur during startup. Therefore, it is necessary to use the /Boot switch. Answer A is incorrect because GPUpdate does not have a /Reboot switch. Answer B is incorrect because GPResult is used to report on which polices are applied; it cannot refresh policies. Answer D is incorrect because GPResult is the wrong tool.

# Need to Know More?

 Jones, Don and Mark Rouse. *Windows Server 2003 Delta Guide.* Sams Publishing. Indianapolis, IN, 2003. ISBN 0789728494.

 Morimoto, Rand, et al. *Windows Server 2003 Unleashed.* Sams Publishing. Indianapolis, IN. 2003, ISBN 0672321548.

# Active Directory Maintenance

## Terms you'll need to understand:

✓ Extensible Storage Engine
✓ **Ntds.dit**
✓ Active Directory log files
✓ Garbage collection
✓ Tombstoning
✓ Defragmentation
✓ Nonauthoritative restore
✓ Authoritative restore
✓ ADSIEdit
✓ System state data

## Techniques you'll need to master:

✓ Performing an authoritative restore
✓ Using NTDSUtil to move AD data files
✓ Using NTDSUtil to move AD log files

Active Directory (AD) is a transactional database. This means that it has built-in recovery techniques that are performed automatically should a system fail because of a hardware problem. It also means that you should know how to both back up and recover the database in the event of failure.

This chapter discusses the structure of the AD, including details of the database and log files used to process updates to the data. We examine how data can be backed up and restored. You will see that the AD replication process can be used to update a domain controller (DC) that has been offline for a period of time. It is also possible to force restored data to be propagated throughout the network via AD replication, even if that data is technically out of date.

# Introducing AD Maintenance

Because so many areas of AD operation are automatic, you would be forgiven for thinking that there is little reason to be concerned about maintenance tasks. However, this assumption would be incorrect. Maintaining the AD database on each DC is an essential task that should be performed regularly. Backup and restore procedures allow you to recover lost or corrupted data.

With regards to maintenance, we will look at four key tasks. Two of these tasks should be scheduled to run on a regular basis. You should also test these procedures periodically to make sure that you can recover from a problem and that you are enjoying optimal performance.

These tasks are as follows:

➤ Backing up AD data

➤ Restoring AD data

➤ Defragmenting AD data

➤ Moving the AD database

You can use the backup utility that ships with Windows Server 2003 to back up the AD database. In addition, several third-party utilities are available that can perform the same task (indeed, NTBackup is merely a stripped-down version of Veritas Backup Exec). Whichever tool you decide to use, this task should occur on a regular schedule.

It is possible for the AD database to become corrupt or accidentally deleted. When this occurs, you must restore the database. Generally, you use the same tool you used for your backup to do this. However, some tape formats allow you to use different restore software.

There are two instances when the AD database must be moved. The first is during the defragmentation process. This ensures that the process does not corrupt the database. The second instance is performance related. If the hard disk that contains AD is becoming full, performance can be affected. To alleviate this problem, you could move the database.

Defragmentation increases the performance of both writing data to the database and querying the AD data. It can also be used to reduce the amount of disk space the database takes up.

# Active Directory Data Files

Active Directory uses the Extensible Storage Engine (ESE), which was first pioneered in Microsoft Exchange Server. It uses the concept of transactions to ensure that the database does not become corrupted by partial updates and so it can recover in the case of a power failure. Each transaction is a call to modify the database. A modification can be the addition of new data or a change being made to data that is already stored.

For the transactional system to work, the AD database must have associated log files. These log files are used to store modifications before the data is written to the physical database file. We'll look at how this works in a moment. Before we do that, however, we must define which files are used by the database. Five files make up the AD database system:

➤ `ntds.dit`

➤ `edb*.log`

➤ `ebd.chk`

➤ `res1.log`

➤ `res2.log`

Each of these files has a role to play in ensuring that data can be written to the directory in a safe and recoverable fashion. You should note that these files exist on every DC in your environment. The AD database is not centralized in any way; it exists on each server that is promoted to the role of DC. Each instance must be maintained separately.

## ntds.dit

This is the single file that holds all the AD data, including all objects and the schema information. This file is stored by default in the <systemroot>\ NTDS folder, although it can be moved. The `ntds.dit` file works in conjunction with the log files. The `.dit` extension stands for *directory information tree*.

## edb*.log

The `edb*.log` file is the transaction log for `ntds.dit`. The file that is currently being used is called simply `edb.log`. When that file reaches a specified size (by default, 10MB), the file gets renamed to `edb*****.log`, where the asterisks are incremented from 1 upward. When the files are no longer needed, they are deleted by the system.

## edb.chk

There can be two copies of changes to AD data. The first copy is kept in log files; these changes occur as data is accepted from an administrative tool. The second copy is the database file itself. This checkpoint file keeps track of which entries in the log file have been written to the database file. In the case of failure, Windows Server 2003 uses this file to find out which entries in the log file can safely be written out to a database.

## res1.log and res2.log

Essentially, `res1.log` and `res2.log` are two placeholders that exist to simply take up space. In the event that a DC runs out of disk space, the AD replica can become inoperable. It is far better for the DC to shut down gracefully. These two files, each 10MB in size, exist to prevent a DC from being able to write to the log files. If a DC runs out of disk space, AD can be sure that it has at least 20MB of space to write out any necessary log data.

# Garbage Collection

*Garbage collection* is the process in which old data is purged from the AD. Because all DCs in a Windows Server 2003 network act as peers, deleting objects is a little more difficult than it might first appear. If an administrator wants to delete a user object from the network, he or she can simply hit the Delete key. However, how will Windows Server 2003 make sure that all DCs in the enterprise are aware that this deletion is taking place? If the deletion happens in real time, it can't. Hence, the use of *tombstoning*.

Data is never immediately deleted from AD. Instead, the object's attributes are deleted and the object is moved to a special container called *Deleted Objects*. The object is then assigned a tombstone. By default, this tombstone is 60 days, although it can be changed. The tombstone means that the physical deletion of the object will occur by the configured interval. This gives AD time to replicate this change to all DCs. It also means that the deletion can take place at around the same time, no matter how distant the DCs may be.

Garbage collection also defragments the database by using the online defragmentation process. We will take a closer look at defragmentation in a moment.

To change the interval for garbage collection, you must use the ADSIEdit tool included with Windows Server 2003. Connect to the Configuration container and edit the **garbageCollPeriod** and **tombstoneLifetime** attributes. By default, the period is 60 days. This is displayed in ADSIEdit as **<not set>**. Be careful about setting the value too low; this can prevent your restores from working. Microsoft recommends leaving the value set at the default.

# Performing Backups

A Windows Server 2003 DC can be backed up while it is online, thereby minimizing disruption. It is not enough to back up only the database and log files. Instead, you must back up the system state data.

*System state data* is a collection of data that makes up a functioning AD infrastructure. It includes the AD database, along with other folders and files. These files collectively can be used to recover from even the most catastrophic failure. System state data includes the following:

➤ AD database file

➤ SYSVOL folder

➤ Registry

➤ System startup files (`Ntdetect.com`, `Ntldr`, and `Bootsect.dat`)

➤ Class Registration database

➤ Certificate Services database

Not all these may exist on your server; for instance, the Certificate Services database is an optional component. You need all these folders because, in one-way or another, they support the server.

The SYSVOL folder is a shared folder that exists on all DCs. This folder is used to replicate Group Policy Object (GPO) data and logon scripts. The Class Registration database is composed of component services that are installed on a system.

You can back up the system state data without buying third-party utilities. To do this, simply use the built-in backup utility and follow these steps:

1. Select Start, All Programs, Accessories, System Tools, Backup. When you do this, an informational screen appears. Click the Advanced Mode link. This introductory screen is shown in Figure 10.1.

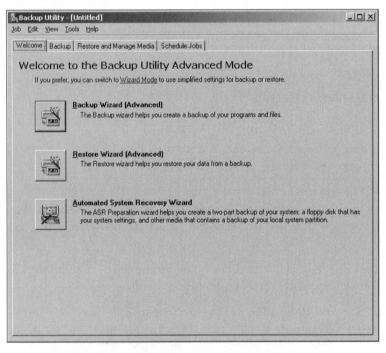

**Figure 10.1** The built-in backup utility.

**2.** This displays the main Backup/Restore window, as shown in Figure 10.2.

**Figure 10.2** Welcome Screen for Backup/Restore utility.

**3.** You must change to the backup options. Click the Backup tab. Once this is done, select System State, as shown in Figure 10.3.

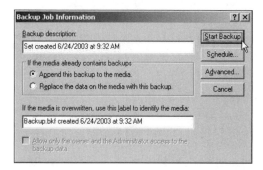

**Figure 10.3**   Selecting System State.

**4.** You will see an informational screen next. This is shown in Figure 10.4. Once you have read this screen, click Start Backup.

**Figure 10.4**   Backup job information screen.

NOTE

You might be familiar with the concept of an *emergency repair disk (ERD)* from previous versions of Windows. Note that this feature is not part of the Windows Server 2003 operating system.

# Recommendations for Backing Up Data

You can't restore a DC fully if you do not have a backup of the system state data. However, even having that data might not be enough if an entire server has been lost in, say, a flood. Make sure you are also backing up all other folders and disk drives on the server periodically. To do this, you can use the built-in backup tool or a third-party utility.

You must be a member of the Administrators, Backup Operator, or Server Operators group before you can back up data. These are built-in groups; if you do not want to use them, you must assign permissions yourself.

The backup utility built in to Windows Server 2003 can only be used locally when backing up system data. This means it cannot be configured from a single server to back up system data on all DCs in your enterprise. For this reason alone, you might want to consider purchasing a utility that offers more features.

 Remember that the backup utility built in to Windows Server 2003 can only be used locally when backing up system data.

## Windows Server 2003 Automated System Recovery (ASR)

Windows Server 2003 has a new tool that can be used for system disaster recovery. Automated System Recovery (ASR) is a two-part system-recovery tool that includes ASR backup and ASR restore. ASR should be a last resort in system recovery, used only after you have exhausted other options such as Safe Mode Boot and Last Known Good. This is a feature that was first introduced with Windows XP and now can be used to recover a machine from complete disaster.

# Restoring AD

Depending on the backup options you have implemented in your environment, you might have three methods to choose from when restoring a Windows Server 2003 DC. If you have performed a backup by following the steps outlined in the previous section, you could simply perform a restore operation with the built-in backup tool.

When you perform a restore, you have two options: You can perform an *authoritative restore* or a *nonauthoritative restore*. We will take a closer look at these two options in a moment.

Be careful about performing restores when utilizing external trusts. The password on an external trust is renegotiated by Windows Server 2003 every 7 days. If a restore is performed that is older than this (say, 14 days), then you should reestablish the trust.

Alternatively, you can simply rely on AD replication to take care of updating a new DC. In this scenario, a failed DC is simply reinstalled from scratch. Once the DC is online, it updates itself via normal replication techniques. This would occur automatically and would not require any additional administrative tasks. Because this is a simple process, we won't discuss it any further in this chapter.

In order to perform a restore at a DC, you must be able to log on with the local administrator password. This password is stored in the local SAM, and not within Active Directory. In Windows Server 2003, it is now possible to change the local Administrator password from within NTDSUtil. Because the local Administrator password allows for AD restores, it should be kept confidential.

## Nonauthoritative Restore

The nonauthoritative restore is the simplest form of restore when you are using backup media. A nonauthoritative restore is simply a restore of data from backup. Because the data will probably be out of date (presumably, some changes were made to the data in AD after the last backup), normal AD replication processes make sure that the missing data elements are updated.

This would be a common practice if a hard disk failure had taken place. If a hard disk fails, the server might become inoperable. You would simply replace the failed hardware, perform a nonauthoritative restore, and then wait for AD replication to bring the DC up to date. This process is faster than simply reinstalling the server and promoting it to a DC with dcpromo.exe, because less data will have to be replicated to the restored DC.

Performing a nonauthoritative restore is fairly simple. However, you cannot restore AD data while it is in use. For this reason, the server must be taken offline before a restore can happen. To do this, follow these steps:

1. Restart the server, pressing F8 during startup. The Advanced Startup Options are displayed.

2. Select Directory Services Restore Mode. This starts the server, but it does not start AD.

3. Log in to the server using the Administrators account. This is stored locally on each DC and can be different for each DC in your enterprise.

**4.** Use the backup tool to restore the system state data.

**5.** Restart the DC.

After the server has been restarted, it is updated by its replication partners. An integrity check also takes place, and various indexes on AD data are rebuilt. This places a temporary additional load on the server during boot time.

## Authoritative Restore

The authoritative restore can be used to restore individual pieces of AD. This is useful if an error has taken place and an object has been deleted by mistake. Let's look at an example to clarify this process. An administrator is working with the AD Users and Computers tool, and he accidentally deletes an Organizational Unit (OU). The OU contained user objects, and they are deleted as well. Because this change was accepted by a DC, it will be replicated to all AD replicas in the enterprise. If nothing is done, this mistake will eventually be replicated to all the DCs in the environment.

If the OU contained a small number of accounts, it might not be a problem to simply re-create it; however, if a large number of user objects were involved, it could take some time. An authoritative restore allows an administrator to restore the deleted OU from backup. When an authoritative restore takes place, the Update Sequence number (USN) of the object is, by default, incremented by 100,000 each day since the last backup. Because the USN is higher than the copy currently held by the DC's replication partners, the restored object is assumed to be the most up-to-date copy. This change is then forced out to all other DCs via normal AD replication processes.

 It is assumed that more than 100,000 changes have not been made to the restored data since the backup took place.

The process for performing an authoritative restore is somewhat different from the process outlined for a nonauthoritative restore. Once you have restored the system state data, you must not restart the computer. Instead, perform these additional steps:

**1.** Open a command prompt. Type **ntdsutil** and press Enter.

**2.** Type **authoritative restore** and press Enter.

3. Type `restore subtree <distinguished name>`, where `<distinguished name>` is the full path to the object. For an OU called `Finance` in a domain called `HCSNET.COM`, this would be `OU=finance,DC=HCSNET,DC=COM`.

4. Type `quit`. Type `quit` again and press Enter to exit NTDSUtil.

5. Restart the DC.

The one exception to the ability to do authoritative restores is when you want to restore objects stored in the Schema partition. The Schema is "owned" by the Schema Master operations master. In order to restore the schema, you must restore the Schema Master. Any changes made since the backup was performed are lost.

Restore operations are highly dependent on the tombstone period discussed in the "Garbage Collection" section earlier in the chapter. If you leave the default tombstone lifetime in place (60 days), you won't be able to restore system state data from tapes that have backups on them older than 60 days. This is because data is deleted once the tombstone lifetime has expired, and introducing a DC with older data that has now been erased from other DCs will cause database inconsistencies. Be careful not to set the tombstone lifetime for too short a time.

## Moving the AD Database

Because AD is a transactional database, you are able to benefit from some of the standard optimization techniques employed with this type of system. One of the most common suggested techniques is to move the database file to a separate physical hard disk from the log files.

Moving the database to a different physical hard disk from the log files prevents disk contention. The log files are being written to constantly, which means the hard disk heads are fairly busy. When a query is made against the AD database, the heads have to move to read from `ntds.dit`. This contention reduces performance of the disk subsystem.

Moving **ntds.dit** does not mean you should pay less attention to the need to protect your data. Your DCs should be running RAID-5. With a single RAID-5 array, you cannot ensure that the database file and log files are on different physical hard disks. If you decide to move the database file to a different disk, make sure that this disk has either RAID-1 (disk mirroring) or RAID-5 enabled.

You can move the database with the NTDSUtil command-line utility. For this to work, you must have booted your server in Directory Services Restore Mode. Remember that for most of the major database-maintenance tasks (other than performing a backup), you must have booted the server into this mode.

Following are the steps for moving the database file to another hard disk:

1. Restart the server, pressing F8 during startup. The Advanced Startup Options appear.

2. Select Directory Services Restore Mode. This starts the server, but it does not start AD.

3. Log in to the server using the Administrators account. This is stored locally on each DC and can be different for each DC in your enterprise.

4. Open a command prompt. Type **ntdsutil** and press Enter.

5. Type **files** and press Enter.

6. Type **move db to <drive>\<folder>**, where <drive> and <folder> make up the full path to the new location. Press Enter.

7. Type **quit** and press Enter. Then type **quit** again and press Enter to exit.

8. Restart the DC.

These commands do not simply move the database file; they also update the Registry so it points to the new location. Simply moving the file will cause the DC to fail.

If you want to move the log files, enter **move logs to <drive>\<folder>** instead of **move db to <drive>/<folder>** in the preceding steps. This moves the log files and also updates the Registry.

# Defragmenting the AD Database

Fragmentation has existed on personal computers for many years. The AD database suffers from it just like any other file. Fragmentation of the AD database occurs during the normal operation of a DC. Put simply, as database entries are made and then deleted, gaps can occur in the database file. These gaps cause subsequent records to be written randomly across the hard disk sectors, which reduces performance. Read and write operations are much faster if the database reads and writes are made to consecutive sectors of the disk. This is because the disk head moves much less if the sectors are contiguous.

Windows Server 2003 includes a defragmentation program that works at the file level to make sure each file is written to consecutive sectors of the disk. The defragmentation utility for AD goes one step further and reorders records within the database file.

Fragmentation within a database occurs in the same way that fragmentation of files occurs. As an example of how this works, imagine that an object is created within AD. This data is written to 150 consecutive sectors of the hard disk. Two properties of the object are then deleted. The properties' data was stored in sectors 50, 51, 90, and 99. New data is then written to the database. This data requires four sectors. Because it takes the first available sectors, it ends up in sectors 50, 51, 90, and 99. This data is now fragmented. It will take longer to retrieve this data than it would if the sectors that contained the data were consecutive.

AD defragmentation can occur in two modes: online mode and offline mode. These are defined in the following sections.

## Online Defragmentation

Online mode means that the server remains online while the process takes place. The online defragmentation method is slower than offline defragmentation, because the DC must service requests while the defragmentation is taking place, and it offers fewer benefits than offline defragmentation.

Online defragmentation is an automatic process that kicks off, by default, every 12 hours. This method is part of the garbage-collection process discussed in the "Garbage Collection" section earlier in this chapter. Full defragmentation can take place with this method, but the size of the AD database file will never be reduced. The records in the database are moved so they exist on contiguous sectors, but even if there is a lot of empty space in the database file (for instance, after a mass deletion process), the space will not be returned to the file system.

## Offline Defragmentation

Offline mode offers greater benefits, but the DC must be taken offline. Because this process is more vulnerable to being corrupted through an unexpected power failure or hardware issue, an offline defragmentation never occurs on the live database file. Instead, a copy of the database is made, and the defragmentation occurs against it. When defragmentation is complete, you must archive the current version of ntds.dit that is being used and move the defragmented version into its place.

Do not delete the old copy of **ntds.dit** until the DC has been rebooted and proven to work with the new defragmented file.

Offline defragmentation is the only way to return space from the database to the file system. This is useful after you have performed mass deletions in the database. By default, if you have a database that contains 50MB of data, and 50% of that data is deleted, the file remains at 50MB. The only way to return the 25MB to the file system is to perform an offline defragmentation.

### Performing an Offline Defragmentation

You must use the NTDSUtil command-line utility to perform an offline defragmentation. For the process to run, you must reboot your server and bring it up in Directory Services Restore Mode. The steps for performing an offline defragmentation are as follows:

1. Restart the server, pressing F8 during startup. The Advanced Startup Options are displayed.

2. Select Directory Services Restore Mode. This starts the server, but it does not start AD.

3. Log in to the server using the Administrators account. This is stored locally on each DC and can be different for each DC in your enterprise.

4. Open a command prompt. Type `ntdsutil` and press Enter.

5. Type `files` and press Enter.

6. Type `compact to <drive>\<folder>`, where `<drive>` and `<folder>` are the location where the compacted file will be stored. Press Enter.

7. Once the process is complete, a new `ntds.dit` file will exist at this location. Type `quit` and press Enter. Type `quit` and press Enter again to exit NTDSUtil.

8. Copy the new `ntds.dit` file over the old version of `ntds.dit`.

9. Restart the DC.

# Recommendations for AD Database Maintenance

The first recommendation for maintaining an AD database is to do it! Make sure that you understand which options are available to you and that they are scheduled to be performed on a regular basis. You should be especially careful of changing the default settings for the tombstone lifetime. This is 60 days by default, and reducing this timeframe can prevent you from being able to restore system state data that is past the tombstone lifetime. (Think of this as a sell-by date; you cannot use the backup if the sell-by date—that is, the tombstone lifetime—has expired.)

You should separate the AD database file from the log files. This prevents disk contention and increases the performance of a DC.

Keep in mind that you do not have to perform an offline defragmentation regularly. Instead, you should rely on the online defragmentation process. You should only perform an offline defragmentation if you think you can compact the database and return a significant amount of space back to the file system. This happens when mass deletions have taken place or when a server that used to be a Global Catalog server will now operate simply as a DC.

# Monitoring Active Directory

Restoring Active Directory data after the event of a failure is still, even with all the correct processes and tapes in place, a harrowing experience. The purpose of monitoring is twofold. First of all, monitoring helps you maintain performance over time. It should alert you to dips in performance, allowing for proactive maintenance. Monitoring can also help you in investigating problems on your system, such as sudden failures of hardware components.

Active Directory, and some of its ancillary services, relies heavily on replication. *Replication* can be defined as the process of making domain controllers (DC) consistent. It should be noted that two areas of replication must be working for a reliable Windows Server 2003 environment.

As mentioned earlier in this chapter, AD is a database. Properties within that database, when they are updated, must be replicated within the environment. This type of replication is commonly called *Active Directory replication*.

At the same time, there are services that rely on AD that store data that is not part of the database. An example of this is Group Policy. Group Policy is actually made up of two sets of data. The first is called the *Group Policy Container (GPC)*. The GPC data is stored within AD and is therefore replicated using standard AD replication processes. Associated with this data are objects called *Group Policy Templates (GPTs)*. These are physical files. For instance, they might be .reg files that store changes that must be applied to the Registries on client machines.

GPTs are stored in SYSVOL on every DC within a domain. All instances of SYSVOL must be kept consistent (a Group Policy cannot be applied if only one or the other of these two items, the GPC or the GPT, exists at a DC). Replication of the GPT data is performed not by AD replication but by the File Replication Service (FRS).

These two replication systems operate using different technologies, and even different topologies. Therefore, for proper monitoring of a Windows Server 2003 environment, you must know what tools are available to monitor them.

# Monitoring Active Directory Replication

The Active Directory replication process is fairly complex, and it relies on other systems to make it work. For instance, DNS is an integral part of any Windows Server 2003 deployment, and a failure in DNS will undoubtedly cause problems with AD replication.

There are three main tools you can use to troubleshoot replication problems with AD:

➤ Event Viewer

➤ The command-line utility Repadmin

➤ The graphical user interface tool Replmon

Any one of these tools can be used to troubleshoot issues or to alert you to problems as they develop.

 Although you might be familiar with Event Viewer from previous versions of Windows, you should note that it is somewhat more complex in a Windows Server 2003 AD environment. Depending on the services you have installed, there are likely to be many different logs to view. For example, problems might appear in the Directory Services log that actually are a response to a problem somewhere else, such as in DNS. Make sure you look at all relevant logs when troubleshooting.

## Event Viewer

Event Viewer contains log files generated by the operating system. The level of detail in the recorded events, and the number of the events themselves, can vary, depending on the level of logging you have turned on.

You can change the level of logging in the Registry. The Registry setting is HKLM, SYSTEM, CurrentControlSet, Services, NTDS, Diagnostics. Four settings can affect the level of logging:

➤ **0**—Disabled

➤ **1**—Minimum Reporting

➤ **2**—Moderate Reporting

➤ **3**—Full Reporting

Logging takes processing time, not to mention disk writes. Therefore, it is not a good idea to turn on full reporting unless it is really necessary, such as when you are actively trying to track down an error.

The events recorded in the logs can be exported for reporting and analysis. Common file types are CSV and TXT. These can easily be imported into applications such as Microsoft Excel.

It used to be possible to use a resource kit utility called Dumpel to analyze event logs. However, this tool has not been updated for Windows Server 2003. It is limited in that it can only be used for the Application, System and Security logs.

## Repadmin

*Replication Administrator*, or *Repadmin*, is a tool that ships with the resource kit. It has many of the same functions as Replmon, with the added benefit (or negative, depending on your point of view) of being command-line based.

Repadmin allows you to monitor replication, while at the same time complements other console functions. For example, if you want to know whether a DC is a Global Catalog (GC) server, you can either view it in the Active Directory Sites and Services console or use Repadmin (with /options).

Repadmin can provide a lot of information and functions. Among other things it can do the following:

➤ Give status of the Knowledge Consistency Checker (KCC)

➤ Provide the last replication event received from a DC's partner or partners

➤ Be used to delete objects restored accidentally with an authoritative restore (such as when the tombstone value has been exceeded)

➤ Disable compression of AD replication data intersite

Repadmin is not a tool you use every day, but it does offer a method of drilling down into the replication process and getting to the heart of a DC's functions.

## Replmon

*Replication Monitor* is basically the same tool as Repadmin, with the addition of a graphical user interface (GUI). This makes it easier to use while you're at a server console. Replmon is provided with System Tools in a Windows Server 2003 installation.

Because Replmon has a GUI, some might find it easier to use. When it starts, it displays a standard set of data. This can be useful to give you basic information at a glance. The following information is provided:

> *Naming context*—Provides the naming contexts supported on the server. If the server is a GC, all naming contexts in the forest are provided.

> *Replication partners*—Lists the names of the inbound replication partners.

> *Icons*—A double server icon is an intrasite partner. A server and phone icon is an intersite partner. A mini PC means local server.

> *Log entries*—The right pane shows the replication history (new entries are added at the end).

Replmon also enables you to see objects that have been tombstoned but not yet deleted. Along with the ability to configure email notification if a connection to a replication partner fails, Replmon represents a useful tool for monitoring AD replication.

# Introduction to FRS

FRS is an integral part of the Windows Server 2003 AD environment. As mentioned earlier, without it, Group Policy would be unable to work. Another instance where FRS plays a key role is when you're using the Distributed File System (Dfs). With Dfs, it is possible to replicate folders between servers. This means the contents of the Dfs source folder must be copied from one place to another; this is done with FRS.

Some significant changes to FRS have been made since Windows 2000. The main difference is that in previous versions, FRS was forced to use the same replication topology as AD. In Windows Server 2003, it is possible to set up a unique topology. This is useful when configuring FRS for use with Dfs, where the AD topology might not be relevant.

Basic knowledge of FRS should include the following items:

> FRS is multithreaded. By default, eight files can be transferred at once.

> Replication occurs based on notification of changes. No polling is ever done.

> FRS servers notify their partners immediately if there is a change to a file. They do not wait 5 minutes (as seen for AD replication).

> FRS replicates on the file level. This means that an entire file must be replicated, even if there is only a minor change.

> FRS uses RPC calls; it never uses SMTP.

Along with this information, it is important to note two weaknesses to FRS:

➤ FRS can only work between Windows 2000 and Windows Server 2003 servers.

➤ FRS does not replicate security descriptors when replicating files. Permissions must be set at each replica.

# Monitoring FRS Replication

We'll now take a look at two different ways to monitor FRS replication. Along with these tools, you can also monitor FRS through inference. What is meant by this is that tools such as Gpotool, which is used to monitor Group Policy, also give information about FRS (because FRS is used to replicate SYSVOL).

## Event Log

FRS has its own log on every DC. This log, known as the *File Replication Service*, can be used to view status, warnings, and errors. Along with other logs (such as DNS), you should be able to form a complete picture of the FRS process.

## Log Files

An option known as *debug logging* can be used for FRS. Debug logging increases the amount of logging that takes place when FRS is running. You set this option through the Registry at HKLM, System, CurrentControlSet, Services NtFrs, Parameters, DebugSeverity (REG_DWORD). Setting this value to 5 imposes the highest level of logging. These logs are stored in the <systemroot>\debug folder.

It is also possible to specify the number of log files that can be created, along with their maximum size.

# Exam Prep Questions

## Question 1

> Younes has just performed a large number of updates and deletions from Active Directory. This was done because his company has been downsizing, and some divisions are being moved outside of the company. Which of the following procedures should he perform? [Check all correct answers.]
>
> ❏ A. Backing up the AD data.
>
> ❏ B. Defragmentating the AD data.
>
> ❏ C. Moving the AD database.
>
> ❏ D. Nothing. Just wait 24 hours before doing any more administrative work for the replication to settle.

Answers A and B are correct. Before performing a defragmentation of the AD database, it is a good idea to perform a backup first. Once this is done, a defragmentation can take place. Answer C is incorrect because moving the AD database is a decision made outside of the process being considered here. That is related to performance and/or capacity requirements. Answer D is incorrect because convergence of the changes will happen regardless of whether additional administrative tasks are being performed.

## Question 2

> Bertram Rawe has just received an email message from a consultant who is coming in to perform a health check on the network. The consultant has told Bertram that he must be prepared to move the AD database on several domain controllers. What are the reasons why he would want to do this? [Check all correct answers.]
>
> ❏ A. The consultant might be bothered about performance on the domain controller. On at least a few of them, hard disk space is getting low on the partition on which AD is installed. During his last visit, the consultant installed a new set of mirrored disks; these are a better choice for the AD database.
>
> ❏ B. The consultant might be bothered about performance on the domain controller. On at least a few of them, hard disk space is getting low on the partition on which AD is installed. During his last visit, the consultant created a new partition on the RAID-5 controller. This is a better choice for the AD database.

❏ C. The consultant wants to move the database to another machine to facilitate better overall performance.

❏ D. The consultant wants to perform a database defragmentation. This is best done with a copy of the AD database in case corruption occurs.

Answers A and D are correct. Two of the most common reasons to move the AD database are to optimize performance by moving it to a dedicated physical hard disk and for the purposes of defragmentation. Answer B is incorrect because moving the database to a different partition on a RAID-5 controller does not mean the data is being moved to a different physical hard disk. The DC would still suffer from disk contention. Answer C is incorrect because the correct procedure for creating a new DC is to run Dcpromo.

# Question 3

Siobhan Chamberlin is a system administrator for a large bank. While running statistics on her servers, she finds that one of her domain controllers is running extremely low on hard disk space. Currently, it is losing 10MB per week. She calls her manager and he tells her not to worry. He will have a support technician add a new hard disk early next week. Siobhan is concerned that the DC will fail before that. Why is the manager confident that this will not be a problem?

○ A. The manager is mistaken. With 10MB being consumed every week, it is highly likely that within days, the DC will fail with a lack of disk space.

○ B. AD will soon discover that the hard disk is getting full. When it does, it will lock the partition that contains the database, thereby preventing any additional space being consumed.

○ C. The manager is correct. AD will send an alert email to all administrators when failure is imminent due to lack of disk space.

○ D. The manager is correct. Two files, each consuming 10MB each, are stored along with the AD data files. These files exist to consume disk space should the disks on a DC fail.

Answer D is correct. There are two files that exist simply to consume disk space. If needed, they are deleted to allow AD to function. Answer A is incorrect because the relatively low weekly consumption, along with the two files, will ensure the server will stay up for more than a week. Answer B is incorrect because there is no built-in function with AD that allows it to lock hard disks if they run out of disk space. Answer C is incorrect because, once again, this function does not exist.

# Question 4

AD is made up of several files. Which of the following represents part of the file set used by AD?

- ○ A. **Ntds.db**
- ○ B. **Ntds.dit**
- ○ C. **Res.log**
- ○ D. **Res3.log**

Answer B is correct. `Ntds.dit` is the file that contains the AD data. Answer A is incorrect because this is clearly a misspelling of `Ntds.dit`. Answers C and D are incorrect because neither of them are the correct name for placeholder files used by AD to conserve space on the hard disk. The correct names for these files are `res1.log` and `res2.log`.

# Question 5

Zevi Mehlman is a system administrator for a charitable organization in Washington, DC. He has been cleaning up an inherited AD-based network by clearing out a lot of objects within AD. These deletions constituted about a third of the total AD data. Over the last few days, Zevi has been monitoring the **ntds.dit** file. He is expecting the size of this file to reduce because it now holds a lot less data. However, he has seen nothing yet. Why is this?

- ○ A. When objects are deleted from AD, they are not immediately deleted. Instead, they are assigned a tombstone of 60 days. The size of the file will not be reduced until after this tombstone has expired.
- ○ B. Zevi is wasting his time because the file will never reduce in size. The space, once consumed by the objects, simply remains empty space within the database file.
- ○ C. Zevi must wait for 24 hours.
- ○ D. Zevi should back up and restore the database. This compresses the file.

Answer B is correct. Zevi would have to perform an offline defragmentation of the database to gain back the space. Answer A is incorrect because, although tombstoning exists as described, it does not affect the space consumed by the database file. Answer C is incorrect because waiting will not change the end result. Answer D is incorrect because backing up and restoring data will not change the overall file size.

# Question 6

Dennis Leibich is a system administrator for a large enterprise. Dennis would like to increase the performance of AD reads and writes. He remembers reading that that to do this he should move the AD database to a different physical hard disk from the log files. This is a single hard disk, with the operating system installed on it, along with a RAID-5 array that includes the AD database file. Dennis decides to move the database file to the single hard disk. During a conversation with the IT Manager, however, he is told he must not do this. Why was he told this?

○ A. His boss does not understand AD. He is wrong; the database *should* be moved.

○ B. Although Dennis will gain some performance benefits from making the move, the lack of data protection in this particular instance means it is not a good idea.

○ C. If performance can be gained by moving the database, Windows Server 2003 will do it automatically.

○ D. RAID-5 is a superior system. Disk writes and reads on a RAID-5 system are substantially faster than any other RAID system; therefore, the files are best left where they are.

Answers B is correct. When considering moving the AD database file, Dennis should consider many factors, not just performance. Answer A is incorrect because moving the database can be a good idea. Answer C is incorrect because Windows Server 2003 will never move the database automatically. Answer D is incorrect because RAID-5, although widely used and effective, is not the fastest performing member of the RAID family for reads and writes.

# Question 7

Scott Keating is a system administrator who has been diligently performing backups of his system state data every 90 days. After 85 days, a server fails because of a hard disk failure. Scott installs a new hard disk and then reinstalls Windows Server 2003. When this is complete, he intends to restore from his last backup. Scott calls a friend to refresh his mind on the correct steps, and he is surprised when his friend advises him that his backups are too old and that he is better off simply running Dcpromo. Scott doesn't agree with this. Who is correct?

○ A. Scott is correct. The age of backed-up files does not matter.

○ B. The friend is correct. AD has a time limit of 30 days on AD restores. Data that is older than this will be replaced by the AD replication process anyway, so Windows 2003 prevents it from being restored.

○ C.  Scott is correct. Although the data is old, he can rely on AD replication to clear up any problems that might arise.

○ D.  His friend is correct. Because the backed-up files are older than the garbage-collection process, Scott could introduce inconsistencies into AD.

Answer D is correct. One can adjust the garbage-collection process to fit in with a backup schedule. However, one should never attempt to restore data from a backup that is older than the garbage-collection process interval (default, 60 days). Answer A is incorrect because the age of the files does indeed matter. Answer B is incorrect because there is no 30-day limit to restores. Answer C is incorrect because AD replication will not fix the bad data.

# Question 8

By default, garbage collection takes place on a system every 60 days. The DCs in Eric's network have plenty of disk space. In addition, he would like to extend the usefulness of his backups. He decides to change the garbage-collection process to occur every 90 days. Which tool will Eric use?

○ A.  Eric will use ADSIEdit to change this.

○ B.  Eric will use NTDSUtil to change this.

○ C.  Eric must use NTDSUtil and AD Domains and Trusts to change this.

○ D.  Eric must use AD Domains and Trusts to change this.

Answer A is correct. Eric will use ADSIEdit to change the garbage-collection process. Answer B is incorrect because, although NTDSUtil has many uses, changing the garbage-collection interval is not one of them. Answers C and D are incorrect because Active Directory Domains and Trusts is a tool used for domain management and has no role here.

# Question 9

Moira Chamberlin is a system administrator for an insurance company. Moira accidentally deleted an OU and wants to get it back. Fortunately, she performed a backup of AD one hour before the deletion. Moira starts the DC and does a restore. When she is done, she restarts the server. The server comes back perfectly. However, within 30 minutes, the OU she has just restored is once again deleted. Why did this happen?

O A. Although it is possible to get this object back from a restore, it must be an authoritative restore. Moira must have performed a nonauthoritative restore.

O B. The backup worked fine. However, because the object had previously been deleted, it must now be re-created. This assigns a new SID and allows the object name to be reused.

O C. Once an object is deleted, it is gone forever. Moira should rename one of her current OUs so it is the same as the deleted object.

O D. Moira must wait. AD replication follows a prescribed methodology. Although it looks like the object is deleted, after an hour or so, replication will stop, and the object will be restored once again.

Answer A is correct. An authoritative restore would allow the object to be restored and would force it to be replicated out to all other DCs. If this is not done, AD replication will detect that the object has come back and will simply have it removed. Answer B is incorrect because objects can indeed be restored with their original SIDs. Answer C is incorrect because renaming an OU would not restore all the permissions and members that once belonged to the original OU. Answer D is incorrect because replication would not fix this problem without an authoritative restore taking place.

# Question 10

Joanne works for a banking organization. Joanne knows that she should back up her DC regularly, but she has not done so in awhile because of several urgent projects that have been going on. Also, the server should never be taken offline. She decides to place a call with Microsoft technical support to ask them for advice about protecting herself due to server failure. What was she told? [Choose the best answer.]

O A. Joanne was told that she should take the server offline so a backup can be performed. Losing a server for a night while it is being backed up is far better than losing it for an extended time due to server failure.

O B. Joanne was told that she should still perform a backup even if the server is being used. Although she won't be able to back up the log files for AD because they are in use, she can still back up the AD database and Registry files. This alone would get the DC functional again.

O C. Joanne was told not to worry. The database is transactional and can protect itself from failures automatically. Backing up to a file or tape is a precautionary measure that is desirable, but not necessary.

O D. Joanne was told to go ahead and perform a backup of system state data. The DC does not have to be taken offline for this process to take place.

Answer D is correct. The built-in backup utility can be used to perform an online backup. Answer A is incorrect because it is not necessary to take a server offline before performing a backup. Answer B is incorrect because an online backup can indeed back up the log files. Answer C is incorrect because a system state backup is an important part of the recovery process for large enterprises.

# Need to Know More?

 Jones, Don and Mark Rouse. *Windows Server 2003 Delta Guide.* Sams Publishing. Indianapolis, IN, 2003. ISBN 0789728494.

 Morimoto, Rand, et al. *Windows Server 2003 Unleashed.* Sams Publishing. Indianapolis, IN. 2003, ISBN 0672321548.

# Practice Exam 1

# Question 1

Duncan is a network administrator who is responsible for migrating a Windows NT domain to Windows Server 2003. The PDC has the following specifications:

- ➤ Dual processors
- ➤ Pentium III 900MHz
- ➤ 128MB RAM
- ➤ A RAID-5 hard drive configuration with four 18.2GB hard drives

After the new installation of Windows Server 2003 is promoted, Duncan notices that the system is performing extremely sluggishly. What might the problem be? [Choose the best answer.]

- ○ A. The server needs a RAM upgrade.
- ○ B. Replication of the new AD data is causing a temporary performance slowdown.
- ○ C. Duncan should change the hard drive configuration to move the system partition to its own separate mirrored partition.
- ○ D. Duncan should promote a BDC to take some of the AD load off of this domain controller.

# Question 2

You are a network administrator who is installing your first Windows Server 2003 server in your organization. Your installation of Active Directory halts because the SYSVOL folder cannot seem to be placed where you've specified. What is the most likely cause of the problem? [Choose the best answer.]

- ○ A. You've requested it go on a partition that doesn't have enough space.
- ○ B. You've formatted the partition with NTFS.
- ○ C. The drive letter you've specified doesn't exist.
- ○ D. The partition you are specifying is FAT or FAT32.

# Question 3

To allow for backward compatibility with Windows NT 4 domain controllers, what functional level should your domains be running at? [Choose the best answer.]

- ○ A. Windows 2000 native mode
- ○ B. Windows 2000 mixed mode
- ○ C. Windows 2003 functional level
- ○ D. Windows NT compatibility mode

# Question 4

Melissa Wise is the network manager responsible for a Windows Server 2003 forest that contains three domain trees with a total of eight domains. She is wanting to raise the forest functional level from Windows 2000 mixed mode to Windows 2003 in order to take advantage of new functionality, and in the process she verifies that each of the parent domains in each tree has been raised to Windows 2003. However, when she goes to raise the forest functional level she is unable to. What might Melissa have missed? [Check all correct answers.]

❏ A. Some domains are not at the Windows 2003 functional level.

❏ B. She has to raise the functional level to Windows 2000 native mode first and then she can raise it to the Windows 2003 functional level.

❏ C. She has a trust relationship in place with a Windows NT 4 domain that must be removed prior to raising the forest functional level.

❏ D. She has to log in with an account that is a member of the Enterprise Admins group.

# Question 5

Kathy works for a worldwide organization based in the United States. Currently the organization has 50,000 employees with five different locations (Singapore, France, England, Canada, and the United States). The domain is a single domain tree with three configured domains in individual sites: one for Singapore, one for France and England, and one for Canada and the United States. The connection to the Singapore site is very unreliable. What can Kathy do to configure replication better between the Singapore site and the U.S./Canada site? [Choose the best answer.]

○ A. Configure a bridgehead server between the two sites.

○ B. Change the configuration to allow Singapore into the U.S./Canada site.

○ C. Configure IP over RPC replication to use a schedule between the two sites.

○ D. Configure SMTP replication between the two sites.

# Question 6

Jon Brock is a network administrator who is trying to demote a Windows Server 2003 domain controller, but it isn't responding. This particular DC holds no FSMO roles, and Jon is sure he no longer needs it (he's planning on formatting it and reinstalling for a different purpose). He needs to do the reformat as quickly as he can. What would be his best option here? [Choose the best answer.]

○ A. Jon should run **dcpromo /forceremoval**.

○ B. Jon should simply reboot the server and reformat it.

○ C. Jon should wait until all replication completes and try demoting the DC again.

○ D. Jon should turn off the server and leave it off for a few days in order for it to be purged from AD.

# Question 7

Daniel is logging on to a Windows 2000 domain that is in native mode. He is a member of a universal group called Managers. Which of the following will assist in the creation of Daniel's access token? [Choose the best answer.]

○ A. The PDC Emulator

○ B. Global Catalog servers

○ C. The Kerberos transaction server

○ D. The Infrastructure Master

# Question 8

Tom is the owner of a cardboard container corporation that manufactures boxes for shipping computer products. The company has a registered namespace of **stretchandshrink.com**, which it utilizes for its AD domain. Tom has just purchased an office supply company that currently has no registered namespace and no AD domain. In the planning discussions, it has been determined that the combination of both companies will require each to maintain a separate security configuration under a contiguous namespace. Which of the following design types should be implemented? [Choose the best answer.]

○ A. Single domain

○ B. Domain tree

○ C. Empty root domain tree

○ D. Forest

# Question 9

You manage the Active Directory forest for a branch of your parent company, W&W, Inc. Users are frustrated because when they connect to resources with their DNS domain name, they have to type their name plus **@sanfran.california. na.wwinc.com**. As the administrator, what can you do to alleviate their problems?

○ A.  Reinstall the domain and create it with a shorter name.

○ B.  Tell the users to log in with just **@wwinc.com** because your domain is a child domain in that tree and transitive trusts will allow it.

○ C.  Create a shortcut trust with the parent domain so users can log in with the shorter **wwinc.com** name.

○ D.  Create an alternate UPN suffix and assign it to the user accounts in the domain.

# Question 10

There is an OU called DocProc for the document-processing department in your company, which happens to be an investment banking firm. There are two security groups in the DocProc OU—one is DocProc for the users, and the other is Managers for the management staff. You have a GPO that enforces a specific wallpaper and removes the Display option changes. Managers are complaining that they do not like having this policy enforced on them. What should you do? [Choose the best answer.]

○ A.  Remove the Managers group from the OU.

○ B.  Select the Block Policy Inheritance option from the OU.

○ C.  Change the permissions on the policy to Deny Read and Apply Group Policy for the Managers security group.

○ D.  Remove the policy from the OU and apply it directly to the DocProc security group.

# Question 11

Charles Thompson is a junior system administrator who has been delegated the task of connecting the new Windows Server 2003 Active Directory forest, **metalmilitia.com**, to the existing Windows NT 4 domain, VOA. The senior administrator, Ken Lord, has requested that when Charles configures the trust, users in VOA should have access to resources in **metalmilitia.com**, but only administrators of **metalmilitia.com** should have access to resources in VOA. What would be the best method for Charles to use to configure this? [Choose the best answer.]

- ○ A.  Charles should configure a one-way realm trust where **metalmilitia.com** trusts VOA.

- ○ B.  Charles should configure a one-way forest trust where **metalmilitia.com** trusts VOA.

- ○ C.  Charles should configure a two-way external trust between **metalmilitia. com** and VOA and then use security groups to limit access from **metalmilitia.com** to VOA to only administrators.

- ○ D.  Charles should configure a one-way external trust where **metalmilitia. com** trusts VOA.

# Question 12

Kim is the network administrator for a global training corporation. She has created a large number of universal groups with several hundred users in each group. She has noticed that a great deal of network traffic has resulted. What is the recommended way of handling universal groups that Kim should apply? [Choose the best answer.]

- ○ A.  The universal groups are established properly in the scenario; the traffic is being generated from other sources.

- ○ B.  Kim should place the users into local groups and then place the local groups into universal groups.

- ○ C.  Kim should place the users into global groups and then place the global groups into universal groups.

- ○ D.  Kim should place the users into universal groups and then place the universal groups into domain local groups.

# Question 13

Ian Worcester is a network manager for a complex Active Directory forest that consists of six domain trees and a total of 28 individual domains, which represents the infrastructure of the Willis Guitar Company, Inc. A partial diagram of the domain structure follows.

Trees:

**ww-inc.com**, **mm-corp.us**, **virtual-realm.com**, **willwillis.us**, **wwguitars.com**, and **wwamps.com**

Users in **development.texas.na.ww-inc.com** often need to collaborate with their Asian counterparts in **development.japan.asia.wwguitars.com**, and users in both domains complain about how long it takes for shared folders to open even though there is excellent connectivity between physical locations. Is there anything Ian can do to help the situation? [Choose the best answer.]

- ○ A.  Ian can create a shortcut trust between **development.texas.na. ww-inc.com** and **development.japan.asia.wwguitars.com**.
- ○ B.  Ian can purchase additional bandwidth to reduce the delay in opening shared resources.
- ○ C.  Ian can move the users from the two domains into a common domain.
- ○ D.  Ian can create a forest trust between the **ww-inc.com** and **wwguitars.com** domain trees.

# Question 14

You are the network administrator of a single domain tree called **braincore.net** with several child domains (**ny.braincore.net**, **utah.braincore.net**, and **delaware.braincore.net**). In the NY domain there is an OU named Marketing. Inside that OU is a user named Joe User. You have implemented a number of Group Policies within the domain. They are as follows:

- ➤ Site Group Policy: Wallpaper is set to Red. Task Manager is disabled.
- ➤ Domain Group Policy: Display Properties tab is disabled. (No Override is set to On.)
- ➤ OU1 Policy: Wallpaper is set to Blue. The Display Properties tab is enabled. (Block Inheritance is set to On.)
- ➤ OU2 Policy: Wallpaper is set to Green.

The OU policies are set in the order of OU1 being on top and OU2 on the bottom of the application order list. What is the resultant set of policies? [Choose the best answer.]

○ A. Joe logs on and his wallpaper is green. Task Manager is not disabled. Display Properties is disabled.

○ B. Joe logs on and his wallpaper is red. Task Manager is disabled.

○ C. Joe logs on and his wallpaper is blue. Task Manager is not disabled. Display Properties is disabled.

○ D. Joe logs on and his wallpaper is red. Task Manager is disabled. Display Properties is enabled.

# Question 15

The first domain controller within your domain contains all five FSMO roles. There are several domain controllers within the domain. The first domain controller fails. What do you need to do to allow the FSMO roles to continue? [Choose the best answer.]

○ A. FSMO roles automatically transfer when the domain controller holding those roles goes down.

○ B. You need to seize the roles by using the Ntdsutil tool.

○ C. You can transfer the roles by using the AD Domains and Trusts tool.

○ D. FSMO roles will not be able to continue.

# Question 16

Matt Rutherford is a Unix administrator who works side by side with Nick Smith, who is a Windows administrator of a Windows Server 2003 forest and one domain. The CIO of the company, Rebekah Willis, has asked Matt and Nick to reduce the total cost of ownership of the separate systems by improving user efficiency in accessing resources from one system to the other and to reduce the current duplication of resources that exists in the Unix and Windows networks. What should Matt and Nick do? [Choose the best answer.]

○ A. Create a realm trust between the Windows Server 2003 forest and the Unix network.

○ B. Create a realm trust between the Windows Server 2003 domain and the Unix network.

○ C. Create an external trust between the Windows Server 2003 forest and the Unix network.

○ D. Migrate the Unix network to Windows Server 2003 Active Directory.

# Question 17

You have installed and configured a new domain controller for an existing Windows Server 2003 domain in a forest that consists of five sites. After a few days you notice that replication isn't behaving the way it should. After troubleshooting you find out that for some reason the domain controller was installed into the wrong site. What can you do to fix the problem? [Choose the best answer.]

- ○ A. Move the DC to the correct site.
- ○ B. Demote the DC and rerun Dcpromo.
- ○ C. Modify the TCP/IP configuration so the DC goes to the correct site.
- ○ D. Remove the site that the DC currently belongs to in order to reallocate the DCs to other sites.

# Question 18

Brandon has designed and implemented a single Windows Server 2003 domain for his company. The company's headquarters is in Fort Lauderdale, Florida. Smaller branch locations include San Francisco, California and London, England. Each location has its own DCs and separate subnet configurations, which are connected through ISDN lines that barely support existing traffic. Brandon notices an extreme amount of replication traffic. He checks the Active Directory Sites and Services tool. What will he notice when he checks this tool? [Choose the best answer.]

- ○ A. He will see that the replication topology is incorrectly set, and he will have to run the Knowledge Consistency Checker.
- ○ B. He will see that the sites configured are missing bridgehead servers.
- ○ C. He will be able to determine the performance of his ISDN traffic and see which traffic is generating the most harm.
- ○ D. He will see that all DCs will be contained within the same default site, and he will need to break them up according to subnet.

# Question 19

You have three site locations for your domain **bluemoose.com**. The sites are Taiwan, Brazil, and South Africa. Replication is configured between the three sites. There is a site link between South Africa and Brazil that is close to T1 connectivity. A slower 56Kbps link connects South Africa and Taiwan. Taiwan and Brazil are connected at T1 speeds. How can you configure these sites to ensure replication between the three in the best possible way, while still providing a backup plan? [Choose all correct answers.]

❏ A. Configure the site link for the South Africa–Brazil connection to be 100.

❏ B. Configure the site link for the South Africa–Brazil connection to be 10.

❏ C. Configure the site link for the South Africa–Taiwan connection to be 100.

❏ D. Configure the site link for the South Africa–Taiwan connection to be 10.

# Question 20

W&W, Inc., is an organization that has a Windows Server 2003 Active Directory infrastructure consisting of four domains in a single forest. The domains are named after the cities in which the offices are located: Dallas, Omaha, StLouis, and Boston. The V.P. of Finance, Warren Selby, has recently transferred from the Boston office to the St. Louis office, and as a result his user account was moved from the Boston domain to the StLouis domain. A few days later, Warren calls the domain administrator in the Dallas office about getting access to a shared finance folder on a Dallas file server. When Jim, the domain admin, attempts to add Warren's account to the shared permissions list, he can't find the account in the StLouis domain. After checking he finds it in its original Boston domain. Jim calls up Brian Patrick, the domain admin in St. Louis, and asks him to check on Warren's user account. Brian reports that Warren's user account is part of the StLouis domain, as it should be. Jim calls up Suresh Doss, the domain admin in Boston, who tells him that he also shows Warren's user account as belonging to the StLouis domain and not the Boston domain. Tim Pfeiffer in Omaha reports the same thing to Jim.

Jim obviously has a problem, but what is the likely cause? [Choose the best answer.]

○ A. The Infrastructure Master in the Dallas domain is down.

○ B. The Global Catalog server in Dallas is down.

○ C. The trust relationship connecting Dallas to the rest of the forest is broken.

○ D. Replication is not taking place as scheduled.

# Question 21

Alexandra Jade is a senior analyst for Yeatts Global Photo. She has configured a design for site replication that takes into consideration the company's five branch offices and their 56Kbps speed connections to the headquarters in Glenn Burnie, Maryland. What further consideration should she give to site design and implementation? [Choose the best answer.]

○ A. Her next consideration should be the purchase of faster links between branches.

○ B. Her next consideration should be the establishment of one unique sub-net that will work for all sites.

○ C. Her next consideration should be designing subnets for each site, where one and only one subnet per site is used.

○ D. Her next consideration should be designing subnets for each site, where one or more subnets in a site are used, without using the same subnet in different sites.

# Question 22

Scott Herrick changed his network password a few days ago on his Windows NT 4 workstation. His workstation belongs to a Windows Server 2003 Active Directory mixed-mode domain consisting of a couple Windows Server 2003 domain controllers and three Windows NT 4 BDCs that have yet to be upgraded. However, ever since he made the change and logged off, he has had to reboot several times in order to get logged in. He is irritated in that sometimes he gets an error that his password is rejected, but then sometimes it takes just fine and logs him in. Scott calls you up and asks you to help fix the problem. What are the most likely causes for Scott's login problems? [Choose two.]

❑ A. The PDC emulator is down.

❑ B. Scott needs to make sure his CAPS LOCK key isn't on or that he is entering his password wrong.

❑ C. Something went wrong with the password change and he should manually change it on a domain controller to something different.

❑ D. Replication of the password change did not reach all domain controllers.

# Question 23

Don Simpson is the senior systems administrator for W&W, Inc., which has recently acquired a competitor that was struggling to stay afloat in the tough economy. The decision has been made to merge the companies rather than have the acquired company continue to operate under its own brand. As a result, Don is bulk-adding roughly 5,000 user accounts to the **wwinc.com** domain, which already has approximately 3,500 accounts. When he runs the import it stops after 4,023 accounts have been created, with an error that the object can't be created. While troubleshooting the problem, Don gets a request to go ahead and create a few essential user accounts manually because they are needed ASAP. When Don opens up Active Directory Users and Computer and tries to create the accounts, the process fails. What problem might he be having in his domain? [Choose the best answer.]

- ○ A. The RID Master in the domain is down.
- ○ B. The PDC Emulator in the domain is down.
- ○ C. Don has reached the physical limit on the amount of user objects a domain will support.
- ○ D. The CSV file Don is trying to import from is corrupt and should be re-created.

# Question 24

Which of the following Operations Masters are forestwide roles? [Choose two.]
- ❑ A. Schema Master
- ❑ B. RID Master
- ❑ C. PDC Emulator
- ❑ D. Domain Naming Master
- ❑ E. Infrastructure Master

# Question 25

Ben Bailey is the systems administrator for a mid-sized company that has a main office plus seven small satellite offices. Three of the satellite offices are connected by 56Kbps WAN connections, mainly just to support email traffic and telnet access to the database server at the main office. The Windows Server 2003 infrastructure is a single Active Directory domain with each office being its own site. As a result of the slow bandwidth and small number of users at three of the offices, those offices have a server, but they are not Global Catalog servers. Ben wants to make logons more reliable and quicker for these three offices, yet he doesn't want to burden the 56K lines with the ongoing replication traffic that would occur if he made the local servers GC servers. What can he do to alleviate the problem? [Choose all correct answers.]

❑ A.  Raise the domain functional level to Windows 2003.

❑ B.  Place the global groups containing users at each site into appropriate universal groups.

❑ C.  Increase the bandwidth to the sites to more fully support the infra-structure's requirements.

❑ D.  Enable universal group caching.

# Question 26

Which of the following can be used to describe the data involved with an inter-site replication scenario? [Choose all correct answers.]

❑ A.  Data is sent uncompressed.

❑ B.  Data is sent compressed.

❑ C.  Data is sent through a schedule.

❑ D.  Data is sent by default replication parameters.

# Question 27

Jon Brock is the network administrator for a company that is looking to migrate from Windows NT 4 to Windows Server 2003 and Active Directory. The company currently has four domains to support one location because of varying administrative requirements. The CIO has asked Jon for a proposal for the new Windows Server 2003 deployment. What type of structure would be best for him to recommend? [Choose the best answer.]

○ A.   Jon should recommend upgrading each domain to Windows Server 2003 and using OUs within each domain to define the administrative structure.

○ B.   Jon should recommend moving all the user accounts into a single accounts domain for administrative purposes, leaving the other three domains as resource domains.

○ C.   Jon should recommend collapsing the four domains into a single domain and using OUs to create the organizational structure.

○ D.   Jon should recommend just upgrading each of the four domains in order to maintain their existing structure.

# Question 28

You are a network administrator for a company that uses smartcard technology extensively for user logon. The company has recently closed one of its branch offices, and at the same time is offering a new kiosk service to its clients. Because of the office closing, you decide to utilize those computers for the new kiosk setup, which will include the smartcard readers that have been in use for some time at the branch office. To enhance security, you remove the workstations from the domain and put them in their own workgroup. When you test the computers after they've been hooked up at the kiosk, you find that they are unable to log on to the network, using your user account or others, even though you are able to hook up your own laptop and log on with your smartcard. What might be happening? [Choose the best answer.]

○ A.   You need to open up the corporate firewall to allow the kiosk computers' traffic to pass.

○ B.   You need to grant "logon locally" permissions to the user accounts.

○ C.   You need to configure the user accounts the kiosk computers will use to log in with smartcards.

○ D.   You need to rejoin the workstations to the domain.

# Question 29

You are in the process of rolling out a smartcard deployment to replace password logons. You are using a Windows Server 2003 member server in your domain as the enrollment station, and you have configured the initial group of cards. However, some users are reporting problems logging in with their cards, although for other users the cards work. After troubleshooting you determine that the logon problems are limited only to Windows 2000 Professional users, and Windows XP Professional users are not having problems logging in. You check that the card readers are installed, and you are not seeing any errors. What might the problem be? [Choose the best answer.]

- O  A.  Windows 2000 Professional can't use smartcards created on Windows Server 2003.
- O  B.  Smartcard authentication requires Windows XP or Windows Server 2003.
- O  C.  Not all the users are properly configured to use smartcards in Active Directory Users and Computers.
- O  D.  The Windows 2000 Professional systems likely need the device driver for the smartcard reader updated.

# Question 30

Nick Smith is the network administrator for a Windows Server 2003 network. He has delegated the control of the Developers OU to the Developer Admins security group, but after he completes the wizard he realizes he only gave permission to reset passwords and not to create and delete user accounts. What does Nick need to do to fix the problem? [Choose the best answer.]

- O  A.  Nick needs to edit the properties of the Developer Admins security group and change the permissions.
- O  B.  Nick needs to remove the Developer Admins security group and re-create it. Then he needs to run the Delegation of Control Wizard to set the permissions back up.
- O  C.  Nick needs to run the Delegation of Control Wizard a second time to grant the desired permissions.
- O  D.  Nick needs to open the properties of the OU and go to the Security tab.

# Question 31

Bertram Rawe has been asked to plan a migration from Windows NT 4.0 to Windows Server 2003. Bertram's network consists of 30 servers. Because he is under a time constraint, he has decided to upgrade the servers as quickly as he can, while ensuring that users are not affected by the upgrade. The user workstations are Windows XP. In this case, this means upgrading 10 per day. He also wants to make sure he moves to a Windows 2003 mode domain as quickly as possible. To this end, he intends to install the first server in Windows 2003 mode. Then, as he upgrades additional servers, they, too, will be in this mode. Bertram hires a consultant to look over his plan but is disappointed to hear that his plan is not going to work. Why is this?

○ A. The only way to perform an upgrade over multiple days without affecting the users is to install the Windows Server 2003 servers in interim mode first. Once all servers are upgraded, then Bertram can switch to Windows 2003 mode.

○ B. Bertram's plan is good; however, he should use RIS to perform the upgrade.

○ C. Bertram's plan is too ambitious. The issue here is that it is unlikely that he could upgrade 10 servers a night; therefore, he should scale back his plan.

○ D. Bertram should plan on going to Windows 2003 native mode. Windows 2003 mode is an interim step designed to give backward compatibility with Windows 2000 servers. Because there are no Windows 2000 servers in this environment, Bertram should simply use native mode.

# Question 32

Scott Keatinge is a systems engineer working for an insurance company. He has been asked to make a presentation to his department about the inner workings of Active Directory with a view to helping the department troubleshoot problems. In Scott's network diagram, he has a root domain and two child domains. His asks his team members which things these domains necessarily have in common. What is the correct response? [Choose all correct answers.]

❑ A. Contiguous namespace

❑ B. A shared schema

❑ C. A shared configuration partition

❑ D. Backward compatibility with Windows NT 4.0 domain controllers

# Question 33

Siobhan Chamberlin has finished her plans for integrating the Windows Server 2003 DNS into Active Directory. She knows of the benefits and believes this would be a good move for her company. However, having shown her plans to a consultant, he has told her that she must be careful due to the additional burden of replication. Siobhan, on the other hand, believes that the replication burden of integrated DNS in Windows Server 2003 is much less than in Windows 2000. Who is right?

○ A. The consultant is right. When you integrate DNS into Active Directory, you are storing it in the domain partition. This means that every domain controller in the environment would have to copy and store DNS data, even if they are not running the DNS service.

○ B. Siobhan is right. Although there were considerations in the past, by default, Windows Server 2003 stores DNS data in an application partition, not the domain partition, as in Windows 2000.

○ C. The consultant is correct. However, there is actually no difference in the replication burden between Windows 2000 and Windows Server 2003.

○ D. Siobhan is correct. Microsoft has fine-tuned replication in Windows Server 2003, and although the replication topology remains the same, less data has to be transmitted and stored.

# Question 34

Denis Leibich is a systems administrator. He is having problems with Group Policy where a GPO that is supposed to change a user's wallpaper setting is not being applied to several computers. He calls a friend to ask her if she has any advise. The friend explains to Denis that GPOs are stored in two distinct places on a domain controller and that Denis must look in both locations to troubleshoot the issue. What are the names of these two locations, and where are they stored? [Choose all correct answers.]

❑ A. Group Policy Template. This is stored in Active Directory.

❑ B. Group Policy Container. This is stored on the SYSVOL share.

❑ C. Group Policy Template. This is stored on the SYSVOL share.

❑ D. Group Policy Container. This is stored in Active Directory.

# Question 35

Zevi Mehlman has deleted 500 objects from Active Directory. These objects were associated with a project that is now complete. When Zevi monitors the size of Active Directory, he is disappointed to see that the overall size of **NTDS.DIT** has not changed. He continues to monitor it for several days, but he never sees the size reduce. Why is this?

- ○ A. Space consumed in Active Directory cannot be reclaimed. This is for auditing purposes and to ensure that objects can be undeleted.

- ○ B. The time it takes for the size to be reclaimed is based on the tombstone settings. Because the default tombstone is 90 days, Zevi will have to wait at least that long before seeing a change.

- ○ C. Deletions never cause the size of the file to reduce; they merely create empty space within the **NTDS.DIT** file.

- ○ D. Space can only be reclaimed once full replication has taken place. Only when all copies of the database know about the deletion will space be reclaimed.

# Question 36

Volker Wiora has asked a consultant to review his network to make sure performance is optimal. On reviewing the Windows Server 2003 Active Directory structure, the consultant informs Volker that he should reduce the number of members in some security groups. Volker is approaching the maximum number of groups members, 5,000, and this can cause replication issues when members are added or taken away. Volker disputes this because his network is fully Windows Server 2003, with all domains running in Windows 2003 mode. Who is correct?

- ○ A. The consultant is correct. Due to the way group member additions are handled by Active Directory replication, the number of members in a group should be kept below 5,000.

- ○ B. Volker is correct. The replication of group membership additions has changed in Windows Server 2003 and is now more efficient.

- ○ C. Both are correct. Group membership replication is more efficient in Windows Server 2003, but still, membership should be kept below 5,000.

- ○ D. The consultant is correct. However, the mode that Active Directory is running in will affect the impact of the replication issue.

# Question 37

A new user created on a Windows Server 2003 domain controller must be replicated to all domain controllers in the domain. It takes time for this process to
take place. What is the term used to describe this period of time?

- ○ A.  Overlap period
- ○ B.  Latency
- ○ C.  Change notification
- ○ D.  Journal updates

# Question 38

Here are four actions commonly performed by Ron Porter, administrator of a
Windows Server 2003–based network:

- ➤  Adding a user
- ➤  Creating a new domain
- ➤  Adding a new object type in Active Directory
- ➤  Adding a group

Which of the following statements are correct?

- ○ A.  Two of these changes will cause enterprisewide replication, and two
       will cause domainwide replication.
- ○ B.  One of these changes will cause enterprisewide replication, and three
       will cause domainwide replication.
- ○ C.  Three of these changes will cause enterprisewide replication, and one
       will cause domainwide replication.
- ○ D.  None of these changes will cause enterprisewide replication, and all
       will cause domainwide replication.

# Question 39

Moira Chamberlin is a system administrator in a Windows Server 2003 enterprise running in Windows 2003 mode. She is explaining to a consultant that Active Directory can only have three replication topologies: domain, configuration, and schema. Because the configuration and schema topologies must be replicated to the same locations, they tend to be the same. The consultant corrects her and says she has forgotten one Active Directory replication topology type. Who is correct?

- A. Moira is correct. There are three, as listed.
- B. The consultant is correct. Active Directory can have a fourth partition known as an application partition.
- C. Neither is correct. There are only two—one for the domain, and one for the configuration and schema partitions.
- D. Neither are correct. There is only one replication topology.

# Question 40

Younes is a system administrator for a large company. One of his users, Eric, has to have an application targeted at him. Eric is the manager of finance, and he belongs to a finance security group and OU. Once he has tested the application, he will want it targeted to his employees. Younes wants to minimize the amount of work he must do now as well as when the testing has finished. Where is the most logical place to target this GPO?

- A. Site
- B. Domain
- C. OU
- D. Finance security group

# Question 41

Active Directory data is stored in a file on all domain controllers. What is the name of this file?

- A. **NTDS.DIT**
- B. **ADDS.ADT**
- C. **NTDS.ADS**
- D. **ADDS.DIT**

# Question 42

Which of the following are the names given to the partitions of data stored within Active Directory? [Choose all correct answers.]

❑ A. Domain

❑ B. Configuration

❑ C. Schema

❑ D. Application

# Question 43

Justin Rodino is troubleshooting a Group Policy problem. He has applied settings that target computers in an Organization Unit, but one client has not received them yet. He goes to the workstation and wants to apply the settings immediately. He cannot afford to restart the computer. What is the best way to achieve this?

○ A. Justin should use the Secedit command-line utility.

○ B. Group Policy can only be applied at startup. Therefore, he must restart the computer.

○ C. Group Policy does not require a restart; the user simply needs to log on and off.

○ D. Justin should use the Refreshgpo command-line tool.

# Question 44

Paul Butler is preparing some questions for a consultant who is going to visit him to discuss his company's Active Directory configuration. One of the concerns Paul has is with account lockouts. Paul has calculated that if he changes a password at a remote site, it will take 15 minutes before that change is replicated to all domain controllers in his organization. Paul is worried that a user might get locked out of the domain while he or she is waiting for replication to take place. When he presents this scenario to the consultant, the consultant tells Paul that he does not need to worry about this because Windows Server 2003 takes care of it automatically. What does the consultant mean?

○ A. The consultant knows that account lockout would not occur. If a user enters a bad password, he or she will simply be logged on with cached credentials.

○ B.  The consultant is wrong. The user would have to wait, but 15 minutes is an accessible window.

○ C.  The consultant is correct. If a user enters a password that is different from the one stored at a single domain controller, the domain controller simply polls all other domain controllers to see whether there has been an update for this account.

○ D.  The consultant is right. In this case, the domain controller that is trying to authenticate the user would poll the PDC Emulator to see whether the password had been changed. Password changes are replicated to the PDC Emulator on an urgent basis.

# Question 45

Active Directory is replicated through the domain and enterprise. Replication partners and site links define the replication paths. Partners between sites can be manually configured or automatically configured. What is the name of the automatic process that performs this function?

○ A.  Knowledge Consistency Checker

○ B.  Knowledge Replication Partner

○ C.  Knowledge Consistency Process

○ D.  Knowledge Case Checker

# Question 46

Jaime Rodriquez is a system administrator. He is having a problem extending the schema to add a new object type. When he does this, he gets an "access denied" message. He is worried about this because he is a domain administrator. He calls a colleague to discuss it, and his colleague says that Jaime does not have sufficient permissions—he needs to be added to a new security group. Jaime says that because he is a domain administrator, this should be all he needs. He is worried Active Directory is corrupt. Who is correct?

○ A.  The colleague is correct. In order to edit the schema Jaime would have to be a domain administrator in every domain in the enterprise.

○ B.  Jaime is correct. To edit the schema in a single domain, he simply needs to be a domain administrator. Jaime should run Ntdsutil.

○ C.  Jaime is correct. However, the database is not corrupt. Jaime simply needs to boot his server into Active Directory Maintenance Mode.

○ D.  The colleague is correct. Jaime must be made a member of the Schema Admins group in order to edit the schema.

# Question 47

Ester Helwig is a system administrator for a law firm. One of the primary functions on her network is time synchronization, because the company uses this in its documents. Ester is therefore concerned when she starts to see time-synchronization errors in the logs on her servers. Where is one of the main places Ester should look for this error?

○ A.  Ester should check the PDC Emulator. This machine is tasked with time-synchronization duties.

○ B.  Ester should search for the server running the Time Service. This synchronizes all other servers.

○ C.  Ester should simply check the motherboard of the servers that are experiencing problems. It is not unusual for a server to lose time, and it should be replaced on the next maintenance cycle.

○ D.  Ester should simply restart the servers experiencing the problem. This causes the servers to resynchronize their time.

# Question 48

Jorg Rosenthal is putting the finishing touches on his Windows Server 2003 Active Directory design. He has come up with a plan for three domains all within the same forest. He has a naming scheme and a DNS design. He has the plan examined by a consultant who has done a lot of work for the company in the past. The only change this consultant made was to remind Jorg to add two-way trusts between each of the three domains. Jorg realizes that the consultant probably has never used Windows Server 2003 with Active Directory before. How did he come to this realization?

○ A.  The consultant used the wrong terminology. Windows Server 2003 has *shortcut trusts*, not *two-way trusts*.

○ B.  The consultant is correct. Two-way trusts will speed up the logon process.

○ C.  Jorg realized this because there is no need to create old-style two-way trusts—trusts within a forest are created automatically in Windows Server 2003, and they're transitive.

○ D.  Jorg realized this because, in order to install a domain, one must explicitly set up a two-way trust. Therefore, there is no reason to create them after the fact.

# Question 49

Ron Porter wants to make sure that searches for objects across domains are faster. His environment has two buildings, each having its own domain in the same tree. In order to make searches faster, Ron intends to move a domain controller from his own building into the remote one, and vice versa. Will this make searches across domains faster?

O A. No. In order to search for an object, the remote domain controller will still have to query servers in its home domain.

O B. No. Searches across domains are made at a Global Catalog server. Merely being a domain controller will not help.

O C. Yes. Because the server will be local to the people doing the search, it will reply faster.

O D. Yes. Because the server will be in the remote domain, it could query local servers for any data it needs.

# Question 50

John Watts is busy at work designing a Windows Server 2003–based Active Directory design. John has just gotten feedback on his initial proposal, and one of his key items has been denied. In his design, John created two distinct domains. This is because of a group of workers in a remote office (50 in number) who must have passwords that are more complex than other users on the network (who number 1,000). However, the design review committee has said it would prefer him to take this requirement into his Organizational Unit design. John decides he must attend the next committee meeting to make his case because he knows his original proposal was right. Who is correct?

O A. The committee is correct. Either option would work, but the committee's suggestion is far easier to administrate and change over time.

O B. The committee is correct. John should simply use Group Policy to alter these settings for the users.

O C. John is correct. Although Organizational Units would work, delegation of authority within a domain is easier than delegation of authority to an OU.

O D. John is correct. In fact, John's proposed solution is the only one that would work.

# Question 51

Peter Chamberlin is a system administrator. He has been tasked with fine-tuning Group Policy in his organization. He decides that one of the things he will do is to disable certain policies. If he wanted to disable unused portions of a GPO to improve processing times, which portions could he disable? [Choose all correct answers.]

- ❑  A.  Specific settings within a GPO
- ❑  B.  The Windows Settings subcontainer
- ❑  C.  The Computer Configuration container
- ❑  D.  The User Configuration container
- ❑  E.  The Software Settings subcontainer
- ❑  F.  The Administrative Templates subcontainer

# Question 52

Which of the following types of scripts are applied to computer accounts? [Choose all correct answers.]

- ❑  A.  Startup
- ❑  B.  Logon
- ❑  C.  Logoff
- ❑  D.  Shutdown

# Question 53

Which Windows Server 2003 service has replaced the older Windows NT Directory Replication service?

- ○  A.  Netlogon
- ○  B.  Active Directory Replication
- ○  C.  SYSVOL
- ○  D.  FRS

# Question 54

Robert Rose wants to document the use of command-line scripts for his fellow system administrators. To this end he is writing an administrator's guide. He is just writing the section on scripting. What is the name of the executable for the command-line version of the Windows Script Host?

- ○ A. **WScript.exe**
- ○ B. **CScript.exe**
- ○ C. **WSH.exe**
- ○ D. **CMD.exe**

# Question 55

Christof Mayer is writing contingency plans for recovery of his domain controllers. One of the things he is most concerned about is having the servers run out of space, thereby preventing Active Directory from being able to make writes to the database. However, Christof's colleague, Colin Martin, tells Christof that he need not worry about this, because Active Directory has a reserve of 20MB on each domain controller to account for this very eventuality. In fact, the names of these files are **NTDS.RES** and **MTDS.RE2**. Christof doubts whether Colin is correct. Who is right?

- ○ A. Colin is right. These files are "placeholders" that exist to simply consume disk space. This space is used when the server hard disk runs out of space.
- ○ B. Colin is almost right. There are indeed files that act as "placeholders" to consume disk space. However, they are called **res1.log** and **res2.log**.
- ○ C. Christof is right. There are no placeholders. Monitoring is the only way to make sure disk space does not run out.
- ○ D. Christof is right. Active Directory automatically shuts down the server if it runs out of hard disk space. This ensures that database corruption does occur.

# Question 56

As a system administrator of a Windows Server 2003 domain environment, which is not performing as expected, you wish to create a more detailed listing of events so that you can see what is happening in detail. How can you best modify the level of logging for the Microsoft Event Viewer.

- A.  Right-click the Event Viewer and select Full Logging.
- B.  Modify the Registry and set the level of logging to 0.
- C.  Modify the Registry and set the level of logging to 3.
- D.  Create a Group Policy Object to write all events to the Event log.

# Question 57

Several tools exist for monitoring Active Directory replication. Which of the following tools can you use to troubleshoot replication problems with AD?

- A.  Event Viewer
- B.  The command-line utility Repadmin
- C.  The command-line utility Replmon
- D.  The Graphical User Interface tool Replmon
- E.  The Graphical User Interface tool Repadmin

# Question 58

Ruby is the system administrator for a holistic dog food company based in Portland, Oregon. During a standard review of the Active Directory files on her server, she notices that the hard drive containing the **NTDS.DIT** file is running out of space. However, there is plenty of space available on the RAID-5 array attached to her server. She decides to move the file to the RAID-5 array. How should she best perform this operation?

- A.  Restart the server in Directory Services Restore Mode and use the Ntdsutil utility to move the file.
- B.  Shut down the server, restart it in Directory Services Restore Mode, and use Windows Explorer to move the file.
- C.  While the server is running, use Windows Explorer to move the file.
- D.  With the servers running, open a command prompt and use Ntdsutil to move the file.

# Question 59

While performing some standard maintenance on the server, Roger accidentally deleted an OU containing 500 user accounts, 200 printers, and several groups. Now, Roger realizes his mistake and wishes to restore all the deleted items in the most efficient way possible. Fortunately for Roger, he does have the backup of the Active Directory structure from the previous evening. Roger restores from the backup; however, within an hour the OU is once again deleted. How can Roger restore the deleted OU without having it automatically delete during the next replication cycle?

- ○ A. Roger needs to perform a nonauthoritative restore of Active Directory while in Directory Services Restore Mode.
- ○ B. Roger needs to perform an authoritative restore of Active Directory while in Directory Services Restore Mode.
- ○ C. Roger needs to perform a nonauthoritative restore of Active Directory while Active Directory is running.
- ○ D. Roger needs to perform an authoritative restore of Active Directory while Active Directory is running.

# Question 60

Randy is the system administrator for a small organization that recently purchased another small organization. When these two companies became one network, Randy created an external trust from the Active Directory domain of the first organization to a Unix-based domain of the second organization. Because both of the organizations are small, needing only a few changes, Randy sets up the backup schedule to only back up the Active Directory every 30 days. However, 22 days after the last backup the Active Directory database becomes corrupted and Randy decides to restore it. The restoration is successful, and all the objects are re-created as expected. Shortly thereafter, a failure occurs on the external trust between the Active Directory and the Unix-based domains. What should Randy do in order to ensure that the external trust functions as expected?

- ○ A. Run **trustrestore.exe**.
- ○ B. Use the built-in backup tool to restore the system data.
- ○ C. The external trust between a Windows AD domain and a Unix-based domain can only be created on a temporary basis.
- ○ D. The trust needs to be reestablished because the passwords are negotiated every 7 days, and the backup exceeds this timeframe.

# Practice Exam 1 Answer Key

| | | |
|---|---|---|
| 1. A | 21. D | 41. A |
| 2. D | 22. A, D | 42. A, B, C, D |
| 3. B | 23. A | 43. A |
| 4. A, D | 24. A, D | 44. D |
| 5. D | 25. A, B, D | 45. A |
| 6. A | 26. B, C | 46. D |
| 7. B | 27. C | 47. A |
| 8. B | 28. D | 48. C |
| 9. D | 29. A | 49. B |
| 10. C | 30. D | 50. D |
| 11. D | 31. A | 51. C, D |
| 12. C | 32. A, B, C | 52. A, D |
| 13. A | 33. B | 53. D |
| 14. C | 34. C, D | 54. B |
| 15. B | 35. C | 55. B |
| 16. B | 36. B | 56. C |
| 17. A | 37. B | 57. A, B, D |
| 18. D | 38. A | 58. A |
| 19. B, C | 39. B | 59. B |
| 20. D | 40. C | 60. D |

# Question 1

Answer A is correct. The bare minimum amount of RAM to even install Windows Server 2003 is 128MB, and that doesn't include the requirements of any applications you are running. A Windows NT 4 PDC with 128MB of RAM may have been perfectly adequate, even if a bit on the low side, but Windows Server 2003 has steeper requirements. That is something to consider when performing an upgrade. Answer B is incorrect because since this is the first AD domain controller, the only replication taking place is related to user account information to the NT 4 BDCs, which isn't likely to overwhelm the system on an ongoing basis. Answer C is incorrect because although performance-placement issues are related to the location of the system partition, the RAID-5 configuration is unlikely to cause the performance drop. Answer D is incorrect in that although it would be helpful to have additional BDCs, being able to offload the FSMO roles would still not improve performance that dramatically on a system starved for memory.

# Question 2

Answer D is correct. The SYSVOL folder structure must be on an NTFS partition. Answers A and C are incorrect because, although these are possible causes of the problem, the question asks for the "most likely" cause. Answer B is incorrect because putting the SYSVOL folder on an NTFS partition would have actually been a good thing.

# Question 3

Answer B is correct. Windows 2000 mixed mode allows for backward compatibility and synchronization with the Accounts Manager. Answers A and C are incorrect because Windows 2000 native mode and the Windows 2003 functional level would ensure incompatibility with Windows NT 4 domain controllers. Answer D is incorrect because there is no Windows NT compatibility mode.

# Question 4

Answers A and D are correct. In order to raise the functional level of a forest to Windows 2003, all domains in the forest must have been raised to the Windows 2003 functional level first, not just the parent domains of each tree. Because not all the domains in the forest have had their functional levels raised, the forest cannot be raised. Furthermore, the account used to perform the task must be a member of the Enterprise Admins group and not simply a domain administrator. Answer B is incorrect because Melissa does not have to raise the functional level in increments; she can go straight from Windows 2000 mixed mode to Windows 2003 if the requirements are in place. Answer C is incorrect because an existing trust relationship would have no bearing on raising the forest's functional level.

# Question 5

Answer D is correct. When dealing with an unreliable connection and site replication, it is better to go with SMTP because it ignores the scheduling issues and will ensure that replication occurs regardless of the connection being available at the time necessary. Answer A is incorrect because bridge-head servers are already a requirement for intersite replication. (One note: If you have a proxy server that serves as a firewall, you have to make the proxy server your bridgehead server.) Answer B is incorrect because it's obvious that Kathy doesn't want to combine the Singapore site into a functional one. Answer C is incorrect because IP over RPC replication is better for reliable connectivity and allows scheduling to take place properly.

# Question 6

Answer A is correct. Because Jon knows he will not be using this particular server again in its current role, he can simply run dcpromo /forceremoval to override AD's usual checks and requirements prior to demoting the domain controller. Answer B is incorrect because by not demoting the DC first, Active Directory will not know the server has been removed. Even forcing the removal will remove the server's information from the directory. The solution in answer C would be preferable, except the scenario suggests that there is an urgent need to reallocate this server, and waiting is not desirable. Therefore, answer C is incorrect. Answer D is incorrect because powering off the server for a period of time would not cause it to be removed from AD.

## Question 7

Answer B is correct. Global Catalog servers search for the domain information necessary during logon when an individual uses his or her user principal name. When a user logs on to a native-mode domain (these are the only ones to include universal groups), the GC updates the DC as to the universal group information for that particular user's access token. Answers A and D are incorrect because PDC Emulator and Infrastructure Master are FSMO roles that are not involved with the generation of an access token. The PDC Emulator is useful in backward-compatibility issues with Windows NT 4. Answer C is incorrect because the Kerberos server is used for domain and forest user verification through tickets.

## Question 8

Answer B is correct. A domain tree would include one or more domains. In this case, there is a need to maintain separate security policies, which would require two domains under one domain tree. Answer A is incorrect because a single domain would not allow for separate security policies. Answer C is incorrect because an empty root is unnecessary; no guidelines for strict separation of control have been requested. Answer D is incorrect because a forest arrangement would involve two noncontiguous namespaces.

## Question 9

Answer D is correct. By creating an alternate UPN suffix, you can make it more manageable for users to log on. In this example, you could create the alternate UPN suffix @sanfran so that users can log on with user@sanfran rather than the lengthy FQDN of their domain. Answer A is incorrect because reinstalling the domain would not result in a shorter name length, unless it was installed at a different level of the domain, which would have other implications as well as being a lot more work than required. Answer B is incorrect because the user account would not be found in the parent domain (it doesn't exist there), and the users would be unable to log on. Answer C is incorrect because a shortcut trust is used to speed up the access of resources between domains in a forest, but this wouldn't change the lengthy UPN a user in a multilevel-deep child domain would have to type.

# Question 10

Answer C is correct. You can prevent a Group Policy from applying to individuals (or entire groups) by altering the permissions to Deny Read and Apply Group Policy. Answer A is incorrect because, although this will work, you should not move a group to stop a policy. Answer B is incorrect because blocking inheritance will only prevent policies from above from applying; it won't stop the policy from affecting managers. Answer D is incorrect because you cannot apply a policy directly to a group, even though it's called "Group Policy."

# Question 11

Answer D is correct. When connecting an Active Directory domain to a Windows NT 4 domain, Charles would use an external trust. Charles would only want to use a one-way trust in this scenario, because with the exception of the domain administrators, metalmilitia.com should not have access to VOA. There are a few different options where admins in metalmilitia.com could access resources in VOA without a trust relationship being in place, such as having accounts created in the VOA domain to use for accessing resources. As a result, answer C is incorrect because a two-way trust is not desirable—it would open up a potential security hole of users in the VOA domain being able to grant permissions to shared resources to users in the metalmilitia.com domain. Answer A is incorrect because a realm trust is used to connect an Active Directory domain to a Unix realm. Answer B is incorrect because a forest trust is used to connect two Active Directory forests.

# Question 12

Answer C is correct. It is recommended that Kim place the users into global groups and then place the global groups into universal groups. Because of the replication of universal group content, the user objects are being referenced and creating excess replication. It would be better to place the users into several key global groups and then place those groups into universal groups. This will reduce the replication load. Answer A is incorrect because this method actually creates tremendous amounts of replication. Answer B is incorrect because local groups would not be available for the domain. Answer D is incorrect because, although this situation is possible, the replication would not be reduced using this step.

# Question 13

Answer A is correct. The way Kerberos authentication works, when a domain requests access to resources in a domain in a different tree within the forest, the access request is passed upwards to each successive domain in the tree and then down the other tree until it reaches the desired domain. Then the access token is passed back in reverse. A shortcut trust directly links domains within a forest, causing authentication traffic to pass directly between the two domains. Answer B is incorrect because throwing more bandwidth at the problem would not only be an expensive solution, but it likely would only have a minimal impact. Answer C is incorrect because there are likely administrative and organizational reasons why separate domains exist, and making such a significant network change is unnecessary in this scenario. Answer D is incorrect because a forest trust is used to connect Active Directory forests, not domain trees within a forest.

# Question 14

Answer C is correct. The final policy blocked the site policy, so Task Manager is not disabled. The No Override setting on the domain policy should enforce the Display Properties tab being disabled. Because OU1 is first in the priority list and the priorities are processed from bottom to top, the OU2 wallpaper setting is ignored. Answers A, B and D provide alternative solutions but do not correctly combine the rules into a final resultant set of policies.

# Question 15

Answer B is correct. Because the server is not operational, it will be necessary for you to seize the roles. Answer A is incorrect because FSMO roles do not automatically transfer. Answer C is incorrect because FSMO roles are transferred smoothly with the AD Domains and Trusts tool only when the DC with those roles is still functional. Answer D is incorrect because there is a method to salvage FSMO roles.

# Question 16

Answer B is correct. Matt and Nick can create a realm trust between the Windows Server 2003 domain and the Unix realm, which would allow them to reduce the duplication of resources and user inefficiency in accessing resources between the two. Answer A is incorrect because, although Microsoft may like this answer, it may not be feasible or desirable to migrate the Unix realm at this time. Answer C is incorrect because external trusts are used to connect Windows Server 2003 Active Directory domains to Windows NT 4 domains. Answer D is incorrect because a trust is created between a domain and a Unix realm, not a forest and a Unix realm.

# Question 17

Answer A is correct. Using Active Directory Sites and Services, you can easily move a domain controller between sites if you don't like where the KCC decided to put the domain controller. Answer B is incorrect because removing and reinstalling the DC may or may not accomplish the task and requires more effort than required. Answer C is incorrect because, although site membership is typically indicated by what subnet a server belongs to, changing the TCP/IP configuration on the server likely will have undesirable consequences for connectivity. Answer D is incorrect because removing the site would cause more problems and wouldn't solve anything.

# Question 18

Answer D is correct. All DCs usually go into the default site, although if you have defined subnets and the server IP address matches a defined subnet, the server will be placed in the one it matches rather than Default-First-Site-Name. In this scenario, it is necessary to establish multiple sites based on subnet and then set replication schedules. Answer A is incorrect because Brandon cannot use the AD Sites and Services tool to determine site topology; he would use it to manage the sites and create new sites based on his bandwidth capabilities. Answer B is incorrect because there will be no sites unless they are manually established, and there are no such components as bridgehead servers in Active Directory; they are components of Exchange Server. Answer C is incorrect because the AD Sites and Services tool is not for this purpose either.

## Question 19

Answers B and C are correct. The faster the connection, the lower the cost you want to establish. The slower the connection, the higher the cost you want to establish. In this case, the South Africa–Brazil connection is faster and should get a cost of 10, whereas the South Africa–Taiwan connection is slower and should get a cost of 100.

## Question 20

Answer D is correct. There is a problem with replication to Dallas because it is the only site that doesn't have the updated account information. Answer A is incorrect because the Infrastructure Master is responsible for tracking user-to-group mappings between domains, but in this case, the account information simply hasn't replicated to the Dallas site. Answer B is incorrect because a GC server being down would have no impact on whether the account shows up in the correct domain in the Dallas site. Answer C is incorrect because trusts between domains in a forest are transitive and not manually configured, and the problem isn't with accessing resources but with a user account that hasn't properly updated, which is a replication issue.

## Question 21

Answer D is correct. Sites should be made up of separate subnets, but they can contain more than one subnet per site. Answer A is incorrect because it would not be part of the analyst's job to purchase faster links. Answer B is incorrect because one subnet would not create separate sites. Answer C, although technically correct, isn't the best choice because there can be more than one subnet per site. As a result, there is no need to set a limit on only one subnet per site.

## Question 22

Answers A and D are correct. The PDC emulator is responsible for replicating password changes to the down-level Windows NT 4 BDCs. If it is down, changes are not replicated in an Active Directory domain to these BDCs. As a result, when Scott is trying to log in, his attempt fails when a BDC that has not received the update responds, and it succeeds when the BDC that initially accepted the change responds. Answers B and C are incorrect because the fact that Scott is able to log on successfully sometimes shows that there's not a problem with the password itself and that he probably is not entering it incorrectly on a regular basis.

## Question 23

Answer A is correct. The RID Master is responsible for maintaining unique IDs for Active Directory objects within a domain, and RIDs are assigned from a pool. If the RID Master is unavailable and the pool is depleted, no additional objects can be created. Answer B is incorrect because the PDC Emulator being down would affect account changes from being replicated to Windows NT 4 BDCs, but would not affect account creation. Answer C is incorrect because an Active Directory domain can support millions of user accounts. Answer D is incorrect because a corrupt CSV file might break the import procedure, but it wouldn't stop Don from creating a user account manually in Active Directory Users and Computers.

## Question 24

Answers A and D are correct. The Schema Master is the domain controller in the forest that is responsible for maintaining and distributing the schema to the rest of the forest. The Domain Naming Master is the domain controller for the forest that records the additions and deletions of domains to the forest. The Relative Identifier (RID) Master is responsible for assigning blocks of RIDs to all domain controllers in a domain. Therefore, answer B is incorrect. The Primary Domain Controller (PDC) Emulator is responsible for emulating Windows NT 4.0 for clients that have not migrated to Windows 2000 or above. Therefore, answer C is incorrect. The Infrastructure Master records changes made concerning objects in a domain. Therefore, answer E is incorrect.

## Question 25

Answers A, B, and D are correct. By implementing universal group caching, Ben can eliminate the need for a GC server to be available for user logon. In order to utilize universal group caching, however, Ben must first raise the domain functional level to Windows Server 2003 and place the global groups containing users into universal groups. Answer C is incorrect because the needs of the users do not require additional bandwidth; it would be a more expensive ongoing solution, and a better solution exists using universal group caching.

# Question 26

Answers B and C are correct. Replication that occurs "intersite" requires data to be compressed and occurs under a schedule. Answer A is incorrect because uncompressed data is utilized in intrasite replication only. Answer D is incorrect because default replication parameters are used for intrasite, non–schedule–based replication, whereas intersite replication requires defined schedules. The exception to this rule is that intersite replication that uses SMTP rather than RPC ignores schedules and tries to replicate on each interval regardless.

# Question 27

Answer C is correct. When migrating to Windows Server 2003 from Windows NT 4, it is a perfect time to utilize the new features of Windows Server 2003 to overcome the limitations imposed by Windows NT. By utilizing OUs, Jon would not be required to administer multiple domains just to control access to resources. Answer A is incorrect because the only reason four domains currently exist is due to Windows NT 4 limitations, which should be addressed during the migration. Answer B is incorrect because this is the Windows NT 4 way of doing things, having a multidomain environment with a master accounts domain and multiple resource domains. Answer D is incorrect because, although it would be the easiest, it doesn't take advantage of the improvements made in Windows Server 2003 and would undermine a lot of the advantages of migrating in the first place.

# Question 28

Answer D is correct. A basic requirement for using smartcard authentication is that the workstation must be a member of a domain. Answer A is incorrect because if the firewall wasn't open, you wouldn't be able to log on from your own laptop from that network. Answer B is incorrect because the only change that has been made from when the computers previously worked is removing them from the domain. Answer C is incorrect because your user account is obviously configured correctly; it works on your laptop, although it doesn't work on the workstations in question.

# Question 29

Answer A is correct. A limitation with using Windows 2000 systems in a smartcard deployment is that they can only use smartcards created on a Windows 2000 enrollment station. Windows XP and Windows Server 2003 systems can use cards created on either Windows 2000 or 2003. Answer B is incorrect because, although smartcards are supported on Windows 2000, there is the requirement to create them on a Windows 2000 enrollment station. Answer C is incorrect because since the problem is limited strictly to Windows 2000 users, it is unlikely to be a problem with just those user accounts. Answer D is incorrect because, although a device driver problem would cause the readers not to function correctly, in this scenario you are not seeing any errors related to the hardware.

# Question 30

Answer D is correct. Once control has been delegated, Nick can easily go to the Security tab in the OU's properties and change the permissions, if required. Answer A is incorrect because the permissions would be assigned on the OU, not on the Developer Admins security group itself. Answer B is incorrect because there is no need to remove and re-create the Developer Admins security group; in fact, this would likely cause more problems than it would solve because the SID associated with the security group would be lost in the process. Answer C is incorrect because, although it would technically work, it wouldn't be the *best* solution. When Nick reruns the Delegation of Control Wizard, he would be unable to see which security groups and users currently have any privileges on the OU. Furthermore, he won't be able to see what permissions have been granted. As a result, it would be difficult for him to know what permissions he has already granted and still needs to grant, which can only be done through the Security tab of the object's properties.

## Question 31

Answer A is correct. The main concern here is that the user community must not be affected by this upgrade. Because a domain in Windows 2003 mode cannot accommodate Windows NT 4.0 domain controllers, the users would have trouble accessing resources. Answer B is incorrect because RIS is used to install operating systems; it is not used to upgrade a server operating system. Answer C is incorrect because the number of servers upgraded per night is not relevant. Answer D is incorrect because native mode is a mode that first appeared in Windows 2000—for upgrades to a purely Windows Server 2003 environment, the ultimate goal should be to get to Windows 2003 mode.

## Question 32

Answers A, B and C are correct. Because each of the child domains shares the same root domain, their namespace is contiguous. Also, the two Active Directory partitions—schema and configuration—are also common to all domains. Answer D is incorrect because each domain might be running in a different mode—some modes are not compatible with Windows NT 4.0 domain controllers.

## Question 33

Answer B is correct. Windows Server 2003 stores DNS data in the application partition, which replicates data to targeted servers, rather than all domain controllers. In the case of DNS, this data would replicate to DNS servers only, and not every domain controller in the domain. Answer A is incorrect because this describes the behavior of Windows 2000, not Windows Server 2003. Answer C is incorrect because Microsoft has indeed improved upon replication in Windows Server 2003. Answer D is incorrect because the replication topology of DNS data is in fact different in Windows Server 2003.

# Question 34

Answers C and D are correct. The Group Policy Template is a folder on the SYSVOL share, which will contain any physical files associated with a GPO. In this case, it might contain a REG file or the new wallpaper graphic. A Group Policy Container is the object created in Active Directory. Therefore, answers A and B are incorrect because they are stored in different locations.

# Question 35

Answer C is correct. The only process that can reclaim space in NTDS.DIT is defragmentation. Otherwise, empty space is simply reserved for new data to be written. Answer A is incorrect because, although deletions do not reclaim space, the space can be reclaimed through defragmentation. Answer B is incorrect because the tombstone lifetime does not affect the reclamation of space for deleted objects. Answer D is incorrect because reclamation of space is on a per-database basis, not domainwide.

# Question 36

Answer B is correct. In Windows 2000, group members were replicated as a single value. This meant that if a group had 4,999 members, and one more was added, 5,000 names had to be replicated. However, group membership in Windows Server 2003 is at the attribute level, and only the change would be replicated. Answer A is incorrect because this describes Windows 2000, not Windows Server 2003. Answer C is incorrect because the replication changes in Windows Server 2003 means the number of members in a group is no longer an issue. Answer D is incorrect because the mode will have no effect on this issue.

# Question 37

Answer B is correct. The term that is used to describe this process is *latency*. Answers A, C, and D are incorrect because these terms are not used in this context.

## Question 38

Answer A is correct. The scope of replication depends on the change being made. Some changes cause replication enterprisewide, and some cause replication domainwide. Adding a user causes a change to the domain partition; this is replicated to all domain controllers in a domain. Creating a new domain causes a change to the configuration partition of Active Directory; this is an enterprisewide change. Adding a new object type causes a change to the schema partition; this is enterprisewide. Adding a security group is a change to the domain partition and therefore would only be replicated to domain controllers in the domain. Answers B, C, and D are incorrect because they do not represent the correct mix of domainwide and enterprisewide changes.

## Question 39

Answer B is correct. There is a new replication topology in Windows Server 2003 for replicating data stored in an application partition. Answer A is incorrect because Moira forgot about the application partition. Answers C and D are incorrect because there are four replication topologies.

## Question 40

Answer C is correct. The most logical place to target is an OU. This will allow Younes to target Eric for testing and then target everyone else in the finance group once the testing is complete. Answer A is incorrect because this would target everyone in the same site as Eric, which likely includes users outside of finance. Although this would work for testing, it would make rolling out to other finance members, later, difficult. Answer B is incorrect for similar reasons, except in this case everyone in the domain would be targeted. Answer D is incorrect because security groups cannot be explicitly targeted.

## Question 41

Answer A is correct. The name of this file is NTDS.DIT. It exists on every domain controller. Therefore, answers B, C, and D are incorrect.

# Question 42

Answers A, B, C, and D are correct. All four are names given to the partitions of data stored within Active Directory. The application partition is new to Windows Server 2003.

# Question 43

Answer A is correct. The Secedit command-line tool can be used to refresh settings at a client computer. Answers B and C are incorrect because different settings are applied at different times. For instance, settings targeting a computer are applied at startup, whereas setting targeting users are applied at log on. Either way, to get all the new settings, the computer would have to be restarted and the user would have to log on again. Using just one or the other would not achieve the desired result. Answer D is incorrect because it refers to a nonexistent tool.

# Question 44

Answer D is correct. Password changes are replicated urgently to the PDC Emulator, which in turn passes the changes down to the domain controller making the request. Answer A is incorrect because cached credentials are only used when the network is not available. Answer B is incorrect because the user would not have to wait. Answer C is incorrect because there is no need for the domain controller to contact other domain controllers; it simply goes to the PDC Emulator.

# Question 45

Answer A is correct. The correct name is Knowledge Consistency Checker. None of the other options exist or describe the correct name. Therefore, answers B, C, and D are incorrect.

# Question 46

Answer D is correct. By default, only Schema Admins can edit the schema; it is not sufficient to be a domain administrator. Answer A is incorrect because it is not necessary to be a domain administrator in every domain. Answer B is incorrect because this is indeed a permissions issue. Answer C is incorrect because, once again, this is not a corruption issue.

# Question 47

Answer A is correct. Time synchronization is taken care of by the PDC Emulator. This machine can be configured to contact an outside time source if necessary. Answer B is incorrect because the Time Service is not an issue in this scenario. Answer C is incorrect because, although it's not unusual for a computer to lose time, it is usually not necessary to change the motherboard. Adequate synchronization should work fine. Answer D is incorrect because restarting the servers would not fix the problem because there is a larger issue with the PDC Emulator.

# Question 48

Answer C is correct. Two-way trusts were commonly used in Windows NT 4.0, but they are rarely needed in Windows Server 2003. In this scenario, they serve no purpose at all. Transitive trusts are created automatically. Answer A is incorrect because this is not merely a terminology issue; two-way trusts still exist, in some instances, in Windows Server 2003. Answer B is incorrect because two-way trusts will not aid the logon process in this case. Answer D is incorrect because this step is not required when installing Windows Server 2003.

# Question 49

Answer B is correct. A Global Catalog server performs searches for objects in other domains. If searches are slow, it's most likely because there is a problem with the Global Catalog server or because there are not enough of them. Answer A is incorrect because, as stated, these queries are done to a Global Catalog server, not between domain controllers. Answer C is incorrect because local searches will not hit the new domain controller. Answer D is incorrect because this process simply does not exist.

## Question 50

Answer D is correct. Password complexity settings can only be set at the domain level. It is not possible to have different password settings for groups of users; once set at the domain level, these settings apply to all users in the domain. Answer A is incorrect because the committee's solution simply does not address the problem. Answer B is incorrect because the Group Policy settings cannot be changed on a per-user basis. Answer C is incorrect because this issue has nothing to do with delegation of authority.

## Question 51

Answers C and D are correct. Windows Server 2003 Group Policy allows an administrator to disable the Computer Configuration and User Configuration containers from being processed. If either container is disabled, the Windows Settings, Software Settings, and Administrative Templates subcontainers for that container would be disabled along with it. Specific settings cannot be filtered within a GPO.

## Question 52

Answers A and D are correct. Startup and shutdown scripts are applied to computer accounts. Answers B and C are incorrect because logon and logoff scripts are applied to users.

## Question 53

Answer D is correct. The File Replication Service (FRS) is a Windows Server 2003 service that expands on the capabilities of the older-style Directory Replication Service. Answer A is incorrect because Netlogon is the share name for the directory that logon scripts are stored in on a domain controller. Answer B is incorrect because, even though Windows Server 2003 uses Active Directory, the name of the service that manages the replication is FRS. Answer C is incorrect because FRS will replicate the entire SYSVOL tree between domain controllers.

## Question 54

Answer B is correct. CScript is the command-line version of the Windows Script Host. Answer A is incorrect because WScript is the Windows GUI version of Windows Script Host. Answer C is incorrect because WSH is the abbreviation for Windows Script Host. Answer D is incorrect because CMD.exe is the command interpreter for Windows Server 2003.

## Question 55

Answer B is correct. There are two files, each 10MB in size, that act as place-holders. Their names are res1.log and res2.log. Answer A is incorrect because the placeholder file names are incorrect. Answer C is incorrect because the placeholders do exist. Answer D is incorrect because the place-holders would free up disk space to give administrators time to free up space before a shutdown becomes necessary.

## Question 56

Answer C is correct. You should modify the Registry and set the level of log-ging to 3. This will set the level of logging to Full Reporting. Answer A is incorrect because this option does not exist. Answer B is incorrect because setting the level of logging to 0 disables logging. Answer D is incorrect because this is not a standard option for Group Policy and is administrative-ly complex.

## Question 57

Answers A, B, and D are correct. Answer C is incorrect because Replmon is not a command-line tool. Answer E is incorrect because Repadmin is not a Graphical User Interface tool.

# Question 58

Answer A is correct. Ruby should restart the server in Directory Services Restore Mode and use the Ntdsutil utility to move the file. In order to move this file, she must use this utility to ensure that the appropriate Registry settings are also modified. This file cannot be moved while it is in use. Answer B is incorrect because using Windows Explorer to move the file will not allow the Registry to be automatically modified. Answer C is incorrect because Ruby cannot move the file while it's in use. Also, this method will not automatically modify the Registry. Answer D is incorrect because, once again, Ruby cannot move the file while it's in use.

# Question 59

Answer B is correct. Roger needs to perform an authoritative restore of Active Directory while in Directory Services Restore Mode. Roger needs to restart the server, pressing the F8 key during startup, and enter the Directory Services Restore Mode. An authoritative restore will increment the version number by 100,000, ensuring that the restored OU is viewed by the other domain controllers as being the most recent. Answer A is incorrect because this is likely what Roger was doing. In this case, the restoration occurs without problem; however, during the next replication cycle, the restored OU is overwritten by the other domain controllers. This is because the other domain controllers see their version of the database file (the one in which the OU has been deleted) as being the most recent. Answers C and D are incorrect because the restoration cannot occur while Active Directory is running.

# Question 60

Answer D is correct. The trust needs to be reestablished because the passwords are negotiated every 7 days, and the backup exceeds this timeframe. Answer A is incorrect because there is no such utility. Answer B is incorrect because the most recent backup is 22 days old, and passwords for an external trust are renegotiated every 7 days. Answer C is incorrect because external trusts can be created between AD domains and Unix-based domains on a permanent basis.

# Practice Exam 2

# Question 1

You would like to ensure that passwords within your domain are complex, and you know that this is possible to enforce through a policy. Which of the following should you perform? [Choose the best answer.]

○ A. Edit the Local Security Policy on each of the DCs within your AD domain to require password complexity.

○ B. Edit the Default Domain Security Policy to require password complexity.

○ C. Edit the Default Domain Controller Policy to require password complexity.

○ D. Edit the Site Policy for your domain to require password complexity.

# Question 2

Which of the following is the Operations Master role that handles interaction with Windows NT 4 BDCs? [Choose the best answer.]

○ A. Schema Master

○ B. Infrastructure Master

○ C. PDC Emulator

○ D. Domain Naming Master

○ E. RID Master

# Question 3

Maverick Corporation is a multinational company that includes several subsidiaries. It is organized into a single forest with two noncontiguous domain trees, and off one of those trees are three child domains. What would be the total number of FSMO role servers involved? [Choose the best answer.]

○ A. One Domain Naming Master, one Schema Master, one RID Master, one PDC Emulator, and one Infrastructure Master

○ B. One Domain Naming Master, one Schema Master, five RID Masters, five PDC Emulators, and five Infrastructure Masters

○ C. One Domain Naming Master, one Schema Master, three RID Masters, three PDC Emulators, and three Infrastructure Masters

○ D. Three Domain Naming Masters, three Schema Masters, three RID Masters, three PDC Emulators, and three Infrastructure Masters

# Question 4

Your company has a Windows Server 2003 domain tree with three domains (**root.com**, **east.root.com**, and **west.root.com**). Your company recently purchased another organization that is using a Windows NT domain. The domain will eventually be upgraded but currently will remain as is. You would like for the Windows NT domain to be able to access a printer located in the **east.root.com** domain. What type of trust relationship should you configure and which way? [Choose the best answer.]

○ A. A two-way transitive trust with **root.com**

○ B. A one-way trust from **east.root.com** to the Windows NT domain

○ C. A one-way trust from the Windows NT domain to **east.root.com**

○ D. A two-way trust between **east.root.com** and the Windows NT domain

# Question 5

You work for an organization with three domains. Two of the domains (**root.com** and **samerica.root.com**) are connected by a high-bandwidth connection. The third domain (**spacific.root.com**) is located in Fiji and is connected to the rest of the organization by a 56Kbps connection. All three domains have 10 OUs configured. The first two domains use Group Policy for their software deployment, management, upgrades, and removal. The remote domain would like to use software deployment through Group Policy but doesn't want to run the deployment over the 56Kbps connection. What should you do to allow the third domain to have the ability to handle its software without using the bandwidth? [Choose the best answer.]

○ A. Configure a Group Policy for each OU in the **spacific.root.com** domain. Configure a software package for each Group Policy that uses software installer files off a local server.

○ B. Configure a Group Policy at the site level. Configure a software package for the Group Policy that uses Software Installation files off a server in the **namerica.root.com** domain.

○ C. Configure a Group Policy for the **spacific.root.com** domain. Configure a software package for the Group Policy that uses Software Installation files off a local server.

○ D. Configure a Group Policy for the **root.com** domain. Configure a software package for the Group Policy that uses Software Installation files off a server in Fiji.

# Question 6

Shannon wants to make sure that all replication takes place only during the evening hours of the day when nobody is on the network. She can do this by adjusting which portion of the site link? [Choose the best answer.]

○ A. Frequency

○ B. Cost

○ C. Transport

○ D. Schedule

# Question 7

When adding DCs to your existing domain, what should you take into consideration? [Choose the best answer.]

○ A. Nothing. The more DCs on the domain, the better.

○ B. Bandwidth usage on the network.

○ C. You can only have three DCs in a domain.

○ D. To promote a server to a DC, you must reinstall the operating system.

# Question 8

When you look at your automatically configured topology through the Replication Monitor, you notice that connection paths are not established the way you would like. What can you manually do to change this? [Choose the best answer.]

○ A. Create a manual connection object on the servers you need connected.

○ B. Force the KCC to update the topology.

○ C. Change the Registry to indicate the new paths you need.

○ D. The KCC will not allow you to modify the replication paths. These are set in stone.

# Question 9

Your organization has three office locations. One in Newark, New Jersey, one in New York, New York, and one in Orlando, Florida. Each is configured with a different subnet unique to its site. Newark and New York are connected by a T1 connection. Orlando is connected with a 56Kbps connection. The T1 is at 92% bandwidth utilization, and the 56Kbps is a dial-up connection that is only used when needed. How would you configure sites in this case? [Choose the best answer.]

○ A. Establish two sites—one for Newark and New York, and one for Orlando.

○ B. Establish three sites, one for each location.

○ C. Establish one site.

○ D. Establish two sites—one for Orlando and Newark, and one for New York.

# Question 10

Vanessa Lord is the WAN administrator for a small company that has a main corporate location and a one branch office. Each location is in its own Active Directory site. Connecting each site is a T1 line, with a demand-dial 56Kbps modem connection as a backup in case the T1 goes down. Vanessa hears complaints from users that sometimes the connection to the other office is fast, and sometimes very slow. As she troubleshoots the problem, she finds that the demand-dial link is being used regularly even when the T1 circuit is up. What can she do so the T1 circuit is always used when it is available? [Choose the best answer.]

○ A. Vanessa can configure the site link using the T1 to have a lower cost than the demand dial.

○ B. Vanessa can configure the site link using the T1 to have a higher cost than the demand dial.

○ C. Vanessa can remove the site link using the demand dial and just add it later if the T1 goes down.

○ D. Vanessa can configure the site link properties of the demand dial to only use the connection if the T1 site link is unavailable.

# Question 11

Paulette Deutman is a systems administrator responsible for a Windows Server 2003 Active Directory domain. She has recently installed a new Windows Server 2003 server in her domain and promoted it to a domain controller, giving her two domain controllers (DC01 and DC02). Now she wants to take some of the load off of the original server by making DC02 the Global Catalog server and taking away that role from DC01. How would she best accomplish this? [Choose the best answer.]

- ○ A. Use Active Directory Sites and Services to make DC02 a GC server and remove the role from DC01.
- ○ B. Use Active Directory Domains and Trusts to gracefully transfer the role from DC01 to DC02.
- ○ C. Use NTDSUtil on DC02 and seize the GC role from DC01.
- ○ D. Reinstall AD on DC02 and choose the option to make the server a GC server during the AD Installation Wizard; then repeat this on DC01 and choose not to make it a GC server this time.

# Question 12

Paulette Deutman is a systems administrator responsible for a Windows Server 2003 Active Directory domain. She has recently installed a new Windows Server 2003 server in her domain and promoted it to a domain controller, giving her two domain controllers (DC01 and DC02). Now she wants to take some of the load off of the original server by making DC02 the Schema Master and PDC Emulator for the domain. How would she go about doing this? [Choose all correct answers.]

- ❑ A. Register the **schmmgmt.dll** dynamic link library.
- ❑ B. Create a custom console for schema management and then use it to transfer the Schema Master role.
- ❑ C. Use Active Directory Users and Computers to transfer the PDC Emulator role.
- ❑ D. Use Active Directory Domains and Trusts to transfer the PDC Emulator role.
- ❑ E. Use Active Directory Sites and Services to transfer the PDC Emulator role.
- ❑ F. Use NTDSUtil on DC02 to seize the roles of Schema Master and PDC Emulator.
- ❑ G. Use Active Directory Domains and Trusts to transfer the Schema Master role.

# Question 13

You are the senior network administrator for a mid-sized company. Your company's main office is in Dallas, and there are branch offices in New York, Los Angeles, and St. Louis. The local administrators at each branch office need to be able to control local resources, but you want to prevent the local administrators from controlling resources in the other branch offices. You want only the administrators from the Dallas office to be allowed to create and manage user accounts. You want to create an Active Directory structure to accomplish these goals. What should you do? [Choose the best answer.]

- ○ A. Create a domain tree that has a top-level domain for the Dallas office and a child domain for each branch office. Grant the local administrators membership in the Domain Admins group in their child domains.

- ○ B. Create a domain tree that has a top-level domain for the Dallas office and a child domain for each branch office. Grant the local administrators membership in the Enterprise Admins group in the domain tree.

- ○ C. Create a single domain. Create a group named Branch Admins. Grant the local administrators membership in this group. Assign permissions to the local resources to this group.

- ○ D. Create a single domain. Create an OU for each branch office and an additional OU named CorpUsers. Delegate authority for resource administration to the local administrators for their own OUs. Delegate authority to the CorpUsers OU only to the Domain Admins group.

# Question 14

You are the administrator of your company's network. Your company has its main office in Seattle and branch offices in London, Paris, and Rio de Janeiro. The local administrator at each branch office must be able to control users and local resources. You want to prevent the local administrators from controlling resources in branch offices other than their own. You want to create an Active Directory structure to accomplish these goals. What should you do? [Choose the best answer.]

- ○ A. Create a top-level OU. Delegate control of this OU to administrators at the main office.

- ○ B. Create child OUs for each office. Delegate control of these OUs to administrators at the main office.

- ○ C. Create child OUs for each office. Delegate control of each OU to the local administrators at each office.

- ○ D. Create user groups for each office. Grant the local administrators the appropriate permissions to administer these user groups.

# Question 15

David Sparks is the network administrator for TSBC, which consists of one Windows Server 2003 Active Directory domain. He is trying to improve security by implementing a password policy that requires users to have passwords that are at least six characters long. He edits the Default Domain Controllers GPO in the **trinitysouthern.org** domain and sets the password policy, but after testing he finds out that users are still able to create passwords composed of fewer than six characters. What should he do? [Choose the best answer.]

- ○ A. Edit the Default Domain GPO and set the password policy to require at least six characters.
- ○ B. Edit the Default Domain Controllers GPO and enable the policy option for passwords to meet complexity requirements.
- ○ C. Configure each client computer with a local password policy requiring a minimum of six characters.
- ○ D. Check and make sure replication is functioning properly in the domain.

# Question 16

You are the administrator of your company's network. Your company's main office is in Seattle. Large regional offices are located in Chicago, Los Angeles, and New York.

Three smaller branch offices are located within each region. The regional offices are connected to the main office by T1 lines. The branch offices are connected to the regional offices by ISDN lines. Branch offices in Boston, Dallas, and San Diego also have direct ISDN connections with Seattle. The network consists of one Windows Server 2003 domain. For fault tolerance and load-balancing purposes, each office has its own Windows Server 2003 domain controller. Each office is configured as its own site. All site links have been created. You want to create a replication topology that allows only the regional offices to communicate with the main office. You want to ensure that each branch office communicates only with the closest regional office. What should you do? [Choose the best answer.]

- ○ A. Manually create connection objects between the domain controllers in the main office and the regional offices. Use SMTP as the transport protocol.
- ○ B. Manually create connection objects between each branch office and the closest regional office. Use SMTP as the transport protocol.
- ○ C. Allow the Knowledge Consistency Checker (KCC) to automatically create the connection objects between the main office and all other offices.
- ○ D. Allow the Knowledge Consistency Checker (KCC) to automatically create the connection objects between the branch offices and the regional offices.

# Question 17

Mike Pal is the senior network administrator for WWGuitars.com, which consists of a single domain spanning 10 sites. Each site has its own domain controller. Users are complaining to Mike that during the middle of the day it seems like the network gets very slow when they try to access resources. The only users not complaining are the ones at the main corporate location. What can Mike do to alleviate the problems? [Choose the best answer.]

○ A. Make a domain controller at each site in a GC server.

○ B. Create additional domain controllers in each site to balance the load.

○ C. Make the most powerful server at the corporate office the GC server for the entire domain.

○ D. Move all the domain controllers into a single site.

# Question 18

C.G. Smith is the systems administrator for a mid-sized company that has its corporate office in Omaha and branch offices in Miami, Albuquerque, Palo Alto, Billings, Seattle, and Boston. Each location is connected to the Omaha office by a T1 line. Active Directory was deployed at each location using the default settings, and the entire network is encompassed in a single domain. Lately C.G. has noticed that replication traffic is consuming a large portion of his bandwidth, and users are complaining that the network is slow when accessing resources at other locations. What can C.G. do to correct the problem? [Choose all correct answers.]

❑ A. Create a site that spans all locations.

❑ B. Create a site for each location.

❑ C. Move each server from Default-First-Site-Name to its appropriate site.

❑ D. Make every domain controller a GC server.

# Question 19

You are the administrator of your company's network. While reviewing the security log one morning, you see that a hacker has been using brute-force attacks to attempt to gain access to your network. You do not want user accounts to be easily accessible, so you decide to create a policy in order to strengthen password security to protect against brute-force attacks, including requiring passwords to be at least eight characters. What should you do? [Choose all correct answers.]

❏ A. Enable the Users Must Log On to Change the Password setting.

❏ B. Enable the Password Must Meet Complexity Requirements setting.

❏ C. Enable the Store Password Using Reversible Encryption for All Users in the Domain setting.

❏ D. Increase the Minimum Password Length setting.

# Question 20

Bill Long is the network administrator for his company, which has three sites in its Active Directory domain. Connectivity is such that there are T1 circuits between St. Louis and Dallas, and St. Louis and Omaha, and a 128Kbps ISDN connection between Dallas and Omaha. Each site has its own GC server, but Bill wants to configure Dallas so that if its GC server goes down, it would contact St. Louis first rather than Omaha. What can Bill do to accomplish this? [Choose the best answer.]

○ A. Bill can configure the GC server in St. Louis as a preferred bridgehead server.

○ B. Bill can remove the site link between Dallas and Omaha so it won't be used.

○ C. Bill can configure the site link between Dallas and St. Louis to have a higher cost than the link between Dallas and Omaha.

○ D. Bill can configure the site link between Dallas and St. Louis to have a lower cost than the link between Dallas and Omaha.

# Question 21

Melissa Willis is the network administrator for a company that has 2,500 users in a single Windows Server 2003 domain. She set up the network about a year ago and has recently discovered that most users are still using the same passwords that were configured when the accounts were created. Melissa wants to ensure that people change their passwords on a regular basis and that they don't reuse passwords they've previously used. What settings should she configure in her password policy? [Choose all correct answers.]

❑ A.  Minimum Password Age

❑ B.  Maximum Password Age

❑ C.  Enforce Password History

❑ D.  Password Must Meet Complexity Requirements

# Question 22

Bill Duncan is the WAN administrator for Struggle Hill Ranch, a company that exports ranching and farming supplies worldwide. The company is headquartered in Texas but has overseas offices in Beijing, London, and Berlin in addition to other U.S. offices. WAN connectivity is very unreliable between Dallas and Beijing, but Bill needs to be able to replicate Active Directory data between the two offices. What can he do to ensure replication works reliably? [Choose the best answer.]

○ A.  Bill can create an SMTP site link between Dallas and Beijing.

○ B.  Bill can create an IP site link between Dallas and Beijing.

○ C.  Bill can create an SMTP site link bridge between Dallas and Beijing.

○ D.  Bill can create an IP site link bridge between Dallas and Beijing.

# Question 23

Veronica DuBose is the domain administrator for a staffing company. She has a single Windows Server 2003 domain and uses OUs to manage the various departments within the company. Veronica has a user, Chris Cobern, who is a member of the Accounting OU and has been delegated permission to reset passwords for that group. Chris is now moving into sales and will no longer be in the accounting department, and he therefore will not need permission to reset passwords any longer. What would be the easiest way for Veronica to prevent Chris from resetting passwords in the Accounting OU? [Choose the best answer.]

- ○ A. She can rerun the Delegation of Control Wizard and revoke Chris's permissions to the Accounting OU.
- ○ B. She can go into the security properties of the Accounting OU and remove Chris's permission to reset passwords.
- ○ C. She can move his user account from the Accounting OU to the Sales OU, which will change his permissions automatically.
- ○ D. She can delete Chris's account and re-create it in the Sales OU.

# Question 24

You have been a junior administrator for the Dallas division of W&W, Inc., a company that has a parent domain, **wwinc.com**, for the Lewisville office, where the company was founded, and child domains named **dallas.wwinc.com**, **houston.wwinc.com**, **sanantonio.wwinc.com**, and **austin.wwinc.com**. Even as a junior admin your user account has been a member of the **dallas.wwinc.com** Domain Admins group. Recently you received a promotion to network administrator and transferred to the Lewisville office. One of your first tasks is to promote an existing Windows Server 2003 member server to a domain controller. You run **dcpromo.exe** on the server but get an "accessed denied" error. What can you do to correct the situation so that Dcpromo will run? [Choose all correct answers.]

- ❑ A. Have your user account added to the Domain Admins group in the **wwinc.com** domain.
- ❑ B. Have your user account moved from **dallas.wwinc.com** to **wwinc.com**.
- ❑ C. Have your user account added to the Enterprise Admins group in **wwinc.com**.
- ❑ D. Have your user account added to the local administrators group on the member server.

# Question 25

You are the network administrator for several Windows Server 2003 domains running at the Windows 2000 mixed-mode domain functional level. You still have many Windows NT 4 member servers in your domains, but you have a need to implement universal groups and specifically universal group caching on your network. What is the easiest way to get universal group caching implemented? [Choose all correct answers.]

- ❑ A. Upgrade all Windows NT 4 member servers to Windows Server 2003.
- ❑ B. Raise the domain functional levels to Windows 2003.
- ❑ C. Raise the domain functional level to Windows 2000 native mode.
- ❑ D. Create universal groups and configure universal group caching.

# Question 26

You are an Active Directory design consultant who has been called in by a small development company that is working on a database application that will run on Windows Server 2003. The company has concerns about running its application on a WAN because of the amount of replication traffic the application currently generates. Knowing the features of Windows Server 2003, what advice could you give the company to deal with the data-replication situation? [Choose the best answer.]

○ A. The company should design the application to support Kerberos authentication.

○ B. The company should design the application to use scheduled replication.

○ C. The company should utilize application data partitions in its application.

○ D. The company should design the application to be aware of sites and to utilize site link costs.

# Question 27

Dawn Arispe is a network administrator who is responsible for two Windows Server 2003 Active Directory domains and a Windows NT 4 domain. Users in the Windows NT 4 domain need to be able to access resources in the two Active Directory domains, but the Active Directory domains do not need to access the Windows NT 4 domain. How would Dawn best configure this? [Choose the best answer.]

○ A. She should configure one-way external trusts, where the Windows NT 4 domain trusts the Active Directory domains.

○ B. She should configure one-way external trusts, where the Active Directory domains trust the Windows NT 4 domain.

○ C. She should configure a single forest trust between the Active Directory forest and the Windows NT 4 domain.

○ D. She should configure one-way realm trusts, where the Active Directory domains trust the Windows NT 4 domain.

# Question 28

You are the senior network administrator for a large company that has offices in Dallas, Houston, Omaha, St. Louis, Boston, and New York. Site links connect all the locations. The Omaha office is a smaller branch that, until recently, has had a single domain controller running on an older system that had been upgraded from Windows NT 4. The office has added a new server as a second DC in response to complaints from users that access to the old server was slow. Even after the new server has been added though, the old server performance doesn't seem to have gotten any better. What can you do to improve performance? [Choose all correct answers.]

❑ A. Manually configure the new server as the preferred bridgehead server.

❑ B. Format and reinstall the old server to clean it up.

❑ C. Demote the old server back to a member server.

❑ D. Transfer all the FSMO roles to the new server.

# Question 29

You are the WAN administrator for a company that has three sites: one in Dallas, one in Houston, and one in Austin. There are site links between Dallas and Austin, and Houston and Austin. You have manually configured site link bridges to connect the sites. Your company has just opened a new office in San Antonio, which is physically connected to Austin through a T1 line. However, although connectivity between San Antonio and Austin works fine, users in Dallas and Houston cannot access San Antonio, and vice versa. What should you look at to troubleshoot the problem? [Choose the best answer.]

○ A. You should reenable Bridge All Site Links.

○ B. You should acquire T1 circuits to connect the new San Antonio office to Dallas and Houston.

○ C. You should have the ISTG recompile the routing table.

○ D. You should configure site link bridges between Houston and San Antonio, and Dallas and San Antonio.

# Question 30

You are the WAN administrator for a large company that spans several sites. Because of traffic concerns, you have decided to use site link bridges to manu- ally configure some specific replication paths. However, after creating the site link bridges and testing them, you find that they are not functioning as you anticipated. What are you likely doing wrong? [Choose the best answer.]

- ○ A. You need to enable the automatic bridging of site links.
- ○ B. Site link bridges are configured automatically and therefore you cannot configure them manually.
- ○ C. You need to disable the automatic bridging of site links.
- ○ D. You must define the site link costs so traffic will flow in the desired manner.

# Question 31

As a system administrator of a Windows Server 2003 server, you notice that it's not performing as expected. You wish to create a more detailed listing of events so that you can see what is happening in detail. How can you best modify the level of logging for the Microsoft Event Viewer.

- ○ A. Right-click the Event Viewer and select Full Logging.
- ○ B. Modify the Registry and set the level of logging to 0.
- ○ C. Modify the Registry and set the level of logging to 3.
- ○ D. Create a Group Policy Object to write all events to the Event log.

# Question 32

You need to force replication between domain controllers in your AD environ- ment. Which of the following tools can you use to initiate replication between domain controllers in AD? [Choose all correct answers.]

- ❑ A. Event Viewer
- ❑ B. The command-line utility Repadmin
- ❑ C. The command-line utility Replmon
- ❑ D. Active Directory Sites and Services
- ❑ E. The Graphical User Interface tool Repadmin

# Question 33

Ruby is the system administrator for a holistic dog food company based in Portland, Oregon. During a standard review of the Active Directory files on her Server, she notices that the hard drive containing the **NTDS.DIT** file is running out of space. However, there is plenty of space available on a secondary hard drive attached to her server. She decides to move the file to the secondary hard drive. How should she best perform this operation?

○ A.  Restart the server in Directory Services Restore Mode and use the NTDSUtil utility to move the file.

○ B.  Shut down the server, restart it in Directory Services Restore Mode, and use Windows Explorer to move the file.

○ C.  While the server is running, use Windows Explorer to move the file.

○ D.  With the servers running, open a command prompt and use NTDSUtil to move the file.

# Question 34

While performing some standard maintenance on the server, Steve accidentally deleted several OUs containing over 750 user accounts, 120 printers, and 50 groups. Now, Steve realizes his mistake and wishes to restore all the deleted items in the most efficient way possible. Fortunately for Steve he does have the backup of the Active Directory structure from the previous evening. Steve restores from the backup; however, within an hour the OU is once again deleted. How can Steve restore the deleted OU without having it automatically deleted during the next replication cycle?

○ A.  Steve needs to perform a nonauthoritative restore of Active Directory while in Directory Services Restore Mode.

○ B.  Steve needs to perform an authoritative restore of Active Directory while in Directory Services Restore Mode.

○ C.  Steve needs to perform a nonauthoritative restore of Active Directory while Active Directory is running.

○ D.  Steve needs to perform an authoritative restore of Active Directory while Active Directory is running.

# Question 35

Bob is the system administrator for a small organization that recently purchased another small organization. When these two companies became one network, Bob created an external trust from the Active Directory domain of the first organization to a Unix-based domain of the second organization. Because both the organizations are small, needing only a few changes, Bob sets up the back-up schedule to back up the Active Directory every 25 days. However, 22 days after the last backup, the Active Directory database becomes corrupted and Bob decides to restore it. The restoration is successful, and all the objects are re-created as expected. Shortly thereafter, a failure occurs on the external trust between the Active Directory and the Unix-based domains. What should Bob do in order to ensure that the external trust functions as expected?

- ○ A.  Run **trustrestore.exe**.
- ○ B.  Use the built-in backup tool to restore the system data.
- ○ C.  The external trust between a Windows AD domain and a Unix-based domain can only be created on a temporary basis.
- ○ D.  The trust needs to be reestablished because the passwords are negotiated every 7 days, and the backup exceeds this timeframe.

# Question 36

Which of the following files make up the AD database system? [Choose all correct answers.]

- ❏ A.  **ntboot.ini**
- ❏ B.  **ntds.dit**
- ❏ C.  **nslookup.txt**
- ❏ D.  **edb*.log**
- ❏ E.  **edb.chk**
- ❏ F.  **edb.txt**
- ❏ G.  **res1.log**
- ❏ H.  **res2.log**
- ❏ I.  **ntds.txt**

# Question 37

Allison is a system administrator at a hotel. In the lobby of the hotel, she has set up a terminal for guest use. Occasionally, a staff member will use this terminal to retrieve information using his or her user account. Allison wants to ensure that the computer settings for this terminal take precedence over the user settings specified in her Group Policies. However, when she applies the Group Policies to the OU that contains this computer, the user settings override the computer settings. What can she do to ensure that this does not occur?

- ○ A. Set up loopback with replace.
- ○ B. Set up loopback with merge.
- ○ C. Disable user settings for the Group Policy in the OU.
- ○ D. Disable the computer settings for the Group Policy in the OU.

# Question 38

Bernard has just created several new Group Policies for an OU called Accounting. These new policies affect the user settings, such as the background, access to Control Panel, and other display options. When Bernard logs on as a test user to ensure that the policies are taking effect, the settings he configured are not applied. Why is this happening and what can Bernard do to see whether his Group Policies are correct?

- ○ A. This is happening because Bernard has incorrectly configured the Group Policies. He must redo the Group Policies correctly.
- ○ B. This is happening because Group Policies refresh on a schedule. This occurs every 90 minutes, plus or minus 30 minutes. He can run RSoP to correct the problem.
- ○ C. This is happening because Group Policies refresh on a schedule. This occurs every 90 minutes, plus or minus 30 minutes. He can run GPUpdate to force a refresh.
- ○ D. This is happening because Bernard must first enable Group Policies through GPOEnable.

# Question 39

Cassandra is running Group Policies for an OU called Engineering that resides in a single site. She modifies a Group Policy that installs a new piece of software to all the computers in this OU. After creating this policy, she waits 3 hours but notices that none of the computers have the new piece of software installed except for one computer, which is being used by an engineer who has just come in to work the evening shift. Why is this happening and what can Cassandra do to ensure that the new piece of software is installed?

○ A. This is happening because she has incorrectly configured the Group Policy to only affect users who log in during evenings. She can correct this by rewriting the Group Policy.

○ B. This is happening because the Group Policy has not refreshed. She can correct this by running the GPUpdate utility.

○ C. This is happening because the Group Policy has not been refreshed. She can correct this by running **GPUPDATE /Target:Computer**.

○ D. This is happening because the Group Policy has not been refreshed. She can correct this by running **GPUPDATE /Target:User**.

○ E. This is happening because the Group Policy has not been run. She can correct this by either restarting the computers or running **GPUPDATE /Boot**.

# Question 40

Dennis is the network administrator of a small organization consisting of a single domain and a single site. He decides to implement Group Policies in order to control the users' environment. Dennis decides to use the computer currently in charge of the DNS as a file server. He then plans on redirecting all the users' folders to shares on this server. He begins by uninstalling DNS, creating a share called Users, and then creating a separate folder for each user account he has. When he creates the Group Policy, it does not seem to take effect. He waits 4 hours to ensure that the Group Policy has enough time to automatically refresh. Yet, after this time, it still does not seem to work. What's more, a number of other problems seem to be occurring. What might be the problem?

○ A. Dennis cannot use the server that was used for DNS as a file server.

○ B. By Dennis uninstalling the DNS, clients will not be able to locate the domain controller and, hence, will not be able to receive the Group Policy.

○ C. Dennis cannot use Group Policy to redirect users' folders.

○ D. Dennis must allow the users' folders to be created automatically through the **%username%** placeholder.

# Question 41

Edward is a system administrator of a company specializing in security alarm systems for other businesses. Much of the information exchanged within his organization is confidential as well as highly secure. To this end, he wants to ensure that certificates are used for both computers and users within this environment. Edward sets all his systems for auto-enrollment but notices that users running Windows 2000 and Windows NT do not automatically enroll with the certificate server. What must Edward do in order to fix this problem?

○ A. Edward should upgrade all the Windows 2000 and NT clients to run Windows XP.

○ B. Edward should set auto-enrollment for computers only.

○ C. Edward cannot use auto-enrollment; he must enroll all computers and users individually.

○ D. Edward cannot use auto-enrollment; he must first upgrade all the systems to Windows 2003 Enterprise Edition.

# Question 42

Frank is configuring his environment to support Folder Redirection for user documents. He has created a single network share where he would like all the users' files to be stored. This share is a RAID-5 array with 50GB of data storage. What must Frank do in order for Folder Redirection to occur?

○ A. Nothing. Folder Redirection automatically occurs when Windows Server 2003 is installed.

○ B. Frank must use the Group Policy Editor and choose Properties. He should choose Basic and then specify the network share.

○ C. Frank must use the Group Policy Editor and choose Properties. He should choose Advanced and then specify the network share.

○ D. Folder Redirection is no longer supported within Windows Server 2003 networks.

# Question 43

Georgette is the network administrator for a graphics design company. Her company has been having problems with users saving files to their local hard drives and not having them backed up. This has caused problems in the past when a file is needed but has not been properly backed up. She wants to control several user folders to ensure that they are redirected to a network share that is backed up on a regular basis. Which of the following folders can be redirected?

❑  A.  Application Data

❑  B.  Desktop

❑  C.  My Documents

❑  D.  Start Menu

# Question 44

Stephanie is the system administrator of a large organization consisting of over 5,000 Windows XP professional client systems. As part of her responsibilities, she is in charge of the creation of Group Policy Objects. The organization is divided into multiple domains for the purposes of security and administrative control. Although Stephanie is responsible for creating all GPOs, other users have the responsibility for which GPOs will be applied to the domains that they oversee. Stephanie wishes to give the users permission to apply the GPOs but not to modify them. How can Stephanie maintain control over the creation of GPOs while allowing other users the ability to determine where to apply them?

○  A.  Stephanie should right-click the desired domain or OU in Active Directory Users and Computers and select Delegate Control. She should then select the option Manage Group Policy Links for the appropriate users.

○  B.  Stephanie should right-click the desired users in Active Directory Users and Computers and select Delegate Control. She should then select the option Manage Group Policy Links for the appropriate users.

○  C.  Stephanie should right-click the desired domain or OU in Group Policy Administrator and select Delegate Control. She should then select the option Manage Group Policy Links for the appropriate users.

○  D.  Stephanie should right-click the desired domain or OU in Group Policy Administrator and select Delegate Control. She should then select the option Delegate Group Policy Control for the appropriate users.

# Question 45

Ingrid is the system administrator for a law firm with a Windows Server 2003 environment. In order to provide a consistent set of security settings for all users, Ingrid has decided to use security templates. She asks her friend Jane which security settings she should use for the environment based on the fact that the law firm continues to use a legacy application that was custom-developed for them. Jane suggests that Ingrid should use the High security template. Ingrid disagrees. She thinks she should use the Compatible security template. Who is correct?

- ○ A. Jane is correct. The High security template will allow the legacy application to run while maintaining the optimal security configuration for the Windows Server 2003 environment.

- ○ B. Ingrid is correct. The Compatible security template will ensure that legacy applications are still allowed to run without granting users the Power User permissions.

- ○ C. Neither is correct. The Secure security template should be used. This template will allow the legacy application to run within the context of the Power User's group.

- ○ D. Neither is correct. Ingrid will have to create a custom security template because legacy applications are not supported in Windows Server 2003.

# Question 46

Jonathan is the network administrator of a medium-sized company running a Windows Server 2003 network environment. This is not a highly secure environment, and functionality does not need to be limited. The computers are used by several different people throughout the day, and Jonathan wants to ensure that each user receives a standard desktop no matter where he or she logs on to the network. There is no need for each user to have a customized environment; a standard desktop for all users is sufficient. What Jonathan does wish to avoid, though, are situations in which someone changes the background or screensaver on a computer. What can Jonathan do in order to successfully create an environment that matches these requirements?

- ○ A. Jonathan can modify the Registry settings for each computer individually.

- ○ B. Jonathan can implement a Group Policy that specifies a computer start-up script, which modifies the Registry of each computer individually.

- ○ C. Jonathan can implement a Group Policy that modifies the Control Panel/display properties to disable changing the wallpaper and to specify a specific screensaver.

- ○ D. Jonathan can create a single login account for all users. This will ensure that all users maintain the same desktop environment.

# Question 47

Windows Server 2003 includes four standard administrative templates. Which of the following are standard administrative templates?

- ❏ A. **System.adm**
- ❏ B. **Inetconf.adm**
- ❏ C. **Inetres.adm**
- ❏ D. **Conf.adm**
- ❏ E. **Conf.Int**
- ❏ F. **Wmplayer.adm**
- ❏ G. **Wmplayer.conf**
- ❏ H. **Admin.adm**

# Question 48

Lenny attempts to install a software package through the use of Group Policies. The software-installation medium supplies the appropriate software-installation package as well as instructions on how to use it. When Lenny uses this package, an error message is returned: "Cannot prepare the package for deployment." Lenny knows that the package has worked in the past and has not been corrupted. What might the problem be?

- ○ A. The workstation on which Lenny is trying to deploy the package is incompatible.
- ○ B. The server on which Lenny is trying to host the application does not support the application.
- ○ C. The workstation on which Lenny is trying to deploy the package does not meet the necessary hardware requirements.
- ○ D. The workstation on which Lenny is trying to deploy the application cannot communicate with the SYSVOL share.

# Question 49

Mary is the network administrator of a small college that specializes in teaching Microsoft Office applications. Mary wants to ensure that users always have the necessary applications available to them. One of her concerns is that users may attempt to delete files that are part of the applications. Mary also wishes to avoid having to visit every desktop in the event that an application has corrupted files. She speaks to her friend Nancy, who suggests that Microsoft Office applications are self-healing. Mary then remembers reading something about Microsoft Office applications having the ability to repair themselves. What can Mary do so that the applications in her environment perform self-repair in the event that the files are corrupted or deleted, with the least amount of administrative support?

- ○ A. Using Group Policy, Mary can set up the Microsoft Office applications to be assigned to each computer account. In the event of a corrupted or deleted file, the affected application will redeploy.

- ○ B. Using Group Policy, Mary can publish each application to each computer account. In the event of a corrupted or deleted file, Mary can have the user reinstall the application.

- ○ C. Mary is not required to do anything. Microsoft Office automatically has this function built in to it.

- ○ D. Mary must install the Microsoft Office administration pack. This includes a tool called **selfheal.exe**, which will ensure self-healing applications.

# Question 50

Place the following phases of software deployment in the correct order:

- ❑ A. Distribution phase
- ❑ B. Pilot program phase
- ❑ C. Targeting phase
- ❑ D. Installation phase
- ❑ E. Preparation phase

# Question 51

Oliver is the network administrator for a coal mining company with 75 client computers. Each of the computers uses the same set of productivity software, which includes Microsoft Word, Microsoft Excel, and Microsoft PowerPoint. Oliver wishes to ensure that any new computer added to the network, as well as those already on the network, receive this software automatically. Fifty of the computers are running Windows XP Professional. Twenty of the computers are running Windows 2000 Professional. Oliver also has five computers running Windows NT Workstation. The server infrastructure has completely been switched over to Windows Server 2003 machines acting as standalone servers. When Oliver attempts to deploy the software, the options to do so are not available. What must Oliver do in order to allow 100% deployment of these applications into the environment? [Choose two.]

- ❑ A. Oliver must promote all Windows Server 2003 servers to act as PDC Emulators.
- ❑ B. Oliver must promote at least one Windows Server 2003 server to act as a domain controller.
- ❑ C. Oliver must promote his Windows NT workstations to Windows 2000 Professional or Windows XP.
- ❑ D. Oliver must promote both his Windows NT workstations and his Windows 2000 Professional clients to Windows XP.

# Question 52

Peter is the network administrator for a vending machine company. The company's office contains 25 Windows XP computers and three Windows Server 2003 servers. The servers are configured as follows: two domain controllers and one member server acting as a file server. The Windows XP computers are all running Windows XP Professional with the latest service packs. Peter has created a Group Policy in order to lock the users' environment and prevent users from changing any of the display settings on the computers. When users log on to the network, they report that the time it takes has increased. Peter determines that this is due to the processing of the Group Policies. Peter wishes to maintain the Group Policy he has created, but also wants to speed up the login process. How can Peter meet this objective?

- ○ A. Peter should disable the GPOs and individually configure each computer.
- ○ B. Peter should disable the user portion of Group Policies.
- ○ C. Peter should disable the computer portion of Group Policies.
- ○ D. Peter should disable both the user and computer portions of computer policies.

# Question 53

Hubert is the system administrator for a kayak tour company. As part of its reservation system, the company has employed 20 kiosk computers in various hotels around the city from which it operates. These kiosk computers are accessible by the hotel staff in order to take commission bookings for kayak tours. Each hotel has its own login and requires Group Policies to control which applications can be run from these terminals. Specifically, Hubert has to ensure that only the reservation-booking application can be run from these terminals. Also, because these terminals are within the public view, Hubert has to ensure that display settings and the wallpaper cannot be modified. Hubert creates and tests Group Policies that configure the desired environment. He uses a standard Group Policy test account he created earlier and is able to meet the objectives successfully. However, once Hubert begins deploying these kiosk terminals into the hotels, the Group Policies do not restrict the hotel users, but they still restrict the test user. Hubert reviews the permissions on the Group Policies and notices that all hotel users do have the Read permission to the Group Policies but no other permissions. What must Hubert do in order to have the Group Policies affect the hotel users?

- ○ A. The hotel users must be added into the Test OU.
- ○ B. The Group Policies must be dropped or re-created.
- ○ C. The hotel users must be assigned the Write permission to the Group Policies.
- ○ D. The hotel users must be assigned the Apply Group Policy permission.

# Question 54

Rachel is the network administrator for an elementary school computer lab. This lab contains 20 computers running Windows XP Professional as well as a single domain controller running Windows Server 2003. Recently, the school district has created a single forest Active Directory structure, which connects seven elementary schools together as a single site, but with each acting as its own domain. Rachel has been assigned the Enterprise Administrator for this forest and is in charge of implementing Group Policies to restrict system access and deliver application support. Rachel creates a Group Policy she wishes to be applied to all computers across all seven schools. At which level should Rachel apply this Group Policy?

- ○ A. At the OU level
- ○ B. At the domain level
- ○ C. At the site level
- ○ D. At the local level

# Question 55

Theodore is the network administrator for a recording studio company. The studio rents out editing suites in several locations that contain computers running audio-editing software. Theodore wishes to ensure that the computer configuration is consistent in each studio environment. The company's Active Directory structure consists of two sites: Downtown and Valley Side. The company runs a Windows Server 2003 environment consisting of a single domain. There are four OUs within the domain: sales, administration, support, and clients. All the systems that are part of the recording suites fall within the clients OU. The following Group Policies are in effect:

➤ The Downtown site sets the wallpaper to red.

➤ The Valley Side site sets the wallpaper to blue.

➤ The client OU specifies that the wallpaper should be black.

➤ The domain GPO specifies that the wallpaper should be green.

When a user logs on to a computer in the editing suite, what color will the wallpaper be?

○ A.  Red

○ B.  Blue

○ C.  Black

○ D.  Green

# Question 56

Ursula is a network administrator for an international import/export company with offices located across the globe. The company is running a Windows Server 2003 environment with Windows 2000 and Windows XP Professional clients. The Active Directory environment for this company consists of a single forest with multiple domains and sites. For ease of administration, Ursula is considering using Universal groups for all security access. Her friend Veronica advises against this. Veronica claims that by using Universal groups exclusively, replication will be slowed. Ursula disagrees and actually thinks that replication will be improved through the use of Universal groups. Who is correct?

○ A.  Ursula is correct. Universal groups will speed replication traffic because they can be used across multiple sites.

○ B.  Veronica is correct. Universal groups will slow replication traffic because they contain more information, which is replicated.

○ C.  Neither is correct. Universal groups will neither slow down nor speed up replication.

○ D.  Neither is correct. Universal groups are not replicated.

# Question 57

Wilma is the network administrator for a quarry. The quarry is running a Windows server environment consisting of four Windows NT Enterprise servers, three Windows 2000 Enterprise servers, and four Windows Server 2003 Enterprise servers. The Active Directory is running in mixed mode in order to support the Windows NT 4 clients. The Windows NT 4 Enterprise servers will be retired soon. However, the clients running Windows NT 4 Workstation will continue to do so for the foreseeable future in order to support a legacy application. Wilma has done some research on Universal groups and decides to use them in order to create a more efficient network. When she creates a Universal group, she is successful, but she's not given the option to make this a Security group. Why is Wilma unable to create a Windows Universal Security group?

- ○ A. Universal groups are only used for distribution groups.
- ○ B. Wilma must be a member of the Enterprise Administrators group in order to create Universal groups.
- ○ C. Before Wilma can create Universal groups, she must take the Windows NT 4 servers offline.
- ○ D. Universal groups may only serve as distribution groups in mixed mode.

# Question 58

Zeke is the network administrator for a sailboat manufacturing company. In order to increase security and ensure that only authorized users are able to access sensitive keel design documents, the company has decided to not use passwords but rather to use smartcards. The environment consists of 20 Windows 2000 Professional clients and 20 Windows XP Professional clients. Zeke configures all systems to use smartcards and tests them successfully. Users continue to use their smartcards for several weeks. Zeke then upgrades all the client systems to run Windows XP Professional. Now, however, those clients previously running Windows 2000 are no longer able to use smartcards to authenticate users on the network. Why is this happening?

- ○ A. Smartcards have an expiry date. In this case, the expiry date has been reached.
- ○ B. Smartcards will only work in a Windows XP Professional environment.
- ○ C. Smartcards for Windows 2000 must be enrolled on a Windows 2000 enrollment station; they are no longer valid with the Windows XP enrollment station.
- ○ D. Smartcards are not supported in Windows XP Professional.

# Question 59

Alexander is the network administrator for a securities company. As part of its security planning, the company wants to ensure that users are only able to log on to the network using smartcards. However, some users continue to use their passwords, rather than their smartcards, to log on to the network. Alexander wishes to prevent this behavior. How can Alexander best force users to use their smartcards for login authentication?

○ A. Alexander should select all the appropriate user accounts, right-click, and check the box that requires authentication via smartcard.

○ B. Alexander should select each individual user account, right-click, and check the box that requires authentication via smartcard.

○ C. Alexander should select the Organizational Unit containing the user accounts, right-click, and check the box that requires authentication via smartcard.

○ D. Alexander should select the domain containing the user accounts, right-click, and check the box that requires authentication via smartcard.

# Question 60

Brian is the network administrator for a large college. Several of the instructors take two months off during the summer. During this time, they do not require access to the college network. Therefore, Brian wants to ensure that no users are able to use their accounts. He speaks with his friend Charles, who suggests that Brian delete these accounts and then re-create them a few days before the instructors return from vacation. Brian's main concern is ensuring that all the appropriate permissions to objects within the network are maintained for each user. How can Brian best accomplish this objective?

○ A. Take Charles's advice. By deleting all the accounts, he can ensure that the users cannot use their accounts while they are gone.

○ B. Take Charles's advice. He can use Microsoft Excel to keep track of all the permissions for each user.

○ C. Don't listen to Charles. He can use Microsoft Excel to keep track of all the permissions for each user and then move all the accounts into a new OU.

○ D. Don't listen to Charles. He should disable all the accounts and then, as the instructors return from vacation, reenable them. This way, they will maintain their permissions.

# Practice Exam 2 Answer Key

1. B
2. C
3. B
4. B
5. C
6. D
7. B
8. A
9. B
10. A
11. A
12. A, B, C
13. D
14. C
15. A
16. C
17. A
18. B, C
19. B, D
20. D

21. A, B, C
22. A
23. B
24. A
25. B, D
26. C
27. B
28. A, D
29. D
30. C
31. C
32. B, C, D
33. A
34. B
35. D
36. B, D, E, G, H
37. A
38. C
39. E
40. B

41. A
42. B
43. A, B, C, D
44. A
45. B
46. C
47. A, C, D, F
48. D
49. A
50. E, A, C, B, D
51. B, C
52. C
53. D
54. C
55. C
56. B
57. D
58. C
59. A
60. D

# Question 1

Answer B is correct. Password requirements can only be established at the domain level, regardless of their ability to appear as if you can change them elsewhere. Answers A, C, and D are incorrect because these policies will not affect the security for the domain.

# Question 2

Answer C is correct. The PDC Emulator handles backward-compatibility issues. Answer A is incorrect because the Schema Master is necessary for changing the schema. Answer B is incorrect because the Infrastructure Master is used to handle references to objects without them existing in the directory partitions. Answer D is incorrect because the Domain Naming Master enables all objects to be unique. Answer E is incorrect because the RID Master is responsible for assigning and removing relative IDs (RIDs) from the domain and processing RID requests from all DCs in a domain.

# Question 3

Answer B is correct. You are allowed one Domain Naming Master and one Schema Master per forest. In addition, you need one PDC Emulator per domain, one Infrastructure Master per domain, and one RID Master per domain. In the given scenario, Maverick Corporation has two domain trees within a single forest and three child domains, for a total of five domains. Therefore, answer B is the only correct answer, making answers A, C, and D incorrect.

# Question 4

Answer B is correct. Remember, the trusting domain extends the trust to the trusted domain. You only need a one-way trust relationship, and it must go to the domain with the resource. Transitive trusts are only formed with Windows Server 2003 domains and only when the domains are part of the same tree or forest. A two-way trust between the two domains is not needed because there is no specification requesting a need for users in the Windows Server 2003 domains to access resources in the Windows NT domain. Therefore, answers A, C, and D are all incorrect.

# Question 5

Answer C is correct. To visualize the entire scenario, you need to first realize that the only way to reduce the traffic over the 56Kbps connection is to have the software package located on a server in Fiji, which is local. The next problem is that you need to establish a Group Policy that will affect everyone in the domain. Answer A is incorrect because it wants to use the OUs, which will work, but its much more effective to use Group Policy at the highest level possible (in this case, right at the domain level). Answer B is incorrect because it tries to place the policy at the site level, which is, again, too high up. Answer D is incorrect because it tries to use the `root.com` domain, but this will not affect the users in the `spacific.root.com` domain. The flow of the policy doesn't extend that deeply.

# Question 6

Answer D is correct. By adjusting the schedule of the site link, Shannon can restrict replication from taking place or permit replication to take place at a certain time. Answer A is incorrect because replication frequency is the time interval a DC will wait before checking for changes on other DCs. Answer B is incorrect because replication cost refers to the amount of bandwidth the replication process will use. Answer C is incorrect because there is no such thing as a replication transport value.

# Question 7

Answer B is correct. When you add DCs to a domain, you improve logon performance. However, the DCs will cause traffic on the domain because of the replication of data between the DCs. Therefore, the more DCs that are on the domain, the more replication that will take place. Replication will use up network bandwidth. Answer A is incorrect because the more DCs you add, the more this will increase bandwidth usage. Answer C is incorrect because you can have more than three domain controllers in a domain. Answer D is incorrect because promoting a server to be a DC does not require a reinstallation of the operating system.

## Question 8

Answer A is correct. In this case, you can manually configure your own connection objects. The KCC manually creates a topology, but you can edit this. Answer B is incorrect because this will most likely generate the same functioning topology, but the KCC is not able to update the topology according to what is in your mind. Answer C is incorrect because you don't update the Registry for this problem. Answer D is incorrect because the KCC does allow this.

## Question 9

Answer B is correct. Sites should be established based on the physical connectivity and subnets. This is a logical grouping of DCs to ease replication traffic. In this scenario, you might think it's a good idea to create a single site between New York and Newark because of the T1 connection, but the bandwidth utilization is too high between the two locations. Answer A is incorrect because of the excessive bandwidth utilization between the two locations. Answer C is incorrect because this doesn't utilize sites correctly at all. Answer D is incorrect because the 56Kbps connection should be kept separate altogether.

## Question 10

Answer A is correct. Site link costs are used to determine the preferred path network traffic should take, with the lower-cost route being the most preferred. Vanessa should set the T1 site link to have a lower cost than the demand dial, which makes answer B incorrect. Answer C is undesirable because, although she could remove the demand-dial link, the whole idea behind having it as a backup is that network communications will be uninterrupted if the T1 circuit goes down. Answer D is incorrect because it is not possible to configure a site link to monitor another site link and only go active if the other is unavailable.

## Question 11

Answer A is correct. Any domain controller can easily be made a GC server through Active Directory Sites and Services, by editing the NTDS Settings and checking the box to make the server a GC. Likewise, an existing GC server can have the role removed in the same manner by unchecking the box. Answers B and C are incorrect because they refer to ways of transferring FSMO roles, and the GC setting is not an FSMO role. Answer D is incorrect because there is no option to configure a GC during the AD Installation Wizard. By default the first domain controller in a domain is automatically made a GC, and all subsequent GCs must be manually configured by the administrator.

## Question 12

Answers A, B, and C are correct. In order to transfer the PDC Emulator role, Paulette would use the Active Directory Users and Computers utility. Transferring the Schema Master role is different in that, by default, Paulette can't run the schema management administrative snap-in. She has to first register the `schmmgmt.dll` file for schema management and then create a custom console and add the schema management snap-in to the console. Once she has done that, she can transfer the Schema Master role to another domain controller. Answers D and E are incorrect because they refer to the wrong utilities to use to transfer the PDC Emulator role. Answer F is incorrect because, although Paulette would use NTDSUtil to seize the role if the domain controller hosting the Schema Master role is permanently offline, she could not gracefully transfer the role in this manner. Answer G is incorrect because Paulette must register the `schmmgmt.dll` file and create a custom console in order to access schema management.

## Question 13

Answer D is correct. With Windows Server 2003, you do not need to use multiple domains in order to control access to resources or delegate administrative authority; you can instead use OUs within a single domain to accomplish the same thing. As a result, answers A and B are incorrect because they add unnecessary administrative overhead. Answer C doesn't work because without using OUs and delegating control to them specifically, you aren't meeting the requirement of preventing administrators from controlling resources in other branches.

## Question 14

Answer C is correct. You will need to use OUs in order to delegate permissions only over the desired resources. In this scenario, you should create child OUs for each branch and then delegate authority to the local admins for their specific OUs. This way, they can effectively administer their own resources without having access to other branches. Answer A is incorrect because the scenario isn't concerned with the main office. Answer B is incorrect because it doesn't meet the requirements of the local administrators being able to administer their own resources. Answer D is incorrect because using groups doesn't let you delegate authority only over specific parts of the domain. That's what OUs are for.

## Question 15

Answer A is correct. In order to set the password policy for the domain, David needs to edit the Default Domain Policy rather than the Default Domain Controllers Policy. Answer B wouldn't help even if he was editing the Default Domain Policy because, although the password complexity and minimum password length settings are often used in conjunction with each other, they are not interchangeable. Answer C would work, but it would be an administrative headache to maintain policies on each individual client computer. Answer D is incorrect because the problem is related to David not setting the policy in the proper place.

## Question 16

Answer C is correct. The Knowledge Consistency Checker (KCC) will automatically attempt to configure the most efficient path for network traffic to take. The way the network is designed, with a star topology rather than a mesh, the KCC will naturally build a topology that uses the most efficient route. Answers A and B are incorrect because the administrative overhead of maintaining all those individual connection objects would be extremely inefficient and unlikely to do a better job than the KCC. Answer D is incorrect because the KCC wouldn't be limited to just part of a domain. It's an all-or-nothing configuration.

# Question 17

Answer A is correct. By default, only the first domain controller in a domain is a GC server. As a result, in this scenario there would be a lot of authentication traffic passing over the WAN connections, which could cause delays during peak usage parts of the day. By making a DC at each site a GC, Mike could eliminate this type of traffic. Answer B is incorrect because adding additional DCs won't result in the creation of new GC servers. Answer C is incorrect because the problem isn't that the GC at the main office is overwhelmed, but rather that the traffic over the slower WAN links is causing delays during peak periods of usage. Answer D would cause more problems because sites are used to control replication, and if all the servers were in a single site, it would dramatically increase replication traffic over already burdened WAN links. Therefore, answer D is incorrect.

# Question 18

Answers B and C are correct. Sites are most commonly used to control replication traffic by defining areas that are well-connected versus areas that are not. Intrasite replication takes place immediately whenever a change is made, whereas intersite replication can be scheduled. Once C.G. creates new sites, he would then need to take the step of moving the existing servers to appropriate sites using Active Directory Sites and Services. Answer A is incorrect for obvious reasons; the problem is he only has a single site presently. Answer D is incorrect because making every server a GC would only increase replication traffic while the servers were contained within a single site.

# Question 19

Answers B and D are correct. The two settings most commonly used in conjunction to create strong passwords are Minimum Password Length and Passwords Must Meet Complexity Requirements. By using these two options, you can ensure that passwords are much harder to crack with a dictionary-style brute-force attack. By enabling Password Must Meet Complexity Requirements, the minimum password length required would be six characters, but you can set the minimum length at eight using the Minimum Password Length setting. Complex passwords must also contain three of the four following types of characters: uppercase, lowercase, numbers, and special characters ($, *, &, #, and so on). Answer A is incorrect because if a hacker gets the password, it doesn't matter whether he has to log on to change it. Answer C is incorrect because storing passwords using reversible encryption won't help against a brute-force attack, which simply guesses at passwords. Another policy option not listed in this question that would be helpful would be to set an account-lockout threshold.

## Question 20

Answer D is correct. Site link costs are used by Active Directory to determine the best path for traffic to take. By setting the site link cost of the Dallas–St. Louis link lower than the cost of Dallas–Omaha link, Bill can ensure that if the Dallas GC goes down, the St. Louis site would be contacted first, thus making answer C incorrect. Answer A is incorrect because a preferred bridgehead server is the server in a site that handles intersite replication. It would have no bearing in this scenario on what site is contacted first, which is a site link cost issue. Answer B is incorrect because removing the site link between Dallas and Omaha would have other undesirable side effects.

## Question 21

Answers A, B, and C are correct. In order for Melissa to have users change passwords on a regular basis, she needs to enable the Maximum Password Age policy option. In order for her to prevent users from simply reusing their existing passwords, she must enable the Enforce Password History option. To prevent users from getting around the password history by changing their passwords over and over until they can get back to their original passwords, Melissa should use the Minimum Password Age option, which requires a specified amount of days to elapse from a password change before a user can change his or her password again. Answer D is incorrect because, although enabling complexity requirements is good, it goes beyond the requirements of the scenario, which is just that passwords must be changed regularly and changed to something different.

## Question 22

Answer A is correct. There are two transport types for carrying intersite communications: IP and SMTP. The IP transport is used when there is reliable connectivity, thus making answer B incorrect. The SMTP transport is used when links are unreliable. In this situation, Bill would want to configure an SMTP site link between Dallas and Beijing to compensate for the unreliable WAN connection. Answers C and D are incorrect because site link bridges are collections of site links used by AD to determine the least-cost route to transport network traffic; they don't define the actual site link.

# Question 23

Answer B is correct. The easiest way for Veronica to remove Chris's permissions is through the security properties of the Accounting OU. Answer A is incorrect because the Delegation of Control Wizard allows you to grant permissions, not remove permissions. Answer C is incorrect because moving Chris's account to the Sales OU will not change his permissions on the Accounting OU. An OU is just a container; by itself, it has no influence on permissions or access to resources of user accounts and groups. Answer D would work as far as removing Chris's permission to the Accounting OU goes, but it would have the unintended side effect of removing his access to everything, because his new user account would have a new SID, even though it has the same name as the old account. All his group memberships and permissions would have to be re-created. Therefore, answer D is incorrect.

# Question 24

Answer A is correct. In the present situation, your user account is a member of the Domain Admins group of dallas.wwinc.com, but not the wwinc.com domain. Domain Admin permissions are required to run the AD Installation Wizard, so you need to have that level of access granted to your account. Answer B is incorrect because moving your account to wwinc.com would not help unless you were made a member of the Domain Admins group, which actually doesn't require moving the account given the transitive nature of automatic trusts between parent and child domains. Answer C is incorrect because, in general, only the bare permissions necessary to complete a task should be given, and being a member of Enterprise Admins is not required for this. Answer D is incorrect because you are promoting a domain controller in an existing domain. If you were setting up a new domain, your account would need to be a member of the local administrators group, but in an existing domain the Domain Admins group is a member of all local administrator groups of member servers.

# Question 25

Answers B and D are correct. This question is a bit tricky in that people tend to see "Windows NT 4" and automatically assume Windows 2000 mixed mode is required. However, you only need to stay in Windows 2000 mixed mode as long as you have Windows NT 4 *domain controllers*. Member servers don't replicate AD account information; therefore, raising the domain functional level will not orphan these servers. Once you raise the domain functional level to Windows 2003, you can create universal groups and implement universal group caching. Although Windows 2000 native mode supports universal groups, it does not support universal group caching, thus making answer C incorrect. Answer A is incorrect because only Windows NT 4 domain controllers would need to be upgraded to continue working after you raise the domain functional level.

# Question 26

Answer C is correct. Windows Server 2003 supports a new feature called *application data partitions* that allows application developers to create partitioned-off areas specific for application data storage. The advantage of application data partitions is that you can control how they are replicated in AD, even to which servers. This helps control the replication traffic generated by the database application. Answer A is incorrect because, although utilizing Kerberos could improve authentication security, it wouldn't have any impact on the requirements of this scenario. Answers B and D are incorrect because they describe functions of the operating system that cannot be controlled by applications.

# Question 27

Answer B is correct. External trusts are used to connect Windows NT 4 domains to Active Directory domains, and in this situation Dawn would want to configure the trusts so that the AD domains trust the Windows NT 4 domain. This is because users in the Windows NT 4 domain need to access the AD domains, but not the other way around, thus making answer A incorrect. Answers C and D are incorrect because a forest trust is used to connect two AD forests, and realm trusts are used to connect AD domains with a Unix realm.

# Question 28

Answers A and D are correct. Generally you don't need to manually configure the preferred bridgehead server for a site, which is the server all intersite replication flows through, because the ISTG does a good job of this. However, you could manually specify that the new server be the preferred bridgehead server, which should reduce the load somewhat on the old server. Additionally, you could manually transfer all the FSMO roles to the new server, which should improve performance on the older DC. Although maybe not ideal, demoting the old server back to a member server would get rid of all the overhead of AD. However, this is not the *best* choice, thus making answer C incorrect. Answer B is incorrect because the problems with the server are related to the load placed on it, which is something that a format/reinstall would not correct.

# Question 29

Answer D is correct. Because you have manually configured site link bridges, you have disabled Bridge All Site Links, which is the default setting. As a result, whenever you add new sites you must manually configure communication paths between them. Answer A is incorrect because, although reenabling Bridge All Site Links would work to establish communication, it would break your existing manually configured site link bridges. Answer B is incorrect because there is no need to purchase additional T1 circuits, which is an expensive solution for this scenario. Answer C is incorrect because the ITSG and KCC work automatically in the background and update as necessary.

# Question 30

Answer C is correct. By default, all site links are bridged automatically, thus making answer A incorrect. Therefore, when you manually configure site link bridges, they won't work as intended until you disable automatic bridging in Active Directory Sites and Services. Answer B is incorrect because site link bridges can be configured manually if desired; you just first have to disable automatic bridging. Answer D is incorrect because, although the costs play a role in how traffic flows through a site link bridge, the manually configured site link bridge won't work until automatic bridging is disabled.

## Question 31

Answer C is correct. Modify the Registry and set the level of logging to 3. This will set the level of logging to Full Reporting. Answer A is incorrect because this option does not exist. Answer B is incorrect because setting the level of logging to 0 disables logging. Answer D is incorrect because this is not a standard option for Group Policy and is administratively complex.

## Question 32

Answers B, C, and D are correct. Answer A is incorrect because Event Viewer is used to view events logged on the server. Answer E is incorrect because Repadmin is not a Graphical User Interface tool.

## Question 33

Answer A is correct. Ruby should restart the server in Directory Services Restore Mode and use the NTDSUtil utility to move the file. In order to move this file, she must use this utility to ensure that the appropriate Registry settings are also modified. This file cannot be moved while it is in use. Answer B is incorrect because using Windows Explorer to move the file will not allow the Registry to be automatically modified. Answer C is incorrect because Ruby cannot move the file while it's in use. Also, this method will not automatically modify the Registry. Answer D is incorrect because, once again, Ruby cannot move the file while it's in use.

## Question 34

Answer B is correct. Roger needs to perform an authoritative restore of Active Directory while in Directory Services Restore Mode. Roger needs to restart the server, pressing the F8 key during startup, and enter the Directory Services Restore Mode. An authoritative restore will increment the version number by 100,000, ensuring that the restored OU is viewed by the other domain controllers as being the most recent. Answer A is incorrect because this is likely what Roger was doing. In this case, the restoration occurs without a problem; however, during the next replication cycle the restored OU is overwritten by the other domain controllers. This is because the other domain controllers see their version of the database file (the one in which the OU has been deleted) as being the most recent. Answers C and D are incorrect because the restoration cannot occur while Active Directory is running.

# Question 35

Answer D is correct. The trust needs to be reestablished because the passwords are negotiated every 7 days, and the backup exceeds this timeframe. Answer A is incorrect because there is no such utility. Answer B is incorrect because the most recent backup is 22 days old, and passwords for an external trust are renegotiated every 7 days. Answer C is incorrect because external trusts can be created between AD domains and Unix-based domains on a permanent basis.

# Question 36

The correct answers are B, D, E, G, and H. Answer A is incorrect because ntboot.ini is part of the system files, not the AD database files. Answer C is incorrect because nslookup is a command, and the .txt extension is not correct. Answers F and I also have incorrect extensions, making these answers incorrect as well.

# Question 37

Answer A is correct. She should set up loopback with replace. This ensures that the computer settings are applied last and that they take precedence. Answer B is incorrect because this will merge both the user and the computer settings, resulting in a combined set of policies rather than having the computer's settings take precedence. Answer C is incorrect because disabling the user settings in the OU will not just affect the computer in the lobby but also all the computers and users in that OU, regardless of where they log on from. Answer D is incorrect because disabling the computer settings in the OU will not just affect the computer in lobby but also all the computers and users in that OU, regardless of where they log on from.

# Question 38

Answer C is correct. This is happening because Group Policies refresh on a schedule, which occurs every 90 minutes, plus or minus 30 minutes. Bernard can run GPUpdate to force a refresh. Answer A is incorrect because, although it may be true until the Group Policies refresh, it is unknown whether or not they are correct. Answer B is incorrect because RSoP is used to see the resultant set of policies, not to refresh them. Answer D is incorrect because the GPOEnable utility does not exist.

# Question 39

Answer E is correct. This is happening because the Group Policy has not been run. She can correct this by either restarting to computers or running GPUDATE /Boot. Cassandra knows that the Group Policy is running correctly because the one user did receive the new installation. The reason the other users have not received the new installation is because software installations only occur when the computer restarts if they are set against the computer object in Group Policy. Using the /Boot switch will force the policy to refresh and the systems to reboot. Answer A is incorrect because there is nothing indicating that there is a difference between evening workers and daytime workers. They are all part of the same OU. Answer B is incorrect because the Group Policy would have refreshed within the timeframe of 3 hours. Answer C is incorrect because, although this will refresh the Group Policy, software installations require a reboot. Answer D is incorrect because the policies are directed toward the computers, not the users.

# Question 40

Answer B is correct. Because Dennis has uninstalled the DNS, clients will not be able to locate the domain controller and, hence, will not be able to receive the Group Policy. Active Directory requires that a DNS server be available and functioning in order for Group Policies (as well as a number of other services) to function correctly. Answer A is incorrect because Dennis can use any server as a file server. In this case, DNS was removed, which would be okay as long as there's another DNS server to take its place. However, it's not recommended that he run both the DNS and a file server on the same machine. Answer C is incorrect because Group Policy does support the redirection of folders. Answer D is incorrect because, although the use of this placeholder is a good idea, it is not mandatory.

## Question 41

Answer A is correct. If Edward wants to take advantage of both user and computer auto-enrollment, his environment must consist of Windows Server 2003 and Windows XP. Answer B is incorrect because he specifically wants to auto-enroll users. Answer C is incorrect because it does not allow for auto-enrollment. Answer D is incorrect because only the servers need to be running Windows 2003 Enterprise Edition.

## Question 42

Answer B is correct. Frank must use the Group Policy Editor and choose Properties. He should then choose Basic and specify the network share. The Basic option redirects all files to the same network share. Answer A is incorrect because Folder Redirection is not automatic. Answer C is incorrect because the Advanced property is intended for directing folders to different locations. Answer D is incorrect because Folder Direction is supported.

## Question 43

Answers A, B, C, and D are correct. All these folders can be redirected.

## Question 44

Answer A is correct. Stephanie should right-click the desired domain or OU in Active Directory Users and Computers and select Delegate Control. She should then select the option Manage Group Policy Links for the appropriate users. Answer B is incorrect because delegation occurs at the container object level, not at the user object level. Answers C and D are incorrect because there is no Group Policy Administrator tool.

# Question 45

Answer B is correct. Ingrid is correct. The Compatible security template will ensure that legacy applications are still allowed to run without granting users the Power User permissions. The Compatible security template increases security over the basic template to allow members of the local users group to run applications that are not Windows Server 2003 compliant with elevated Power User privileges. Answer A is incorrect because the High security template will invoke extreme security measures, without regard for functionality, performance, or connectivity with non–Windows Server 2003 clients. Answer C is incorrect because the Secure security template removes all members from the Power Users group. Answer D is incorrect because Windows Server 2003 will support legacy applications.

# Question 46

Answer C is correct. Jonathan can implement a Group Policy that modifies the Control Panel/display properties to disable changing the wallpaper and to specify a specific screensaver. By specifying a Group Policy that prevents the changing of the wallpaper and screensaver, Jonathan is effectively creating a standard desktop environment. Answer A is incorrect because this involves a large amount of administrative overhead. Answer B is incorrect because the startup script would be unnecessarily complex and require the computer to restart in order to take effect. Answer D is incorrect because this will not allow for other individual settings for each user, such as a unique My Documents folder.

# Question 47

Answers A, C, D, and F are correct. The four standard administrative templates are System.adm, Inetres.adm, Conf.adm, and Wmplayer.adm. The other files do not exist, making answers B, E, G, and H all incorrect.

# Question 48

Answer D is correct. The workstation on which Lenny is trying to deploy the application cannot communicate with the SYSVOL share. This error message indicates that the package is corrupt or that communication with the

SYSVOL share has failed. Because the question states that the package is not corrupt, the only possible explanation is the lack of connectivity. To solve this problem, Lenny should attempt to install the application on another workstation that has connectivity. Answer A is incorrect because an incompatible workstation will cause an application error message, not a Group Policy error message. Answer B is incorrect because there is no indication that the server is required to run the application. In this case, the server is only acting to deliver the application, not host it. Answer C is incorrect because failing to meet the necessary hardware requirements would result in a different error message.

## Question 49

Answer A is correct. Using Group Policy, Mary can set up the Microsoft Office applications to be assigned to each computer account. In the event of a corrupted or deleted file, the affected application will redeploy. Assigning an application through Group Policy will place a shortcut on the user's Start menu that, when clicked, will ensure proper installation without user intervention. Answer B is incorrect because it requires each user to reinstall the application, which is administratively costly. Answer C is incorrect because Microsoft Office does not support automatic recovery in this matter. Answer D is incorrect because the administration pack does not include such a tool. This tool selfheal.exe is fictitious.

## Question 50

The correct order is E, A, C, B, D.

## Question 51

Answers B and C are correct. Oliver must promote at least one Windows Server 2003 server to act as a domain controller, and he must promote his Windows NT workstations to Windows 2000 Professional or Windows XP. The requirements for software installations are Active Directory and Group Policies. Active Directory requires a domain controller, and Group Policies require that the clients are running Windows 2000 or Windows XP. Answer A is incorrect because the PDC Emulator is only required for login authentication of legacy clients. Answer D is incorrect because Windows 2000 is supported by Group Policies.

# Question 52

Answer C is correct. Peter should disable the computer portion of Group Policies. The options to modify the desktop and display settings are found within the user settings portion of Group Policies. Therefore, Peter wants the user settings to run but does not necessarily require the computer settings to run. By Peter disabling the computer settings from running, Group Policies will process more quickly. Answer A is incorrect because it involves a prohibitive amount of administration. Answer B is incorrect because disabling the user portion of Group Policies from running will prevent the desired settings from being enforced. Answer D is incorrect because disabling both the computer and user portions of group policy will effectively render Group Policies completely disabled.

# Question 53

Answer D is correct. The hotel users must be assigned the Apply Group Policy permission. In order to be affected by Group Policy, users must have both the Read and the Apply Group Policy permission set. Answer A is incorrect because the Group Policies will apply to any site, domain, or OU to which they are applied. Answer B is incorrect because dropping and re-creating the Group Policies will not solve Hubert's problem. Answer C is incorrect because the Write permission could potentially allow these users to modify the Group Policies. The desired behavior is to have the Group Policies affect the users without giving them the ability to modify the Group Policies.

# Question 54

Answer C is correct. Rachel should apply this Group Policy at the site level. By Rachel applying the Group Policy at the site level, it will affect all computers that fall within the site boundary. Answer A is incorrect because each school may have multiple OUs, which would require Rachel to apply the Group Policy to many different OUs. Answer B is incorrect because each school runs its own domain, which would require Rachel to apply the Group Policy at each school. Answer D is incorrect because applying the Group Policy at the local level would require Rachel to visit every single computer.

# Question 55

Answer C is correct. When a user logs on to a computer in the editing suite, the color of the wallpaper will be black. Group Policies are processed in the following order: site, domain, and then OU. Generally speaking, unless specific behaviors are modified, the policies applied later will overwrite the policies previously applied. In this case, the final background color specified for the client OU is black, and this is the color that will appear.

# Question 56

Answer B is correct. Universal groups will replicate all information about each object within the group to all sites. This means that user accounts added to a Universal group will have all their information completely replicated, thus slowing down the replication process. A best practice is to use Universal groups and nest other groups within them in cases where access to all domains is required by a group of users. Answer A is incorrect because more information will take a longer period of time to replicate. Answer C is incorrect because Universal groups will slow replication. Answer D is incorrect because Universal groups are replicated.

# Question 57

Answer D is correct. Universal groups may only serve as distribution groups in mixed mode. This answer may seem confusing at first, because in many cases it is stated that Universal groups *cannot be used at all* within an environment running in mixed mode. However, the fact is that Universal groups can be used—just not as security groups. They can only be used as distribution groups while running in mixed mode. Answer A is incorrect because Universal groups can be used for more than just distribution groups, but the environment cannot be running in mixed mode. This answer is actually an example of an absolute statement. To say that Universal groups are only used for distribution groups is false. If the statement were "Within mixed mode, Universal groups are only used for distribution groups," then the statement would be true. Answer B is incorrect because the question states that Wilma is able to create a Universal group—just not one used for security. Answer C is incorrect because the problem is not with the Windows NT 4 servers; it is the fact that the entire environment is running in mixed mode.

# Question 58

Answer C is correct. Smartcards for Windows 2000 must be enrolled on a Windows 2000 enrollment station; they are no longer valid with the Windows XP enrollment station. Answer A is incorrect because it is unlikely that smartcards, which were working previously, would have expired at the exact same time the upgrade occurred. Answer B is incorrect because smartcards can be used in a Windows 2000 environment. Answer D is incorrect because smartcards can be used in a Windows 2003 environment.

# Question 59

Answer A is correct. Alexander should select all the appropriate user accounts, right-click, and check the box that requires authentication via smartcard. Active Directory Users and Computers allows this option to be applied to multiple user accounts at the same time. By selecting all the accounts he wishes to change the option for and then right-clicking once, Alexander is able to perform this action against several accounts at the same time. Answer B is incorrect because it would require far more administrative work. Answer C is incorrect because this option is not configured from the OU level. Answer D is incorrect because this option is not configured from the domain level.

# Question 60

Answer D is correct. Brian shouldn't listen to Charles. Instead, he should disable all the accounts and then, as the instructors return from vacation, reenable them. This way, they will maintain their permissions. Because the accounts are disabled, nobody will be able to use them, and they will be available to use once they are reenabled when the staff returns. Answers A and B are incorrect because deleting all the accounts will require significant administrative effort in re-creating them when the staff returns. Answer C is incorrect because, although using Excel to maintain a list of permissions will help, moving the accounts to a new OU will not prevent them from being used if someone has the appropriate name and password.

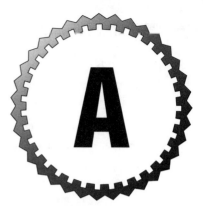

# What's on the CD-ROM

This appendix is a brief rundown of what you'll find on the CD-ROM that comes with this book. For a more detailed description of the *PrepLogic Practice Tests, Preview Edition* exam-simulation software, see Appendix B, "Using the *PrepLogic Practice Tests, Preview Edition* Software." In addition to the *PrepLogic Practice Tests, Preview Edition* software, the CD-ROM includes the electronic version of this book in Portable Document Format (PDF), several utility and application programs, and a complete listing of test objectives and where they are covered in the book.

## *PrepLogic Practice Tests, Preview Edition*

PrepLogic is a leading provider of certification training tools. Trusted by certification students worldwide, PrepLogic is, we believe, the best practice exam software available. In addition to providing a means of evaluating your knowledge of the *Exam Cram 2* material, *PrepLogic Practice Tests, Preview Edition* features several innovations that help you to improve your mastery of the subject matter.

For example, the practice tests allow you to check your score by exam area or domain to determine which topics you need to study more. Another feature allows you to obtain immediate feedback on your responses in the form of explanations for the correct and incorrect answers.

*PrepLogic Practice Tests, Preview Edition* exhibits most of the full functionality of the *Premium Edition* but offers only a fraction of the total questions. To get the complete set of practice questions and exam functionality, visit PrepLogic.com and order the *Premium Edition* for this and other challenging exam titles.

Again, for a more detailed description of the *PrepLogic Practice Tests, Preview Edition* features, see Appendix B.

# Using the *PrepLogic Practice Tests, Preview Edition* Software

This *Exam Cram 2* includes a special version of *PrepLogic Practice Tests*—a revolutionary test engine designed to give you the best in certification exam preparation. PrepLogic offers sample and practice exams for many of today's most in-demand and challenging technical certifications. This special *Preview Edition* is included with this book as a tool to use in assessing your knowledge of the *Exam Cram 2* material while also providing you with the experience of taking an electronic exam.

This appendix describes in detail what *PrepLogic Practice Tests, Preview Edition* is, how it works, and what it can do to help you prepare for the exam. Note that although the *Preview Edition* includes all the test-simulation functions of the complete, retail version, it contains only a single practice test. The *Premium Edition*, available at PrepLogic.com, contains the complete set of challenging practice exams designed to optimize your learning experience.

## Exam Simulation

One of the main functions of *PrepLogic Practice Tests, Preview Edition* is exam simulation. To prepare you to take the actual vendor certification exam, PrepLogic is designed to offer the most effective exam simulation available.

# Question Quality

The questions provided in the *PrepLogic Practice Tests, Preview Edition* are written to the highest standards of technical accuracy. The questions tap the content of the *Exam Cram 2* chapters and help you review and assess your knowledge before you take the actual exam.

# Interface Design

The *PrepLogic Practice Tests, Preview Edition* exam-simulation interface provides you with the experience of taking an electronic exam. This enables you to effectively prepare for taking the actual exam by making the test experience a familiar one. Using this test simulation can help eliminate the sense of surprise or anxiety you might experience in the testing center because you will already be acquainted with computerized testing.

# Effective Learning Environment

The *PrepLogic Practice Tests, Preview Edition* interface provides a learning environment that not only tests you through the computer but also teaches you the material you need to know to pass the certification exam. Each question comes with a detailed explanation of the correct answer and often provides reasons the other options are incorrect. This information helps to reinforce the knowledge you already have and also provides practical information you can use on the job.

# Software Requirements

*PrepLogic Practice Tests* requires a computer with the following:

➤ Microsoft Windows 98, Windows Me, Windows NT 4.0, Windows 2000, or Windows XP.

➤ A 166MHz or faster processor (recommended).

➤ A minimum of 32MB of RAM. (As with any Windows application, the more memory, the better your performance.)

➤ 10MB of hard drive space.

# Installing *PrepLogic Practice Tests, Preview Edition*

Install *PrepLogic Practice Tests, Preview Edition* by running the setup program on the *PrepLogic Practice Tests, Preview Edition* CD-ROM. Follow these instructions to install the software on your computer:

1. Insert the CD-ROM into your CD-ROM drive. The Autorun feature of Windows should launch the software. If you have Autorun disabled, click Start and select Run. Go to the root directory of the CD-ROM and select setup.exe. Click Open and then click OK.

2. The Installation Wizard copies the *PrepLogic Practice Tests, Preview Edition* files to your hard drive; adds *PrepLogic Practice Tests, Preview Edition* to your Desktop and Program menu; and installs test engine components to the appropriate system folders.

## Removing *PrepLogic Practice Tests, Preview Edition* from Your Computer

If you elect to remove the *PrepLogic Practice Tests, Preview Edition* product from your computer, an uninstall process has been included to ensure that it is removed from your system safely and completely. Follow these instructions to remove *PrepLogic Practice Tests, Preview Edition* from your computer:

1. Select Start, Settings, Control Panel.

2. Double-click the Add/Remove Programs icon.

3. You are presented with a list of software installed on your computer. Select the appropriate *PrepLogic Practice Tests, Preview Edition* title you want to remove. Click the Add/Remove button. The software is then removed from your computer.

# Using *PrepLogic Practice Tests, Preview Edition*

PrepLogic is designed to be user friendly and intuitive. Because the software has a smooth learning curve, your time is maximized because you start practicing almost immediately. *PrepLogic Practice Tests, Preview Edition* has two major modes of study: Practice Test and Flash Review.

Using Practice Test mode, you can develop your test-taking abilities as well as your knowledge through the use of the Show Answer option. While you are taking the test, you can expose the answers along with detailed explanations of why the given answers are right or wrong. This gives you the ability to better understand the material presented.

Flash Review is designed to reinforce exam topics rather than quiz you. In this mode, you will be shown a series of questions but no answer choices. Instead, you will be given a button that reveals the correct answer to the question and a full explanation for that answer.

# Starting a Practice Test Mode Session

Practice Test mode enables you to control the exam experience in ways that actual certification exams do not allow:

➤ *Enable Show Answer Button*—This option activates the Show Answer button, allowing you to view the correct answer(s) and full explanation(s) for each question during the exam. When this option is not enabled, you must wait until after your exam has been graded to view the correct answer(s) and explanation(s).

➤ *Enable Item Review Button*—This option activates the Item Review button, allowing you to view your answer choices and marked questions, and to facilitate navigation between questions.

➤ *Randomize Choices*—This option randomizes answer choices from one exam session to the next. This makes memorizing question choices more difficult, thus keeping questions fresh and challenging longer.

To begin studying in Practice Test mode, click the Practice Test radio button from the main exam-customization screen. This enables the options detailed in the preceding list.

To your left, you are presented with the option of selecting the preconfigured practice test or creating your own custom test. The preconfigured test has a fixed time limit and number of questions. A custom test allows you to configure the time limit and the number of questions on your exam.

The *Preview Edition* included with this book has a single preconfigured practice test. You can get the compete set of challenging PrepLogic practice tests at PrepLogic.com and make certain you're ready for the big exam.

Click the Begin Exam button to begin your exam.

# Starting a Flash Review Mode Session

Flash Review mode provides you with an easy way to reinforce topics covered in the practice questions. To begin studying in Flash Review mode, click the Flash Review radio button from the main exam-customization screen. Select either the preconfigured practice test or create your own custom test.

Click the Best Exam button to begin your Flash Review of the exam questions.

# Standard *PrepLogic Practice Tests, Preview Edition* Options

The following list describes the function of each of the buttons you see. Depending on the options, some of the buttons will be grayed out and inaccessible or missing completely. Buttons that are appropriate are active. The buttons are as follows:

➤ *Exhibit*—This button is visible if an exhibit is provided to support the question. An exhibit is an image that provides supplemental information necessary to answer the question.

➤ *Item Review*—When you click this button, you leave the question window and go to the Item Review screen. From this screen you will see all questions, your answers, and your marked items. You will also see correct answers listed here when appropriate.

➤ *Show Answer*—This option displays the correct answer with an explanation of why it is correct. If you select this option, the current question is not scored.

➤ *Mark Item*—Check this box to tag a question you need to review further. You can view and navigate your marked items by clicking the Item Review button (if enabled). When grading your exam, you will be notified if you have marked items remaining.

➤ *Previous Item*—Use this button to view the previous question.

➤ *Next Item*—Use this button to view the next question.

➤ *Grade Exam*—When you have completed your exam, click this button to end your exam and view your detailed score report. If you have unanswered or marked items remaining, you will be asked whether you would like to continue taking the exam or view your exam report.

# Time Remaining

If the test is timed, the time remaining is displayed in the upper-right corner of the application screen. It counts down minutes and seconds remaining to complete the test. If you run out of time, you will be asked if you want to continue taking the exam or if you want to end it.

# Your Examination Score Report

The Examination Score Report screen appears when the Practice Test mode ends—as the result of time expiration, completion of all questions, or your decision to terminate early.

This screen provides you with a graphical display of your test score with a breakdown of scores by topic domain. The graphical display at the top of the screen compares your overall score with the PrepLogic Exam Competency Score.

The PrepLogic Exam Competency Score reflects the level of subject competency required to pass this vendor's exam. Although this score does not directly translate to a passing score, consistently matching or exceeding this score does suggest you possess the knowledge to pass the actual vendor exam.

# Reviewing Your Exam

From your Examination Score Report screen, you can review the exam you just completed by clicking the View Items button. Navigate through the items, viewing the questions, your answers, the correct answers, and the explanations for the questions. You can return to your score report by clicking the View Items button.

# Getting More Exams

The *PrepLogic Practice Tests, Preview Edition* that accompanies this *Exam Cram 2* book contains a single PrepLogic practice test. Certification students worldwide trust PrepLogic practice tests to help them pass their IT certification exams the first time. You can purchase the *Premium Edition* of *PrepLogic Practice Tests* and get the entire set of all the new challenging practice tests for this exam. PrepLogic Practice Tests—Because You Want to Pass the First Time.

## Contacting PrepLogic

If you would like to contact PrepLogic for any reason, including to obtain information about our extensive line of certification practice tests, we invite you to do so. Please contact us online at www.preplogic.com.

# Customer Service

If you have a damaged product and need a replacement or refund, please call the following phone number:

800-858-7674

## Product Suggestions and Comments

We value your input! Please email your suggestions and comments to the following address:

feedback@preplogic.com

## License Agreement

YOU MUST AGREE TO THE TERMS AND CONDITIONS OUT-LINED IN THE END USER LICENSE AGREEMENT ("EULA") PRESENTED TO YOU DURING THE INSTALLATION PROCESS. IF YOU DO NOT AGREE TO THESE TERMS, DO NOT INSTALL THE SOFTWARE.

# Glossary

**access control entry (ACE)**
An entry within an access control list that grants or denies permissions to users or groups for a given resource.

**access control list (ACL)**
Contains a set of access control entries that define an object's permission settings. ACLs enable administrators to explicitly control access to resources.

**Active Directory (AD)**
The Windows Server 2003 directory service that replaces the antiquated Windows NT domain structure. Active Directory forms the basis for centralized network management on Windows Server 2003 networks, providing a hierarchical view of network resources.

**Active Directory Service Interfaces (ADSI)**
A directory service model implemented as a set of COM interfaces. ADSI allows Windows applications to access Active Directory, often through ActiveX interfaces such as VBScript.

**Active Directory Users and Computers**
The primary systems administrator utility for managing users, groups, and computers in a Windows Server 2003 domain, implemented as a Microsoft Management Console (MMC) snap-in.

**application data partition**
A partitioned section of Active Directory that is replicated only to specified domain controllers. Application data partitions are used by applications to store their application-specific data.

## assigned applications

Through the Software Installation utility in Group Policy, administrators can assign applications to users and computers. Assigned applications are always available to the user, even if the user attempts to uninstall them. Applications assigned to a computer will automatically be installed on the next restart.

## asynchronous processing

Occurs when one task waits until another is finished before beginning. This is typically associated with scripts, such as a user logon script not running before the computer startup script has completed. This is the default behavior in Windows Server 2003.

## attribute

The basic unit of an object, an *attribute* is a single property contained in the schema that through its values defines the object. For example, an attribute of a standard user account is the account name.

## auditing

A security process that tracks the usage of selected network resources, typically storing the results in a log file.

## authentication

The process by which a user's logon credentials are validated by a server so that access to a network resource can be granted or denied.

## backup domain controller (BDC)

A Windows NT 3.x or 4.0 server that contains a backup read-only copy of the domain security accounts manager (user account and security information). BDCs take the load off the primary domain controller (PDC) by servicing logon requests. Periodic synchronizing ensures that data between the PDC and BDCs remains consistent.

## baseline

A term associated with performance monitoring, a *baseline* is the initial result of monitoring typical network and server performance under a normal load, and all future results are measured against the baseline readings. A baseline will typically have performance readings for the processor(s), memory, disk subsystem, and network subsystem.

## bridgehead server

The contact point for the exchange of directory information between Active Directory sites.

## Certificate Authority (CA)

A trusted authority either within a network or a third-party company that manages security credentials such that it guarantees the user object that holds a certificate is who it claims to be.

## checkpoint file

Indicates the location of the last information successfully written from the transaction logs to the database. In a data-recovery scenario, the checkpoint file indicates where the recovery or replaying of data should begin.

## circular logging

When a log file fills up, it is overwritten with new data rather than a new log file being created. This conserves disk space but can result in data loss in a disaster-recovery scenario.

## Computer Configuration

The portion of a Group Policy Object that allows for computer policies to be configured and applied.

## connection object

An Active Directory object stored on domain controllers that is used to represent inbound replication links. Domain controllers create their own connection objects for intrasite replication through the Knowledge Consistency Checker (KCC), whereas only a single domain controller in a site creates connection objects for intersite replication, through the Intersite Topology Generator.

## container

An object in Active Directory that is capable of holding other objects. An example of a container would be the Users folder in Active Directory Users and Computers.

## convergence

The process of stabilization after network changes occur. Often associated with routing or replication, *convergence* ensures each router or server contains consistent information.

## counters

The metrics used in performance monitoring, *counters* are what you are actually monitoring. An example of a counter for a CPU object would be %Processing Time.

## DCPROMO

The command-line utility used to promote a Windows Server 2003 system to a domain controller. DCPROMO could also be used to demote a domain controller to a member server.

## delegation

The process of offloading the responsibility for a given task or set of tasks to another user or group. Delegation in Windows Server 2003 usually involves granting permission to someone else to perform a specific administrative task such as creating computer accounts.

## directory

A database that contains any number of different types of data. In Windows Server 2003, the Active Directory is a database that contains information about objects in the domain, such as computers, users, groups, and printers.

## Directory Service (DS)

Provides the methods of storing directory data and making that data available to other directory objects. A directory service makes it possible for users to find any object in the directory given any one of its attributes.

## Directory System Agent (DSA)

Makes data within Active Directory accessible to applications that want it, acting as a liaison between the directory database and the applications.

## disk quota

An administrative disk space limitation set on the server storage space, on a per volume basis, that can be used by any particular user.

## distinguished name

The name that uniquely identifies an object. A distinguished name is composed of the relative distinguished name, the domain name, and the container holding the object. An example would be CN=WWillis,CN=Inside-Corner,CN=COM. This refers to the WWillis user account in the inside-corner.com domain.

## Distributed File System (Dfs)

A Windows Server 2003 service that allows resources from multiple server locations to be presented through Active Directory as a contiguous set of files and folders, resulting in more ease of use of network resources for users.

## distribution group

An Active Directory group of user accounts, or other groups, that is used strictly for email distribution. A distribution group cannot be used for granting permissions to resources. That type of group is called a *security group*.

## domain

A logical grouping of Windows Server 2003 computers, users, and groups that share a common directory database. Domains are defined by an administrator.

## domain controller (DC)

A server that is capable of performing authentication. In Windows Server 2003, a domain controller holds a copy of the Active Directory database.

## domain functional level

Windows Server 2003 domains can operate at one of four functional levels: Windows 2000 mixed mode, Windows 2000 native mode, the Windows Server 2003 interim level, or the Windows Server 2003 functional level. Each functional level has different tradeoffs between features and limitations.

## domain local group

A domain local group can contain other domain local groups from its own domain, as well as global groups from any domain in the forest. A domain local group can be used to assign permissions for resources located in the same domain as the group.

## Domain Name System (DNS)

A hierarchical name-resolution system that resolves host names into IP addresses, and vice versa. DNS also makes it possible for the distributed Active Directory database to function, by allowing clients to query the locations of services in the forest and domain.

## Domain Naming Master

One of the two forestwide Flexible Single Master Operations (FSMO) roles, the Domain Naming Master's job is to ensure domain name uniqueness within a forest.

## Dynamic Domain Name System (DDNS)

An extension of DNS that allows Windows 2000 and Windows XP Professional systems to automatically register their A records with DNS at the time they obtain an IP address from a DHCP server.

## Dynamic Host Configuration Protocol (DHCP)

A service that allows an administrator to specify a range of valid IP addresses to be used on a network, as well as exclusion IP addresses that should not be assigned (for example, if they were already statically assigned elsewhere). These addresses are automatically given out to computers configured to use DHCP as they boot up on the network, thus saving the administrator from having to configure static IP addresses on each individual network device.

## enrollment agent certificate

A special certificate issued by a CA that grants the owner of the certificate the authority to enroll users into advanced security and issue certificates on behalf of the users.

## enrollment station

This station is the physical workstation or server where the enrollment agent certificate is installed and used by the authorized person to enroll users and issue certificates.

## Extensible Storage Engine (ESE)

The Active Directory database engine, ESE is an improved version of the older Jet database technology. The ESE database uses the concept of *discrete transactions* and *log files* to ensure the integrity of Active Directory. Each request to the DSA to add, modify, or delete an object or attribute is treated as an individual transaction. As these transactions occur on each domain controller, they are recorded in a series of log files that are associated with each Ntds.dit file.

## external trust

A trust relationship created between a Windows Server 2003 Active Directory domain and a Windows NT 4 domain, or between Active Directory domains in different forests.

## File Replication Service (FRS)

A service that provides multimaster replication between specified domain controllers within an Active Directory tree.

## File Transfer Protocol (FTP)

A standard TCP/IP utility that allows for the transfer of files from an FTP server to a machine running the FTP client.

## firewall

A hardware and software security system that functions to limit access to network resources across subnets. Typically a firewall is used between a private network and the Internet to prevent outsiders from accessing the private network and limiting what Internet services users of the private network can access.

## flat namespace

A namespace that cannot be partitioned to produce additional domains. Windows NT 4 and earlier domains were examples of flat namespaces, as opposed to the Windows Server 2003 hierarchical namespace.

## Flexible Single Master Operations (FSMO)

Five roles that are required by Windows Server 2003 not to follow the typical multimaster model, and instead are hosted on only a single domain controller in each domain, in the case of the Infrastructure Master, PDC Emulator, and RID Master, or on only a single domain controller in the forest, in the case of the Domain Naming Master and the Schema Master.

## Folder Redirection

A Windows Server 2003 feature that allows special folders, such as My Documents, on local Windows XP Professional system hard drives to be redirected to a shared network location.

## forest

A grouping of Active Directory trees that have a trust relationship between them. Forests can consist of a noncontiguous namespace and, unlike domains and trees, do not have to be given a specific name.

## forest functional level

The three forest functional levels are Windows 2000, Windows Server 2003 interim, and Windows Server 2003. The default forest functional level is Windows 2000. When the forest functional level is raised to Windows Server 2003 interim or Windows Server 2003, advanced forestwide Active Directory features are available.

## forest root

The first domain created in a forest.

## forest trust

A trust relationship established between two Active Directory forests.

## forward lookup query

A DNS name-resolution process by which a hostname is resolved to an IP address.

## fully qualified domain name (FQDN)

A DNS domain name that unambiguously describes the location of the host within a domain tree. An example of an FQDN would be the computer www.inside-corner.com.

## functional level

A concept first introduced in Windows Server 2003 that determines what level of features and interoperability with other Windows operating systems is available in a domain or forest. In Windows 2000, functional levels were referred to as *nodes*.

## Global Catalog (GC)

Contains a partial replica of every Windows Server 2003 domain object within the Active Directory, enabling users to find any object in the directory. The partial replica contains the most commonly used attributes of an object, as well as information on how to locate a complete replica elsewhere in the directory, if needed.

## Global Catalog server

The Windows Server 2003 server that holds the Global Catalog for the forest.

## global group

A global group can contain users from the same domain that the global group is located in, and global groups can be added to domain local groups in order to control access to network resources.

## globally unique identifier (GUID)

A hexadecimal number supplied by the manufacturer of a product that uniquely identifies the hardware or software. A GUID is in the form of eight characters, followed by three sets of four characters, followed by 12 characters. For example, {15DEF489-AE24-10BF-C11A-00BB844CE637} is a valid format for a GUID (braces included).

## gpresult

A command-line utility that displays information about the current effect Group Policy has had on the local computer and logged-in user account.

## Group Policy

The Windows Server 2003 feature that allows for policy creation, which affects domain users and computers. Policies can be anything from desktop settings to application assignments to security settings and more.

## Group Policy Editor

The Microsoft Management Console (MMC) snap-in that is used to modify the settings of a Group Policy Object.

## Group Policy Object (GPO)

A collection of policies that apply to a specific target, such as the domain itself (Default Domain Policy) or an Organizational Unit (OU). GPOs are modified through the Group Policy Editor to define policy settings.

## hierarchical namespace

A namespace, such as with DNS, that can be partitioned out in the form of a tree. This allows great flexibility in using a domain name because any number of subdomains can be created under a parent domain.

## Infrastructure Master

The FSMO role that is responsible for receiving replicated changes from other domains within the forest and replicating these changes to all domain controllers within its domain. There is one Infrastructure Master per domain, and it also is responsible for tracking what Active Directory container an object is located in.

## inheritance

The process by which an object obtains settings information from a parent object.

## Intersite Topology Generator (ISTG)

The Windows Server 2003 server that is responsible for evaluating and creating the topology for intersite replication.

## Just-In-Time (JIT)

Technology that allows software features to be updated at the time they are accessed. Whereas in the past missing application features would need to be manually installed, JIT technology allows the features to be installed on the fly as they are accessed, with no other intervention required.

## Kerberos

An Internet standard security protocol that has largely replaced the older LAN Manager user-authentication mechanism from earlier Windows NT versions.

## Knowledge Consistency Checker (KCC)

A Windows Server 2003 service that functions to ensure consistent database information is kept across all domain controllers. It attempts to ensure that replication can always take place.

## latency

The delay that occurs in replication from the time a change is made to one replica and to the time that change is applied to all other replicas in the directory.

## Lightweight Directory Access Protocol (LDAP)

The Windows Server 2003 protocol that allows access to Active Directory. LDAP is an Internet standard for accessing directory services.

## linked policy

A Group Policy that exists in one object and is linked to another object. Linked policies are used to reduce administrative duplication in applying the same policies to multiple OUs.

## local area network (LAN)

A network where all hosts are connected over fast connections (4MBps or greater for Token Ring; 10MBps or better for Ethernet). LANs typically do not involve any outside data carriers (such as Frame Relay lines or T1 circuits) and are generally wholly owned by the organization.

## local group

A security group that exists on a local workstation or server and is used for granting permissions to local resources. Typically, global groups from a domain are placed inside a local group to gain access to resources on a local machine.

## Local Group Policy Objects

Objects that exist on the local Windows Server 2003 system. Site-, domain-, and OU-applied GPOs all take precedence over local GPOs.

## member server

A server that is a member of a domain but is not a domain controller. A Windows Server 2003 domain can have Windows NT, Windows 2000, and Windows Server 2003 member servers, regardless of the domain functional level.

## Microsoft Management Console (MMC)

An extensible management framework that provides a common look and feel to all Windows Server 2003 utilities.

## multihomed

A server that has two or more network cards is said to be *multihomed*. This allows a server either to function as a router or to belong to more than one subnet simultaneously. Alternatively, multiple network adapters can be used for load balancing or fault tolerance.

## multimaster replication

A replication model in which any domain controller will replicate data to any other domain controller. This is the default behavior in Windows Server 2003. It contrasts with the single-master replication model of Windows NT 4, in which a PDC contained the master copy of everything and BDCs contained backup copies.

## name resolution

The process of resolving a hostname into a format that can be understood by computers. This is typically resolving a DNS name or NetBIOS name to an IP address but could also be a MAC address on non-TCP/IP networks.

## NetBIOS

An application programming interface (API) used on Windows NT 4 and earlier networks by services requesting and providing name resolution and network data management.

## network operating system (NOS)

A generic term that applies to any operating system with built-in networking capabilities. All Windows operating systems beginning with Windows 95 have been true network operating systems.

## non-local Group Policy Objects

GPOs that are stored in Active Directory rather than on the local machine. These can be site-, domain-, or OU-level GPOs.

## NSLOOKUP

A TCP/IP utility used in troubleshooting DNS name-resolution problems.

## NTDSUTIL

A command-line utility that provides a number of Active Directory management functions.

## NTFS

The Windows NT/2000 file system that supports a much more robust feature set than either FAT16 or FAT32 (which is used on Windows 9x). It is recommended to use NTFS whenever possible on Windows Server 2003 systems.

## object

A distinct entity represented by a series of attributes within Active Directory. An object can be a user, computer, folder, file, printer, and so on.

## object identifier

A number that uniquely identifies an object class or attribute. In the United States, the American National Standards Institute (ANSI) issues object identifiers, which take the form of an x.x.x.x dotted decimal format. Microsoft, for example, was issued the root object identifier of 1.2.840.113556, from which it can create further sub-object identifiers.

## Operations Master

A Windows Server 2003 domain controller that has been assigned one or more of the special Active Directory domain roles, such as Schema Master, Domain Naming Master, PDC Emulator, Infrastructure Master, and Relative Identifier (RID) Master.

## Organizational Unit (OU)

An Active Directory container object that allows an administrator to logically group users, groups, computers, and other OUs into administrative units.

## package

A collection of software compiled into a distributable form, such as a Windows Installer (.msi) package created with WinInstall.

## parent-child trust relationship

The relationship whereby a child object trusts its parent object, and the parent object is trusted by all child objects under it. Active Directory automatically creates two-way transitive trust relationships between parent and child objects.

## patching

The process of modifying or updating software packages.

## ping

A TCP/IP utility that tests for basic connectivity between the client machine running ping and any other TCP/IP host.

## policy

Settings and rules that are applied to users or computers, usually Group Policy in Windows Server 2003 and System Policy in Windows NT 4.

## preferred bridgehead server

Rather than letting the KCC decide what server should be a bridgehead server, you can designate preferred bridgehead servers to be used if the primary goes down. Only one preferred bridgehead server can be active at a time.

## primary domain controller (PDC)

A Windows NT 4 (and earlier) server that contains the master copy of the domain database and the only writable copy of the database. PDCs authenticate user logon requests and track security-related changes within the domain.

## PDC Emulator

The domain-level FSMO role that serves to replicate data with Windows NT 4 BDCs in a domain, in effect functioning as an NT 4 PDC.

## Public Key Infrastructure (PKI)

An industry standard technology that allows for the establishment of secure communication between hosts based on a public key/private key or certificate-based system.

## published applications

Through the Software Installation utility in Group Policy, administrators can publish applications to users. Published applications appear in Add/Remove Programs and can be optionally installed by the user.

## realm trust

A trust relationship in Windows Server 2003 that is created between an Active Directory domain and a Unix realm.

## Registry

A data repository on each computer that contains information about that computer's configuration. The Registry is organized into a hierarchical tree and is made up of hives, keys, and values.

## relative distinguished name (RDN)

The part of a DNS name that defines the host. For example, in the FQDN www.inside-corner.com, www is the relative distinguished name.

## relative identifier (RID)

The part of the security identifier (SID) that uniquely identifies an account or group within a domain.

## Resultant Set of Policy (RSoP)

A Windows Server 2003 Group Policy tool that lets you simulate the effects of Group Policies without actually implementing them. RSoP has two modes: logging mode and planning mode. Logging mode determines the resultant effect of policy settings that have been applied to an existing user and computer based on a site, domain, or Organizational Unit. Planning mode simulates the resultant effect of policy settings that are applied to a user and computer.

## RID Master

The domain-level FSMO role that is responsible for managing pools of RIDs and ensuring that every object in the domain gets a unique RID.

## replica

A copy of any given Active Directory object. Each copy of an object stored on multiple domain controllers is a replica.

## replication

The process of copying data from one Windows Server 2003 domain controller to another. Replication is a process managed by an administrator and typically occurs automatically whenever changes are made to a replica of an object.

## Request for Comments (RFCs)

Official documents that specify Internet standards for the TCP/IP protocol.

## resource records

Standard database record types used in DNS zone database files. Common types of resource records include Address (A), Mail Exchanger (MX), Start of Authority (SOA), and Name Server (NS), among others.

## return on investment (ROI)

A business term that seeks to determine the amount of financial gain that occurs as a result of a certain expenditure. Many IT personnel today are faced with the prospect of justifying IT expenses in terms of ROI.

## reverse lookup query

A DNS name-resolution process by which an IP address is resolved to a hostname.

## router

A dedicated network hardware appliance or a server running routing software and multiple network cards. Routers join dissimilar network topologies (such as Ethernet to Frame Relay) or simply segment networks into multiple subnets.

## scalability

Measurement (often subjective) of how well a resource such as a server can expand to accommodate growing needs.

## schema

In Active Directory, a schema is a description of object classes and the attributes that the object classes must possess and can possess.

## Schema Master

The Windows Server 2003 domain controller that has been assigned the Operations Master role to control all schema updates within a forest.

## security group

A type of group that can contain user accounts or other groups and can be used to assign levels of access (permissions) to shared resources.

## security identifier (SID)

A number that uniquely identifies a user, group, or computer account. Every account is issued one when created, and if the account is later deleted and re-created with the same name, it will have a different SID. Once an SID is used in a domain, it can never be used again.

## security templates

Collections of standard settings that can be applied administratively to give a consistent level of security to a system.

## shortcut trust

A Windows Server 2003 trust relationship between two domains within the same forest. Shortcut trusts are used to reduce the path authentication needs to travel by directly connecting child domains.

## single-instance store (SIS)

A RIS component that combines duplicate files to reduce storage requirements on the RIS server.

## single-master operations

Certain Active Directory operations that are only allowed to occur in one place at any given time (as opposed to being allowed to occur in multiple locations simultaneously). Examples of single-master operations include schema modifications, PDC elections, and infrastructure changes.

## site

A physical component of Active Directory. Sites are created for the purpose of balancing logon authentication with replication. They can have zero (in planning), one, or multiple IP subnets. These subnets should be well-connected with fast LAN links.

## site link

A connection between sites, a *site link* is used to join multiple locations together.

## site link bridge

A collection of site links that helps Active Directory work out the cost of replicating traffic from one point to another within the network infrastructure that is not directly connected by a single site link. By default, all site links are bridged, but this can be disabled in favor of manually configured site link bridges.

## site link cost

A way for AD to determine what path to replicate traffic over on a routed network. The lower the cost, the more preferable it is for AD to use a particular site link. For example, if you have a T1 and an ISDN site link connecting the same sites, the T1 site link would have a lower cost than the ISDN site link, making it the preferred path for traffic.

## slow link

A connection between sites that is not fast enough to provide full functionality in an acceptable timeframe. Site connections below 512KBps are defined as slow links in Windows Server 2003.

## smartcard

A credit card–sized device that is used with an access code to enable certificate-based authentication and single sign-on to the enterprise. Smartcards securely store certificates, public and private keys, passwords, and other types of personal information. A *smartcard reader* attached to the computer reads the smartcard.

## Software Installation

A Group Policy component that allows administrators to optionally assign applications to be available to users and computers or publish applications to users.

## snap-in

A component that can be added or removed from a Microsoft Management Console (MMC) console to provide specific functionality. The Windows Server 2003 administrative tools are implemented as snap-ins.

## static IP address

Also called a *static address*, this is where a network device (such as a server) is manually configured with an IP address that doesn't change rather than obtaining an address automatically from a DHCP server.

## store

Implemented using the Extensible Storage Engine, a *store* is the physical storage of each Active Directory replica.

## subnet

A collection of hosts on a TCP/IP network that are not separated by any routers. A basic corporate LAN with one location would be referred to as a *subnet* when it is connected by a router to another network, such as that of an Internet service provider.

## synchronous processing

Synchronous processing occurs when one task does not wait for another to complete before it begins. Rather, the two run concurrently. This is typically associated with scripts in Windows Server 2003, such as a user logon script running without waiting for the computer startup script to finish.

## System Policies

System Policies are Windows NT 4 Registry-based policy settings that have largely been replaced in Windows Server 2003 by Group Policy. System Policies can still be created using `poledit.exe`, however, for backward compatibility with non–Windows Server 2003 clients

## Systems Management Server (SMS)

A product in Microsoft's BackOffice server line that provides more extensive software distribution, metering, inventorying, and auditing than what is capable strictly through Group Policy.

## SYSVOL

A shared folder on an NTFS partition on every AD domain controller that contains information (scripts, Group Policy info, and so on) that is replicated to other domain controllers in the domain. The SYSVOL folder is created during the installation of Active Directory.

## TCP/IP

TCP/IP (Transmission Control Protocol/Internet Protocol) is the standard protocol for communicating on the Internet and is the default protocol in Windows Server 2003.

## Time To Live (TTL)

The amount of time a packet destined for a host will exist before it is deleted from the network. TTLs are used to prevent networks from becoming congested with packages that cannot reach their destinations.

## total cost of ownership (TCO)

A change and control management concept that many IT professionals are being forced to become more aware of. TCO refers to the combined hard and soft costs (initial price and support costs) of owning a given resource.

## transitive trust

An automatically created trust in Windows Server 2003 that exists between domain trees within a forest and domains within a tree. Transitive trusts are two-way trust relationships. Unlike with Windows NT 4, transitive trusts in Windows Server 2003 can flow between domains. This way, if Domain1 trusts Domain2, and Domain2 trusts Domain3, Domain1 automatically trusts Domain3.

## tree

A collection of Windows Server 2003 domains that are connected through transitive trusts and share a common Global Catalog and schema. Domains within a tree must form a contiguous namespace. A tree is contained within a forest, and there can be multiple trees in a forest.

## universal group

An Active Directory security group that can be used anywhere within a domain tree or forest, the only caveat being that universal groups can only be used when an Active Directory domain has been converted to native mode.

## universal group caching

A feature that can be used once a domain has been raised to the Windows Server 2003 functional level, *universal group caching* allows users in universal groups to log on without the presence of a GC server.

## Update Sequence Number (USN)

A 64-bit number that keeps track of changes as they are written to copies of the Active Directory. As changes are made, this number increments by one. Every attribute in Active Directory has a USN value.

## UPN suffix

The part of the user principle name (UPN) that comes after the @ symbol and is typically the domain name for a user account. Alternate UPN suffixes can be created to allow for improved logon security or simply shorter UPNs for users.

## user configuration

The portion of a Group Policy Object that allows for user policy settings to be configured and applied.

## user principle name (UPN)

The full DNS domain name of an Active Directory user account that could be used for authentication purpose. An example of a UPN would be `wwillis@inside-corner.com`.

## user profile

Contains settings that define the user environment, typically applied when the user logs on to the system.

## well-connected network

A network that contains only fast connections between domains and hosts. The definition of "fast" is somewhat subjective and may vary from organization to organization.

## wide area network (WAN)

Multiple networks connected by slow connections between routers. WAN connections are typically 1.5MBps or less.

## Windows 2000 mixed mode

Allows Windows NT 4 domain controllers to exist and function within a Windows Server 2003 domain. This is the default setting when Active Directory is installed, although it can be changed to native mode.

## Windows 2000 native mode

The mode in which all domain controllers in a domain have been upgraded to Windows Server 2003 and there are no longer any NT 4 domain controllers. An administrator explicitly puts Active Directory into native mode, at which time it cannot be returned to mixed mode without removing and reinstalling Active Directory.

## Windows Server 2003 functional level

The highest functional level of either the domain or forest in Windows Server 2003, this functional level implements all the new features of Windows Server 2003 Active Directory but at the expense of some backward compatibility.

## Windows Internet Naming System (WINS)

A dynamic name-resolution system that resolves NetBIOS names to IP addresses on Windows TCP/IP networks. With Windows Server 2003, WINS is being phased out in favor of DNS, but it will be necessary to keep WINS in place as long as any legacy clients or applications on the network use it.

## Windows Management Instrumentation (WMI)

A Windows Server 2003 management infrastructure for monitoring and controlling system resources.

## Windows Script Host

Enables the running of VBScript or JavaScript scripts natively on a Windows system, offering increased power and flexibility over traditional batch files.

## WinInstall

An optional utility that ships with Windows Server 2003 and can be used to create Windows Installer packages.

## workgroup

A group of workstations and servers that are not networked within the concept of a domain. In other words, each machine maintains its own local accounts database and can be difficult to administer as the number of computers in the workgroup grows.

## WScript

The Windows interface to Windows Script Host (WSH).

## X.500

A set of standards developed by the International Standards Organization (ISO) that defines distributed directory services.

# Index

# H-I

# Q-R

# U

# V-W

# X-Z